THE TECHNIQUE OF
ELECTRONIC MUSIC

THE TECHNIQUE OF ELECTRONIC MUSIC

Thomas H. Wells

SCHIRMER BOOKS
A Division of Macmillan Publishing Co., Inc.
NEW YORK

Collier Macmillan Publishers
LONDON

SCHIRMER BOOKS
A Division of Macmillan Publishing Co., Inc.
866 Third Avenue, New York, N.Y. 10022

Collier Macmillan Canada, Ltd.

Library of Congress Catalog Card Number: 78–8819

Printed in the United States of America

printing number

1 2 3 4 5 6 7 8 9 10

Library of Congress Cataloging in Publication Data

Wells, Thomas H.
    The technique of electronic music.

    Includes bibliographies and index.
    Discography: p.
    1. Electronic music—Instruction and study.
I. Title.
MT723.W44   1980   789.9'9   78-8819
ISBN 0-02-872830-0

To my parents

Ein neuer Klang ist ein unwillkürlich gefundenes Symbol,
    das den neuen Menschen ankündigt, der sich da ausspricht.

A new sound is an involuntarily discovered symbol,
    which heralds the new man who expresses himself therein.

Arnold Schoenberg

CONTENTS

PREFACE

This book is concerned with the presentation and explanation of the techniques of electronic music production and is intended as a textbook for college courses in electronic music. The material has been employed and developed over eleven years of teaching at the University of Texas at Austin and the Ohio State University. Wherever possible, technically correct terminology will be used in place of the sometimes equivocal layman's terms so often encountered in writings on the subject. However, the author is aware that in writing a comprehensive essay on the techniques of electronic sound generation for use *chiefly by musicians,* one must seek a mean between comprehensibility through use of musical analogies and accuracy in technical description. Some of the features of this book include: problems sections at the ends of chapters to assist the student in understanding concepts presented in the text; block diagrams (patchings) at the ends of most chapters to show the student in general, usually nonequipment-specific terms, how the equipment he uses is interconnected to employ sound synthesis principles discussed in the preceding text: extensive end-of-chapter bibliographies; appendixes, including tables of frequencies of notes in equal temperament, power and voltage ratios to decibels, trigonometric tables, basic algebraic relationships, and others; and a glossary of electronic music terminology.

The book is extensively illustrated, with over 300 oscilloscope and spectrum analyzer photographs, line drawings, and equipment photographs.

This book has been used over the past five years in electronic music courses at the beginning, intermediate, and graduate levels, as well as in audio production courses and seminars.

Although a discussion of detailed compositional techniques per se is beyond the scope of this book, certain compositional aspects are treated in connection with the description of electronic music compositions and compositional resources inherent in certain technical processes. This book does not deal directly with the history of electronic music. The reader is referred to the bibliography in Chapter 1 of this book for a partial listing of the many books and articles on this subject.

It should go without saying that a knowledge of the basic technical processes of electronic music production is essential for those working in this medium. An understanding of these basic techniques gained from a systematic presentation should prove more valuable to the student, both in his creative work and later on in teaching, than is provided by empirical approaches. Although technology continues to advance at a rapid rate, the basic analog electronic music processes are well known, have been in use for almost thirty years, and will continue to serve as a foundation for future developments in the field.

In the opinion of the author, prerequisites for a beginning professional course in electronic music should ideally include: *at least* one semester of instrumental composition or the equivalent; a course in the acoustical foundations of music; a *basic* knowledge of mathematics; and, hopefully, a basic electronic engineering course for non-majors. Of course, local situations and resources will determine the extent to which such prerequisites are required. Some of the above mentioned prerequisites may be taken concurrently with the student's first quarter or semester in electronic music. Moreover, these prerequisites are specifically recommended for composition and audio engineering majors; for those majoring in other disciplines, or for an appreciation/survey course, the prerequisites should be less stringent. An example of a syllabus for a beginning professional course in electronic music is outlined below. Of course, some instructors might wish to emphasize the creative aspects of such a course; others might teach the course chronologically, beginning with projects in musique concrète (or earlier); some might emphasize the technical aspects of the course.

Beyond the introductory course, the author recommends private instruction for advanced students, if possible. Depending on the size of the studio(s) and programs, the introductory courses might be taught in smaller studios, reserving the main studio for advanced students. Questions of studio access and policies of the director of the studio must be clear and unequivocal (cf. Chapter 9).

This book assumes a rudimentary knowledge of algebra, trigonometry, and *fundamental* concepts of analytic geometry and calculus, not necessarily gained from formal course study. Familiarity with these concepts is most important for the composer of electronic music—these concepts constitute the foundations for an understanding of an important part of his craft. The user should not be put off by the mathematical and technical content of this book. Verbal explanations and musical analogies are provided to aid those not so familiar with mathematics. For example, in the case of the equations in Chapter 6 concerning frequency modulation, the *result* is important, that is, a general description of the capabilities of the FM process to generate distributions of frequency components. This deductive approach is representative of the manner in which subjects are treated in this book, and the importance of musical intuition and the employment of aural skills is stressed throughout. Certainly there are many ways in which composers may come to grips with the electronic music medium. Some need only be shown a few patchings and operations and then proceed on their own; others will learn best with a structured curriculum. Although knowledge of technical information is as helpful for the student's immediate understanding as it will be later on in his teaching, he certainly

**Example Syllabus for a Beginning Electronic Music Course Designed
for Composition (and Theory) Majors**

I. Review of Basic Concepts in Acoustics and Psychoacoustics of Music
   A. Standards and Levels
   B. Test and Measurements

II. Selected Topics from Audio Engineering
   A. Standards and Levels
   B. Sound Recording and Reproduction; Demonstration of Professional Recording Techniques

III. Introduction to Sound Synthesis Methods
   A. History of Sound Synthesis
   B. Additive, Subtractive Synthesis; Modulation Synthesis; Waveform Synthesis
   C. Signal Generators
   D. Signal Processors
   E. Control Signal Generators

IV. Areas of Specificity in Electronic Music (include scores, recorded examples [and ideally performances, where applicable] in each area)
   A. Tape Music
   B. Live Electronic Music
      1. Purely Electronically Generated
      2. Electroacoustically Modified Instrumental Music and/or Natural Sounds (live or transcribed)
      3. Combinations of 1 and 2 Above
   C. Applications of Digital Computers
      1. Direct Digital Synthesis
      2. Hybrid Systems
   D. Commercial Applications of Electronic Music (popular music, transcription of scores, commercial advertising, etc.)

V. History of Electronic Music
   A. Bibliography and Chronology
   B. Aesthetics and Criticism

VI. Projects: As many projects from Category IV as possible. Emphasis on collaborative works (radio, television, film, computer graphics, drama, dance, etc.)

does not have to understand the electronic engineering refinements of a voltage-controlled oscillator or to be fully conversant with every equation in this book. A program of instruction in electronic music should be taught systematically—presenting the student with simple constructs in some logical sequence and later connecting and elaborating these simple cases to include more complex situations—or such a program may become a kind of therapy session.

While this book is not intended as a source of circuit diagrams and patchings, a large number of schematics and block diagrams are included. However, since a given patching can yield a wide variety of sounds, verbal description of patchings is limited to a cursory explanation. Through a basic understanding of the processes involved in a given patching, the student should realize what the variables in a given patching are, and how, working interactively with the equipment, he may control the variables in such a way as his ear and intuition demand.

The symbols used in block diagrams of patchings have been adapted

Symbols Used for Block Diagrams of Patchings

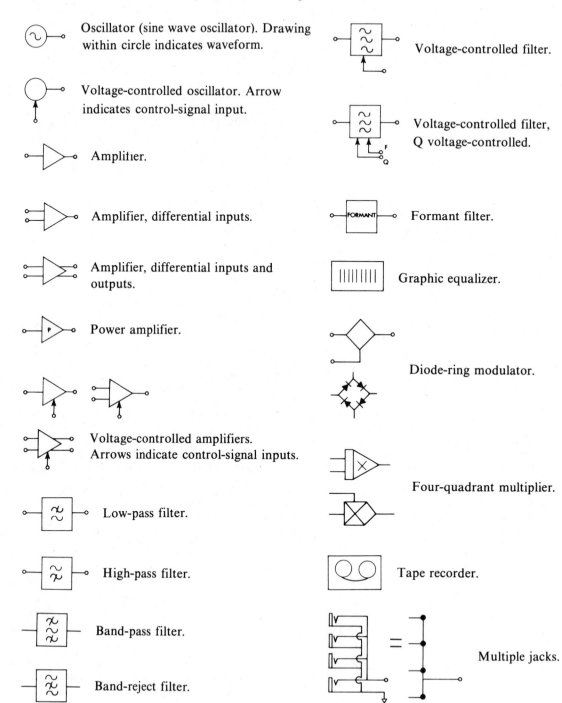

Oscillator (sine wave oscillator). Drawing within circle indicates waveform.

Voltage-controlled oscillator. Arrow indicates control-signal input.

Amplifier.

Amplifier, differential inputs.

Amplifier, differential inputs and outputs.

Power amplifier.

Voltage-controlled amplifiers. Arrows indicate control-signal inputs.

Low-pass filter.

High-pass filter.

Band-pass filter.

Band-reject filter.

Voltage-controlled filter.

Voltage-controlled filter, Q voltage-controlled.

Formant filter.

Graphic equalizer.

Diode-ring modulator.

Four-quadrant multiplier.

Tape recorder.

Multiple jacks.

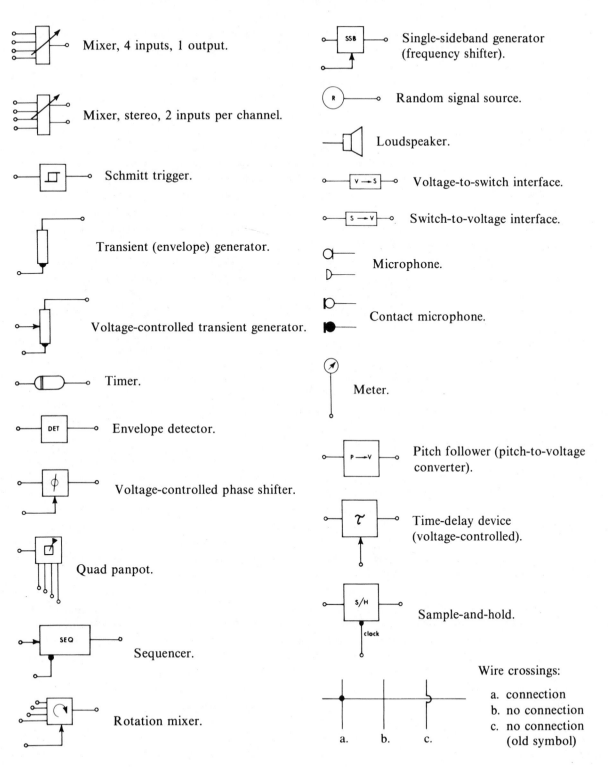

Mixer, 4 inputs, 1 output.

Mixer, stereo, 2 inputs per channel.

Schmitt trigger.

Transient (envelope) generator.

Voltage-controlled transient generator.

Timer.

Envelope detector.

Voltage-controlled phase shifter.

Quad panpot.

Sequencer.

Rotation mixer.

Single-sideband generator (frequency shifter).

Random signal source.

Loudspeaker.

Voltage-to-switch interface.

Switch-to-voltage interface.

Microphone.

Contact microphone.

Meter.

Pitch follower (pitch-to-voltage converter).

Time-delay device (voltage-controlled).

Sample-and-hold.

Wire crossings:
a. connection
b. no connection
c. no connection (old symbol)

a.   b.   c.

from engineering practice and have evolved through many years of teaching and studio work. The author feels that the use of these general symbols should largely preclude difficulties in communication resulting from disparities in equipment from studio to studio, making this book usable with all types of analog electronic music instrumentation. Further, by keeping these symbols on a conceptual level, the student must translate the patchings to his own equipment, reinforcing the learning process and, hopefully, deepening the student's understanding of the function of the equipment. On the other hand, disparities in equipment capabilities may present problems that may be solved only by altering the patching.

Electronic music is an integral part of our culture, having achieved commercial viability, institutional acceptance, and the approval of the avant-garde. Although many important works of the last 30 years have employed electronic media, many musicians still regard electronic music more as an ineresting anomaly than as a vehicle for serious musical expression. Many electronic music compositions seem to be deficient in those qualities that make the best instrumental music of the last 30 years interesting: a sense of timing; adequate differentiation of musical resources; a sense of tension and release; *kinesis;* interesting and attractive sounds—to name but a few admittedly subjective criteria. Often the difficulty lies with the composer who, lacking a thorough understanding of the capabilities of the equipment with which he works, is forced to compromise his compositional ideas.

Although equipment designed specifically for electronic music production includes certain features of automation to facilitate sound generation, some composers never progress beyond the superficial capabilities of such time-saving refinements. Yet many early electronic compositions were produced using equipment not originally intended for the production of music; and, in the opinion of the author, some of these pieces remain the most impressive works in the literature of electronic music, both from technical and musical standpoints.

I am especially indebted to my colleague, Professor David Butler, for writing the chapter on psychoacoustics and electronic music. I wish to thank the following persons for their assistance: Eric S. Vogel, co-author of the private edition of this book; David Richards; Roger Chiodo; David Grote; David Hough; Dr. Martha Cone; Robert Hare; Russ Kacir; and Britt, Graf, Campbell, and Nagel attorneys. Special thanks to Robert L. Nelson, Jr. for his invaluable assistance and criticism of the private edition of the book, and to Charmayne Wells for her reading and typing the final draft of this revision.

1

BASIC CONCEPTS

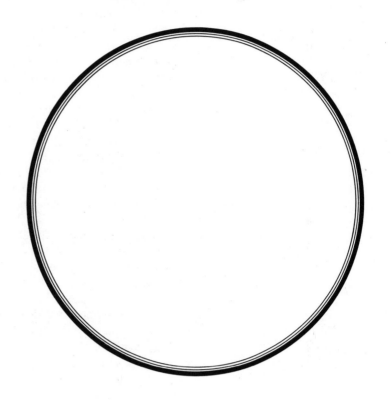

In general, sound is perceived when the human ear is subjected to a series of alternate compressions and rarefactions of the air, above and below the ambient pressure, at rates of approximately 15 to 15,000 times per second. Fluctuations of air pressure above and below this range do exist (for example, periodic changes in barometric pressure or bat echo rangings), but these are *not* perceived as sound by humans. These periodic changes in air pressure are usually caused by a vibrating body—a string, metal rod, metal plate, or membrane—in contact with the air.†

Although we are primarily concerned with sound waves generated by vibrating bodies, there are other means by which sound waves may be generated in air. Throttled airstream generators such as sirens, lip-modulated brass instruments, clarinets, and so on, employ a vibrating valve to produce a periodically interrupted airstream. Explosion-type generators, such as bursting balloons and chemical explosions that produce violent gas expansion, produce a sound wave consisting of a short-duration, high-amplitude compression wave followed by a larger duration contraction wave. Thermal sound generators such as the hot-wire generator have been employed in the calibration of microphones. The hot-wire generator requires a DC bias in order to operate the wire in the linear part of its range. Arc-type sound generators figure in the history of electronic music in the late nineteenth century. Such sound generators are still used for experimental applications in which large sound pressures are required. Radiators that employ a flame that is modulated by an electrostatic field have been built. The Aeolian sound generator, familiar to many musicians (Aeolian harp), is yet another type of sound generator.

To understand the nature of vibration, we shall examine a simple case in which a spherical weight W is attached to one end of an elastic rod R, the other end of which is securely attached to a support S (figure 1.1). At first the system is in equilibrium (figure 1.1a). We then apply a force F_a downward on the sphere and hold it in equilibrium (figure 1.1b). In this position F_a, the force exerted downward, is balanced by a force F_r, the restoring force due to the elasticity of the rod. Let force F_a be removed. The system is now unbalanced, and force F_r causes the sphere to accelerate upward through the original equilibrium position of figure 1.1a. The upward momentum of the sphere carries it to the position shown in figure 1.1c, where the sphere is temporarily at rest. At this point a restoring force F_r' causes the sphere again to accelerate toward the equilibrium position of figure 1.1a. However, the sphere's momentum carries it to the position shown in figure 1.1b, at which point the system is again temporarily at rest. Again, a restoring force causes the sphere to accelerate toward the equilibrium position of figure 1.1c, and the process repeats over and over.

One *cycle* of vibration is one complete excursion from a given point, for example, the point of equilibrium of figure 1.1a, through the extremes of

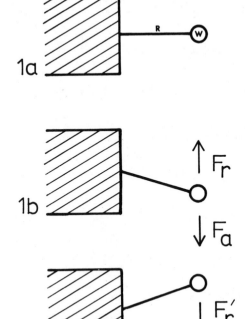

FIGURE 1.1

†An event is said to be *periodic* and to have a period T units of time if, after every time interval T, the event repeats exactly the behavior of the previous T sec.

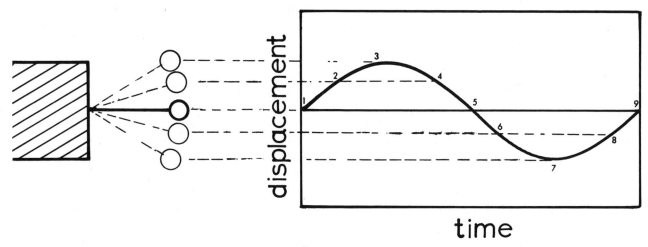

FIGURE 1.2

displacement shown in figures 1.1b and 1.1c, and back to the equilibrium position of figure 1.1a. The distance from the equilibrium position of figure 1.1a to either extreme of displacement is called the *amplitude* of the vibration. The motion of this system is called *simple harmonic motion*. It is periodic, and repeats *ad infinitum* as long as there is no energy loss.

The time in seconds required to complete one cycle of vibration is called the *period* of vibration. Another term, *frequency*, indicates the number of cycles completed per unit of time. Thus, frequency = 1/period, that is, frequency is the inverse of period. Frequency is measured in *cycles per second*, or an equivalent term *Hertz* (Hz).

As stated above, the ear perceives alternate compressions and rarefactions of the air as sound when the frequency of vibration is 15 to 15,000 cycles per second, or 15 to 15,000 Hz. We would like to examine the displacement of the sphere in figure 1.1 as a function of time.

Figure 1.2 shows the displacement of the sphere projected against the *y*-axis of a coordinate system and the resulting values of *y* plotted as a function of time. The curve $\sim$ represents the displacement versus time function of the spherical weight. If two variables (in this case *y* = displacement and *x* = time) are related in such a way that whenever a value is assigned to *x* there is automatically assigned a unique value to *y* by some relationship, *y* is called a single-valued function of *x*.

In the case cited above, the relationship between the displacement, *y*, and the time, *x*, is the *sine function* (Latin *sinus:* a pleat or a fold). The sine function can also be derived in the following manner: consider the rotating arm of unit length (figure 1.3). At *t* = 0 the arm is set at an arbitrary starting angle θ with respect to the horizontal axis. If the arm rotates at a constant angular velocity about a circle, the vertical projection of the tip of the arm plotted against time generates a sinusoidal function.

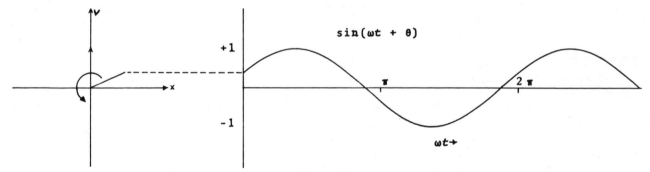

FIGURE 1.3

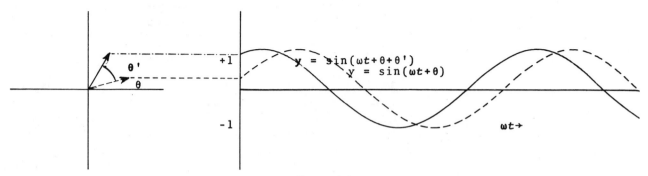

FIGURE 1.4

Angular velocity is defined as the time rate of angular motion about an axis. Thus, if the angle described in time t is θ, the angular velocity ω equals θ/t. Angular velocity is measured in *radians per second*. One radian equals $360°/2\pi$, or approximately $57.3°$. The rotating arm makes one complete revolution every 2π radians. For every complete revolution of the arm, the sinusoidal function (generated by plotting the vertical projection of the tip of the arm versus time) completes one cycle. Thus $\omega = 2\pi f$, where ω is the angular velocity measured in radians per second, $\pi = 3.1416$, and f is the frequency measured in cycles per second (Hz).

Thus, an expression for the sinusoidal function above may be written as $y = A \sin (\omega t + \theta)$, where A is the *amplitude* (displacement on the y-axis).† See figure 1.3: $y = A \sin (\omega t + \theta)$. When θ, the arbitrary initial starting angle, equals zero, this expression becomes $y = A \sin \omega t$, which is traditionally called the *sine function*. The expression for the sine function can also be written as $y = \sin x$, where $x = \omega t$. The use of the dummy variable x facilitates looking up the values of the sine function in a table when one plots functions. A table of sine function values for different angles is given in Appendix 1.

Figure 1.4 shows two equal-length arms that rotate at the same speed.

†From trigonometry, the sine of an angle is the ratio of the side opposite an acute angle of a right triangle to the hypotenuse.

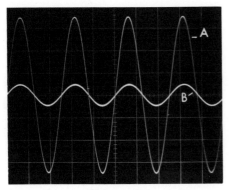

FIGURE 1.5

One arm leads the other by a constant angle θ'. The sinusoidal functions generated by these rotating arms are shown to the right. The solid-line sinusoid is said to lead the dashed-line sinusoid by an angle of θ'. The two sinusoids are out of phase by θ' degrees.

Consider the expression for a certain sine function in radian notation: $y = 0.7 \sin 2763t$. From this expression we may determine: the *amplitude*, 0.7 (arbitrary) units; the *angular frequency*, ω, 2,763 radians per second; the *repetition frequency*, $2763/2\pi$, or 440Hz; and the *period*, 1/440 second.

Consider the sinusoidal displacement versus time functions of two vibrating bodies (figure 1.5). The system with the greater amplitude of vibration (function a) will cause greater pressure changes in the surrounding air, resulting in a louder sound (in this case a single-frequency, or pure, tone). (See Appendix 4: Sound Power Output from a Simple Source in Terms of Maximum Volume Displacement.)

Sound pressure level is measured in dynes per square centimeter (dynes/cm^2) or in microbars (μB). One *microbar* equals one dyne per square centimeter, or $1.4504 \cdot 10^{-5}$ pounds per square inch. One *dyne* is the force that will accelerate a one gram mass one centimeter per second per second. We may get some idea of the force of one dyne by placing just under a quarter teaspoon of table salt in the hand. The force exerted on the hand by the salt is roughly one dyne.

The sound pressure level that corresponds to the threshold of human hearing is 0.0002 μB at a frequency of 1,000 Hz.† A frequency notation is included in this measurement, since the response of the ear to sound level is frequency dependent. Due to the large ranges of intensities, pressures, and the like, encountered in acoustics, a logarithmic scale of *decibels* is employed (see chapter 4).

Pure tones discussed above occur infrequently both in music and in everyday surroundings. Most sound sources produce complex tones, which are collections of single-frequency, or pure, tones of different amplitudes and frequencies. The number of these pure tones, along with their individual frequencies and amplitudes, determine the tone quality, or *timbre*, of a complex sound. The pure-tone, single-frequency components of a complex sound are called *partials* or *harmonics,* depending on the ratios of their frequencies to the lowest frequency component, or *fundamental*. Because the meaning of the term *overtone* is often equivocal and dependent on the nature of the complex sound being described, the author discourages its use.

Consider two complex tones, both of which have 100 Hz as their lowest single-frequency component, or fundamental. The first tone contains the following frequency components: 100 Hz, 200 Hz, 300 Hz, 400 Hz, 500 Hz, 600 Hz, 700 Hz, 800 Hz, and 900 Hz. The second tone contains the following frequency components: 100 Hz, 190 Hz, 271 Hz, 292 Hz, 303 Hz, 451 Hz, 555.2 Hz, 607.2 Hz, and 835 Hz. In addition, each sinusoidal

†By comparison, the threshold of hearing of a cat is 20 dB below the human threshold.

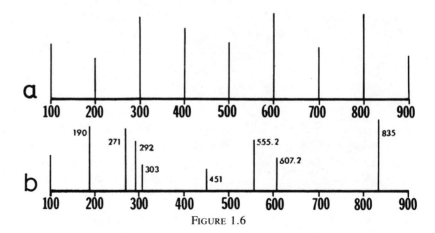

FIGURE 1.6

frequency component has an amplitude value associated with it. A more readily comprehensible tabulation of the frequency components is presented with the following graphs of frequency versus amplitude (figure 1.6). Such a graph of frequency versus amplitude is called a *line spectrum* or *discrete-frequency spectrum*.

The frequencies of the partials of complex sound shown in figure 1.6a are related one to another by integers, namely, 1, 2, 3, 4, 5, 6, 7, 8, and 9. The frequencies of the partials of complex sound shown in figure 1.6b are related one to another by nonintegers, namely, 1, 1.9, 2.71, 2.92, 3.03, 4.51, 5.552, 6.072, and 8.35. From mathematics, the series $1/2 + 1/3 + 1/4 + \ldots 1/n + \ldots$ is called the *harmonic series*. Frequency components related to a fundamental by integer ratios are called *harmonics*. The fundamental is the first harmonic, or first partial. The frequency components in figure 1.6a are harmonics (or partials, or *harmonic partials*), while the frequency components in figure 1.6b are partials (or *inharmonic partials*) but *not* harmonics. The analysis of everyday sounds subjectively called *noises* yields frequency components that are not integrally related to a fundamental. The whole-number-multiple frequency components in figure 1.6a are characteristic of those of most musical instruments of definite pitch. However, the frequency components of many electronically produced sounds are nonintegrally related (see chapter 5). Any periodic waveform may be broken down into a number of single-frequency, sinusoidal components. Figure 1.7 shows the addition of three sine waves of different frequencies and amplitudes to produce a resultant fourth, complex waveform.

A description of a waveform in which the variable(s) involved is/are a function of time is called a *time domain* description. Generally speaking, a description of a waveform in which the sinusoidal components are plotted as a function of frequency is called a *frequency domain* description. Using

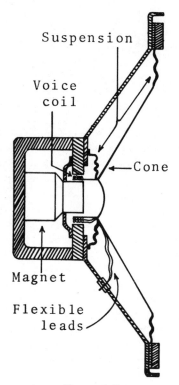

Suspension

Voice coil

Cone

Magnet

Flexible leads

FIGURE 1.8

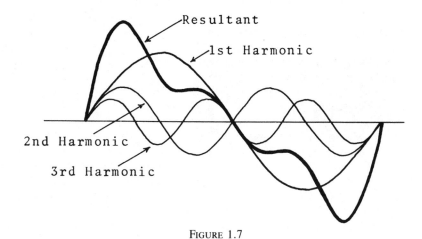

Resultant

1st Harmonic

2nd Harmonic

3rd Harmonic

FIGURE 1.7

a *sound spectrograph,* it is possible to obtain a two-dimensional amplitude-frequency-time plot on which frequency is shown on the y-axis, time is shown on the x-axis, and amplitude is indicated by the blackness of the trace.

Thus far, we have considered only mechanical vibrating systems. In general, in the production of electronic music, one works with sound in terms of electrical analogies to elements of mechanical vibrating systems. The electrical signal, a function of voltage or current with time, may be converted into sound (mechanical energy) using a loudspeaker, a type of transducer. The transduction mechanism generally uses one of a number of possible electromechanical converting principles, which may in some cases be reversible. A diagram of a typical dynamic loudspeaker is shown in figure 1.8.

An *oscillator* is a device that produces a periodic voltage or current-versus-time function. Most oscillators designed specifically for electronic music are capable of producing several different waveforms simultaneously. Such an oscillator is called a *function generator.* These waveforms differ from one another in the number and amplitudes of their sinusoidal harmonic components. As we have seen, the harmonic content of the sine wave includes only one component, the first harmonic, or first partial. The output of most practical sine-wave oscillators does contain higher order harmonics. However, this harmonic distortion is negligible in most good designs; as we shall see in later chapters, after the waveform is subjected to various signal modification processes (such as modulation), a small amount of harmonic distortion can be tolerated.

The sawtooth wave (figure 1.9) is commonly available from most function generators. This waveform may be thought of as resulting from the instantaneous summation at every point in time of its frequency components, which are integral multiples of a fundamental frequency. The

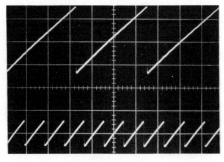

FIGURE 1.9

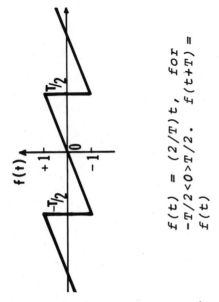

FIGURE 1.10

$$f(t) = (2/T)t, \text{ for } -T/2 < 0 > T/2. \quad f(t+T) = f(t)$$

FIGURE 1.11

amplitude of any given sinusoidal component is the amplitude of the fundamental frequency divided by the harmonic number.

A spectrum of a sawtooth wave is shown in figure 1.10. The sawtooth-wave function may be represented as shown in figure 1.11. In this example, the function is defined over an interval $-T/2$ to $+T/2$, where T is the period, and t is time. The relation $f(t + T) = f(t)$ shows that the time function is periodic, that is, it repeats itself every T seconds.

The function described above may also be represented as a series of sinusoidal terms of different frequencies and amplitudes by Fourier analysis. It was Fourier who first demonstrated that any periodic function satisfying certain conditions may be represented as a sum of sinusoids and a constant:

$$f(t) = a_0 + a_1 \cos \omega_0 t + a_2 \cos 2\omega_0 t + a_3 \cos 3\omega_0 t + \ldots b_1 \sin \omega_0 t + b_2 \sin 2\omega_0 t + b_3 \sin 3\omega_0 t + \ldots.$$

The above equation may be rewritten as

$$f(t) = \sum_{k=1}^{\infty} (a_k \cos k\omega_0 t + b_k \sin k\omega_0 t).$$

Note: Read "the summation $(a_k \cos k\omega_0 t + b_k \sin k\omega_0 t)$ from $k = 1$ to $k = \infty$."

Figure 1.12 shows the first eight partials (harmonics) of the sawtooth-wave spectrum shown in figure 1.10 transcribed into musical notation. Although no indication of frequency of the sine-wave partials is shown in figure 1.10, figure 1.12 is drawn with a bass clef to resolve problems of interval spelling.

The discovery of the Fourier series has permitted engineers to associate

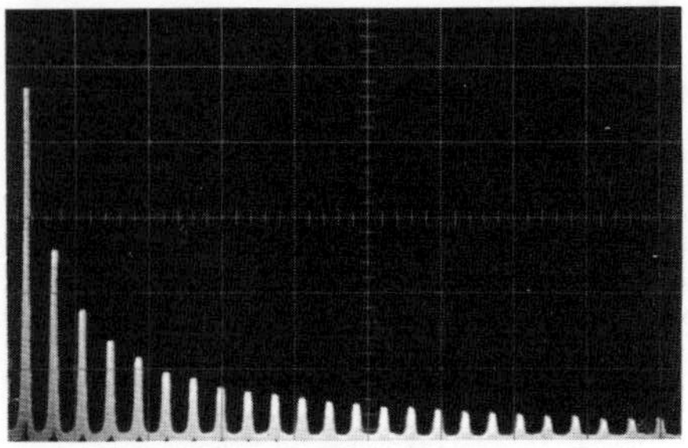

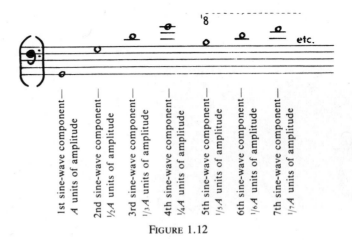

1st sine-wave component— A units of amplitude
2nd sine-wave component— $\frac{1}{2}A$ units of amplitude
3rd sine-wave component— $\frac{1}{3}A$ units of amplitude
4th sine-wave component— $\frac{1}{4}A$ units of amplitude
5th sine-wave component— $\frac{1}{5}A$ units of amplitude
6th sine-wave component— $\frac{1}{6}A$ units of amplitude
7th sine-wave component— $\frac{1}{7}A$ units of amplitude

FIGURE 1.12

specific meanings with the word frequency. Strictly speaking, frequency refers only to a sinusoid. Although the sawtooth wave may be spoken of as having a frequency (1/period, that is, $1/T$), there are, of course, other frequencies present. The Fourier series for the sawtooth-wave function is

$$f(t) = \frac{2}{\pi} \sum_{n=1}^{\infty} \frac{(-1)^{n+1}}{n} \sin n\omega_0 t = \frac{2}{\pi} (\sin \omega_0 t - \frac{1}{2} \sin 2\omega_0 t + \frac{1}{3} \sin 3\omega_0 t - \dots).$$

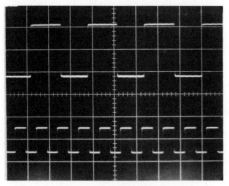

FIGURE 1.13

The sawtooth wave has long been employed in electronic organ circuitry, since harmonic components of the sawtooth wave may be altered selectively using filters to produce various tone colors. Notice that the slope of the sawtooth wave varies with its amplitude and frequency. (Compare the slopes of the two sawtooth waves in figure 1.9.)

The square wave is another waveform commonly available from most function generators. The square wave is a particular case of a rectangular pulse wave for which the pulse width is one half the period. Figure 1.13 shows two square waves of different frequencies and amplitudes. The frequency components that make up the square wave are odd number multiples of a fundamental frequency. The amplitude of any given component is the amplitude of the fundamental divided by the harmonic number. A spectrum of a square wave is shown in figure 1.14. The square wave function may be represented as shown in figure 1.15.

The Fourier series for the square wave function is

$$f(t) = \frac{4}{\pi} \sum_{n=1,3,5,\dots}^{\infty} \frac{1}{n} \cos n\omega_0 t = \frac{4}{\pi} (\cos \omega_0 t + \frac{1}{3} \cos 3\omega_0 t \,^a \frac{1}{5} \cos 5\omega_0 (+ \dots).$$

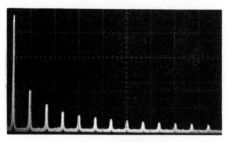

FIGURE 1.14

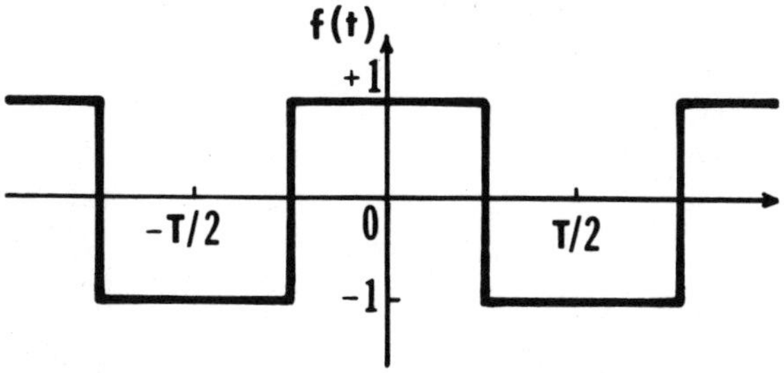

$$f(t) = -1, \quad -T/2 < T > -T/4$$
$$= +1, \quad -T/4 < t > T/4$$
$$= -1, \quad T/4 < t > T/2$$

FIGURE 1.15

Many function generators employed in electronic music provide a variable-width pulse waveform. The spectrum of the pulse wave depends on the pulse width. The ratio of pulse width to the total period is called the *duty cycle,* which is usually expressed as a ratio, for example, 1:2, or a percentage, for example, 50%. Varying the duty cycle, as might be expected, alters the spectrum of the waveform, thus providing the composer with a means of timbral differentiation. In chapter 3, we shall see that pulse width may be voltage-controlled; in chapter 5, pulse-width modulation is discussed.

The following expression may be used to determine the amplitude of a given frequency component of a rectangular wave:

$$A = 1/n \sin (n\pi d/T),$$

where A is the amplitude of the component, n is the harmonic number, d is the duration of the pulse, and T is the period. For example, using this expression to obtain the coefficient of amplitude of the second harmonic of a pulse wave of duty cycle 1:4 gives

$$1/n \sin (n\pi d/T) = 1/2 \sin (2\pi/4) = 1/2.$$

The amplitude of the first harmonic component of the above waveform is

$$1/n \sin (n\pi d/T) = 1/1 \sin (\pi/4) = .707.$$

Thus, the amplitude of the second harmonic is equal to approximately 0.5/0.707, or approximately 71% of the amplitude of the fundamental. (See figure 1.16, Spectra of pulse waves of varying duty cycle: duty cycle 3:4. The line spectra of the 1:4 and 3:4 duty-cycle pulse waves are identical.)

It should be noted that for cases in which the pulse width and period are related to each other by whole numbers, say, pulse width ÷ period = $1/a$ (where a is an integer) the coefficient of amplitude of every a^{th} harmonic is zero.

By varying the pulse duration one can obtain a large number of complex sounds with integrally related frequency components. These pulse-wave signals, like the sawtooth-wave signal, may be filtered in order to create sounds of different timbres. To be sure, with an adequate system of filters to eliminate some of the steady-state† characteristics of these signals, one can generate interesting sound events. Certain composers of electronic music treat the waveforms available from their equipment somewhat like

†Here the author uses the term *steady state* to refer to a condition of no perceptible change (see chapter 2, page 32).

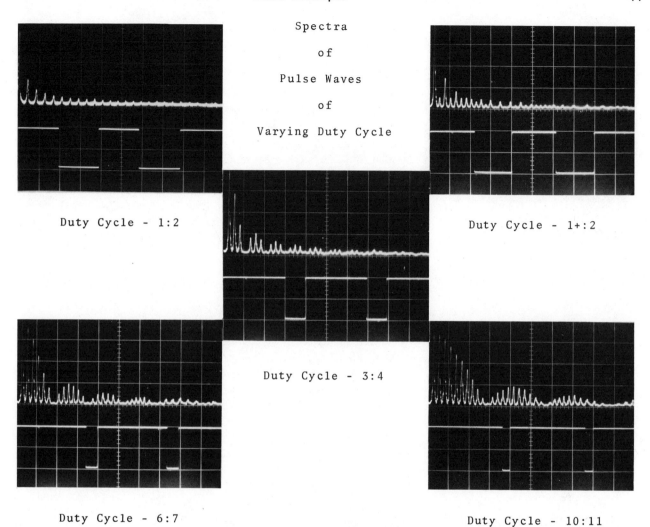

Spectra

of

Pulse Waves

of

Varying Duty Cycle

Duty Cycle - 1:2

Duty Cycle - 1+:2

Duty Cycle - 3:4

Duty Cycle - 6:7

Duty Cycle - 10:11

FIGURE 1.16

Spectra of pulse waves of varying duty cycle

instruments of different timbres. Certainly this approach has proven valuable in electronic music used for commercial advertising and in electronic music transcriptions of music of earlier periods. However, in many respects the waveforms discussed in this chapter represent only the most basic material from which electronic music is made. We shall concern ourselves in later chapters with methods of signal processing by which complex sounds with time-varying spectra may be produced by the interaction of these basic waveforms.

The triangle wave is another waveform commonly available from func-

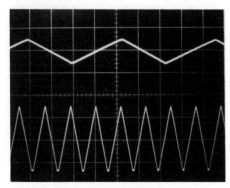

FIGURE 1.17

tion generators. Figure 1.17 shows two triangle waves of different frequencies and amplitudes. (While the timbre of the sawtooth wave and certain rectangular [pulse] wave signals may be described as "buzzy," and the timbre of the square wave as "hollow and clarinet-like," the timbre of the triangle wave is much like that of the sine wave, but with a bit of "edge." Of course these waveforms themselves have different sounds depending on their frequency. The reader should compare sine, sawtooth, rectangular, square, and triangular waves at approximately 70 Hz and approximately 3000 Hz.) The frequency components that make up the triangle wave are odd number multiples of a fundamental frequency. The amplitude of any given component is 1/(*harmonic number*)². A line spectrum of a triangle wave is shown in figure 1.18. The triangle-wave function may be represented analytically as shown in figure 1.19. The Fourier series for the triangular wave function is

$$f(t) = \frac{8}{\pi^2} \sum_{n=1,3,5\ldots}^{\infty} \frac{-1^{\frac{(n-1)}{2}}}{n^2} \cos n\omega_0 t = \frac{8}{\pi^2} \left(\cos \omega_0 t - \frac{1}{3^2} \cos 3\omega_0 t + \frac{1}{5^2} \cos 5\omega_0 t - \ldots\right).$$

The frequency components, like those of the square wave, consist of odd-number multiples of a fundamental frequency. The coefficients of amplitude are, of course, different.

In general, there are four operations that are employed for generating and/or modifying signals for electronic music production: *additive synthesis, subtractive synthesis, modulation synthesis,* and *waveform synthesis.* Each of these processes will be discussed in detail in later chapters. Usually, additive synthesis, subtractive synthesis, and waveform synthesis are suited for applications involving discrete pitch material. Modulation synthesis is often employed (with small modulation indices) as an ornamental

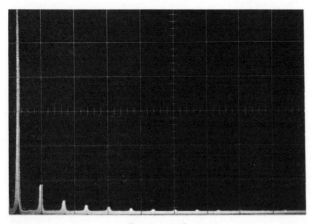

FIGURE 1.18

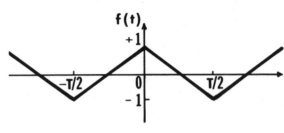

$$f(t) = 1 + 4/T(t), \quad -T/2 < t > 0$$

$$= 1 - 4/T(t), \quad 0 < t > T/2$$

FIGURE 1.19

resource for "coloring" discrete pitch material. As we shall see in chapter 5, large modulation indices, for a given range of modulated and modulating signals, produce complex sounds; changing the frequency of one of the input signals to a modulator by, say, using a keyboard-control device, will not necessarily raise the pitch, or pitch area, of the complex sound by an easily predictable interval. For example, J. W. Beauchamp, writing in the *Journal of the Audio Engineering Society,* states that

> although this method [modulation synthesis] is realizable by inexpensive electronic circuitry and can be made to yield a variety of tone colors, arbitrary spectral distributions cannot be produced.[1]

The ability to specify and realize predetermined spectral distributions could be a tool of considerable importance to the composer of electronic music. Ideally, working interactively with such a system he would be able to make adjustments on his sound material in real time. Except for additive and subtractive synthesis using waveforms of known spectra, most generation of complex sounds in the analog electronic-music studio is accomplished by processes that can be readily understood and predicted, but which do not lend themselves to the production of predetermined spectra without the aid of accurate test equipment. Even then, the time required for measurements would render this deterministic approach unworkable for most compositional purposes. The interactive process, in which a composer controls a system, for example, modulation synthesis, and adjusts the variables as his ear and intuition require, is the usual method of working in the analog studio.

An interesting and useful method for realizing predetermined spectra was employed by Gary Kendall of Northwestern University using a digital sound-synthesis system with a Fast Fourier Transform and Inverse Fourier Transform with interactive graphics. With this system the operator may specify large numbers of sinusoidal components on a cathode-ray tube with a light pen. The time function (waveform resulting from the addition of the sinusoidal components through time) could be viewed if desired and the resulting sound could be heard within a few seconds. Time functions themselves may be drawn with the light pen and may be resolved into sinusoidal components or auditioned.

Digital synthesis offers attractive possibilities for control, accuracy, and realization of sound generating and modifying processes difficult or impossible to accomplish with analog equipment—however, often at the sacrifice of the interactive process. Using a digital-synthesis system, a composer assigns values for variables associated with sound events and waits (turnaround time) for the necessary computations and conversions to be accomplished. Turnaround time may vary from seconds to days depending on the program and conversion facilities. However, real-time digital synthesis is, at this writing, possible with some systems. Digital synthesis and signal processing is employed to an increasing degree in discrete instruments such as oscillators, time-delay, and reverberation units used in conjuction with analog equipment. Certainly the future of electronic sound synthesis will owe much to developments in digital-sound synthesis and signal processing.

Except in the case when the modulated and modulating signals are related by whole numbers, complex modulation-produced sounds are usually characterized by nonharmonically related frequency components. Due to the inharmonic nature of such sounds, and the number and relative amplitudes of their frequency components, certain modulation-produced sounds do not possess a definite pitch. However, the range of complexity of modulation-produced sounds is great—from quasi-discrete-pitched sounds to wide band "noises," components of which might occupy the entire audio-frequency band. Still, one may compose pitch differentiations utilizing the pitch areas determined either by the bandwidth of the complex sound itself, or by the passband of a filter through which the complex signal is processed. The notion of *timbre composition,* in which the role of timbre is elevated from that of an ornamental resource to that of a form-determining musical element has been much polemicized. In the opinion of many critics, those electronic music works that are most representative of the state of the art *do* exhibit a high degree of timbral differentiation. Implicit in the concept of timbre composition is the idea that complex timbres have pitches or pitch areas that themselves must be ordered by the composer, and that the differentiation of pitch is still a most important part of the compositional process.

ELECTRONIC MUSIC SYSTEMS

Electronic music may be divided into several areas of specificity, namely, tape music, real-time performance, and digital-sound synthesis. In practice, these categories are far from autonomous, given the many combinations of these genres that exist.

Tape music relies on analog tape storage of sound events (natural or electronically generated) to achieve time structuring and polyphony. Analog tape storage does provide a convenient means to structure time in terms of tape length ÷ tape velocity.

In the past, tape editing was employed extensively to organize and modify individual sounds in electronic pieces (see chapter 8, page 212–216). The increased use of multichannel recorders (see chapter 8, page 211–212) in electronic music studios has permitted composers to organize and synchronize large sections of pieces by "electronic editing," taking advantage of the possibilities inherent in multitrack recording. Individual sounds and sections of pieces may be assembled by mixing the outputs of several tape machines and regulating the combination with a studio mixer. Close tape editing of sound events may be used to advantage on the tapes to be mixed together, and to adjust timings on the master tape. Editing of multitrack tape is, of course, accomplished at the expense

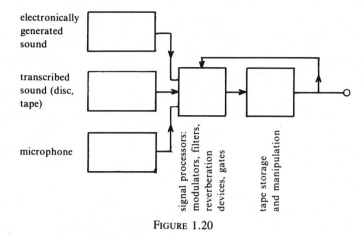

electronically
generated
sound

transcribed
sound (disc,
tape)

microphone

signal processors:
modulators, filters,
reverberation
devices, gates

tape storage
and manipulation

FIGURE 1.20

of track independence. A simplified diagram of a tape music system is shown in figure 1.20.

Real-time performance includes electroacoustical modification of live or transcribed natural sounds, live performance with electronically generated sounds, combinations of these methods, as well as the use of prepared prerecorded material. The large range of possibilities for interconnection of electronic music devices, along with the possibilities for including feedback and interactive control, make real-time performance an intriguing endeavor. The composer can invent patchings that produce highly differentiated series of sound events, with no perceivable order of pitches, timbres, or durations. Many of these patchings, however, produce periodic events, the period of repetition of which is very long.

Sound events may easily be randomly differentiated through the use of noise generators to provide control of sound generating and modifying equipment. Among the liabilities inherent in such real-time systems is the lack of control over *individual* sound events produced (see chapter 7, page 178). Of course, sounds produced by such systems with feedback may be included in a tape music composition (see Subotnick, *Silver Apples of the Moon*) in which the composer may use tape manipulation to achieve additional control. In addition, recorders may be employed in live electronic music works for time delay and storage of audio or control signals. A diagram of a real-time performance system is shown in figure 1.21.

Digital computers have been employed since the mid-1950s for both sound synthesis as well as artifical intelligence (compositional decision making) applications. Certain studios employ digital computers to generate control signals for voltage-controlled analog instruments. Such a configuration is called a *hybrid* system. Using solid-state switches, it is possible to construct a computer-controlled switching array to replace or augment the standard patch-panel switching and signal routing in a studio. Some of the advantages and drawbacks of digital sound synthesis, as well as other

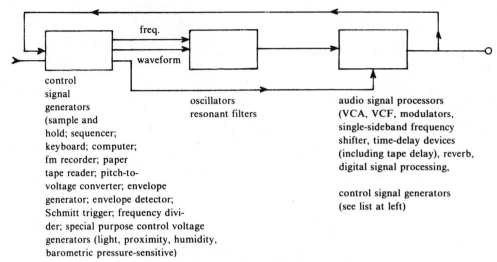

control
signal
generators
(sample and
hold; sequencer;
keyboard; computer;
fm recorder; paper
tape reader; pitch-to-
voltage converter; envelope
generator; envelope detector;
Schmitt trigger; frequency divider; special purpose control voltage
generators (light, proximity, humidity,
barometric pressure-sensitive)

oscillators
resonant filters

audio signal processors
(VCA, VCF, modulators,
single-sideband frequency
shifter, time-delay devices
(including tape delay), reverb,
digital signal processing,

control signal generators
(see list at left)

FIGURE 1.21

applications of digital technology in electronic music, were discussed
earlier in this chapter. It requires a large financial and intellectual invest-
ment to design a workable digital sound synthesis system. Few studios
can afford a complete, dedicated minicomputer system, the new price of
which can easily run $40,000 to $50,000, and time sharing has proven to be
inefficient for digital sound synthesis. In a university it is often possible to
pool resources with departments and areas of similar interest (psychology,
computer graphics, and the like) to solve equipment and software problems. Certain synthesis programs such as the Vercoe-MIT *Music 11* can be
used directly or adapted to run on most Digital Equipment Corporation
PDP 11/ series computers. Two small dedicated digital synthesizers, the
New England Digital *Synclavier* and the Alles/Bell Labs synthesizer are
available in the $20,000 range at this writing. Several reputable used
computer outlets offer minicomputer equipment at considerable savings. In
general, microcomputers are too slow for digital synthesis applications.
However, microcomputers are being used with increasing frequency for
generation of control signals for analog equipment.[2]

PROBLEMS

1. Describe the frequency components of the following waveforms: sine wave,
   sawtooth wave, triangle wave, square wave, pulse wave of 60% duty cycle,
   and pulse wave of 90% duty cycle.

2. What factors influence the tone quality of a sound?

3. Name two instruments that employ a throttled airstream for sound wave generation.

4. Give an example of simple harmonic motion.

5. Convert 6,280 radians/second to Hz.

6. Compare the frequency components of a 100 Hz sawtooth wave with those of a 100 Hz square wave. What is the frequency of the fundamental of each wave? What is the frequency of the third harmonic of each wave? What is the frequency of the sixth partial of each wave? What is the frequency of the third overtone of each wave? Why is the term *overtone* often ambiguous?

7. What is the interval defined by the seventh and eighth harmonics of a sawtooth wave; by the fifth and thirteenth harmonics of a square wave?[3]

8. If the frequency of A_4 (USA Standard; a', Helmholtz) is 440 Hz, using the ratios in the harmonic series, calculate the frequency of D_5; of F_6. These frequency ratios are those of intervals in what type of tuning?[4]

9. If the period of oscillation of a given waveform is 0.125 millisecond, what is the frequency of oscillation in Hz?

10. The two sine waves shown in Example 1 differ in phase by how many degrees?

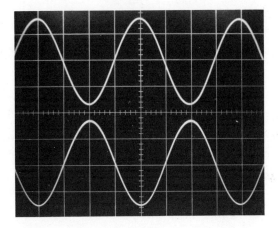

11. Describe the phase relationships of the four sine waves shown in example 2.

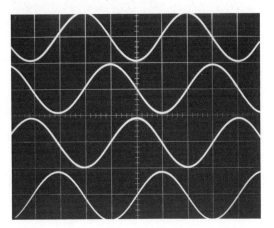

12. What are the approximate duty cycles of the pulse waves the spectra of which are shown in examples 3 and 4?

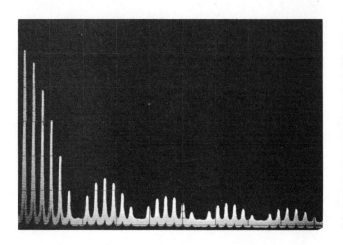 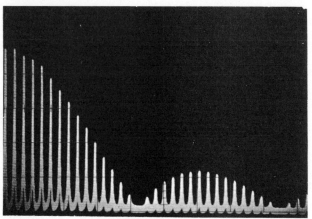

13. Connect a pulse generator to a tunable resonant low-pass filter or band-pass filter of approximately one-third octave bandwidth or less. Tune the pulse generator to approximately c_3 and adjust the duty cycle to 50% (square wave). Use the filter to listen to the frequency components present. Set the filter to pass only the fifth harmonic, and then vary the pulse width until this harmonic disappears. What is the duty cycle of *this* pulse wave? If possible, view the waveform on an oscilloscope. Slow the pulse wave frequency to 1 Hz or less and listen to the rhythm made by the clicks from the loudspeaker. Notate this rhythm and correlate your findings with the duty-cycle value you determined.

NOTES

1. J. W. Beauchamp, "Additive Synthesis of Harmonic Musical Tones," *Journal of the Audio Engineering Society* 14 (1966): 332–342. Mr. Beauchamp's comments should be understood in their proper context: for his particular application—the generation of harmonic tones—modulation synthesis was considered impractical. However, Chowning's article, "The Synthesis of Complex Audio Spectra by Means of Frequency Modulation," *Journal of the Audio Engineering Society* 21 (1973): 526–534, is a discussion of FM as a means for generating harmonic tones, the spectral characteristics of which may be accurately specified and controlled through time. However, to implement Mr. Chowning's method would require a digital computer (his technique), or a special voltage-controlled oscillator (controllable through 0 Hz and having a linear control-voltage–versus–frequency response).

2. See P. Hillen, "A Microprocessor-Based Sequencer for Voltage-controlled Electronic Music Synthesizer," *Audio Engineering Society Reprint Number 1229* (1977).

3. See J. Backus, *The Accoustical Foundations of Music* (New York: Norton, 1964), pp. 115–140.

4. Ibid.

SELECTED BIBLIOGRAPHY
Books

Alley, C. L., and Atwood, K. W. *Electronic Engineering,* 2nd ed. New York: Wiley, 1967.

Appleton, J., and Perera, R. *The Development and Practice of Electronic Music.* Englewood Cliffs, N.J.: Prentice-Hall, 1974.

The ARRL Radio Amateur's Handbook, 1973. Newington, Conn.: ARRL.

Austin, W. *Music in the Twentieth Century.* New York: Norton, 1966.

Backus, J. *The Acoustical Foundations of Music.* New York: Norton, 1969.

Baer, C. *Electrical and Electronics Drawing.* New York: McGraw-Hill, 1973.

Beaver, P., and Krause, B. *The Nonesuch Guide to Electronic Music,* HC73018 New York: Nonesuch Records, 1968.

Beckwith, J., and Kasemits, U. *The Modern Composer and His World.* Toronto: University of Toronto Press, 1961.

Cope, D. *New Music Composition.* New York: Schirmer Books (Macmillan), 1977.

Craig, E. J. *Laplace and Fourier Transforms for Electrical Engineers.* New York: Holt, Rinehart and Winston, 1964.

Cross, L. *A Bibliography of Electronic Music.* Toronto: University of Toronto Press, 1966.

Crowhurst, N. *Electronic Musical Instruments.* Blue Ridge Summit, Pa.: TAB Books, 1971.

Deutsch, H. *Synthesis.* New York: Alfred Publishing, 1976.

Dorf, R. *Electronic Musical Instruments.* Mineola, N.Y.: Radiofile, 1963.

Ernst, D. *The Evolution of Electronic Music.* New York: Schirmer Books (Macmillan), 1977.

Gayford, M. L. *Electroacoustics.* London: Butterworth, 1970.

Ghausi, M. *Electronic Circuits.* New York: Van Nostrand-Reinhold, 1971.

Graf, R. *Modern Dictionary of Electronics.* Indianapolis, Ind.: Howard W. Sams, 1972.

Hayt, W., and Hughes, G. *Introduction to Electronic Engineering.* New York: McGraw-Hill, 1968.

Helmholtz, H. *On the Sensation of Tone.* Translated by A. J. Ellis. New York: Dover 1954.

Hickey, H., and Villines, W. *Elements of Electronics,* 3rd ed. New York: McGraw-Hill, 1970.

Hiller, L., and Isaacson, L. M. *Experimental Music Composition with an Electronic Computer.* New York: McGraw-Hill, 1959.

Horowitz, M. *How to Build Solid-State Audio Circuits.* Blue Ridge Summit, Pa.: TAB Books, 1972.

Howe, H. *Electronic Music Synthesis.* New York: Norton, 1974.

Hsu, H. *Fourier Analysis.* New York: Simon and Schuster, 1970, revised edition.

Jenkins, J., and Smith, J. *Electric Music: A Practical Manual.* Bloomington, Ind.: University of Indiana Press, 1976.

Judd, F. C. *Electronic Music and Musique Concrète.* London: Neville Spearman, Ltd., 1961.

Lefkoff, G., ed. *Computer Applications in Music*. Morgantown, W.Va.: West Virginia University Press, 1967.

Lenk, J. D. *Manual for Integrated Circuit Users*. Reston, Va.: Reston Publishing Co., 1973.

Magrab, E. B., and Blomquist, D. S. *The Measurement of Time-Varying Phenomena*. New York: Wiley-Interscience, 1971.

Mandl, M. *Handbook of Modern Electronic Data*. Reston, Va.: Reston Publishing Company, 1973.

Markus, J. *Source Book of Electronic Circuits*. New York: McGraw-Hill, 1968.

Meyer-Eppler, W. "Elektronische Musik." In *Klangstruktur der Musik*. Edited by F. Winckel. Berlin: 1955.

Moles, A. *Information Theory and Esthetic Perception*. Champaign, Ill.: University of Illinois Press, 1966.

Olson, H. *Music, Physics, and Engineering*. New York: Dover, 1967.

Orr, W. *The Radio Handbook,* 14th ed. Summerland, Calif.: Editors and Engineers Ltd., 1964.

Reference Data for Radio Engineers, 4th ed. Indianapolis, Ind.: Howard W. Sams, 1964.

Risset, J. *An Introductory Catalog of Computer Synthesized Sounds*. Murray Hill, N.J.: Bell Telephone Laboratories, 1970.

Ruscol, H. *Electronic Music: The Liberation of Sound*. Englewood Cliffs, N.J.: Prentice-Hall, 1972.

Salzman, E. *Twentieth-Century Music: An Introduction*. Englewood Cliffs, N.J.: Prentice-Hall, 1967.

Schillinger, J. "Electronic Instruments." In *The Schillinger System of Musical Composition,* Book XII, vol. II. New York: Carl Fischer, 1946.

Schwartz, E., and Childs, B. *Contemporary Composers on Contemporary Music*. New York: Holt, Rinehart, and Winston, 1967.

Schwartz, E. *Electronic Music: A Listener's Guide*. New York: Praeger, 1973.

Sear, W. *The New World of Electronic Music*. New York: Alfred Publishing, 1975.

Stockhausen, K. *Texte*. Vols. 1, 2, and 3. Cologne: DuMont Schauberg.

Strutt, Baron Raleigh J. *The Theory of Sound,* Vol. I. New York: Macmillan, 1929.

Stuckenschmidt, H. H. *Twentieth-Century Music*. New York: McGraw-Hill, World Universal Library, 1969.

Taylor, C. A. *The Physics of Musical Sounds*. New York: American Elsevier, 1965.

Thomas, H. *Handbook of Electronic Circuit Design Analysis*. Reston, Va.: Reston Publishing, 1972.

Tremaine, H. *Audio Cyclopedia,* 2nd ed. Indianapolis, Ind.: Howard W. Sams, 1969.

Trythall, G. *Principles and Practice of Electronic Music*. New York: Grosset and Dunlap, 1973.

von Foerster, H., and Beauchamp, J. W., eds. *Music by Computers*. New York: Wiley, 1969.

Winckel, F. *Music, Sound, and Sensation*. Translated by T. Binkley. New York: Dover, 1967.

Zaffiri, E. *Due Scuole di Musica Elettronica in Italia*. Milan: Silva, 1968.

Zaripov, R. K. *Kobernetika i Muzyka*. USSR 71, VKP.

Zimmerman, H., and Mason, S. *Electronic Circuit Theory*. New York: Wiley, 1962.

Articles

Appleton, J. "Aesthetic Direction in Electronic Music." *Western Humanistic Review* 18, no. 4 (1974).

Babbitt, M. "Who Cares if You Listen?" *High Fidelity* 8 (1958): 38.

Backus, J. "*Die Reihe*—a Scientific Evaluation." *Perspectives of New Music* 1, no. 1 (Fall 1962).

Beauchamp, J. W. "Additive Synthesis of Harmonic Musical Tones." *Journal of the Audio Engineering Society* 14, no. 4 (1966): 332–342.

Benade, A. "The Physics of Brasses." *Scientific American* 229 (July 1973): 24–35.

Blackham, E. "The Physics of the Piano." *Scientific American* 213 no. 6 (December 1965): 88–96, 99.

BMI: The Many Worlds of Music. Summer 1970. New York: BMI, Public Relations Department, 589 5th Avenue, N.Y., N.Y. 10017.

Ciamaga, G. "Some Thoughts on the Teaching of Electronic Music." *Yearbook of the Inter-American Institute for Musical Research* 3 (1967): 69.

De la Vega, A. "Regarding Electronic Music." *Tempo* 75: 2.

Die Reihe 5. English Translation. Bryn Mawr, Pa.: Theodore Presser Company.

Ehle, R. "Inside the Moog Synthesizer." *Audio* 53, no. 12 (December 1969): 30, 32, 34.

Eimert, H. "How Electronic Music Began." *The Musical Times* 113, no. 1550 (April 1972): 347–349.

Electronic Musicians' Handbook and Catalog. Newton, N.H.: C.F.R. Associates, 1976.

Forte, A. "Composing with Electrons in Cologne." *High Fidelity* 6 (October 1956),: 64.

"Four Views of the Music Department at the University of California at San Diego." *Synthesis* 1 no. 2 (1971).

Henning, H. "Applications of Walsh Functions in Communications." *IEEE Spectrum*. November 1969, pp. 82–91.

Hiller, L. "Music Composed with a Computer: A Historical Survey." *Illinois Technical Report*-18, School of Music, University of Illinois at Urbana.

Hutchins, B. "Interview with Robert Moog. Part One: The First Ten Years." *Electronotes* 45, no. 2 (October 1974).

Judd, F. C. "The Composition of Electronic Music." *Audio and Record Review* 1 (November 1961).

Kryter, K. "Impairment to Hearing from Exposure to Noise." *Journal of the Acoustical Society of America* 53, no. 5 (May 1973).

Le Caine, H. "Electronic Music." *IRE Proceedings* 44 (1956): 457.

Luening, O. "Some Random Remarks about Electronic Music." *Journal of Music Theory* 8 (Spring 1964): 89.

McCarty, F. "Electronic Music Systems: Structure, Control, Product." *Perspectives of New Music*. Spring–Summer 1975, pp. 98–125.

Meyers, R. "Technical Bases of Electronic Music [sections 5.00 to 9.04]." *Journal of Music Theory* 8, no. 2 (Winter 1964): 184–250.

Oster, G. "Auditory Beats in the Brain." *Scientific American* 229, no. 4 (October 1973): 94–102.

Pellegrino, R. "An Electronic Studio Manual." Columbus, Ohio: Ohio State University, College of the Arts Publication no. 2 (1969).

Pousseur, H. "Calculation and Imagination in Electronic Music." *Electronic Music Review* 5: 21.

Stockhausen, K. "Elektronische und instrumentale Musik." *Texte zur elektronischen und instrumentalen Musik*. Cologne: DuMont Schauberg, 1963.

————. "Die Entstehung der elektronischen Musik." *Texte zur elektronischen und instrumentalen Musik*. Cologne: DuMont Schauberg, 1963.

————. "The Origins of Electronic Music." *Musical Times* 112, no. 1541 (July 1971): 649–650.

Technische Hausmitteilungen des Nordwestdeutschen Rundfunks 6 nos. 1–2 (1954), trans. National Research Council of Canada, *Technical Translations*, 601–612 (1956).

Ussachevsky, V. "Notes on a Piece for Tape Recorder." *Musical Quarterly* 46 (1960): 202.

————. "The Process of Experimental Music." *Journal of the Audio Engineering Society* 6 (1958): 202.

Winckel, F. "The Psychoacoustical Analysis of Structure as Applied to Electronic Music." *Journal of Music Theory* 7, no. 2 (Winter 1963).

2

PSYCHOACOUSTICS AND ELECTRONIC MUSIC

First performance of Gesang der Jünglinge at
the West German Radio, Cologne, 1956

The electronic music composer can produce sounds that transcend the limits of the listening abilities of the audience. It is a simple feat to generate pitches that are imperceptibly high, or pitch changes that are imperceptibly subtle. It is also simple to generate pitches of such short duration that all pitch information is lost. It is not much more difficult to produce melody-like series that are random note strings of indeterminate length, or rhythmic strings that never duplicate themselves.

It seems sensible then that the composer of electronic music know something about the nature of auditory perception, in the sense both of apprehension and comprehension. Unfortunately, we know little about *musical* perception, in the sense of comprehension. The central processes involved in musical perception remain largely a mystery. They are highly complex, and do not submit easily to objective measurement.

The more peripheral processes, those that take place in the ear, are easier to measure quantitatively. These processes have been studied extensively and are understood fairly well; they relate to the sound elements *pitch, timbre/sonance, loudness,* and *time/space.* It is essential that the reader not consider these elements to be discrete; each is strongly related perceptually to every other. Experimental investigation of the perception of these elements has gone on for more than a century. Still, there is a great deal of confusion concerning the perceptual activities themselves and the significance of their interrelationships.

In their effort to promote experimental rigor, psychoacoustical investigators have sought to approach the goal of steady-state sound as their experimental stimulus. In fact, many of the instruments designed to provide these stimuli have since turned up in the electronic music studio. It is important to realize, though, that music is not steady-state sound. This fact is most apparent when music is generated by traditional instruments, including the human voice, but it also seems that electronic music composers do not favor the steady-state attributes of electronically generated sound. In fact, many composers devote a great deal of attention to the reduction of ''steady-stateness'' in their compositions, trying instead to produce the subjective qualities of ''life'' and ''naturalness.''

One of the greatest problems in the study of music and psychophysics is the fact, validated too often by history, that musicians and psychophysicists tend to misunderstand each other. The psychophysicist's definition of ''music'' often differs from that of the musician. Musical generalizations induced from nonmusical information can be misleading. The author shall try to correct many of these misunderstandings in this chapter.

PITCH

The lower threshold of human pitch perception is about 15 Hz. Below 15 Hz, discrete cycles are heard; between 15 to 30 Hz, these cycles perceptually fuse into an uninterrupted tone. The upper threshold of pitch percep-

This chapter was prepared especially for this publication by David Butler.

tion is commonly considered to be about 15 kHz. This audibility threshold is a rough average; individual responses may vary widely, due to such factors as signal intensity and age of the listener.

The frequency range of 15 Hz to 15 kHz spans a musical range of a little less than 10 octaves. The range of the piano, using U.S.A. Standard octave designations, is A_0 (27.5 Hz. equal-tempered [ET]) to C_8 (4186.0 Hz, ET). The ranges of other musical instruments seldom extend beyond this frequency range. Although this range seems small when viewed as one-fifth of the human audibility range, the musical span is more than eight octaves. In physical terms, the common instrumental range is 20% of the audibility range; in musical terms, the common instrumental pitch range is 80% of the audibility range.

Henry found that the "central pitch information area" of traditional music may be as small as a single octave in some cases, with pitches outside the normal two- to three-octave "central pitch information area" utilized for color, commonly through the compositional device of doubling.[1] Henry states that electronic music composers have the capability to distribute their music more equally across the pitch spectrum, without being constrained by conventional pattern grids such as the octave. There is an important psychoacoustical limit that must temper this assertion: the just-noticeable-difference (jnd) of perceived pitch varies in different registers.[2] At frequencies up to about 1,000 Hz, the jnd of inequal pitches (presented sequentially) is 3 Hz; above 1,000 Hz, the jnd becomes a constant 0.25%. In musical terms, the jnd of inequal pitches at 30 Hz is a 10% shift, or roughly a major second. At 1,000 Hz, the jnd is 0.05 semitones (5 cents). Backus stated that pitch perception is essentially nonexistent above around 10 kHz.[3] There is a perceptible pitch-like sound in this higher frequency range, but we experience much greater difficulty in labeling it than we would if the frequency were divided by two or three. In short, there is a range of maximum accuracy for pitch perception: about seven octaves starting upwards from about 30 Hz.

It may be possible to reconcile Henry's assertion with psychoacoustical limits on one point: Snow found that most of the musical information carried in the above-10-kHz range consists of transient "noises" such as bow scrapings and reed attack transients.[4] Physicists with an interest in musical acoustics have commonly assigned little musical significance to this information, but electronic music composers who wish to add "naturalness" to their compositions might see an important compositional device that physicists have overlooked.

Much of the influential psychoacoustics literature on pitch perception is based on experiments in which sine tones were used as stimuli. Recently, the importance of partials (see the section on timbre and sonance, below) in pitch perception has been better recognized. Plomp has asserted that pitch perception is a function of either frequency-fundamental perception, or periodicity-characteristic perception, depending on the fundamental fre-

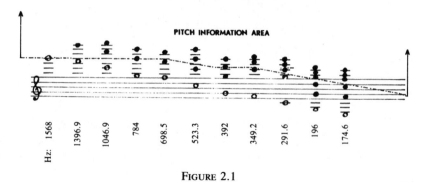

FIGURE 2.1

Pitch information threshold for complex tones,
developed from data given by Plomp (1967).

quency of the stimulus tone.[5] The pitches of frequencies between about 700
Hz and 1,400 Hz (F_5 to F_6) are perceived through the second and higher
partials, and not the fundamental. Above 1,400 Hz, the fundamental carries the pitch information. Pitches within the approximate range F_4 to E_5
(350 to 700 Hz) carry the pitch information in the third and higher partials;
pitches below F_4 contain no pitch information below the fourth partial. This
phenomenon is represented graphically in figure 2.1. Should Plomp's findings be substantiated, they would, in turn, substantiate Winckel's
hypothesis that pitch perception is a function of both place-pattern and
periodicity response existing side-by-side,[6] although Winckel did not have
the experimental data to suggest the frequency-dependent shift. The author
has not been able to replicate Plomp's findings, either when using his own
stimuli or when using Plomp's recordings.

Fundamental tracking is the phenomenon on which Plomp based his
research. This phenomenon is easily demonstrable, musically important,
and forms a strong link between the pitch and timbre perception processes.
The auditory system processes all of the partials of the complex tone
spectrum as it decodes pitch input signals, not just the fundamental. It is
not necessary for all parts of the complex tone, including the fundamental,
to be physically present in order that the listener receive the correct pitch
impression. A correct pitch judgment can be made when the pitch information is limited to any two adjacent partials: as other partials are added, only
a change of timbre (which may variously be characterized as "depth,"
"resonance," "richness," or simply as loudness) will be perceived. This
phenomenon is related to *subjective tone* perception (see the section on
timbre and sonance, below).

For example, the lowest pitch produced by the double bass has a frequency of about 41 Hz, well below the frequency response of smaller or
less sophisticated loudspeakers, including those housed in headphones.
Yet, the listener perceives the correct pitch and in the correct register,
although a spectral analysis of the speaker output will show no physical

energy present at the point in the spectrum that coincides with that of the fundamental. The perceptual process of fundamental tracking works for any pure tones that are harmonically related: that is, tones with the same composite repetition rate, or period.

The *chorus effect* occurs frequently in traditional music and could be of considerable importance to the electronic music composer. Why should an impoverished community symphony not attempt to economize by firing eleven of its twelve first violinists, and amplify the one remaining violinist to twelve times the normal amplitude? The answer, of course, is that the resulting sound would be musically unsatisfactory: even an untrained observer would hear that the first violin part was being played by a single, very loud, violin. The chorus effect, the sensation of several almost identical sounds in near fusion, would be lost.

Chorus effect is commonly attributed to the beats that result from slightly out-of-tune complex tones.[7] This explanation is probably simplistic. When two or more performers attempt to produce a sound that is a perfect unison in every possible way, there is the potential for dissimilarity in every element of that sound. If the performers attack or release any pitch more than 2 milliseconds (msec) apart, the separate attacks and releases will be discernible. It is very unlikely that two similar instruments (or voices) would generate the same spectral envelope, so timbre and sonance differences must also be considered. Even if the same instrument is "dubbed" over itself on multitrack tape, the transient characteristics of the sound will differ, and a small difference in performance dynamics can alter the timbre of the instrument's sound. If a convincing chorus effect is to be produced in the electronic music studio, the composer will need to consider much more than just pitch differences.

Recently, quite a bit of attention has been focused on *dichotic* listening: the input of discrete auditory signals to the two ears. Dichotic listening has its greatest musical influence over pitch perception through three phenomena: diplacusis, melodic channeling, and eradication of beat-tone sensations.

Diplacusis is the apprehension of equal frequencies as inequal pitches when presented to the separate ears. Although there is an abundance of experimental literature concerning diplacusis, there is no general agreement as to its musical importance. Indications are that the phenomenon is of negligible musical significance in a free-sound field environment (that is, when the left ear hears part of what the right ear hears and vice versa). Diplacusis is, however, noticeable in a dichotic listening situation, and might be a problem when stereo headphones are used for monitoring. Van den Brink and others found that "the site in the auditory system where neural excitation patterns that unequivocally determine the perceived pitch [pure tone pitch or residue pitch] are elicited must be beyond the areas where the information descending from the two ears is still separate."[8]

Melodic channeling (also called streaming, stream segregation, and

melodic fission) is a more recent area of study in dichotic musical perception. Deutsch found that the presentation of the melodic pattern

to the left ear and the presentation of the pattern

to the right ear resulted in the perception of the pattern

for the right ear and perception of the pattern

for the left ear.[9]

There is some experimental evidence that the melodic-channeling phenomenon persists even when many of Deutsch's experimental controls are
removed. Two-part contrapuntal specimens have been substituted for the C
major scale patterns, the stimuli have been presented in a stereophonic
free-sound field, musical instruments have been used in place of computer-controlled oscillators, and the frequency responses of the two
channels have been made noticeably inequal, without undoing the channeling phenomenon.[10]

Beat-tones or *beats* are perceived when two pitches are slightly mistuned at the unison. In order to experience the influence of dichotic listening over beat-tones, it is suggested that the reader tune two oscillators
(same waveform) to a near unison in the low frequency range of below
about 90 Hz. These signals should then be driven through separate chan-

nels of a stereophonic amplifier with switching capability to loudspeakers (free-sound field presentation) and stereo headphones (dichotic presentation). Should the signals be mistuned by 1 Hz, the listener will perceive an amplitude fluctuation, or beat, each second when the signals are routed through the loudspeakers. With the speakers switched off and the signals presented dichotically, the beat sensation will disappear. This phenomenon is frequency-dependent: between about 90 and 150 Hz, the beat will be perceived as a "ping-pong" effect, localizing first in one ear, then the other. Above 150 Hz, the dichotic beat sensation resembles the free-sound field beat sensation.

The phenomena attributable to dichotic listening may be quite important to the electronic music composer. If the composer intends to use loudspeakers as the performance medium, it is advisable that monitoring and mixing always be performed with loudspeakers instead of stereo headphones. Otherwise, unfortunate surprises may result.

It was stated at the beginning of this chapter that interrelationships among the perceptions of sound elements are common. Several other relationships will be discussed later in this chapter: the interrelationship of pitch and loudness (see the section on loudness, below); subjective tones and other relationships between pitch and timbre (see the section on timbre and sonance below); and the Doppler effect (see the section on space and time, below).

TIMBRE AND SONANCE

Reviews of the experimental literature on timbre perception usually begin with the disclaimer that this element has been under-researched and is currently little-understood. A more basic problem seems to be that the term *timbre* itself takes on different meanings within different disciplines, and may be defined differently by individuals within the same discipline. Music dictionaries and texts commonly define *timbre perception* as the ability to discriminate one musical instrument's sound from that of another when pitch and loudness are the same.

Yet, timbre is too broad an attribute to be confined only to orchestral instrument sounds, or vocal sounds, or complex steady-state sounds. The discussion in this section will assume that (1) human auditory systems are not imperfect meters, but that meters are imperfect approximations of human auditory systems; (2) the reader is not interested in attempting to duplicate the sounds produced by traditional orchestral instruments—timbre means more than many musicians seem to think; and (3) the reader will agree that timbre is the perceptual manifestation of the combined partials of a complex tone *only at any given instant*. The term *sonance* refers to the transient attributes of tone color: attack and decay characteristics of partial tones, fusion, phase differences, and other aperiodic attributes of the sound.[11] Although this term has never found common usage, it is resurrected in this chapter simply because the interrelationship of time and timbre is vitally important to the electronic music composer.

Timbre

Other than a few tones produced by the flute and organ, musical sound traditionally has been composed of complex tones: that is, tones which contain a fundamental and upper partials that are integer multiples of the fundamental (the inharmonicity of upper partials produced by stretched strings will be discussed later in this section). The individual resonating properties of acoustical instruments enhance or suppress individual partial tones in this spectrum, resulting in the physical manifestation of timbre. The timbral spectrum is discussed at some length in chapter 1, and a graphic representation of a complex waveform that results from sinusoidal partials is given in figure 1.7, chapter 1.

Note that *waveform* is defined as the *physical* description of timbre; there is not a perfect correlation between the physical and perceptual attributes of timbre. Although the waveform is a representation of the relative phases of the partials, as well as their energy levels, the effect of phase has only a subtle perceptual consequence on timbre.[12] This is one of the most misunderstood phenomena related to timbre perception; unfortunately, it is also one of the most basic. Ohm asserted that the ear analyzes a complex wave as does a present-day harmonic-wave analyzer: by breaking the incoming signal down into its Fourier sine components.[13] Helmholtz tested Ohm's theory and summarized his findings with a two-part assertion: (1) two tones with the same waveform will be perceived as having the same timbre and (2) two tones with different waveforms *may not* be perceived as having different timbres.[14] For over a century, most acoustics texts have faithfully repeated Ohm's assertion and only the former of Helmholtz's assertions. Helmholtz's second assertion becomes significant if the reader is more interested in the perceptual, rather than the physical, attributes of timbre. During the 1950s, a great deal of activity was devoted to the simulation of the sounds of traditional musical instruments by additive synthesis of sine components (Fourier transform generation). The success of the resulting sounds was mixed. Some sounds, especially that of the simulated piano, were generally judged unconvincing, even when transient characteristics such as attack and decay attributes were introduced. One cause of this disappointment, in retrospect, is that the harmonic spectrum of the piano is actually slightly inharmonic: the second and higher partials are not perfect integer multiples of the fundamental, but are sharp to a measurable degree.[15] It is for this reason that piano tuners "stretch" octaves on a piano, incrementally flatting pitches in the lower registers, and correspondingly sharping the pitches in the upper registers so that their fundamentals are in tune with coincidental upper partials of the tones struck at the lower end of the keyboard. Ohm's theorem did not account for this inharmonicity; one of the most important descriptive systems in musical psychophysics is not totally descriptive. The intent in this illustration is not to deny the validity of physical data, but to show that they should be applied judiciously in any attempt to explain musical phenomena.

The equipment housed in the average electronic music studio allows the composer to alter timbres through both physical (that is, meter-readable) and perceptual (non–meter-readable) manipulations. Physical alterations are achieved through the use of filters, modulators, and transform generators. They result in an alteration of waveform that may or may not be hearable. Perceptual alterations are generally achieved through mixing and switching devices. By definition they are hearable, but they may not result in a physical alteration that is meter-readable. Of course, a composer will use all of these devices in order to perceptibly alter the sound in the program. It is important to remember, however, that there is no one-to-one correlation between the physical attributes of sounds and their perceptual manifestations. Physical alterations are discussed in the ensuing chapters of this book and will not be discussed here. Perceptual alterations may be caused by temporal separation or by certain signal combinations: *subjective tones* are the most common perceptual phenomena which result from these combinational alterations. Temporal separation effects would relate only to very short tone bursts or to attack transients of longer tones. Hirsh found that

> there are cases in which two acoustic events give rise to one auditory event and, further, the temporal separation between the two acoustic events is responsible for a change in the quality of the single auditory event. If two brief clicks are delivered to one ear and are separated by less than two msec, they will be heard as one sound and, further, the quality of that sound, whether "dull" or "sharp" will be determined by the amount of separation between the two acoustic clicks.[16]

Combinational effects have a much broader relationship to timbre perception. *Subjective tone* perception seems closely related to both beat-tone perception and fundamental tracking.[17] Unlike these phenomena, however, subjective tone perception is loudness-dependent. If two signals, f and ($f + x$) are generated at a sufficient intensity, a third sound, at the frequency level of x, will be heard (so long, of course, as x lies in the audible range). This third sound, or subjective tone, has no physical energy: it is solely a perceptual entity. Since the frequency of this third tone is always the same as the frequency differential between the two source tones, it is commonly called a *difference tone*. The cause of subjective tones has generally been attributed to nonlinear distortion within the inner ear (cochlea) or even within the central nervous system.[18] This explanation, although widely accepted, is objectionable because the model and the reality are confused: the ear/central nervous system/brain complex is depicted as a flawed nonlinear transducer. It seems more acceptable to view subjective tone perception as a manifestation of the same pattern-processing activity as is fundamental tracking. Above a certain loudness level, a sound amplification system will produce distortions that resemble subjective tones. These sounds are not to be confused with subjective tones, since they have a measurable physical energy level.

Sonance

In an unaltered state, the tones produced by electrically driven nonrandom oscillators differ from acoustical instruments in several respects that are important in a discussion of sonance: (1) the sounds approach a steady state to the extent that the energy levels, phase relationships, and frequency ratios of the partials, as well as the listening environment and listener, remain static from the time when the sound is switched on until it is switched off; (2) the sounds are "clean," that is, the signals contain no aperiodic ingredients; and (3) the amplitude patterns of unmodulated complex tone spectra are always decremental: for example, the amplitude characteristics for the spectrum of a sawtooth wave are 1, 1/2, 1/3, 1/4, and so on for the ascending partials, whereas an orchestral instrument is likely to produce a spectrum that does not show this sort of regular, decremental pattern. A line spectrum generated by an orchestral instrument might have the amplitude ratio set of 1, 1.5, 0.75, 0.5, 1.75, and so on for the ascending partials.

As an example of the non–steady-state sound characteristics of acoustical instruments, a short investigation of the sound of a trumpet should be informative. The trumpet's timbral spectrum is frequency dependent: it is not constant throughout the range of the instrument. In addition, the spectrum is loudness dependent (see figure 2.2).

Figure 2.2 illustrates not only the loudness dependency of the timbral spectrum of a trumpet tone, but also that the spectrum can, depending on the amplitude, be either decremental or incremental. Note that the amplitude pattern for the frequency components of the *pianissimo* tone somewhat resembles a spectrum analysis pattern of a sawtooth wave, but that at the *fortissimo* level there is such an incremental energy curve that the ninth partial is about twice the loudness of the fundamental. Remember that figure 2.2 represents only a 13 msec "photograph" of a trumpet sound; the next 13 msec would almost certainly contain some variation in some or all of these curves.

The frequency and loudness dependency of the trumpet's timbral spectrum is not the sole source of its sonance. As was stated earlier in this chapter, tones produced by orchestral instruments are anything but steady-state. Musical "noises" such as bow scrapes, reed-attack noises, and the percussive sounds of piano hammers hitting metal wire exist both within the musical pitch information area of below 5 kHz and upwards in the

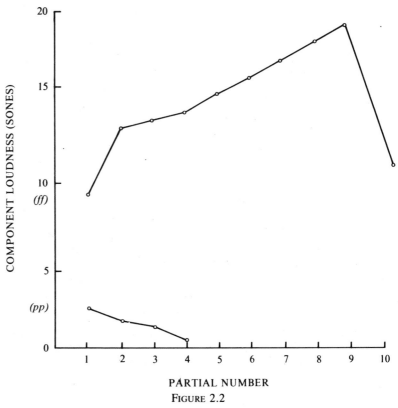

FIGURE 2.2

Line spectrum of a trumpet tone (concert pitch
C_4), at pianissimo and fortissimo levels.

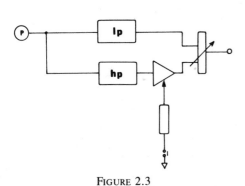

FIGURE 2.3

Patching diagram to add attack transient to
steady-state signal.

frequency spectrum to well above 10 kHz. Musical instruments have
unique attack and decay transients: during the first milliseconds of the
onset of an instrumental or vocal sound, certain partials may have quite
different energy levels than when measured after several hundred milliseconds have passed and the sound has become established. These transients carry important instrument identification information to the musical
listener.[19] In addition, room acoustics plays a role in sonance; attack and
decay transient characteristics, especially, are perceptually modified by
room ambience.

In the discussion of pitch perception, it was suggested that high-
frequency transients might be added to the program to impart the quality of
"life" or "naturalness." The reader will probably find that the most
convincing transient is that added at the attack phase of the tone. This
attack transient may be achieved by using filters to isolate and impart
transient amplitude characteristics to the high frequency components of the
program and gating (see the Glossary, under "gate") this transient so that

it decays within the first 20 to 30 msec of each tone, as shown in figure 2.3. Voltage-controlled comb filters (see chapter 6) are often employed to impart sonance characteristics to steady state sounds.

These sonance characteristics have not been outlined for the purpose of encouraging electronic music composers to use them to build better simulations of traditional musical instrument sounds. Instead, it is hoped that composers who are interested in adding to their compositions the highly subjective qualities of "life" and "naturalness" will find in these sonance characteristics analogs that will help them reach this goal while maintaining the stylistic integrity of their medium.

LOUDNESS

Loudness is perhaps the most interdependent of the auditory sensations. Pitch perception is loudness-dependent, and loudness perception is frequency-dependent.[20] As was stated in the previous section, timbre perception is often loudness-dependent, and subjective tones are perceptible only when the stimulus tones are sufficiently loud. It will be demonstrated in this section that loudness can also be timbre-dependent.

The perceptual measurement of loudness is related to the physical measurement of intensity; for a variety of reasons, there is not a linear correlation between the two measurement systems. The intensity of a tone, that is, its physical energy, is measured by its sound pressure level (SPL) in increments of decibels (dB). The lower threshold of hearing is 0 dB; the upper, known as both the "threshold of feeling" and the "threshold of pain," is about 120 dB. A normal conversational loudness range is 50 to 60 dB. Decibels are measures not of arithmetic, but of logarithmic, increments (see chapter 5). If you decrease the intensity of a tone by a factor of 10, a 10-dB drop results; a decrease of intensity by a factor of 100 results in a 20-dB drop. The 60-dB difference between the threshold of hearing and normal conversational sound level is equal to an intensity differential of 10^6, or a millionfold.

Fletcher and Munson investigated the relationship between sound level and perceptual loudness, using a 1-kHz sine wave as their control tone.[21] This particular waveform was selected because it is easy to define mathematically. The frequency of 1 kHz was selected because it is a round number and lies in the range where human auditory perception is most acute. By asking their test subjects to match perceived loudness of sine tones of various frequencies with the control tone, and repeating this procedure at various sound pressure levels, Fletcher and Munson derived the set of intensity/frequency levels judged to be equal in loudness shown in figure 2.4.

It should be remembered that these curves represent the *averaged* judgments of a large group of subjects; individual responses may differ noticeably. The Fletcher-Munson curves have been cited often in acoustics and psychoacoustics texts and were used as a starting point for a great deal of

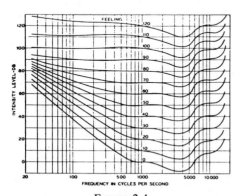

FIGURE 2.4

Fletcher-Munson equal loudness curves. From Harvey Fletcher and W. A. Munson, "Loudness: Its Measurement and Calculation," *Journal of the Acoustical Society of America* 5 (1933): 91

research. The term *phon* was created to describe loudness level; *phons* and decibels are equal at the frequency of 1 kHz, the frequency of the control tone used by Fletcher and Munson. Reference to figure 2.4 will quickly show that phons and decibels are not equal throughout the frequency spectrum. However, as Fletcher noted in his original paper, the two levels are approximately the same within the frequency range of 300 Hz to 4 kHz; this is roughly the central pitch information area of traditional music. There are two anomalies within this range: (1) the rather sharp fall-off of the ear's sensitivity to low-frequency tones at low sound levels, and (2) the higher sensitivity to 3- to 4-kHz tones at all sound levels. Backus asserted that the added sensitivity of the auditory system to tones in the 3- to 4-kHz range is partially due to a resonance frequency of the closed tube formed by the auditory canal (meatus) and the eardrum.[22] The insensitivity of the ear to low-frequency, low sound-level tones that is indicated by the Fletcher-Munson curves leads us to an important problem. It seems plausible that one cause of the low-frequency, low sound-level fall-off is that the curves represent people's responses to sine waves. Fletcher himself warned:

> It should be emphasized here that changes of the level above threshold corresponding to any fixed increase or decrease in loudness will, according to the theory outlined in this paper, depend upon the frequency of the tone when using pure tones, or upon its structure when using complex tones.[23]

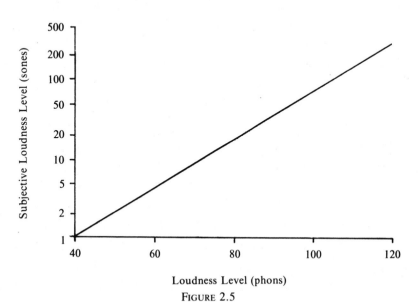

FIGURE 2.5

Relationship between loudness level (phons)
and subjective loudness (sones).

Were complex tones, rich in upper partials, used as stimuli, the low-frequency response curves could be noticeably different. To the author's knowledge, no such study exists.

Stevens coined the term *sones* to describe units of subjective loudness.[24] The sone scale is perceptually based, using the psychophysical method of magnitude estimation (ME), and has broader musical relativity, since complex and random sounds, as well as pure tones, were used as stimuli. Sone levels are related arithmetically: two sones sound twice as loud as one, and three sones sound three times as loud as one. The sone scale is arbitrarily related to the phon scale: one sone is equal to 40 phons. Figure 2.5 is a representation of the phon-sone relationship. Again, an average of responses is shown here—individual responses may vary.

To illustrate the phon-sone relationship shown in figure 2.5, we might ask: how many oscillators, producing the same waveform and frequency, would have to be ganged in order to produce the perception that the sound was twice as loud as one oscillator alone? Reference to figure 2.5 shows that one sone equals 40 phons, and two sones equal 50 phons. The answer to our question, then, is ten oscillators: an increase of 10 phons means a tenfold increase in sound level, and a doubling of loudness (one sone).

This relationship would not hold true if the multiple sound sources yielded different waveforms and/or frequencies, due to the masking phenomenon. A soundwave produces one or many regions of excitation on the basilar membrane (critical bands). Should other soundwaves simultaneously reach these already excited critical bands, the added subjective loudness is quite a bit less than the physical energies of the sounds one might be led to expect. If the excitation patterns of the second sound source were to move outside the critical bands of the first, however, the level of subjective loudness would increase.[25]

TIME AND SPACE

The element of time affects each auditory sensation discussed earlier in this chapter. These time dependencies are reviewed in the next three paragraphs.

The psychoacoustical literature states quite uniformly that, depending on their fundamental frequencies, pitches must have a duration of at least 13 msec to be perceived as having definite pitch.[26] The frequency dependency of this lower durational threshold was shown by Meyer-Eppler[27], and is given below:

Hz:	100	200	500	1000	2000	3000	4000	6000
Msec:	45	30	26	20	13	14	14	18

These figures, though often cited in works purporting to address musical acoustics and psychoacoustics, should be considered as having questionable musical significance. This is not due to perceptual experiments which were poorly done, but to reports of experimental results which were misinterpreted. Psychophysicists have not been concerned, in general, with the measurement of the perceptibility of pitches in a musical context; their testing methods have tended not to permit the test subject to describe auditory sensations in a musical manner. In an informal and unpublished study, the author generated a series of four sine tones, each 5 msec in duration, which had the musical pitch equivalences of C_4, E_4, F_4, and G_4 (A=440 Hz, ET). Observers, all trained musicians, encountered no difficulty in describing this quasi-melodic linear pattern through such means as vocalization and solfeggio syllables.

Timbre perception is time-dependent in several ways. The most basic point to consider is that time defines the difference between timbre and sonance (see the section on timbre and sonance, above): perceived *timbre* results from the perception of the spectral components of a sound at any given instant. *Sonance* is the perceptual dimension that results from the transient (that is, time-loaded) characteristics of that sound—the cumulative perception of a series of spectral instants. It might be argued that timbre, as used in this chapter, has no perceptual existence, since we cannot perceive one instant out of context. Hirsh's experimental results which indicate a time dependency for the perceived quality of almost-simultaneous clicks, are reported in the section on *timbre and sonance*, above.

The time dependency of loudness perception is shown in studies by von Bekesy and Steudel.[28] There is both a physical and psychophysical inertia factor that influences all perceptions of any change in loudness level—any increase or decrease. Without even considering the physical inertia to be found in a loudspeaker system, there is a psychological and/or physiological lag, or "rise time," of about 200 msec. When a sound is abruptly switched on, the listener hears its full loudness 200 msec after full intensity is reached. After the sound has been switched off, there is a perceptual lag of about 50 msec, that is, a subjective decay of 50 msec that is unrelated to such physical phenomena as room reverberation. It seems to be this lag that accounts for pitch fusion: should a series of vibrations surpass the frequency of 20 per second (20 Hz), the 50-msec decay lag would operate as a sample-and-hold mechanism, storing each vibration until the beginning of the next. Thus, the vibrations would perceptually fuse into an apparently steady pitch. It also seems to be more than coincidence that the separate frames in a filmstrip are seen as a series of still photographs until the eye/brain mechanism is forced to process more than 20 to 25 of them per second; in other words, visual fusion occurs at about the same frequency as does auditory fusion. This would seem to indicate that fusion occurs either in the neural pathway or, more likely, in the brain itself, but not in the ear.

Several of these time thresholds, together with others discussed in this

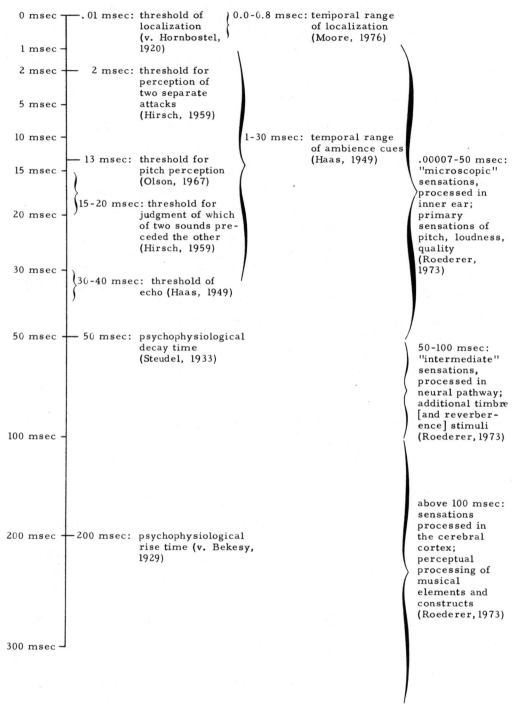

<figcaption>Figure 2.6</figcaption>

chapter, are represented in figure 2.6. There are two other time-related perceptual phenomena of sufficient musical importance to be discussed at some length: (1) auditory localization—the perception of directionality of the sound source, and (2) spatial impression—the sense of room size and reverberance or *ambience*.

Auditory Localization

A sound rarely strikes the two eardrums at exactly the same time; in order to reach both eardrums simultaneously, the sound would have to come from a source equidistant from the two eardrums, that is, on the *median plane* (see figure 2.7).

The chances are slight that a sound will originate on the median plane. In the more common event that the sound source lies somewhere other than on the median plane, the two ears are given different signals to process. The important differences in these signals are their arrival times and amplitudes. The greatest difference is presented when the sound source is placed at a 90° angle to the median plane (see figure 2.8).

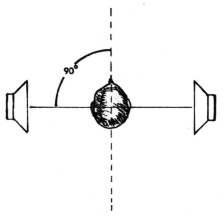

FIGURE 2.8

The discrepancy of arrival times of a single sound at the two ears is simple to illustrate. At a normal humidity level and at about 70° Fahrenheit, a sound will travel through air at about 1,130 feet per second (13,560 inches per second). At an angle of 90° from the median plane a sound will have to travel some 8 to 11 inches farther to reach the more remote eardrum than to reach the nearer eardrum. The reader may respond at this point that he knows of no normal person with an 8- to 11-inch head width. This is a valid point that is commonly ignored in the literature. Actually, the eardrums may be only 4 or 5 inches apart as measured through the middle of the head, since they are somewhat inset. However, sound must travel the outside route, as shown in figure 2.9.

FIGURE 2.9

At the rate of 13,560 inches per second, the sound would traverse 8 inches in just under 0.6 msec. Von Hornbostel and Wertheimer found that temporal differences of as little as 10 μsec (0.01 msec) will cause an apparent shift of sound source direction.[29] More recent literature indicates that the temporal range of localization processing extends from 0.0 msec, when the sound source is at the median plane, to 0.7 to 0.8 msec, when the sound source is 90° from the median plane.[30] It will become apparent later in this section that the less-than-1-msec-time range indicates that it is *direct sound* (that is, that which travels directly from the sound source to the ear) that is involved in auditory localization, not reflected sound.

Interaural amplitude differences are caused primarily by diffraction of sound around the head. After a sound source is moved more than only a few degrees from the median plane, there is no direct route between the sound source and the more remote ear. The sound must travel around the perimeter of the head (diffraction), while the head and hair absorb a portion of the sound's energy. The following several paragraphs will provide a strong argument that the generation of interaural amplitude differences will prove to be more useful than the generation of arrival time differences when the electronic music composer wants to achieve an apparent movement of sound.

Since the 1930s, a great deal of attention has been directed toward the interrelationships of arrival time and amplitude as causative factors in auditory localization. The widely cited 1949 dissertation of Helmut Haas demonstrated that, in an almost anechoic environment, a monaural signal driven through two separate loudspeakers will fuse into a single sound image that seems to come entirely from the loudspeaker that carries the time-delayed signal.[31]

Quite a few more recent publications have expanded this demonstration to include, for instance, the "phantom third channel" that can be "moved" back and forth between stereophonic loudspeakers through a time-delay operation in one of the channels. From a pragmatic point of view, perhaps the most important musical interpretation of the precedence effect is that any work spent trying to build auditory localization effects into an electronic music composition solely through synthetic time delay would result in some disappointment. The critical factor here is that the prededence effect shows itself in a carefully controlled environment that is very unlike a music performance environment. Invariably, the test sounds in precedence effect experiments were presented either dichotically through headphones or routed through loudspeakers, in an anechoic space. Concert halls, by nature, are free sound-field environments; public performances in which each member of the audience is provided headphones are exceedingly rare. There is another problem associated with loudspeaker presentation, even discounting the fact that recital areas are not anechoic. In the Haas dissertation itself is an adequate description of this problem. Haas found that when the signal to one of a pair of loudspeakers was delayed up to 1 msec, the sensation was that the sound "moved" toward whichever speaker produced the undelayed signal. In 1 msec, sound will travel a little over a foot, with a very slight variance for temperature and humidity. However, when Haas increased the time delay to 10 msec (equal to the transit time for about 11 feet) the delayed signal was not heard at all, although its physical energy equalled that of the undelayed signal. Haas had no explanation for this phenomenon and suspected some sort of "blocking reaction" in the central nervous system; that is, our auditory decoding system possibly rejects this delayed input as redundant. The threshold of the Haas effect is given by Gardner: if two speakers with equal in-phase outputs are located at equal angles from the median plane, a phantom image will be apparent at the median plane; the strength of this phantom image is enhanced if a dummy loudspeaker is located midway between the real sources.[32] If one of the speakers is moved as much as 12 inches farther away from the listener, introducing a time delay of about 1 msec to that sound, the phantom image will shift to the closer speaker. This is experimental evidence of what most high-fidelity buffs already know: there is a stereophonic "sweet spot" within which our direction detecting mechanisms work well.

The composer will have to consider carefully what, in all of this information, constitutes an effective compositional technique. Should a composer attempt to introduce localization effects solely through the use of time-delay devices, which are now common items on the market, he will have the span of 0.0 to 0.8 msec in which to work. By routing a given undelayed signal to one speaker and the same signal, delayed, to a second speaker, he will have to place his audience within a few inches of the line that exactly bisects those speakers or the time-delay localization effect will be undone. Time delay as a cause of real-life localization is introduced by the real-life

FIGURE 2.10

Diagram of speaker and microphone placement used in the recording process of Stockhausen's *Kontakte*.

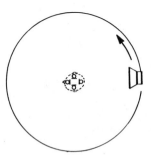

FIGURE 2.11

Diagram of speaker and microphone placement to simulate around-the-head diffraction effects.

Spatial Impressions

factor of relative distance, which is controlled by the performance environment itself. Localization effects, as the reader may have suspected, are best achieved by amplitude differences, that is, relative output levels of the speakers. If one wants a sound to appear as though it comes from speaker x, one should increase the gain to speaker x. Unless speaker x lies on the median plane of the listener, interaural time delay will result from the simple fact that the sound emanated from speaker x.[33]

An effective system for the generation of localization effects in a multiple-channel sound system would have to take into account more factors than interaural amplitude and arrival time differences. The system should account for all of the physical and perceptual factors that serve as localization cues. These factors would include (1) interaural amplitude differences; (2) interaural arrival time differences; (3) room acoustics cues (ambience); (4) around-the-head diffraction effects; and (5) Doppler effect.[34]

Stockhausen devised such a system in the process of recording *Kontakte*.[35] A series of microphones was set in a circle around a highly directional loudspeaker, as shown in figure 2.10.

Stockhausen's rotating speaker system accounts for almost all the physical and perceptual factors listed above; only the effect of around-the-head diffraction is left unsimulated. This diffraction effect could be achieved by means of a revolving speaker method (see figure 2.11), a variation on the system reported by Theile and Plenge.[36] The two essential differences in this method are that the speaker rotates around the microphones and that the microphones are set in a dummy head, which allows for around-the-head diffraction effects.

There is, however, a valid use for time-delay devices in the electronic music studio. When time delays of more than a few msec are introduced to a split signal, the listener will begin to get a sense of added room reverberance, or ambience. Figure 2.12 shows the physical situation that gives rise to the impression of ambience.

Given a room that is about 16 feet by 16 feet, let us assume a listener is positioned 10 feet away from a speaker. The sound that travels directly from the speaker (a_1 and a_2) will reach the listener about 9 msec after being emitted, ± about 0.8 msec to either ear, depending on which direction the listener happens to be facing. This sound is called, understandably, *direct sound,* and the differences between a_1 and a_2, both in relative arrival times and amplitudes, helps determine the impression of sound source direction.†

A loudspeaker emits sound in a spherical pattern; even the most directional of speakers will emit *some* sound in every direction. Some sound

†Note that the 9-msec transit time is not a delay; as far as the listener is concerned, the sound did not exist for that period.

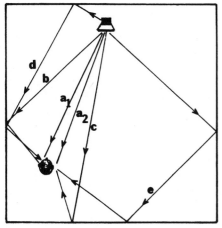

FIGURE 2.12

Pathways of direct sound and some early reflections in a fictitious 16′ by 16′ room.

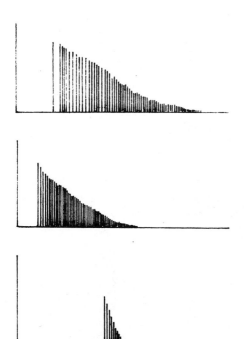

FIGURE 2.13

Examples of simulated reflection patterns that would create altered impressions of room size and ambience. (Note: The graphs are not in scale horizontally.)

that does not travel directly toward the listener will probably encounter a reflective surface: a wall, the floor, the ceiling, or a piece of furniture. In figure 2.12, the sound traveling along path *b* happens to encounter a nearby reflective surface and is the *first reflection* to be heard after the direct sound. This sound has traveled about three feet farther than did the direct sound and is physically weaker because of air friction and some absorption by the wall; it arrives about 3.5 msec after the direct sound. After this first reflection, other early reflections are heard by the listener; they occur at increasingly short time intervals from one another and become increasingly muted as their physical energy is expended. Normally, ambience cues lie in the time range of about 1 to 30 msec. This means that the time delay between the arrival of the direct sound and that of the first reflection should fall within this range. The length of time that it will take the second and later reflections to decay (that is, drop below the threshold of hearing) determines room reverberance. Should the first reflection not occur until about 30 to 40 msec after the direct sound, the listener will perceive an *echo,* as opposed to reverberance. Figure 2.13 shows some possible combinations of ambience and reverberance cues that could be realized with multiple time delay units. The duration of reverberation in the examples in figure 2.13 is highly variable. Similarly, the duration between the direct sound and first reflection is also variable within the range of 1 to 30 msec. An interval of 25 msec between the direct sound and the first reflection will carry the impression of a larger room than will a delay of, say, 15 msec.

At this point, it is advisable to attempt an adequate definition of *echo,* since the term is so commonly confused with reverberation. Certainly, both echo and reverberation are made of the same ingredient: delayed arrivals of the sound impulse. No clear distinction is made between these terms in most psychoacoustics literature; one often finds the terms used interchangeably.[37] The distinction between these terms becomes readily apparent when one compares their perceptual properties. Both echo and reverberation are repetitions of a sound, and both become continuously weaker as their energies dissipate. The only real difference between the two is that echo has an attack that is perceptibly separate from that of any impulses within 30 msec prior to it. This seemingly obvious point would have been dismissed by the author as trivial, except that confusion of these terms appears to be widespread. To gain perspective on this point, consider that most psychoacoustics literature agrees that room acoustics (ambience) information is carried in the time-delay range of about 1 to 30 msec and that echo becomes apparent in the time delay range of 30 to 50 msec. Yet, a reverberation chamber can produce a sustained, even reverberation for a full minute without producing any perceptible echoes. Conversely, echo chambers can be acoustically "dry" (that is, nonreverberant). It should be possible, in fact, to encounter both sustained reverberation and echoes in the same sound. A long succession of progressively weaker repetitions that

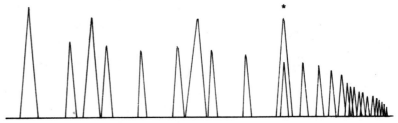

FIGURE 2.14

Amplitude vs. time function of a synthetic
sound containing both reverberation and echo
impulses.

are within 30 msec of one another would produce the reverberation effect,
and a series of repetitions (perceptibly stronger than the reverberation
impulses that precede them) that are separated from one another by more
than 30 msec would produce the echo sensation. In effect, each of these
stronger echo impulses constitutes an added physical energy that will produce the sensation of a separate attack or echo (see figure 2.14).

Although the model represented in figure 2.14 is based on speculation, it is
probable that there would be summation effects when the delayed attacks
coincide, such as at point *.

An oscillographic representation of the amplitude-time function of a
reverberant, echoic sound is given in figure 2.15. The vertical lines of the
reference grid in this figure represent time increments of 100 msec. The
reader should note that there are several "flutter echoes" present at the
early stage of this sound. In this particular case, these flutter echoes have a
greater amplitude than does the direct sound impulse. The reader will also
notice that there is a long, steadily decaying reverberance pattern that
begins at the outset of the tone and continues steadily through the flutter
echo phase of the sound.

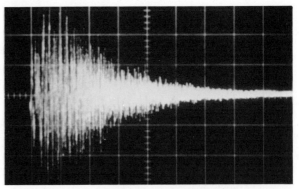

FIGURE 2.15

Amplitude vs. time function of a short tone
burst in a reverberant and echoic room.

PROBLEMS

1. Tune two VCOs (voltage-controlled oscillators) so that they generate the pitch interval of a perfect fifth (for example, begin with the frequency interval of 440 and 660 Hz), routed through separate channels of a stereo amplifier with channel-switching capability, to a stereo headset. By ear, tune the signals so that the interval sounds "pure" (that is, no beats). Switch the channels back and forth. Do you hear an apparent change of pitch(es)? If you do, why do you?

2. Route any complex waveform through a high bandpass filter to any listening medium (free sound field or dichotic presentation). Dial out the fundamental. Do you hear a change in pitch? A change in timbre? Dial out a greater number of lower partials. What is the perceptual result?

3. In order to achieve an authentic chorus effect, try the following procedures:

   a. Gang three or more asynchronous VCOs, tuned to a near unison.

   b. Frequency modulate several VCOs with random noise generators and use either a time-delay device on one of the signals or a time delay modulated with a random noise generator.

   c. Use pulse-width modulation at a slow pulse rate of about 0–8 pulses per second.

   Which of these operations yields the most convincing result?

4. Ask an observer who is given no visual cues to identify correctly the timbres of a sine, sawtooth, and square wave within the frequency range of 100–1500 Hz. Allow the observer to practice this task until he or she attains a perfect success rate. Repeat this identification drill when the frequencies are 5 kHz or above. What is the result?

5. Using figure 2.3 as your patching model, investigate the perceptual effects when transient amplitude characteristics are added to an otherwise steady, "clean" sound.

6. Tune two VCOs (same waveform) so that one is judged to be higher in pitch than the other. Alter the amplitudes of the signals. When does the lower pitch begin to conceal, or mask, the upper pitch? When does the upper pitch begin to mask the lower one? Repeat this activity using a nonrandom VCO and unfiltered random sound. Why is the masking phenomenon unattainable with this sound mix?

7. Tune two VCOs (preferably sine wave) so that they generate a unison in the pitch range above C_5. The amplitudes of the signals should be equal and at a fairly high level; the signals may be routed to monaural or stereophonic loudspeakers. Raise the pitch of one of the signals by an octave or more. Do you hear any sounds in addition to the sinusoidal signals? Are these subjective tones lower or higher in pitch than the sine tones?

SOURCES

1. Otto W. Henry, "The Evolution of Idiomatic and Psychoacoustical Resources as a Basis for Unity in Electronic Music," Ph.D. dissertation, Tulane University, 1970. Ann Arbor, Mi.: University Microfilms.

2. John Backus, *The Acoustical Foundations of Music* (New York: Norton, 1969). Backus cites the findings of Shower and Biddulph (1931), who used sine tones as their stimuli (see note 20 below). Since harmonics are the predominant pitch information vehicle in this low range, it is expectable that pitch jnd of low-frequency complex tones would be smaller than that given by Backus.

3. Backus, p. 111.

4. W. B. Snow, "Audible Frequency Ranges of Music, Speech, and Noise," *Journal of the Acoustical Society of America* 3 (1931): 155–166.

5. Reinier Plomp, "The Ear as a Frequency Analyzer," *Journal of the Acoustical Society of America,* 36 (1964): 1628–1636. See also, Reinier Plomp, "Pitch of Complex Tones" *Journal of the Acoustical Society of America* 41, no. 6 (1964): 1526–1533; see especially p. 1532.

6. Fritz Winckel, "The Psychoacoustical Analysis of Music as Applied to Electronic Music," *Journal of Music Theory* 7, no. 2 (1963): 194–246. A history of conflicting theories of hearing since Helmholtz is given in David Butler, "An Historical Investigation and Bibliography of Nineteenth-Century Music Psychology Literature," Ph.D. dissertation, Ohio State University, 1973.

7. Backus, p. 105.

8. G. van den Brink, et al., "Dichotic Pitch Fusion," *Journal of the Acoustical Society of America* 59, no. 6 (1976): 1471–1476; see especially p. 1476.

9. Diana Deutsch, "Two Channel Listening to Musical Scales," *Journal of the Acoustical Society of America* 57, no. 5 (1975): 1156–1160. See also Diana Deutsch, "Musical Illusions," *Scientific American* 233, no. 4 (1975): 92–104. Reported in Alex Cima, "Illusion and Motion . . .," *Synapse,* November-December (1976), pp. 24–25.

10. David Butler, "A Further Study of Melodic Channeling," *Perception and Psychophysics* 25, no. 4 (1979): 264–268.

11. M. Metfessel, "Sonance as a Form of Tonal Fusion," *Psychology Review* 33 (1926): 459–466.

12. Richard Cabot, et al., "Detection of Phase Shifts in Harmonically Related Tones," *Journal of the Audio Engineering Society* 24, no. 7 (1976): 568–571. The authors could only get positive discriminative judgments from subjects after considerable training in front of an oscilloscope. The conclusion was that phase shifts are detectable, but subtle; the authors questioned the audibility of phase shift compared to the more familiar forms of distortion.

13. G. S. Ohm, "Ueber die Definition des Tones, nebst daran gekneupfter Theorie der Sirene und aehnlicher tonbildener Vorrichtungen," *Annalen der Physik und Chemie* 135 (1843): 497–565.

14. H. L. F. von Helmholtz, *On the Sensations of Tone as a Physiological Basis for the Theory of Music* (1863), 4th ed., 1877. Translated and revised by Alexander T. Ellis (London: Longmans, Green, 1895). 2nd English edition (New York: Dover, 1954).

15. Harvey Fletcher, et al., "Quality of Piano Tones," *Journal of the Acoustical Society of America* 34 (1962): 749–761. See also, E. Donnell Blackham, "The Physics of the Piano," *Scientific* American 213, no. 6 (1965): 88–99.

16. Ira J. Hirsh, "Auditory Perception of Temporal Order," *Journal of the Acoustical Society of America* 31, no. 6 (1959): 759–767; see especially p. 766.

17. Reinier Plomp, "Beats of Mistuned Consonances," *Journal of the Acoustical Society of America* 42 (1967): 462–474.

18. Georg von Bekesy, *Experiments in Hearing* (New York: McGraw-Hill, 1960).

19. E. L. Saldanha and J. F. Corso, "Timbre Cues and the Identification of Musical Instruments," *Journal of the Acoustical Society of America* 36 (1964): 2021–2026.

20. E. G. Shower and R. Biddulph, "Differential Pitch Sensitivity of the Ear," *Journal of the Acoustical Society of America* 3 (1931): 275–287; and Harvey

Fletcher and W. A. Munson, "Loudness, Its Measurement and Calculation," *Journal of the Acoustical Society of America* 5 (1933): 82–108. Shower and Biddulph, using sine waves as their stimuli, demonstrated measurable pitch-judgment differentials at different loudness levels. Harvey Fletcher ("Loudness, Pitch, and the Timbre of Musical Tones and their Relation to the Intensity, the Frequency, and the Overtone Structure," *Journal of the Acoustical Society of America* 6 [1934]: 311–343) asserted that the loudness dependency for pitch judgments was only about one fifth as pronounced when complex tones were used as stimuli.

21. Fletcher and Munson, p. 84.

22. Backus, p. 86.

23. Fletcher and Munson, p. 95.

24. S. S. Stevens, "The Measurement of Loudness," *Journal of the Acoustical Society of America* 27, no. 5 (1955): 815–829.

25. E. Zwicker, G. Flottorp, and S. S. Stevens, "Critical Bandwidth in Loudness Summation," *Journal of the Acoustical Society of America* 29 (1957): 548–557.

26. Harry F. Olson, *Music, Physics, and Engineering,* 2nd ed. (New York: Dover, 1967); see especially p. 250.

27. Werner Meyer-Eppler, *The Mathematical-Acoustical Fundamentals of Electrical Sound Composition.* English translation by H. A. G. Nathan, Technical Translation TT-608: National Research Council of Canada. Meyer-Eppler's figures generally coincide with those given by R. Feldtkeller, "Hoerbarkeit von Verzurrungen bei Uebertragung von Instrumentklaengen," *Acustica* 4, no. 1 (1954).

28. Georg von Bekesy, "Zur Theorie des Hoerens," *Phys. Z.* 30 (1929): 118; and U. Steudel, "Ueber Empfindungen und Messung der Lautstaerke," *Z. Hochfreq. Tech. Elektrotech.* 41 (1933): 116.

29. E. M. von Hornbostel and M. Wertheimer, *Sitzbericht deut. Akad. Wiss. Berlin* 15 (1920): 388–396.

30. Christopher Moore, "Studio Applications of Time Delay," *Lexicon Application Note (AN–3)* (July 1976), Lexicon, Inc., 60 Turner St., Waltham, Mass. 02154.

31. Helmut Haas, "The Influence of a Single Echo on the Audibility of Speech," Ph.D. dissertation, University of Gottingen. English translation by I. K. P. R. Ehrenberg in: *Journal of the Audio Engineering Society* 20 (1972): 146–159. The "precedence" or "Haas" effect hardly seems to have been unearthed by Haas, although he is widely credited with its discovery. For background, see Mark B. Gardner, "Historical Background of the Haas and/or Precedence Effect," *Journal of the Acoustical Society of America* 43 (1968): 1243–1248. See also, Mark B. Gardner, "Some Single- and Multiple-Source Localization Effects," *Journal of the Audio Engineering Society* 21, no. 6 (1973): 430–437; see especially pp. 430–431.

32. Gardner, "Localization Effects," p. 430–437.

33. Gardner, ("Localization Effects," p. 430–437.) and John Eargle (*Sound Recording,* [New York: Van Nostrand, 1976], pp. 37–43) report the generation of phantom sound images or "phasors" that may be perceived as existing outside the range of the two speakers and even "within" or behind the head of the listener. Again, the practicability of these images is questionable, since the listener must be situated on a line equidistant from the two speakers in order to experience these images.

34. R. E. Kelly, "Musical Pitch Variations Caused by the Doppler Effect," *American Journal of Physics* 42, no. 6 (1974): 452–455. Kelly stated that the Doppler effect causes a pitch variation of 2.25 cents (.0225 semitone, ET) for each mile per hour of speed attained by the sound source. This is equal to about 1.5 cents variation for each foot per second.

35. Karlheinz Stockhausen, *Kontakte,* Universal Edition [UE 13678] (Theodore Presser Co., United States, Canada and Mexico, 1969).

36. G. Theile and G. Plenge, "Localization of Lateral Phantom Sources," *Journal of the Audio Engineering Society* 25, no. 4 (1977): 196–200.

37. The author has found that most texts on musical acoustics and psychoacoustics make no attempt to define echo and reverberation separately. Haas used the term *echo* to mean any delayed arrival of a sound impulse.

SELECTED BIBLIOGRAPHY

Books

Beranek, Leo. *Music, Acoustics and Engineering.* New York: Wiley, 1962.

Bergeijk, William A. van; Pierce, J. R; and David, E. E., Jr. *Waves and the Ear,* Science Study Series, S9. Garden City, N.Y.: Doubleday, 1960.

Erickson, Robert. *Sound Structure and Music.* Berkeley, Calif.: University of California Press, 1975.

Farnsworth, Paul. *The Social Psychology of Music.* Ames, Iowa: Iowa State University Press, 1969.

Lundin, Robert. *An Objective Psychology of Music.* 2nd edition. New York: Ronald Press, 1967.

Plomp, Reinier. *Aspects of Tone Sensation: A Psychophysical Study.* New York: Academic Press, 1976.

Roederer, Juan G. *Introduction to the Physics and Psychophysics of Music.* 2nd edition. New York: Springer-Verlag, 1977.

Ward, W. Dixon. "Musical Perception." In *Foundations of Modern Auditory Theory.* Edited by Tobias. New York: Academic Press, 1970.

Winckel, Fritz. *Music, Sound, and Sensation: A Modern Exposition.* New York: Dover, 1967.

Articles

Bariaux, D., et al. "A Method for Spectral Analysis of Musical Sounds: Description and Performances." *Acustica,* 32, no. 5 (1975): 307–313.

Bauer, Benjamin, et al. "A Compatible Stereo-Quadrasonic (SQ) Record System." *Journal of the Audio Engineering Society* 19, no. 7 (1971): 638–646.

Cohen, Alexander. "Further Investigation of the Effects of Intensity upon the Pitch of Pure Tones." *Journal of the Acoustical Society of America* 33, no. 10 (1961): 1363–1376.

Hay, L. R., and J. V. Hanson. "Towards a More Natural Sound System." *Journal of the Audio Engineering Society* 24, no. 1 (1976): 24–26.

Hodgkinson, K. A. "A Versatile Waveform Envelope Generator for the Synthesis of Musical Attack and Decay Transients." *Journal of Physics* E8, no. 2 (1975): 123–126.

Koenig, W. "Subjective Effects in Binaural Hearing." *Journal of the Acoustical Society of America* 22 (1950): 61–62 (letter to the editor).

Milner, Paul. ''Frequency Dependence of Spatial Impression.'' Paper presented to the Audio Engineering Society, 30 October 1976. Typescript, 15 pages.

Poland, William. ''Theories of Music and Musical Behavior.'' *Journal of Music Theory* 7, no. 2 (1963): 150–192.

Sakamoto, K., et al. ''On 'Out of Head Localization' in Headphone Listening.'' *Journal of the Audio Engineering Society* 24, no. 9 (1976): 710–715.

Whitworth, Randolph, and Jeffress, Lloyd A. ''Time versus Intensity in the Localization of Tones.'' *Journal of the Acoustical Society of America* 33, no. 7 (1961): 925–929.

3

OSCILLATORS

The late Hugh LeCaine in the University of
Toronto Electronic Music Studio.

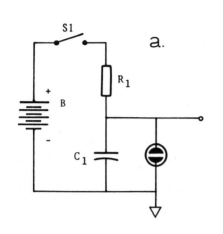

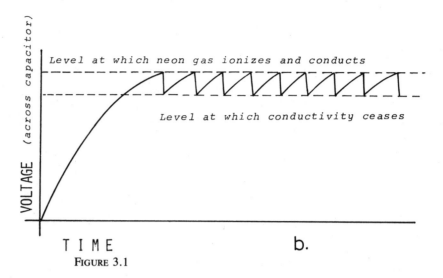

FIGURE 3.1

In chapter 1 we discussed certain types of oscillators in terms of frequency components. In this chapter we shall describe some basic principles of oscillator operation, along with waveshaping techniques.[†]

Figure 3.1a diagrams a simple oscillator, the *relaxation oscillator*. Closing the switch, S_1, allows capacitor C_1 to charge with current from battery B through resistor R_1, resulting in an increasing potential across C_1. At some point the voltage across C_1 reaches a level sufficient to ionize the gas in the neon bulb, forming a path from C_1 to ground through the ionized gas for the charge on the capacitor. As the charge diminishes, the voltage across C_1 decreases until it falls below the level required to keep the neon bulb ionized. At this point, the path from C_1 to ground is broken, and C_1 again begins to charge. The neon bulb thus functions as a voltage-sensitive switch that discharges the capacitor every time the voltage across the switch attains a certain level.

Other devices besides the neon bulb may be employed as voltage-sensitive switches in the relaxation oscillator circuit, provided that the voltage at which the switch closes (providing the path to discharge the capacitor) is greater than the voltage at which the switch opens (allowing the capacitor to recharge). Figure 3.1b shows the output waveform of the oscillator shown in figure 3.1a.

Figure 3.2 shows a relaxation oscillator that uses a unijunction transistor as a voltage-controlled switch. Moog Music and other manufacturers of electronic music instrumentation have utilized this circuit as the basis for a voltage-controlled oscillator. The constant current source shown in figure 3.2 is a device that produces the voltage necessary (within circuit limita-

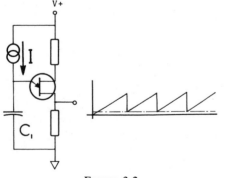

FIGURE 3.2

[†]The reader is urged to refer often to the display of symbols used for block diagrams of patchings given in the Preface, pp. xiv–xv.

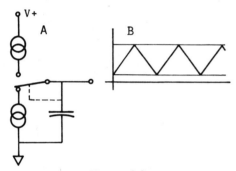

FIGURE 3.3

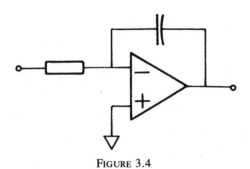

FIGURE 3.4

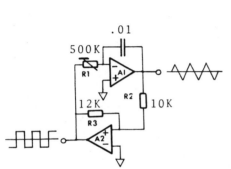

FIGURE 3.5

tions) to pass a constant current through any impedance. Charging a capacitor with current passed through a resistor does not produce a linear charging characteristic, because the voltage drop across the resistor decreases as the capacitor charges. Consequently, progressively less current flows through the resistor, and the charging rate slows. On the other hand, the constant current source presents a varying potential and constant current to C_1 (figure 3.2), resulting in a linear charging curve.

The rate of charging of C_1 may be varied by changing the value of either the resistor or the capacitor in the charging circuit. Variable capacitors of a value large enough to be useful for audio-frequency oscillator applications are impractical. As a result, the capacitor in an oscillator is usually fixed in value (although different value capacitors may be switched in the circuit to change the frequency range), and the resistor (or in figure 3.2 the current supplied by the constant current source) is varied to change the frequency of the oscillator. The constant current source is well suited to the design of a wide-range voltage-controlled oscillator.

The elements that constitute the sawtooth-wave oscillator may be arranged to form a triangle wave generator. An arrangement for alternately charging and discharging a capacitor by using a voltage-sensitive switch along with a constant current source and the complement of the CCS, the constant current *sink,* is shown in figure 3.3a. Figure 3.3b shows the output waveform produced by this configuration. Figure 3.4 shows a diagram of an *integrator,* a device commonly employed in analog computer applications. The integrator shown in figure 3.4 employs a capacitor placed in the feedback loop of an operational amplifier. As the op amp attempts to put a current through the capacitor equal to the current flowing through R into the input terminal (marked −), the capacitor will be a constant rate. This circuit is characterized by the expression

$$V_{out} = -\frac{1}{RC} \int_{t_1}^{t_2} V_{in} dt.$$

From the equation we see that the output voltage changes linearly with time at a rate determined by the amount of current flowing through the input resistor.

Figure 3.5 shows a triangle wave oscillator that employs an integrator. In this figure, A_1 is connected as an integrator, and A_2 is connected as a *comparator,* a device the output of which can be in one of two states depending on the relative signal levels at its two inputs. (In this case, in one state the output of the comparator is a voltage equal to the positive supply voltage; in the other state the output of the comparator is a voltage equal to the negative supply voltage.)

In figure 3.5 the comparator functions as a voltage-sensitive switch. In this circuit the noninverting input of A_2 (marked +) is connected to a

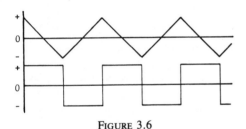

FIGURE 3.6

FIGURE 3.6

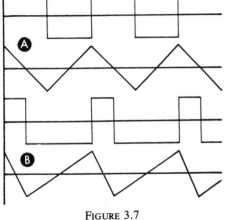

FIGURE 3.7

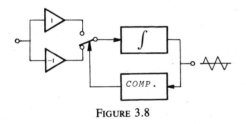

FIGURE 3.8

voltage divider (R_2 and R_3), which is placed between the outputs of A_1 and A_2.

When the output of the comparator (figure 3.6) switches positive, the integrator output voltage begins slewing negative. This negative voltage continues to increase until the voltage level between R_2 and R_3 reaches the point at which the noninverting input of the comparator is negative with respect to the inverting input, at which point the comparator output switches, becoming negative, and the integrator begins slewing in the opposite direction. One may obtain a square wave output from this circuit by tapping off the comparator output. This circuit, called a *function generator,* is the basis of the *voltage-to-frequency converter* (used in digital voltmeters, FM recorders, telemetry, and so on.)

In the voltage-to-frequency converter diagrammed in figure 3.8, an increase in the input voltage causes the integrator to slew more rapidly, causing the comparator to switch more quickly, producing a higher frequency output signal.

With inverting and noninverting amplifiers adjusted for equal gain, the two voltages presented to the integrator are of equal absolute value. Thus, the integrator will slew down to the negative switching point in the same time as it takes to slew back up to the positive switching point, resulting in a symmetrical waveform at both the triangle and square wave outputs (figure 3.7a). If the gains of the inverting and noninverting amplifiers are not equal, the two waveforms will not be symmetrical (figure 3.7b). Manual or voltage control of waveform symmetry is often included in function generator design. This circuit exhibits a linear voltage-to-frequency conversion. However, for electronic music applications, this circuit is usually modified to exhibit an exponential voltage-to-frequency conversion, that is, equal increments of control voltage will produce equal increments in pitch (compare the 1 octave-per-volt control characteristic used in many voltage-controlled oscillators [VCO's] designed for electronic music production).

Figure 3.9 shows the exponential relationship between pitch and frequency. Part of a piano keyboard, A_0 to A_5 (subcontra A to A^2), is shown on the x-axis, while frequency (linear scale) is shown on the y-axis (each small division represents 27.5 Hz). The exponential curve (see the Glossary) results from the plotting of the notes of the piano keyboard (tuned in equal temperament) against the *frequencies* of the notes on the y-axis. As we shall see in later chapters, voltage-controlled oscillators with an exponential control-voltage-versus-frequency response (exponential VCO) are particularly suited to electronic music applications.

Voltage control of the duty cycle of a pulse wave may be achieved by processing the triangle wave output of an oscillator through a comparator (figure 3.10). The comparator switches positive when the level of the triangle wave is greater than that of the control voltage, and switches negative when the level of the triangle wave falls below that of the control voltage. The control voltage determines the point on the triangle wave at which the comparator switches, thereby controlling the duty cycle of the pulse wave at the output of the comparator (see figure 3.10).

Figure 3.11 shows a practical version of a pulse-width modulator using a comparator. (Note that control signals are inverted by the control-voltage-summing amplifier.)

Figure 3.12 shows the output of an integrator used to process a pulse wave that varies between 0 and some negative value. If the negative excursions of the input signal are made sufficiently short, the output of the integrator will (ideally) be a step voltage. By adding a switch to reset the integrator when the output reaches some designated level, a staircase waveform may be produced (figure 3.13). The staircase waveform is useful as a control signal for certain applications (see chapter 7).

The *differentiator* shown in figure 3.14 is another circuit employed for waveshaping. This circuit is characterized by the expression

$$V_{out} = -RC \frac{dV_{in}}{dt} .$$

Figure 3.15 shows a differentiated triangle wave (a) and a differentiated square wave (b). Since the triangle wave presents a voltage to the dif-

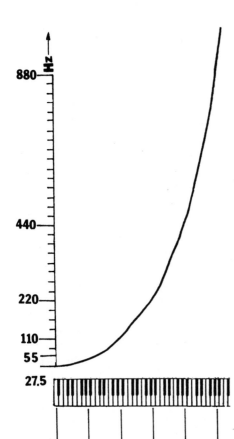

FIGURE 3.9

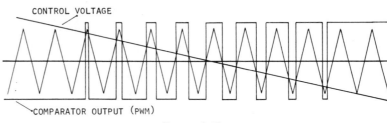

CONTROL VOLTAGE

COMPARATOR OUTPUT (PWM)

FIGURE 3.10

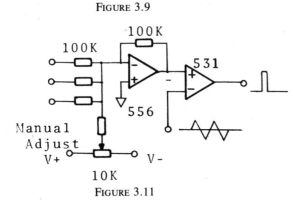

Manual
Adjust
V+   V-
10K

FIGURE 3.11

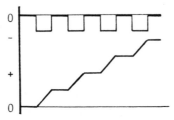

FIGURE 3.12

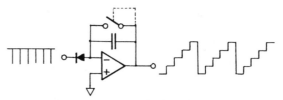

FIGURE 3.13

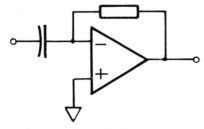

FIGURE 3.14

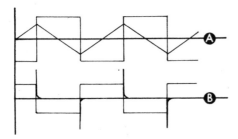

FIGURE 3.15

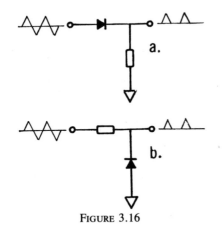

FIGURE 3.16

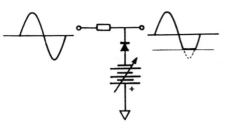

FIGURE 3.17

ferentiator that increases and decreases linearly with time, the differentiated output alternates between a positive constant and a negative constant value $(d(x)/dx = 1; d(-1)/dx = -1)$. Since the square wave presents a voltage to the differentiator that increases and decreases very rapidly, the differentiated output consists of alternating positive and negative large-amplitude, narrow-width pulses. A sine wave passed through a differentiator will theoretically result in no change in waveform $(d/dx[\sin v] = \cos v \, dv/dx)$. However, pure sine waves are rarely encountered in practice, and the differentiator can be used to identify the presence of impurities in a sine-wave generator output. A high quality triangle wave may be employed for examining the performance of a high-fidelity amplifier by passing the triangle wave through the amplifier, differentiating the amplifier output, and examing the resulting square wave.[1]

Nonlinear circuits may be employed to introduce distortion in a sinusoidal (single frequency) signal to obtain various complex (harmonically) waveforms. Figure 3.16a shows a triangle wave processed through a diode-resistor configuration. The circuit in figure 3.16a is a simple *half-wave rectifier,* so named because the diode permits only unilateral current flow, limiting the signal to positive excursions. By reversing the diode polarity, the signal may be limited to negative excursions. In figure 3.16b, the diode and resistor arrangement of figure 3.16a is altered to form a circuit that shunts negative-going signals to ground, while permitting positive-going signals to pass.

By placing a low-impedance, variable voltage source in series with the diode to ground (figure 3.17), the point at which negative signal excursions are limited may be varied. This process by which the amplitude excursions of a signal are restricted (as in figure 3.17) is known as *clipping.* Although clippers may be employed in the electronic music studio for audio-signal wave shaping (for example, clipping a sine wave to produce a squared-off waveform that contains higher order harmonics), these devices are capable of modifying sounds over a limited timbral range. Clippers may also be employed for control signal waveshaping, (for example, limiting the negative excursions of a modulating signal, or processing the output of a transient, or envelope, generator). Many "fuzz-tone" generators used by popular music groups employ some type of clipper circuit, although many fuzz-tone generators employ more complex circuits. In chapter 5, we shall show applications of clipping to limit frequency deviation in FM synthesis.

Figure 3.18 shows a graph of the input-versus-output characteristics of a circuit that clips at $+2V$ and $-2V$. Figure 3.19 shows a circuit of a clipper suitable for electronic music applications. This device permits positive clipping adjustable over the range $0 \rightarrow V+$ and negative clipping adjustable over the range $0 \rightarrow V-$ volts†. Figure 3.20 shows the time function (a) and the frequency spectrum (b) of a clipped sine wave.

†This circuit may be incorporated to good advantage in the control voltage mixer shown in chapter 4, figure 4.9. The R. A. Moog Company at one time marketed a 4-input, differential-output, direct coupled mixer that incorporated a clipper.

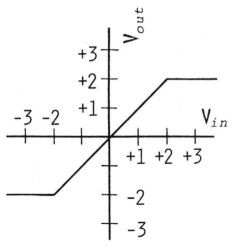

FIGURE 3.18

Figure 3.21a shows a diode-shaping network using several diodes with separate reference voltages and separate resistors to limit the shunt currents. This circuit functions as a series of attenuators that are switched in and out at various points determined by the relationship of the input signal voltage to the reference voltages. Such networks are employed for triangle wave to sine wave conversion. Figure 3.21b shows the input-versus-output characteristics of the circuit of figure 3.21a, along with the waveform of a triangle wave processed by the circuit. Note that the circuit of figure 3.21a shapes the positive-going portion of the waveform; a complementary circuit is necessary to shape the negative-going portion of the waveform to produce a sine wave. Using this waveshaping technique it is possible to produce sine waves of <1% distortion.

Full-wave rectification is a waveshaping technique in which the effective absolute value of a signal is produced. Figure 3.23 shows the input-versus-output characteristics of a full-wave rectifier. The full-wave rectifier is commonly employed in power-supply circuits where its characteristics are used to change alternating current into pulsating direct current that

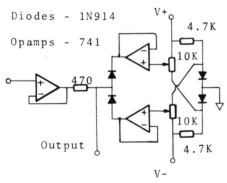

FIGURE 3.19

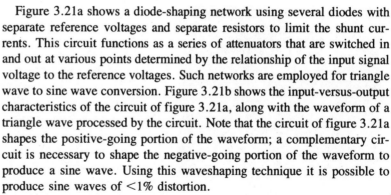

FIGURE 3.20

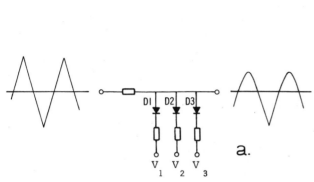

a.

Positive Voltage References

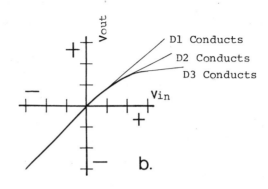

b.

FIGURE 3.21

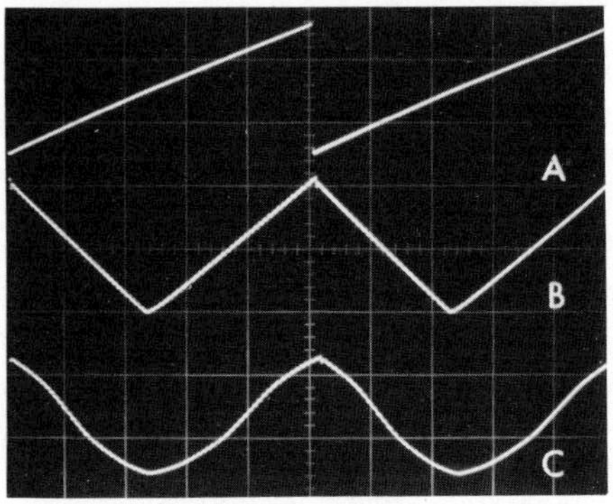

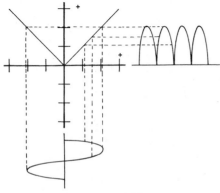

FIGURE 3.22

is then filtered (and in certain cases regulated) to produce direct current (see figure 3.23). A sawtooth wave (figure 3.22a) may be full-wave rectified to produce a triangle wave (figure 3.22b). Due to the flyback time of the sawtooth wave, an anomaly (which may be reduced by filtering) appears, in this case at the positive peak of the waveform. This triangle wave may be shaped into an approximation of a sine wave by means of a diode-shaping network (figure 3.22c). Processing a triangle wave through a full-wave rectifier produces a second triangle wave, the frequency of which is twice that of the unprocessed wave†.

Phase-locking is a useful capability included in many oscillators in electronic music systems to permit more accurate tracking. Figure 3.25 shows a basic phase-locked loop (PLL) that can be patched for demonstration purposes using normal electronic music equipment. In this diagram, a sine-wave oscillator set to frequency f_a is connected to one input of the multiplier M in the phase-locked loop. The other input of the multiplier is connected to the phase-locked loop VCO, set to frequency f_b. Sum and difference frequencies $(f_a + f_b)$ and $(f_a - f_b)$ are present at the output of the multiplier. The low-pass filter (LPF) will tend to attenuate the higher frequency sum: $(f_a + f_b)$ and pass the difference $(f_a - f_b)$ frequency. Assume in this example that f_a and f_b are close in frequency. The output of the low-pass filter is connected to the control-voltage input of the phase-locked loop oscillator, and feedback in this closed system will continue until $f_a - f_b = 0$, in which case the two oscillators will be phase-locked to one another. A divide-by-n circuit ($\div$) may be inserted in the feedback loop to permit phase-locking of frequency ratios other than 1:1. In setting up the phase-locked-loop demonstration patching of figure 3.25, f_a and f_b should be set close together in frequency, since the capture range of this patched PLL will be limited.

Multivibrators are a type of relaxation oscillator the output waveform of which is a pulse wave. *Astabile* multivibrators have long been used in electronic music as square-wave oscillators.[2] Under certain conditions, these oscillators may be synchronized with other oscillators to effect frequency division by integer values.

The *monostabile multivibrator* is a device that is inactive until triggered by an input pulse. The monostabile multivibrator then produces a single

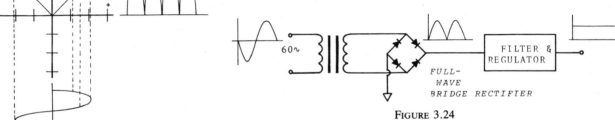

FIGURE 3.24

†Frequency doubling may also be accomplished by processing a signal (sine wave) with a multiplier, the inputs of which are connected in parallel.

FIGURE 3.23

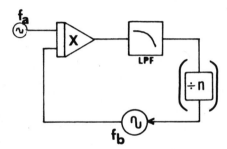

FIGURE 3.25

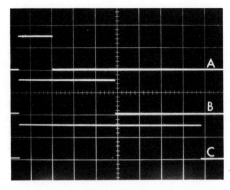

FIGURE 3.26

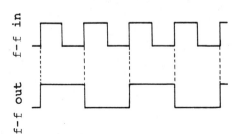

FIGURE 3.27

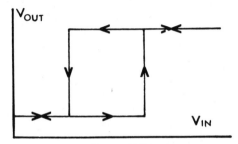

FIGURE 3.28

pulse, the duration of which is determined by the time constant of components in the monostable circuit. This device is useful for pulse stretching and shortening applications. Figure 3.26 shows three output waveforms produced by a monostable multivibrator, triggered in each case by pulses of equal duration. The time constant of the monostable's components was altered in each case so that: duration of pulse a < duration of pulse b < duration of pulse c.

Like the monostable multibrator, the *bistable multivibrator,* or *flip-flop* (f-f), changes states only upon the application of a triggering signal. The bistable multivibrator, however, does not automatically return to the initial state after being triggered, but rather requires a second trigger to reset it to the initial state. By making the flip-flop sensitive only to, for example, positive-going pulses, this circuit can be used to divide the frequency of a pulse wave by 2 (see figure 3.27). Frequency dividers are often employed for real-time modification of natural sounds, in which case the square-wave output of the frequency divider(s) is often processed by filtering to achieve the desired sound result. By cascading a number of flip-flops, frequency division by 2^n (where *n* is any positive integer) is possible. Other circuit configurations permit division by any integer, and in some cases by fractions, for example, 5/2.[3] A flip-flop (in conjunction with the appropriate interfacing) might be used to turn a sequencer's clock *on* with one pulse and *off* with a subsequent pulse.

The *Schmitt trigger* is often employed in electronic music instrumentation. Like the comparator, the Schmitt trigger detects whether an input signal is greater or less than some reference level, and indicates the result of the comparison by an output signal: for example, a high output level if the input signal > reference level. The Schmitt trigger exhibits *hysteresis,* that is, once the device is triggered by an input signal, it returns to its initial state only after the input signal drops below a second reference level. Figure 3.28 shows the hysteresis curve that results from plotting the input-versus-output characteristics of a Schmitt trigger. (Notice that this characteristic resembles the response of the neon bulb [figure 3.1a].)

Figure 3.29 shows two output waveforms produced by processing an analog input signal with a Schmitt trigger and comparator, respectively. By processing a low-pass-filtered random signal through a Schmitt trigger or

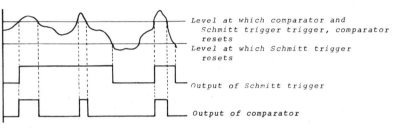

FIGURE 3.29

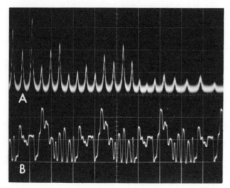

FIGURE 3.30

comparator, one may obtain a train of random-width pulses, useful for clocking sequencers and sample-and-hold circuits, as well as for other applications.

Many techniques are available for generating and modifying periodic waveforms. We have seen how periodic waveforms may be altered to produce a variety of waveshapes by processing through multielement diode shaping (clipping) networks providing adjustable biasing for each clipping element. Other analog techniques for generating complex waveforms have been described in the literature.[4]

In general, digital-waveform generators produce a step-voltage approximation of the desired waveform, which is then usually smoothed by low-pass filtering to produce a continuous function. Burhans has described a simple digital technique for generating a wide range of useful waveforms.[5] Digital computers are employed not only to generate and modify periodic waveforms, but also to produce sound events of a complex nature, for example, speech. The sequencer can be used to generate periodic waveforms (see chapter 7). For example, figure 3.30 shows the spectrum (a) and time function (b) of a low-pass-filtered step voltage produced by a 24-event sequencer (see chapter 7, page 183.)

The noise inherent in certain electronic devices may be amplified and used as a sound source. The most common type of noise source used in the electronic music studio is the *white noise* generator, a device that produces a signal of both random frequency and amplitude that displays equal power per unit bandwidth. Theoretically, white noise is not physically realizable, because to achieve a constant power spectral density over the entire frequency range (0 Hz to ∞ Hz) would require infinite power. White noise used in electronic music applications usually provides band-limited noise over a frequency range from below 1 Hz to less than 20 kHz.

The energy distribution of white noise is such that a Fourier analysis yields a flat plot of noise versus frequency. For example, the same energy is present between 1 and 2 Hz as is present between 10,000 Hz and 10,001 Hz. White noise is also described as *Gaussian noise,* since the amplitude-versus-probability curve of the signal displays a Gaussian distribution (see figure 3.31).

Pink noise, also known as $1/f$ noise, may be produced by passing white noise through a low-pass filter with a slope of -3 dB per octave (figure 3.32), with the result that the filtered signal (pink noise) displays equal power for equal percentages of bandwidth within the spectrum. Pink noise exhibits a $1/f$ noise spectrum: that is, noise power varies inversely with frequency, so that the noise voltage increases as the square root of the decreasing frequency. For example, pink noise contains equal power for any given octave. Pink noise is commonly used for testing the response of audio systems in certain environments by passing the noise through 1/3-octave band-pass filters, sending the filtered noise through the system, and measuring the power level of the processed filtered noise. By taking

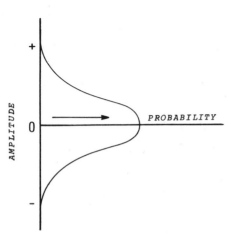

FIGURE 3.31

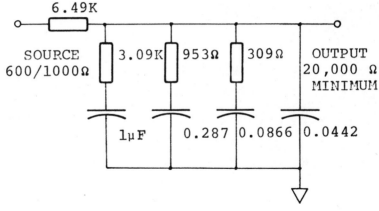

FIGURE 3.32

measurements at each one-third octave throughout the audio range, the overall response of a system may be estimated.

For electronic music purposes, neither white nor pink noise is very useful in its unmodified state, since the wide range of frequencies and amplitudes inherent in such wideband noise produces a steady-state effect for the ear.

Passing white noise through a highly selective filter produces a signal of determinate frequency but random amplitude known as *narrow-band noise* (see chapter 6, figure 6.22). The sound produced by such filtering of noise has been called "an approximation of choral whistling". This narrow-band noise is useful both as an audio signal and as a control signal. Processing white noise with various types of filters enables the composer to produce a wide range of sounds, all of which retain to some degree the original random qualities of the white noise. Entire compositions have been constructed from sounds derived principally from white noise, for example, Henri Pousseur's *Scambi*. Gated filtered noise is often used to simulate attack transients in electronic music synthesis. Figure 3.33 shows a gated program source mixed with a gated filtered noise source (see chapter 4). The duration of the noise component is usually adjusted to be short in relation to the duration of the program.

Hubert Howe relates early speculation regarding applications for white noise:

> One of the first ways that composers thought of making electronic sounds more "realistic" was to introduce random amounts of amplitude and frequency modulation. It was thought that deviations in live sounds were random because no clear patterns could be established for them. The question then became one of finding the right amounts of amplitude and frequency modulation, but the tones that were produced in this way were still quite different from live sounds.[6]

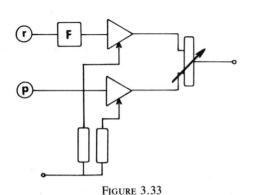

FIGURE 3.33

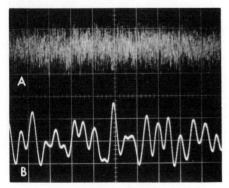

FIGURE 3.34

Low-pass filtering of white noise to frequencies below approximately 20 Hz provides the composer with a control signal with random qualities that may be used to produce random rhythmic sequences, continuous or discrete random pitch changes, and so on. Figure 3.34 shows the time function of white noise (*A*) which has been low-pass filtered (*B*) to produce a subaudio (or infrasonic) random signal. By varying the filter cutoff frequency, the composer may control the range of the rates of change within which the random variations occur.

Specious analogies are often made between the visible light spectrum and the audio frequency spectrum. While the use of admittedly nonspecific terms such as "azure sound" may be broadly descriptive, the reader should note that such names often conflict with certain precisely defined terms, namely, *pink noise* (1/*f* noise), and *red noise* (1/*f²* noise).

The white noise generator shown in figure 3.35 provides a DC-coupled output permitting very low-frequency random voltages to be obtained with proper filtering and amplification.

Figure 3.36 shows an oscillator with an exponential control-voltage-to-frequency response. The circuit utilizes the Intersil 8038 integrated circuit VCO, which features an internal triangle to sine wave convertor capable of producing a sine wave of less than 1% THD (Total Harmonic Distortion).[8] For best temperature stability, the two PNP transistors should be either a matched pair that is mechanically connected (for example, epoxied together) or a monolithic pair, such as is available on the RCA CA3096AE.

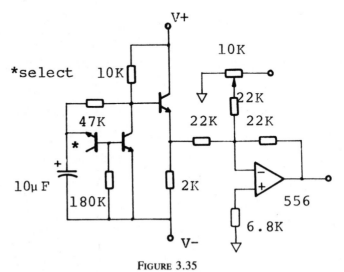

FIGURE 3.35

Transistors - 2N3707 or similar
WHITE NOISE GENERATOR (after Jung)[7]

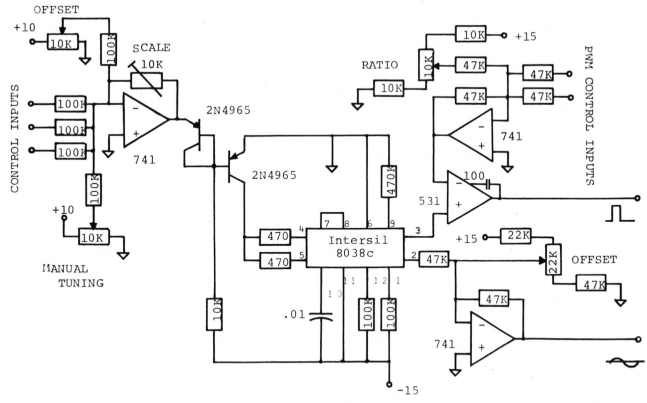

FIGURE 3.36

PROBLEMS

1. What is the result of processing (a) a square wave, (b) a sine wave, (c) a sawtooth wave, and (d) a triangle wave through a differentiator? What is the result of processing each of these waveforms through an integrator?

2. What frequency components are present in a full-wave rectified sine wave?[9]

3. Describe the differences between a comparator and a Schmitt trigger.

4. Generate a complex audio-frequency signal using a low-pass filtered sequencer. Monitor the signal aurally and on an oscilloscope, adjust the voltage levels associated with the various events (counts) of the sequencer, and note the resultant changes in the waveform and timbre. Use a tunable resonant band-pass filter (high Q) to examine the frequency components generated by the configuration described above.

5. In general, the frequency components present in a clipped sine wave consist of

_____ .

6. What is white noise? pink noise?

7. What are some advantages inherent in an exponential control-voltage-versus-frequency characteristic in a VCO? What are some advantages inherent in a linear control-voltage-versus-frequency characteristic in a VCO?

8. Show how each of the four basic waveforms (sine wave, sawtooth wave, square wave, triangle wave) discussed in the text can be transformed into other members of this group, that is, sine→square, square→triangle, and so on.

NOTES

1. M. Horowitz, *Measuring Hi Fi Amplifiers* (Indianapolis, Ind.: Howard W. Sams, 1976).

2. H. Badings and J. W. deBruyn, "Electronic Music," *Phillips Technical Review* 19 (1957–1958): 191–201.

3. "Non-Integer Frequency Division," *Electronic Engineering,* April 1972, p. 60.

4. "Generating Complex Waveforms," *Electronic Engineering,* May 1972, p. 60; and R. A. Schaeffer, "Electronic Musical Tone Production by Nonlinear Wave-shaping," *Journal of the Audio Engineering Society* 18 (1970): 413–416.

5. R. W. Burhans, "Pseudo-Noise Timbre Generators," *Journal of the Audio Engineering Society* 20 (1972): 174–184.

6. H. Howe, "Compositional Limitations of Electronic Music Synthesizers," *Perspectives of New Music,* Spring/Summer 1972, pp. 120–129.

7. "Generating Complex Waveforms," *Electronic Engineering*, May 1972.

8. Intersil, Inc., "Everything You Always Wanted to Know about the 8038," *Intersil Technical Paper,* 1976.

9. See H. Hsu, *Fourier Analysis* (New York: Simon and Schuster, 1970 rev.).

SELECTED BIBLIOGRAPHY

Books

Blake, M., and Mitchell, W. S. *Vibration and Acoustic Measurement Handbook.* New York: Spartan Books, 1972.

Doyle, J. M. *Pulse Fundamentals,* 2nd ed. Englewood Cliffs, N.J.: Prentice-Hall, 1973.

Horowitz, M. *Measuring Hi Fi Amplifiers.* Indianapolis, Ind.: Howard W. Sams, 1976.

Hutchins, B. *Musical Engineer's Handbook.* Ithaca, N.Y.: Cornell University Press, 1975.

Jung, W. *IC Op-Amp Cookbook.* Indianapolis, Ind.: Howard W. Sams Company, 1976.

Littauer, R. *Pulse Electronics.* New York: McGraw-Hill, 1965.

Magrab, E. B., and Blomquist, D. S. *The Measurement of Time-Varying Phenomena: Fundamentals and Applications.* New York: Wiley-Interscience, 1971.

Millman, J., and Taub, H. *Pulse, Digital, and Switching Waveforms.* New York: McGraw-Hill, 1965.

Motchenbacher, C. D., and Fichten, F. C., *Low-Noise Electronic Design.* New York: Wiley, 1973.

Strauss, L. *Wave Generation and Shaping,* 2nd ed. New York: McGraw-Hill, 1970.

Articles

"Analogue Modules Applications." *Electronic Engineering,* March 1970, pp. 64–65.

Badings, H., and deBruyn, J. W. "Electronic Music." *Phillips Technical Review* 19 (1957–1958): 191–201.

Balmer, L., and Brooks, B. "How To Obtain Direct Display of Probability Density Functions." *Electronic Engineering,* April 1972, pp. 37–39.

Barbarello, J. "VCO for Electronic Music." *Popular Electronics,* March 1977, pp. 42–44.

Bombi, F. "High-Performance Voltage-to-Frequency Converter Has Improved Linearity." *Electronic Engineering,* December 1970, pp. 61–64.

Broch, J. T. "The Application and Generation of Audio-Frequency Random Noise." *Technical Review* (Bruel and Kjaer Instruments, Inc., Cleveland, Ohio) 2 (1961).

Burhams, R. W. "Pseudo-Noise Timbre Generators." *Journal of the Audio Engineering Society* 20, no. 3 (April 1972): 174–184.

Chua, L. O. "Synthesis of New Nonlinear Network Elements." *IEEE Proceedings* 56 no. 8 (August 1968): 1325–1340.

Civit, A., and Bracho, S. "IC's Simplify V.-F. and V.-T. Conversions." *Electronic Engineering,* December 1971, pp. 36–38.

Clayton, G. B. "Experiments with Operational Amplifiers no. 6: Straight Line Approximated Nonlinear Response." *Wireless World,* November 1972, p. 524.

Flynne, A. "Improving the Linearity of Voltage-to-Frequency Converter." *Electronic Engineering,* April 1973, pp. 22–29.

Franklin, D. P. "Hypotenuse Function Generator." *Electronic Engineering,* January 1969, pp. 63–65.

Franco, Sergio. "Current-Controlled Triangular/Square-Wave Generator." *Electronic Design* 17 (August 16, 1973): 91.

Fredriksen, Howard Sleeth. "Free-Running Staircase Wave Generator." *Electronic Design,* 18 January 1973.

Gabrielson, B. "A Patchable Electronic Music Synthesizer." *Journal of the Audio Engineering Society* 26, no. 6 (June 1977): 295–399.

"Generating Complex Waveforms." *Electronic Engineering,* May 1972, p. 60.

Glenhill, B. "Nonlinear Elements Offer Analogue Solutions." *Electronic Engineering,* May 1971, pp. 70–73.

Hood, R. B. "Simple 1% Voltage-to-Frequency Converter." *Electronic Engineering,* December 1972, pp. 36–37.

Howe, H. "Compositional Limitations of Electronic Music Synthesizers." *Perspectives of New Music,* Spring/Summer 1972, pp. 120–129.

Intersil, Inc. "Everything You Always Wanted to Know about the 8038." *Intersil Technical Paper,* 1976.

Jung, W. J. "A Transistorized Noise Generator." *dB,* February 1971, p. 32.

Keene, J. P., and Hayden, D. W. "The Uncommon Versatility of the Common Current Generator." *Electronics,* 1 February 1971, pp. 40–43.

Keele, D. B., Jr. "The Design and Use of a Simple Pseudo-Random Pink-Noise Generator." *Journal of the Audio Engineering Society* 21, no. 1 (January/February 1973): 33–41.

Klevenhagen, S. "An Interval to Pulse Rate Conversion Technique Using a Monostable Multivibrator." *Electronic Engineering,* January 1970, pp. 44–48.

Klein, G., and Hagenbenk, H. "Accurate Triangle-Sine Converter." *Electronic Engineering* 39 (1967).

Lampton, M. "A Wide-Range Audio Sweep Oscillator." *Audio,* July 1971.

Lockhart, R. K., Jr. "Nonselective Frequency Tripler Uses Transistor Saturation Characteristics." *Electronic Design* 17 16 August 1973: 86.

"Low-Frequency Function Generator." *Electronic Engineering,* May 1970, p. 99.

McNatt, M. "Use Digital Counting Logic to Generate Precise Waveforms. *Electronic Design,* 18 January 1975.

Moog, R. A. "Voltage Controlled Electronic Music Modules." *Journal of the Audio Engineering Society* 13, no. 3 (July 1965): 200–206.

"Noninteger Frequency Division." *Electronic Engineering,* April 1972, p. 60.

Pease, R. "Ultralinear Voltage-to-Duty-Cycle Converter." *Electronic Engineering,* December 1971, p. 49.

Powner, E. T., et al. "Digital Waveform Synthesis." *Electronic Engineering,* August 1969, pp. 50–54.

"Relaxation Oscillator Uses IC Op-Amp." *Electronic Engineering,* November 1971, pp. 54–55.

Risley, A. R. "Designer's Guide to Logarithmic Amplifiers." *Electronic Design News,* 5 August 1973, pp. 42–51.

Rossum, D. "Chip VCO Using the 8038." *Electronotes* 16, no. 4 (December 1972).

Sankarananarayanan, P. "Constant Amplitude Ramp Generator with Op-Amps." *Electronic Engineering,* September 1974.

Schaeffer, R. A. "Electronic Musical Tone Production by Nonlinear Waveshaping." *Journal of the Audio Engineering Society* 18, no. 4 (August 1970): 413–416.

"A Simple Square-Triangle Waveform Generator." *Electronic Engineering,* October 1972, p. 29.

Smith, D. T. "Versatile Triangle Wave Generator." *Wireless World,* February 1973, pp. 87–89.

Sunstein, D. E. "Photoelectric Waveform Generator." *Electronics,* February 1949, pp. 100–103.

Tribolet, J.-P. "Original Sawtooth Generator." *Electronic Engineering,* December 1972, p. 40.

Vanderkooy, J., and Koch, C. J. "Generate Low-Distortion Sinewaves." *Electronic Design* 14 (5 July 1973): 70–73.

Young, R. "Get .02% VCO Accuracy." *Electronic Design,* 15 March 1973.

4

MIXING

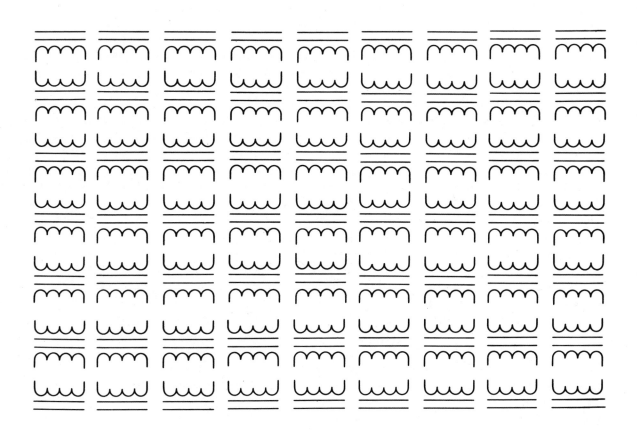

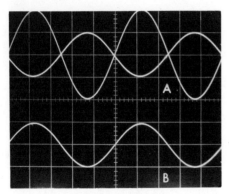

FIGURE 4.1

Signals may be combined in many ways. In the simple mixing process we shall discuss here, the instantaneous amplitudes of several signals are summed to produce a composite signal. For example, if two signals of identical frequency but unequal amplitude are out of phase (figure 4.1a), their summation will cause a partial cancellation (figure 4.1b). (For this reason, good recording studio technique dictates that no more than one microphone output be recorded onto a tape track. For example, if four singers are to be recorded onto a single track and two microphones are used, unpredictable phase cancellations may result, in effect distorting the desired result.) If the signals are of identical amplitude and 180° out of phase, their summation may result in complete cancellation. To avoid phase cancellations with multiple miking of a single instrument, many audio engineers use the 3 to 1 rule: if a microphone is placed one foot from the instrument, do not place the other microphones within three feet of the first.

As has been explained, complex periodic waveforms may be represented as a series of sinusoidal components. Conversely, waveforms may be synthesized by adding sinusoidal components in the proper amplitude and phase relationships. This technique is called *additive synthesis*.† The production of sounds by means of additive synthesis is very time-consuming and requires a large number of oscillators. Several interesting approaches to additive synthesis have been described in the literature.

LeCaine has constructed a device consisting of 30 oscillators, interconnected to produce 200 separate sine waves.[1] The frequencies of these sine waves lie between 5 Hz and 1000 Hz, spaced at 5 Hz intervals. Called the *Sonde*, this device offers the composer an excellent basis for additive synthesis, but the large number of signal sources makes control over time a formidable proposition. LeCaine mentions several control techniques in his article, including a touch-sensitive keyboard with an individual level control for each sine wave.

Beauchamp has constructed a device that generates the first six harmonics of a voltage-controlled fundamental frequency. Provisions are made to give each harmonic a separate envelope, allowing for complex attack and decay characteristics. The latter feature is most important, as we shall see later.

However theoretically appealing additive synthesis may be, in practice it is a most laborious synthesis technique. The problem is not in generating a large number of sine waves, but rather in devising suitable methods of controlling their mixture. An obvious but expensive solution is a programmable memory with provisions for the individual amplitude control of each element in the mixture. To this end, recording studios are exploring automated mix-down techniques that may be applicable to the electronic

---

†Certain sounds may be built up by adding together any set of signals, for example, square waves, prerecorded natural sounds, and the like. However, strictly speaking, additive synthesis refers to the summation of sine waves.

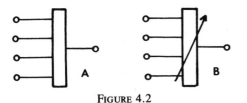

FIGURE 4.2

music studio. Because the cost of a powerful additive synthesis system is beyond the range of most studio budgets, this technique is usually employed on a limited scale. This is not to say that combining signals is not important: in fact, the simplest patching will undoubtedly include some form of signal addition.

The most common type of mixing involves the combining of several signals, which are then fed to a single output for distribution. Throughout this book, mixers will be designated as in figure 4.2. Signal flow is from left to right. The symbol $\nearrow$ indicates that the input and/or output levels are adjustable.

Electronic music applications involve direct-coupled mixers for control signal processing, line-level mixers, and low-level (microphone and phono cartridge) mixers. Most commercially available mixers such as the Tascam Model 3 and Model 5 provide selection between high- and low-level inputs. Although direct-coupled (DC) mixers are usually included in the complement of instruments in synthesizers, it is often desirable to construct extra DC mixers to provide added flexibility in the studio. A circuit of a simple DC mixer is shown later in this chapter.

In general, *impedance* is a description of the voltage-to-current ratio in a given AC circuit. The outputs of most electronic music instruments are designed to deliver *voltage*, not current. A major consideration in the design of equipment is compatability of input and output structures: how the no-load (open circuit) properties of the *driving* instrument will be affected by the connection to it of the *driven* instrument.

Figure 4.3 shows an oscillator with a 1000-ohm output impedance, R_S (S=source), connected to a load, R_L (L=load). The oscillator voltage is adjusted to 2 volts (measured with an oscilloscope or other high-impedance measuring instrument). Assume that an instrument, for example, control-voltage input of a voltage-controlled amplifier with a 100,000-ohm (100-kilohm) input impedance, R_L, is connected to the oscillator. The total series resistance of the circuit is now 101,000 ohms. Using Ohm's law, $E = I \cdot R_S$

$$2 = I \cdot 101,000$$
$$I = 2/101,000 = 0.0000198 \ A = 0.0198 \ mA.$$

The voltage across the load, R_L, is $I \cdot R_L = 0.0000198 \cdot 100,000 = 1.98$ volt, a drop of 0.02 volt, or 1%.

In the case in which the output and input impedances are equal (1000 ohms):

$$E = I \cdot R$$
$$2 = I \cdot 2000$$
$$I = 2/2000 = 1/1000 = 0.001 \ A = 1 \ mA.$$

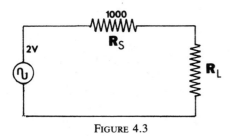

FIGURE 4.3

The voltage across the load, R_L, is now $I \cdot R$, or $0.001 \cdot 1000 = 1$, a drop of 1 volt, or 50%. From this, one can determine a simple method to find the output impedance of a device: measure the open-circuit (no-load) voltage with a high-impedance voltmeter; connect a variable resistor across the device in question as a load; adjust the resistor until the voltage drops to half the unloaded value; and measure the resistor's value. This value equals the impedance of the device.

A voltage source should have a low impedance with respect to the impedance of the device being driven. The opposite is required of a current source (see chapter 3, page 52). Impedance matching is not necessary or desirable for most electronic music modules. As another example, it is common audio engineering practice to operate professional microphones (approximately 50 to 250-ohm impedance) into preamplifiers with high (approximately 4 kilohms) input impedance, with no effort made to match impedances. Impedance matching *is* necessary, however, when maximum power transfer is required, for example, matching speakers to power amplifiers.

Examine figure 4.3 with regard to maximum power transfer. The power transferred to the load, R_L, is $I^2 \cdot R_L$. From Ohm's Law we know that I_{tot}, the total current flowing in the circuit, is equal to E/R_{tot} or $E/(R_S + R_L)$, or $2/(1000 + R_L)$. I^2 is equal to $[2/(1000 + R_L)]^2$, or $4/(1000 + R_L)^2$. Since the power transferred to the load, R_L is equal to $I^2 \cdot R_L$ (see above), we can substitute $4/(1000 + R_L)^2$ for I^2 in that expression and obtain $P = [4/(1000 + R_L)^2] \cdot R_L$. Multiplying, we obtain $P = 4R_L/(1000 + R_L)^2$. Choosing some test values for R_L, say 100 ohms, 1000 ohms, and 100,000 ohms:

for the case $R_L = 100$ ohms: $P = 4 \cdot 100/(1000 + 1000)^2 = 400/(1100)^2 = 0.00033$ watt;

for the case $R_L = 1000$ ohms: P $4000/(2000)^2 = 0.001$ watt;

for the case $R_L = 100,000$ ohms: $P = 400,000/(101,000)^2 = 0.00039$ watt.

It can be seen that maximum power transfer does occur when source and load impedances are equal. John Eargle points out that

recording technology had common origins with the broadcast, motion picture, and telephone industries. Most passive components used in recording, such as faders and certain filters, are still designed around the impedance level of 600 Ohms characteristic of telephone and broadcast transmission lines. Such devices present a 600 Ohm load, and are required to be loaded themselves by 600 Ohms.[2]

In recording studios and certain other installations, the *balanced line* is employed for routing signals. Figure 4.4 compares the balanced and unbalanced line configurations. In the balanced line configuration, the signal path is provided by two wires (a and b), while the outer conductor serves only as a shield, carrying no signal current. Although more expensive and

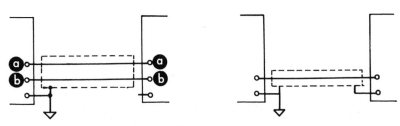

FIGURE 4.4

bulky than the unbalanced line, the balanced line is employed in applications in which maximum signal quality must be maintained. The balanced line configuration is sensitive only to signal differences between the signal lines. Any spurious signal that penetrates the outer shield will be induced in equal amplitude and phase in the two inner conductors. Since the spurious signal presents no instantaneous level difference to the receiving equipment, it is ignored.

Occasionally, signals must be passed between balanced and unbalanced lines. The most common method to interface these configurations employs a transformer whose input and output impedances are chosen to effect an optimum impedance match (figure 4.5a). An alternative method using operational amplifiers is shown in figure 4.5b. This circuit may be treated as a transformer—any input or output may be grounded to provide the desired configuration. The circuit is most useful when going from an unbalanced to a balanced line, since a single opamp may be used to go from a balanced to an unbalanced line (figure 4.4c).†

However, to use a device with balanced outputs in an unbalanced system, it is necessary to connect one side of the balanced line output pair to ground (shield). Either of the pair may be grounded, although the "low

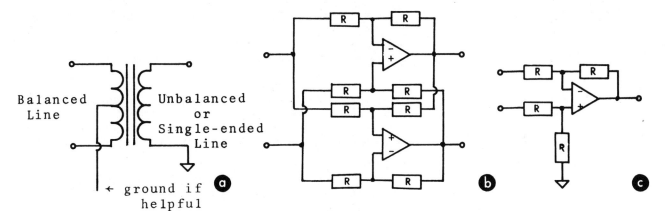

FIGURE 4.5

†In either case the opamps provide an extremely low output impedance. For more details, the reader is referred to the many references on opamps in this book.

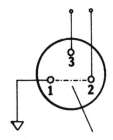

FIGURE 4.6

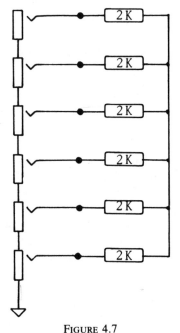

FIGURE 4.7

side'' is, by convention, usually grounded. Inconsistency in grounding will result in a 180° phase-shift between different lines. This condition will be very noticeable when the out-of-phase channels containing the same program material are monaurally mixed. Figure 4.6 shows a rear view of a male Cannon XLR–3 connector. Pins 1 and 2 should be connected together for unbalanced line operation.

In most electronic music studios, balanced lines are not needed because most signal levels in the studio are on the order of volts, rather than the millivolt levels provided by most microphones. Further, studio equipment is commonly designed to deliver voltage, and device input and output impedances do not match. Rather, input impedances are made high (10K to 100K), while output impedances are made as low as practicable (1K to 50 ohms). Because of this, a large number of device inputs may be connected to a single output without causing undue loading effects. On the other hand, the direct interconnection of two or more device outputs should be avoided: their low output impedances will load each other, causing not only a signal reduction, but quite often distortion as well. Such distortion can be a desirable effect, but unless the manufacturer specifically states that device outputs may be interconnected, or one is exactly sure of what he is doing, such a practice should be avoided.

This precaution should be observed when using multiple jacks. Multiple jacks are simply a group of jacks connected in parallel that are used to distribute, or *fan out,* a device output signal to several device inputs. The reverse process involves the interconnection of several outputs to a single point for routing to a single input. This is a common function for a mixer, which combines signals while isolating device outputs from each other. Multiple jacks can be modified for a mixing operation, as shown in figure 4.7. The resistors serve to isolate low output impedance devices from each other, while causing moderate attenuation when the combined signal is fed to a high-input impedance device. Of course, this configuration is not suitable for critical mixing or for combining low level signals that require amplification.

LEVEL MONITORING

The *level* of a quantity is defined as ''the logarithm of the ratio of that quantity to a reference quantity of the same kind.'' The unit employed for measuring electrical and acoustical levels is the *bel,* named for Alexander Graham Bell. The bel is commonly divided into decibels (abbreviated dB), one decibel being one-tenth of a bel. Many mixers incorporate a means for monitoring either the levels present at the mixer inputs and/or the level of the combined signals appearing at the mixer output. The most common monitoring device is a meter whose scale is calibrated in decibels.

†ANSI Standard C 42.65–1957, Def. 65.08.006 (1957).

A power level L_p is defined as

$$L_p = (10 \log_{10} \frac{P_1}{P_2}) \text{ dB},$$

where P_1 and P_2 are two power levels, P_1 being some measured value that is compared to P_2, the reference value.

Often the output signal of a device is measured with respect to its input signal. For example, an amplifier with a power gain of 2 is said to have a power gain of 3 dB. If an attenuator causes a power gain of 1/2, its power gain expressed in decibels is -3 dB. A negative power gain is often referred to as a power loss. (Although $\log_{10} 2 = 0.3010$, and $10 \cdot 0.3010 = 3.010$, we round off the quotient to 3.) Notice that the decibel measurement gives no indication of the actual power values involved. A power loss of 3 dB simply means that only half as much power is available at the output as is applied to the input (assuming that the device is fed from a source impedance equal to the device input impedance).

Voltage and current levels may also be measured in decibels. From Ohm's Law, recall that the power varies as the square of the current or voltage. Hence, for decibel expressions involving voltage and current, we obtain, for expressions involving voltage

$$L_e = (20 \log_{10} E_1/E_2),$$

and, for expressions involving current,

$$L_i = (20 \log_{10} I_1/I_2) \text{ dB}$$

$P = IE$, $P = I^2R$, and $P = E^2/R$; and $10 \log_{10} (E_1{}^2/R)/(E_2{}^2/R) = 20 \log_{10} E_1/E_2$ (recall that $\log M^n = n \log M$). For example, an amplifier with a power gain of 20 dB would have a ratio of power output to power input of 100. An amplifier with a voltage gain of 20 dB would have a ratio of voltage output to voltage input of 10. If the reference value is known, the value of the other quantity may be derived from the level measurement. For example, the Moog Music voltage-controlled amplifier specifications state that the maximum voltage gain for the amplifier is 6 dB. If a one-volt DC signal is applied to the input of this amplifier (we shall not concern ourselves with *which* input or output—differential inputs and outputs will be discussed later in this chapter), we should like to obtain the magnitude of the output signal, assuming the amplifier is operating at maximum gain. From the expressions above:

$$6 \text{ dB} = 20 \log_{10} x \text{ volt/1 volt}$$
$$0.3 = \log_{10} x$$
$$10^{0.3} \simeq x \simeq 2.$$

The decibel can be used an an absolute measure of power or voltage, provided a standard reference level is used (placed in the denominator of the fraction in the expressions given above), for example:

$$L_e = \left(20 \log_{10} \frac{\text{voltage to be measured in dB}}{\text{reference voltage}}\right) \text{dB}$$

Using the standard reference level in audio engineering, one milliwatt into 600 Ω, the voltage level that is present under these conditions is 0.774 volt (774 millivolts). Recall that power in watts is equal to current in amperes multiplied by electromotive force in volts: $P = I \cdot E$. From Ohm's Law, $E = I \cdot R$, and $I = E/R$. Substituting $I = E/R$ for the I of $P = I \cdot E$ gives $P = E^2/R$. Given that $P = 1$ milliwatt (.001 watt) and $R = 600$ ohms, substitution of these values in $P = E^2/R$ gives $0.001 = E^2/600$. $E^2 = 0.001 \cdot 600$. $E^2 = 0.6$. $E = \sqrt{0.6} = 0.774$.

To express voltage levels in terms of dB referred to 1 milliwatt into 600 Ω (dBm), the following expression is used:

$$L_e = (20 \log_{10} \frac{\text{voltage to be measured in dBm}}{0.774}) \text{dBm}$$

Several reference standards are commonly employed. The reader may encounter several of those listed below.

dB   6 milliwatts, 1.73 volts, 500 Ω
dBm   1 milliwatt, 0.774 volts, 600 Ω
dBV   1 volt reference
dBW   1 watt reference
VU   0
      VU= +4 dBm.

Level measurement in dBm is standard in audio engineering: it is very important that the student become familiar with expressing levels in this system. See voltage and power ratios to decibels in the Appendixes, table 2.

VU stands for *volume unit*. A VU meter is an AC voltmeter originally designed to read zero level on its scale when the voltage corresponding to one milliwatt into 600 ohms is applied. Figure 4.8 shows a standard VU meter scale. Monitoring devices should not draw an appreciable amount of power from the device being monitored: that is, the impedance of the monitoring device should be high compared to that of the monitored device. In order to raise the characteristic impedance of the VU meter (3,900 ohms) to a value approximately more than ten times the impedance of standard transmission lines (600 ohms), a series resistor is added before the meter, with the result that the meter is less sensitive and requires more voltage to produce a reading equivalent to that produced before the series resistor was added. In this case, the series resistor (3600 ohms) introduces a 4-dB loss. A 0-dBm (774 millivolts) level will now produce a reading of

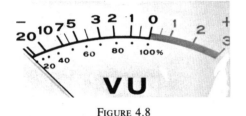

FIGURE 4.8

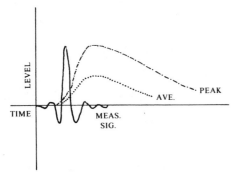

FIGURE 4.9

−4 dB on the VU meter, and a +4-dBm level will be required for the meter to read 0 dB.

The ballistics of the VU meter are such that 1/3 second is required for the meter to reach 99% of full scale when a constant amplitude sine wave of, say, +7 dBm is suddenly applied. Thus, the VU meter is incapable of accurately indicating transient signals shorter than 1/3 second. Short-duration transients in electronic and instrumental music are often 13 to 15 dB higher than the average signal level indicated on the VU meter, and amplifier clipping and tape saturation may result from such transients, especially if the nominal level is on the order of +4 dBm (0 VU) or greater. The peak and average meters' responses to the measured signal and the approximate relationships between peak and average levels are shown as a function of time in figure 4.9.

Peak-level indicators are extensively employed in recording studios to provide a more accurate reading of transient program material. Many peak-level indicators consist of a series of light-emitting diodes, incandescent lamps, or neon lamps, to indicate program level condition. Unlike the VU meter, lamp displays are fast enough to follow signal peaks accurately. (The response of some lamp displays is selectable between peak and "VU" responses.) The lamps are usually arranged vertically, with the maximum level indicator at the top. A circuit of a simple peak-level meter is shown in figure 4.10. Other light-indicating peak-level monitor designs employ television monitors to display bar graphs of the levels of a multichannel system. A transparent red mask is often employed with this system to indicate a critical level. Vertical lamp displays allow a large number of monitors to be built with a small space and permit the operator

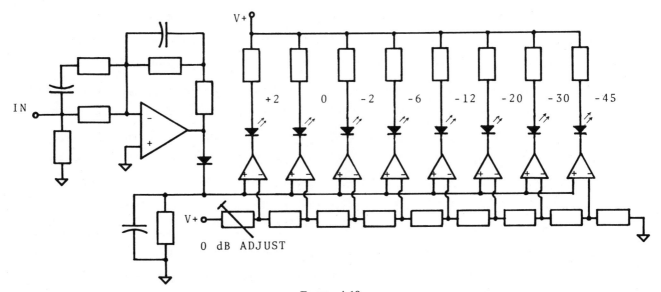

FIGURE 4.10

to quickly recognize signal conditions by scanning the displays comparatively.

Ideally, a studio should employ both VU and peak-level monitoring of program levels. Although the VU meter is sluggish and does not indicate short-duration high-level transients, its slow ballistics often work to the operator's advantage: it encourages the use of a higher program level and, although clipping may result, occasional clipping of high-level transients has been shown to be unnoticeable. On the other hand, the peak-level monitor may encourage the operator to use lower program levels than he would with a VU monitor, thereby degrading the signal-to-noise ratio of the system. Peak-level indicators are, however, desirable in cases in which a number of channels are mixed down to one—cases in which intermodulation distortion may be a problem.

The oscilloscope can provide an extremely sensitive level-monitoring display by routing the signal to be monitored to the y-axis input, and disabling the internal x, or horizontal axis sweep. Program level indication is provided by the length of the vertical trace, which should be calibrated to the desired reference signal amplitude. The resultant display indicates the instantaneous signal level, and as such is a useful adjunct to a VU meter, allowing the operator, for example, to take advantage of the full dynamic range of a tape system to achieve the maximum signal-to-noise ratio of which his equipment is capable.

The peak-level reading meter shown in figure 4.10 designed specifically for use with a tape recorder, is included to illustrate the principle of a meter incorporating a lamp display. The frequency response of this device is shaped by the input circuitry, so that 0 dB on the meter follows a reference level for total harmonic distortion at low frequencies, and the tape saturation characteristic at high frequencies. For a more detailed discussion of such a meter, see E. A. Balik, "Constructing a Peak-Reading VU Meter."[3]

The eight comparators are referenced to a voltage divider with resistor values chosen to reflect the indicated levels. If the rectified output from the amplifier exceeds one of the reference levels, the appropriate comparator switches *on,* lighting the LED, which displays that signal level. The resistor and capacitor following the diode serve to hold the signal peak long enough for the operator to notice the peak level, but not so long as to obscure lower level readings. The construction of this device may be greatly simplified by using a National LM3914 LED bar/dot display driver.

BASICS OF MIXER DESIGN

As has been mentioned before, certain mixers are designed to accept certain types of input signals. Control voltages typically exhibit a range of several volts, and periods from seconds and tens-of-seconds to approximately 0.1 millisecond. Control voltages often include an intentional offset of several volts from ground (figure 4.11). A control-voltage mixer should

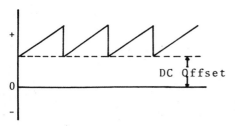

FIGURE 4.11

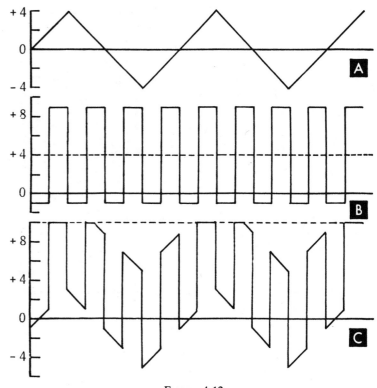

FIGURE 4.12

have a large frequency response, for example, from DC, or 0 Hz,† up into (and, desirably, beyond) the audio-frequency range. A good high-frequency response ensures that the mixer will be able to handle sudden level changes such as step voltages, and so on.

However, a DC response can often cause unexpected results unless the composer understands the special properties of instruments with this characteristic. Assume that a certain control-voltage mixer output can swing ±10 volts before clipping. The mixer in this example has a gain of one. If a triangle wave of 8 volts peak-to-peak and an offset voltage of +4 V is mixed with a square wave of 10 volts peak-to-peak, the mixer will clip at +10 volts (figure 4.12).

Some control voltage mixers are specifically designed to allow the user to adjust both the positive and negative clipping levels. Such a clipping capability is useful not only for processing control-voltage signals, but audio signals as well (see chapter 3, page 56).

†A *direct-coupled* amplifier is an amplifier that omits the customary coupling capacitor to obtain a response extending to 0 Hz. As we shall see in chapter 7, certain modulation and detection schemes also permit system response to DC.

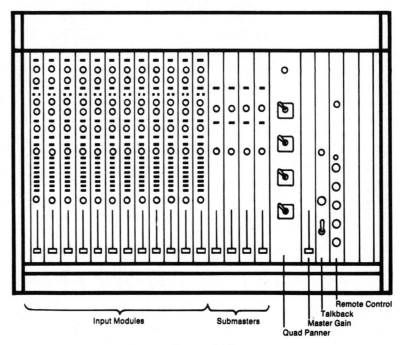

Input Modules　　Submasters

Quad Panner
Master Gain
Talkback
Remote Control

FIGURE 4.13

Specifications for mixers designed for audio signals (whether electronically generated or obtained from a microphone or instrument pickup) differ in several respects from control-voltage mixer specifications. An audio-signal mixer must introduce as little distortion as possible in the signal processed through it. A control-voltage mixer, on the other hand, may include provisions for distorting (clipping) signals. A lower signal-to-noise ratio is allowable when mixing control voltages than when mixing program material. Of course, the effects of distortion and noise are cumulative, and the finished sound can be no cleaner than that which the processing equipment is capable of. Audio-signal mixer design is simplified in the sense that DC response is not required. In fact, DC response in an audio-signal mixer could be a drawback, especially if the studio equipment has DC offset problems, since the offsets could be amplified to the extent that signals might be clipped. The audio-signal mixer's frequency response (flat) must extend at least to the limits intended for the program material.

A central mixing console is a most important instrument, providing signal mixing and routing capabilities as well as monitoring and equalization facilities in the studio. Figures 9.14 and 9.15, chapter 9, show two small studio mixers (Tascam and Fairchild) suitable for electronic music use. Figure 4.13 shows a possible module layout for the Tascam Model 10B mixer, used in many electronic music studios. Figure 4.14 shows a block diagram of a studio mixer with eight inputs and four outputs. Starting

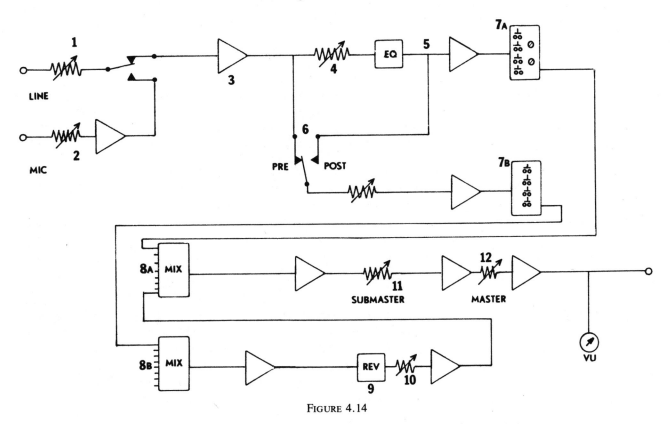

FIGURE 4.14

at the inputs to the mixer, a switch selects either high- or low-level (mic) program (1 and 2). Adjustable attenuators (pads) provide some scaling adjustments so that the settings of the input faders can be normalized (operated in the normal range for input signals of different levels. A pre-amp (3) boosts the program level before the fader (4). A switch (6) selects between taps taken from the fader input and from the output of the equalizer (5) and routes either of these taps through a volume control (echo, or *auxiliary,* send) and booster amplifier to the reverb/auxiliary channel assignment section (7B), which routes the signal through the reverb or auxiliary device to any combination of the four submasters. The channel/pan assignment section (7A) performs the same distribution function as the reverb/auxiliary channel assignment section, but routes the signal directly to the program combining network (mixer) (8A). In addition, this section of the mixer permits panning between various submaster inputs, for example, between 1 and 2; 2 and 3; 1 and 4; 2 and 3; 2 and 4; 3 and 4; (1 and 2) and 3; (1 and 2) and (3 and 4); and so on. This facility is useful when mixing a 4- or 8-channel tape down to 2 channels: the mixer might want to assign channel 1 of the multitrack tape to channels 1 and 2 of the 2-channel tape, 1/3 *left* and 2/3 *right,* and so on.

Both reverberated and nonreverberated programs are mixed in the program combining networks (8A), amplified, and routed to the submaster fader (11), which controls the overall level for one output channel of the mixer (subject to settings of the master (12) volume control, sometimes called *grandmaster*). This control regulates the levels of all output channels together. Switch 6 (pre/post), described above, permits program material to be sent to the reverb or auxiliary device before (pre) or after (post) the action of the fader and the equalizer (EQ). This configuration affords flexibility in mixing reverberated (wet) program with nonreverberated (dry) program in the program combining network. The reverb unit (or any sound processing device: filter, modulator, time-delay device, and the like) is connected at point 9, and the output of the reverb/auxiliary unit is sent through a control (10, echo receiver), amplified, and connected to the program combining network (8A). Equalization facilities for most mixers include: a high-band peak-and-dip filter (fixed-center frequency); a mid-bank peak-and-dip filter (selection between two fixed center frequencies); and a low-band peak-and-dip filter (selection between two fixed center frequencies). One of these filter sets is provided for each input module.

A talkback/slate option permits the operator of the mixer to interrupt the program material and insert a tone and/or verbal message at the input of the program amplifier. This facility is useful in identifying different sections of an electronic piece for later assembly. The term *slating* is derived from the motion picture practice of holding a clapboard/slate tablet in front of the camera at the beginning of a take to identify the scene and take number. In commercial recording applications, the slate/talkback provides the engineer or producer a way to communicate with the musicians in the studio. Pressing the slate button should mute the control-room speakers to avoid feedback. In addition, a low-frequency tone of around 30 Hz is applied to the program output during slating. The low-frequency tone provides a cue to indicate the beginning of a take; during fast forwarding or rewinding, the low-frequency tone is heard as a high pitch.

Most professional mixers provide an output of +4 dBm, with the amplifiers in the unit capable of an additional 20 dB of gain (headroom) before clipping, thereby making the maximum output of the system +24 dBm. This headroom is necessary to accommodate peaks caused by transient signals often encountered in instrumental and electronic music. The operator of the mixing console must be aware of the procedures necessary to obtain the maximum dynamic range and maximum signal-to-noise ratio from the equipment—these procedures apply as well to practically all operations in the electronic music studio. A common mistake involves setting the gain of an amplifier or mixer too low and having to compensate for this low level by raising the gain of the following stage, resulting in reduction of dynamic range of the second stage as well as an increase in the noise level. Figure 4.15 shows the progress of a signal through a mixer: (a) set to take advantage of the maximum dynamic range and (b) improperly operated. In this diagram, noise levels are shown by crosshatching at

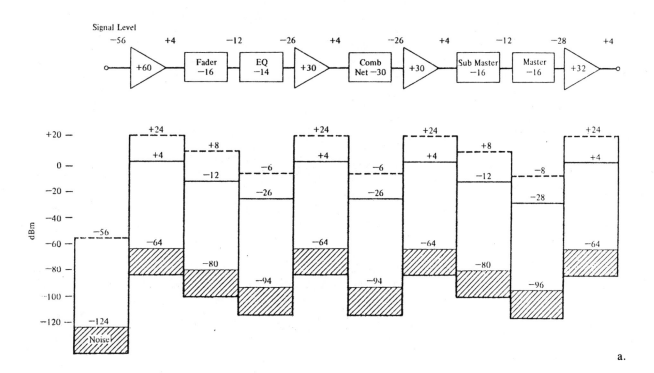

a.

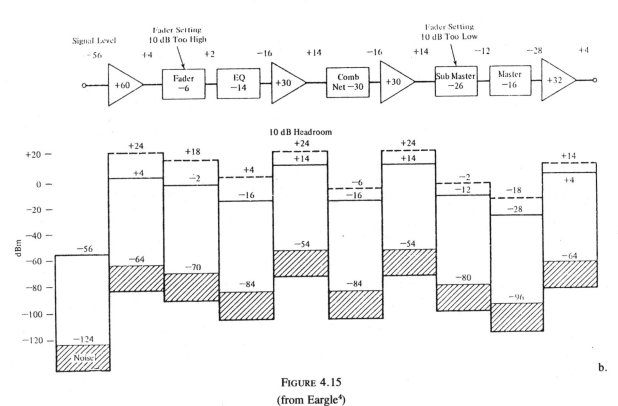

b.

FIGURE 4.15
(from Eargle[4])

the bottom of the figure. Normal signal levels are indicated by solid lines, while clipping levels are shown by dotted lines. Setting the input fader 10 dB too high in Figure 4.15b results in a 10-dB loss in dynamic range throughout the entire system.

Usual practice is to pass signals to be recorded through the mixer. The input level controls of the tape recorder should be adjusted so that a 1,000-Hz tone passed through the mixer (no equalization) at 0 VU will cause the meter of the recorder connected to the mixer to indicate 0 VU as well. Once this calibration is accomplished for all channels of all recorders in the studio, recorder input attenuators may be marked and left at that setting. This calibration permits the operator to monitor only one set of meters—at the mixing console.

MIXER CIRCUITS

Figures 4.16 and 4.17 show two simple mixers that may be used for production work in small studios with limited budgets or as construction projects in a technical course on electronic music. The operational amplifiers in these circuits are 741, 558 (dual 741), 531, or LF351.

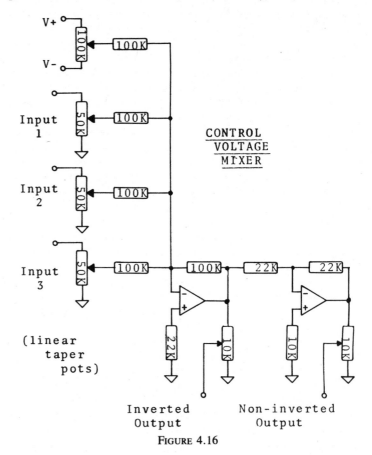

FIGURE 4.16

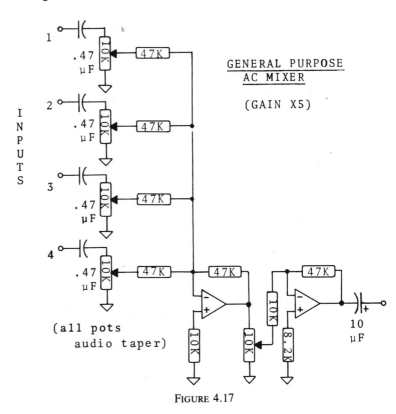

FIGURE 4.17

MULTICHANNEL MIXING AND PANNING

A stereo mixer is employed to mix signals for distribution to two separate channels, as in stereo recording or live performance with a two-channel system. The stereo mixing configuration may be quite simple, consisting of two separate mixers, one for each channel. However, to apportion sound between two channels requires that some signal be fed into each channel. Using two mixers, the mixer inputs should be connected in parallel as shown in figure 4.18. This configuration allows the composer/performer to feed any desired amount of input signal to either channel. By increasing the level of one channel while simultaneously decreasing the level of the other channel, a sound may be made to appear to move from one channel to the other.

A more sophisticated stereo mixer configuration is shown in Figure 4.19. For visual clarity, only two input channels are shown, although six or more are common. In this mixer, each input level is separately controllable, while the two output levels are varied together by means of two pots ganged together on one shaft. The three-position switch allows the signal to be routed to channel A, channel B, or both. In position 1, the signal fed to channel A is grounded, while the signal to channel B is attenuated by the voltage divider R_2-R_3. With the switch in position 3, the reversed situation exists, and the signal is passed to channel A. In position 2, the slider of R_3

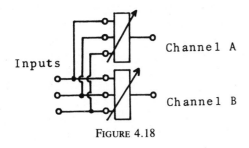

FIGURE 4.18

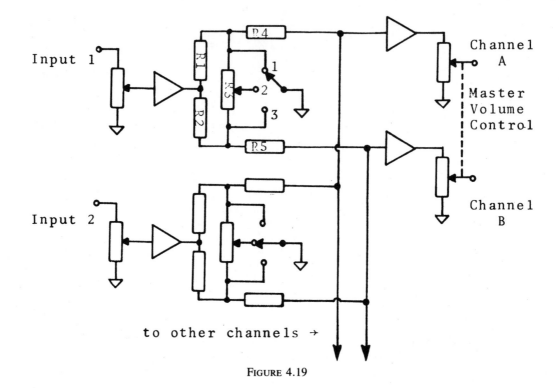

FIGURE 4.19

is grounded, forming two voltage dividers, R_1–R_3 and R_2–R_3. As the slider is moved towards R_1, the attenuation in channel A increases, while the attenuation in channel B decreases. Moving the slider toward R_2 produces an equal but opposite effect. A diagram of signal attenuation versus slider position is shown in Figure 4.20. Such a control is called a *panoramic control*, or *panoramic potentiometer* (or *panpot*). Used with a two-channel playback system, the panpot allows one to position the apparent source of a sound anywhere on a line between two speakers. The process of moving the apparent source of a sound by means of a panoramic control is known as *panning* a sound.

A sound system may be composed of any number of independent channels. To pan sounds along a line requires two channels and two speakers. To move sound in two dimensions, at least three channels are required. The four-channel or quadraphonic system is interesting for the possibilities it provides the composer for moving sounds spatially. Furthermore, such a system permits the reproduction of a sound's reverberation envelope, theoretically yielding more realistic sound reproduction. Blaukopf has commented on the heretofore unresearched capabilities of multichannel sound systems with regard to synthetic reverberation and sound dimensionality.[5] Serge Modular Music Systems has recently developed a series of *equal power* panning and mixing modules, so-called because the sum total power output for a panned program will remain constant, regardless

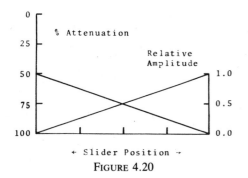

FIGURE 4.20

of the program apportionment selected by the operator, thereby insuring a more even panning effect.

QUAD PANPOT

Four-channel sound may be controlled in a useful manner by extending the stereo panpot configuration. Figure 4.21 diagrams a four-channel or *quad* panpot that is easily understood as a system of three simple panpots. One panpot controls the front-to-back distribution, while the two other panpots control the side-to-side distribution, with one panpot for the front and one panpot for the back. This arrangement has been described by Bluthgen.[6] Mechanical control is effected by means of a so-called joy stick so that the position of the stick corresponds to the position of the apparent sound source. Connected in reverse, the quad panpot operates as a coordinated four-to-one-channel mixer. By using the panpot in this manner, four signals (audio signals, control signals) may be blended in almost any proportion. This arrangement affords many advantages. For example, the composer may make continuous transformations between sound events, an effect that is most difficult to realize with a conventional four-input mixer.

ELECTRONIC LEVEL CONTROL

Any device the resistance of which may be varied electrically can be used as an electronic attenuator. Diodes, transistors, FETs, and so on, have all been used for voltage or current control purposes. Photo-sensitive resistors, or photoresistors, find many applications in electronic attenuator designs. The resistance of the photoresistor decreases as the intensity of light directed upon the photoresistor increases. A lamp or light-emitting diode may be driven by an amplifier so that a voltage may be used to control the lamp intensity, thereby controlling the amount of signal passed through a photoresistor attenuator. Figure 4.22 illustrates such an arrangement.

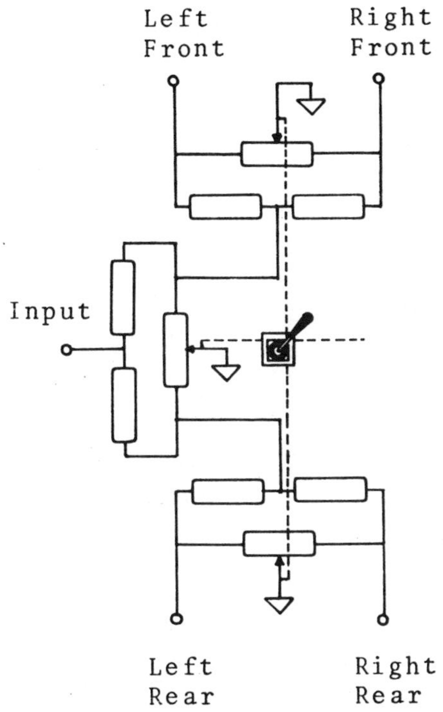

Photoresistors have been used in multichannel mixers designed both for the studio and for live performance.[7] By grouping the photoresistors in some convenient arrangement, channels may be selected with a flashlight. For example, each channel of a four-channel sound system may be connected to a photoresistor attenuator, the photoresistors being mounted in a circle, as shown in figure 4.23. By directing a flashlight beam at a photoresistor, the resistance of the device will lower, causing the input signal to be passed to the respective output channel.

By illuminating the photoresistors one by one rapidly in sequence, the operator can cause program material to appear to rotate among the speakers. The photoresistor mixer described above may be set up either to rotate sounds or to mix sequentially (fade in and out in order) a group of sounds by using the configuration shown in figure 4.24. This illustration shows a battery-powered lamp mounted on a variable-speed phonograph turntable, with the photoresistors placed around the turntable at 90° intervals. The photoresistors are mounted in plexiglas blocks that have been drilled to accept the photoresistor leads. The plexiglas blocks provide mechanical support for the photoresistors, preventing their leads from twisting and

Left Front   Right Front

Input

Left Rear   Right Rear

FIGURE 4.21

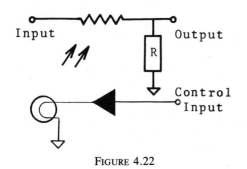

FIGURE 4.22

breaking off. The mercury switch turns on the lamp when the turntable is in motion, although a bypass switch may be provided for manual control. For this and most other light-controlled attenuator applications, Clairex CL 703L photoresistors are recommended. This technique affords a fairly inexpensive solution to the design of an eight-channel panning device.

While photoresistor level controls afford "hands-on" operation, precise and repeatable control is difficult. In addition, these devices must be shielded from ambient light, which can cause undesired bleedthrough in the photoresistor-controlled channels. Many composers have used photoresistor controlled devices for the theatrical quality the moving control lights lend to a live performance. Certain other light-controlled devices will

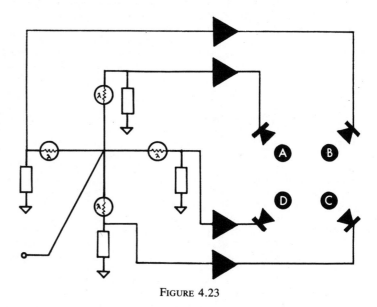

FIGURE 4.23

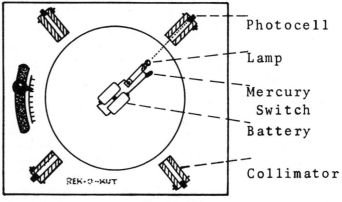

FIGURE 4.24

be discussed in chapter 7. Lamps and photoresistors are available as sealed units, that may be employed as voltage-controlled attenuators. Many guitar (instrument) amplifiers use such a circuit to produce a tremolo effect (see circuit, figure 4.25). In this circuit, a low-frequency (approximately 1 to 12 Hz) is fed to the attenuator control input, causing low-frequency amplitude modulation of the program input. The "depth" of the tremolo is controlled by varying the amount of current fed to the lamp by the driving amplifier.

VOLTAGE-CONTROLLED AMPLIFIER

An amplifier may be built so that its gain may be controlled by a current or voltage. In electronic music studios, the *voltage-controlled amplifier* is most common. Many voltage-controlled amplifiers, or VCAs, have two inputs: one input inverts the signal (causes the signal to be multiplied by −*1 times the gain of the amplifier*); the other input causes no inversion (the signal is multiplied by +*1 times the gain of the amplifier*). In addition, some VCAs provide two complementary outputs. (For example, a signal appearing at one output equals the signal appearing at the other output multiplied by −1.) The signal relationships (using a sinusoidal input signal) between the inputs and outputs of a VCA having both inverting and noninverting inputs and outputs is shown in figure 4.26. In this drawing, the inverting inputs and outputs are indicated by minus signs; noninverting inputs and outputs are indicated by plus signs. Thus, feeding a signal to a + input and taking the − output and vice versa causes signal inversion. Feeding a signal to the + input and taking the + input produces no inversion. Likewise, feeding a signal to the − input and taking the − output produces no inversion.

Such an amplifier is said to have *differential* inputs and outputs. Like a balanced line, differential inputs respond only to instantaneous differences between the two input terminals. Differential outputs are often referred to as *push-pull* (p-p) outputs.

The gain of a VCA is proportional to a voltage applied to its control input. Many VCAs are capable of both *linear* and *exponential* control-voltage-input-versus-amplifier-gain characteristics. In the linear mode, the control-voltage-versus-gain characteristic is

$$A = k \cdot V_c,$$

where A is the voltage gain; k is a constant; and V_c is the control voltage. In the exponential mode, the control-voltage-versus-gain characteristic is

$$A \simeq k^{Vc}.$$

Figure 4.27 shows an oscilloscope photograph of the control-voltage-versus-gain characteristics of a Moog Music voltage-controlled amplifier

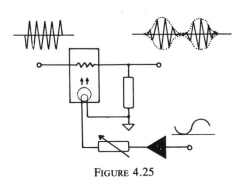

FIGURE 4.25

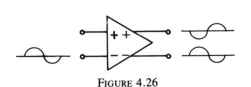

FIGURE 4.26

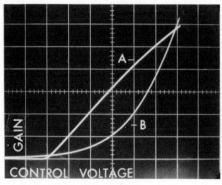

FIGURE 4.27

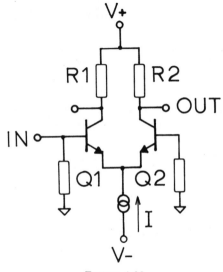

FIGURE 4.28

both in the linear mode (curve a) and in the exponential mode (curve b). Other control-voltage-versus-gain characteristics (namely, logarithmic) are possible but not common.

Voltage-controlled amplifiers may be built simply by combining an amplifier with any electronic attenuator, for example, a photoresistor attenuator. However, these configurations are not easily controllable in more than one mode, and do not provide the accurate and repeatable control that VCAs afford. A means of achieving electronic gain control, popular because of its many inherent advantages, is the differential transistor pair shown in figure 4.28. Descriptions of this circuit are so numerous (see the selected bibliography at the end of this chapter) that only a cursory explanation of the configuration is presented here.

If the bases of Q_1 and Q_2 are suitably biased and are at equal potential, the current provided by the constant current source (CCS) flows equally in R_1 and R_2. If an input signal causes the base of Q_1 to go positive with respect to the base of Q_2, the current flow through Q_1 and R_1 will increase. Because the CCS restricts the total current flow to a constant value I, current flow through Q_2 and R_2 will decrease by an amount exactly equal to the of the increased current flow through Q_1 and R_1. The decreased current flow causes the voltage drop across R_1 to decrease, causing a positive voltage swing at the output. In this manner, the output signal accurately follows the input signal. An identical but *inverted* signal appears at the collector of Q_1, providing a differential output. Differential inputs are obtained by using both transistor bases as inputs. The voltage gain of this circuit is approximately $I \cdot R^2 \cdot 100$. Thus, by varying the current supplied by the CCS, the voltage gain of the circuit may be controlled. A discussion of design considerations for voltage-controlled, temperature-compensated constant current sources is beyond the scope this chapter. The interested reader should pursue this subject in the literature, as well as examine the schematic diagrams of commercial electronic music equipment.

A VCA CIRCUIT

Many VCA configurations have been described in the literature (see the selected bibliography at the end of this chapter). Motorola produces a device, MFC 6040, called an electronic attenuator. However, the harmonic distortion produced by the device (3% at −35dB from full output) makes the MFC 6040 unusable for critical applications. Figure 4.29 shows a VCA of good quality offering differential inputs and a linear control-voltage-versus-gain characteristic.

VCA APPLICATIONS

Although we shall discuss applications of VCAs in subsequent chapters, several VCA panning configurations are shown below. Stereo panning of sounds may be controlled using VCAs as shown in figure 4.30. Since the

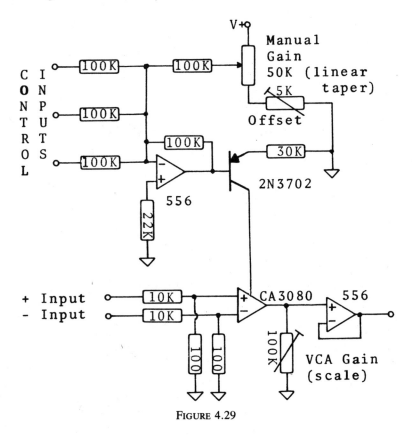

FIGURE 4.29

noninverting output of the control-signal amplifier is connected to the control input of one VCA, and the inverting output is connected to the control input of the other VCA, the gains of the VCAs will change inversely. In this example, the VCAs have a linear control-voltage-versus-gain characteristic, a control range of 0 to +10 volts, and a maximum gain of 1 volt. The manual control on most voltage-controlled devices provides a DC control voltage, variable over a certain range, that is used to set the instrument at a constant level. This control voltage must be taken into consideration when operating voltage-controlled instruments that, in most cases, respond to the sum of all control voltages applied. The manual control of VCA 1 is set to maximum, and the manual control of VCA 2 is set to minimum. With a control voltage of +5 volts applied to the control-voltage amplifier, both VCAs have a gain of ½. At either extreme of control-voltage range, one VCA has a gain of 0 (passing no signal), while the other VCA has a gain of 1 (passing all of the signal). By varying the control voltage, precise control of the panning effect is achieved. The problem of generating useful control voltages will be discussed in detail in chapter 7.

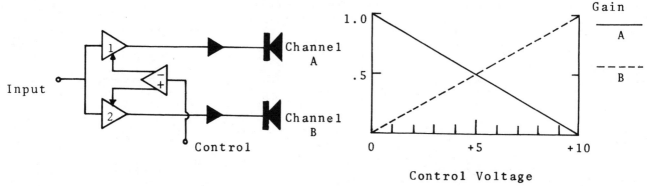

FIGURE 4.30

MULTICHANNEL PANNING USING VCAs

To illustrate the complexity of voltage-controlled systems required to produce effects that are relatively simple to achieve mechanically, we shall consider a simple case—rotating a sound among four loudspeakers. Sound rotation may be accomplished mechanically using the following methods: a quad panpot; a special mechanical device using 360°-turnpots; a photoresistor rotation mixer (described above); or a rotating loudspeaker with four microphones placed around it at 90° intervals in a circle (see Stockhausen *Kontakte, Realisationspartitur*, p. 3).

In the photoresistor mixer, the channels are faded in and out sequentially. To accomplish sound rotation with four VCAs requires control voltages like those shown in figure 4.31. The control voltages serve an

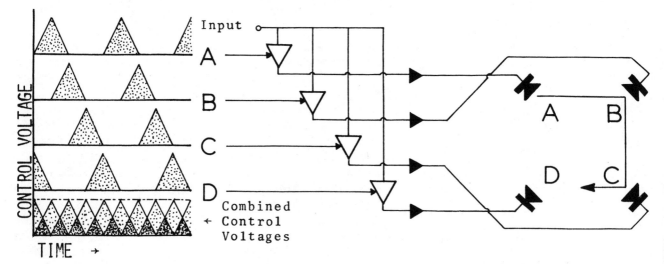

FIGURE 4.31

analagous function to that of the lamp in the photoresistor mixer. The area under each of the triangular regions corresponds to the amount of input signal passed by each VCA over time. Notice that the graphical summation of these regions shows that the signal is always present at a constant level as it pans from speaker to speaker.

Theoretically, the sound should appear to pan in a square, from A to B, B to C, and so on. Chowning has calculated the control functions necessary for a circular pan.[8] However, within certain limits, the waveform of the control signals is less important than their proper phase-relationships.

Several techniques are available for generating the necessary control signals. For example, each VCA may be provided with an envelope generator, and the four envelope generators triggered sequentially with a sequencer or a series of time-delay circuits. Not only does such a patching require fine adjustment to produce a smooth panning effect, but different rotation rates require a readjusting of the envelope generator controls. However, this patching is most useful for other mixing and panning applications.

An oscillator with *quadrature* outputs produces two identical waveforms, one leading the other by 90°. Each output may be inverted, and the resulting outputs then half-wave rectified to produce the control voltages shown in figure 4.32. It is desirable to have the direction and rate of sound rotation voltage-controllable. Since most oscillators will not oscillate down to 0 Hz, much less backwards, some rather special circuitry is required. One method employs a function generator with quadrature outputs capable of voltage control through 0 Hz.[9] An alternate technique

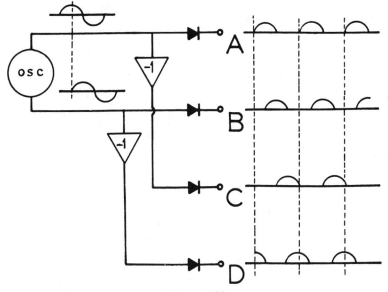

FIGURE 4.32

utilizes two oscillators, both running at a relatively high frequency, approximately 1 kHz, from which a quadrature beat frequency of a much lower value is derived. This technique has been employed in single-sideband generator design.[10] Quadrature sine waves may also be produced by connecting the bandpass output to the program input of a state-variable filter such as the Serge Extended Range VCF so that the filter oscillates. (Make sure that the Q adjustment is set sufficiently high.) The sine wave signals at lowpass and bandpass outputs of the filter will be 90° out of phase. Inverting thse two outputs will produce two additional quadrature sine waves. (See problem 11, example 2, chapter 1.)

A prototype voltage-controlled four-channel panning device has been constructed by E. S. Vogel and is currently in use at the Ohio State University Electronic Music Studios. This device has four input and four output channels, allowing the composer to pan (rotate) four signals in quadrature at rates of 20–0–20 Hz. The device also provides quadrature sine-wave outputs, the frequency of which corresponds to the panning rate. These outputs are used not only as control voltages for filters, phase shifters, and other instruments, but also to provide a visual display of the status of the panned signals by connecting one quadrature output to the vertical input and the other quadrature output to the horizontal input of an oscilloscope. By properly adjusting the vertical and horizontal gains of the oscilloscope, a circular trace (Lissajous figure) will result. The motion of the moving point of light on the oscilloscope face corresponds to the speed and direction of the panning sound.

A voltage-controlled quad panpot is shown in figure 4.33. This device is an electronic version of the quad panpot previously discussed, with the three passive panning devices replaced by three active ones (compare figure 4.34). Manual control is accomplished with a joy-stick controller from a hobby radio-control transmitter. Such a control consists of two variable resistors mounted in a gimbal at right angles, with the joy stick providing x/y control over the resistive elements. A useful feature of this arrangement is that the control voltages generated for the VCAs are made available for other purposes. Access to these voltages allows the composer to coordinate several functions with the pan. Joy-stick controllers used in video games are readily available from parts supply houses such as James Electronics in California for $5 to $8. While these controllers are workable and durable, they do not provide the resolution and ease of control of, for example, the Automated Processes model 480 conductive plastic quad panner.

A coordinated 4:1 mixer may be realized by rearranging the above configuration (see figure 4.34). The control circuitry is identical to that shown in figure 4.33.

Voltage-controlled amplifiers have recently been used in the design of automated mixdown consoles in which the input faders are used as voltage dividers to supply DC control voltages to VCAs, which actually perform the gain regulation in the system. The DC voltages from the faders may be

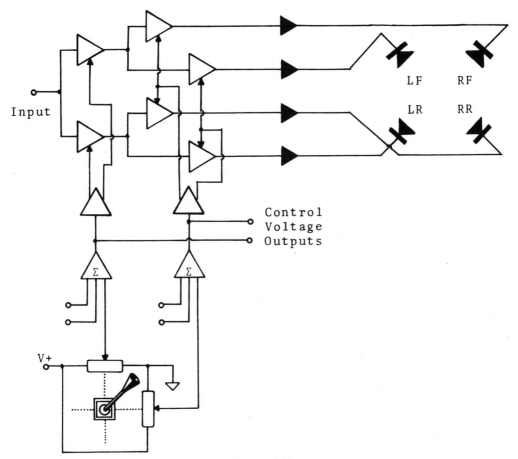

FIGURE 4.33

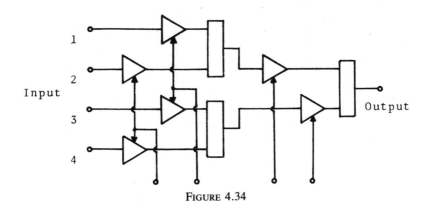

FIGURE 4.34

stored digitally, with the result that one operator may "ride gain" on a large number of channels that would be impossible to regulate effectively with two hands in real time.

REAL AND APPARENT SOUND SOURCES

So far in our discussion of panning we have assumed that loudness differentials are primarily responsible for cuing the angular location of a sound source. Certainly the apparent sound source does appear to move when a signal is panned between two reproducing channels. However, audition is an extremely complicated process, and the author does not wish to imply that a quad panpot and a four channel sound system permit the realization of all spatial effects.

We shall first consider some aspects of a familiar phenomenon—reverberant sound. Figure 4.35a shows a sound source S and a listener L in a room. The loudspeaker is fed a pure tone for a duration of T seconds. The listener hears the onset of the tone, and when the tone ceases, he perceives that the sound does not simply stop, but rather degenerates progressively, even though the speaker has ceased to radiate acoustic energy. This residual phenomenon is called *reverberant sound*. In figure 4.35a, at the onset of the tone, sound radiates from the speaker directly to the listener (arrow 1). Some of the sound bounces off the wall nearest the listener before reaching him (arrow 2). Since the distance traveled by the reflected sound is longer than the distance traveled by the incident sound, the reflected sound reaches the listener *after* the incident sound. Furthermore, the reflected sound reaching the listener has less energy, some of the energy having been absorbed by the wall, and some of the energy having been diffused as the sound travels through the air. Reflected sound continues to reach the listener, causing the energy at point L to grow. The reflected sounds arrive at different times, producing a cumulative effect, as shown in figure 4.35b. The buildup of sound energy measured at L (or any other point in the room) follows a stepwise curve that approximates an exponential function. By smoothing this function and plotting it on a logarithmic scale, we obtain a curve that closely approximates the listener's impression of the sound event (figure 4.35c).

To the listener, the incident sound is usually the strongest element in the sound event, and serves to orient him toward the sound source.[11] The ear is sensitive enough to the pattern of the reflected sound arriving from many directions to distinguish among reverberant rooms of various sizes, and the ear perceives the absence of reverberation as a "dry" quality of sound. If the initial reflections are strong enough and spaced far enough apart, the listener will hear distinct echoes. Often, the arrival times are so close together that a single sound event of "expanded" quality is perceived. At the cessation of the tone in figure 4.35a, the sound energy arriving at L decreases in a manner similar to that in which it built up. Thus, as men-

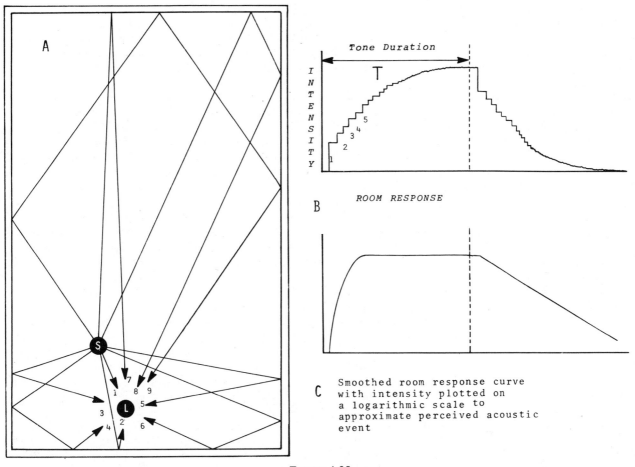

Tone Duration

INTENSITY

ROOM RESPONSE

B

C Smoothed room response curve
with intensity plotted on
a logarithmic scale to
approximate perceived acoustic
event

FIGURE 4.35

tioned above, the sound seems to die away gradually rather than stop
abruptly. The time interval between the cessation of the tone and the point
at which the sound energy has decayed by 60 dB is called the *reverberation
time* of the room. If the reverberation time is too long, speech and music
will be garbled; if the reverberation time is too short, listeners will com-
plain that sounds appear "dry" and "lifeless."

In figure 4.35a, notice that if the sound source is moved to a different
position relative to the listener, a different pattern of reverberant sound
results (although the shape of the reverberant envelope is unchanged). A
sound panned among the four channels of a quad sound system does not
behave like a sound source moving through the same space. Since the
reproducers are fixed in position, their reverberation pattern is fixed,
whereas the reverberation pattern of a moving sound source would be
constantly changing.

Chowning reports creating convincing moving sound images with a four-channel sound system, and has isolated several variables that are of interest here. Since the reverberant sound becomes more directional as the distance between the listener and the sound source increases, Chowning lists two types of reverberation:

1. *global reverberation,* that is, that part of the overall reverberant signal that emanates equally from all channels, is proportional to *1*/distance · *1*/√distance; and

2. *local reverberation,* that is, that part that is distributed between a speaker pair as is the direct signal, is proportional to (*1* − *1*/distance) (*1*/√distance); thus, by increasing the distance of the apparent sound source the reverberation becomes increasingly localized, compensating for the loss of direct energy.[12]

Furthermore, a sound source in motion causes a frequency shift in the perceived sound, the well-known *Doppler effect.* Chowning calculates the required frequency shift "by computing the distance D from the subject to the apparent source and [the] change in frequency proportional to dD/dT."[13]

The reader should have an appreciation for the complexity of sound events produced by natural sound sources. Chowning uses a digital computer to calculate every parameter of his sound events, storing each specification on a disc file. Because of the complexity of the necessary calculations, the sound cannot be produced in real time, but must be played back after the computations are completed. To reproduce Chowning's effects using analog equipment would be a formidable task.

Before the advent of digital and analog time-delay devices, a true Doppler shift was a difficult effect to synthesize. At this writing there are many commercially available voltage-controlled analog and digital time-delay devices with which the composer can easily produce voltage-controlled changes in pitch to imitate Doppler shifts. In addition, component parts for such devices are readily available, and time-delay devices may be built by studio technicians at considerable savings.[14] The amount of pitch change required to simulate the Doppler shift depends on the rate of change of panning and the nature of the program material. It should, nevertheless, be subtle: it was noted in chapter 2 that the relationship between pitch change and the velocity of the sound source relative to the listener is 2.25 cents per mile per hour (1.534 cents per foot per second). Voltage-controlled time-delay devices may be employed by themselves to create the illusion of spatial movement of sounds in a multichannel playback system, as well as to enhance panning effects.[15] Unfortunately, auditory localization effects produced by time-delay effects alone are highly dependent on room acoustics and speaker placement (see chapter 2, pages 39–42).

Time-delay devices are often used in conjunction with spring- and plate-reverberation devices to produce a "more natural" reverberation effect: the program in this case is delayed by, say, 20–30 milliseconds and then routed to the reverberation device. The additional delay simulates initial reflection of the sound in a reverberant environment, while the reverberation device simulates the "fused" multipath reflections (see chapter 2, pages 42–44). Time-delay devices may also be used to produce excellent artificial reverberation,[16] but the best units are at this writing expensive: the EMT digital reverberation unit sells for over $15,000. Time-delay devices also find important applications in filtering (see chapter 6, page 163).

SYNTHETIC REVERBERATION

Many techniques have been employed to add reverberation to a signal. One infrequently used reverberation device employs an ultrasonic carrier that is amplitude-modulated with the program material, propagated through water using a sonar-type transducer, picked up by another transducer, and demodulated. In a more practical method, the program is sent through a loudspeaker placed in a special room and is picked up by one or more microphones located at some distance from the loudspeaker. The advantage of this system is that "real" reverberation may be added to the program. Many professional recording studios have reverberant rooms built especially for reverberating program material (many studios still use elevator shafts, stone staircases, empty basements, and wells for reverberation chambers).[17] Flats of absorbing material may be brought into the chamber if it is desirable to reduce the reverberation time.

Plate-type reverberation units are capable of natural sounding and high audio quality reverberation. These units consist of a metal plate held under tension (usually by springs). Transducers mounted at both ends of the plate produce and receive transverse vibrations propagated through the plate. Plate-type reverberators allow for the adjustment of reverberation time by the varying of the pressure of a damping plate against the reverberation plate. Some designs permit remote control of this damping adjustment.

Spring-type reverberators consist of a spring with transducers attached at both ends. Like the plate-type reverberator, the spring reverberator permits adjustment of the reverberation time by damping. It should be noted that all the reverberators discussed here "color" the program in varying degrees. Of these devices, the spring unit is most obtrusive in this regard (although many spring-type units, namely Fairchild Reverbertron and Quad-Eight reverberation units, are useful devices that cost less than half the price of most plate reverberators). Spring-type reverberators are also quite sensitive to mechanical vibration; in many designs, changing the reverberation-time control will cause unwanted spring noise (although some composers have deliberately employed this sound in their works).

Olson has built a reverberator consisting of a tube with a transducer at one end and several pickup microphones placed in taps along the pipe, spaced at approximately 25-foot intervals. The signals from the microphones are mixed in the proper amplitude relationships and then fed back to the transducer, producing a degenerative echo. Although the process is similar to that of tape echo, in Olson's reverberator the echoes are so closely spaced that the ear hears only a decaying sound, similar to that of room reverberation.[18] The Cooper Time Cube (UREI) is a commercially available acoustical delay device with an extremely good signal-to-noise ratio. The device, however, produces only two fixed delay times.

We have mentioned how synthetic reverberators, besides introducing reverberation, tend to "color" program material according to the frequency-response characteristics of the reverb unit. Schroeder has found that most reverberators produce an insufficient *echo density*. He states that more than 1,000 echoes per second commonly occur at the beginning of a natural reverberant event, while simple delay-type reverberators may produce only approximately 30 echoes per second. For convincing reverberation, echo densities of approximately 1,000 per second seem to be necessary. Schroeder has discussed practical solutions to these problems in detail in his article.[19]

ECHO

Like reverberation, echo effects are produced by delaying a signal and, in some cases, combining the delayed and original signals. Although perceptually distinct, reverberation and echo differ mainly in the time rate at which the delayed signals occur. One method for producing echo effects involves placing several playback heads along the tape path of a magnetic recorder and mixing the outputs of the playback heads (figure 4.36). The delay time may be varied by altering the speed of the tape, as well as changing the position of the playback heads in relation to that of the record head.

Regenerative echo may be accomplished by feeding a portion of the delayed signal back into the record head (figure 4.37). The effect produced by this configuration may be varied from a hint of echo to an unstable regenerative condition by controlling the amplitude of the fed-back delayed signal. In the unstable regenerative condition, the sound builds in intensity until the tape is saturated, causing the sound to be "dissolved" into distortion. Of course, analog or digital delay lines may be substituted for tape delay in the above applications. (see chapter 8 for a discussion of tape-delay techniques.)

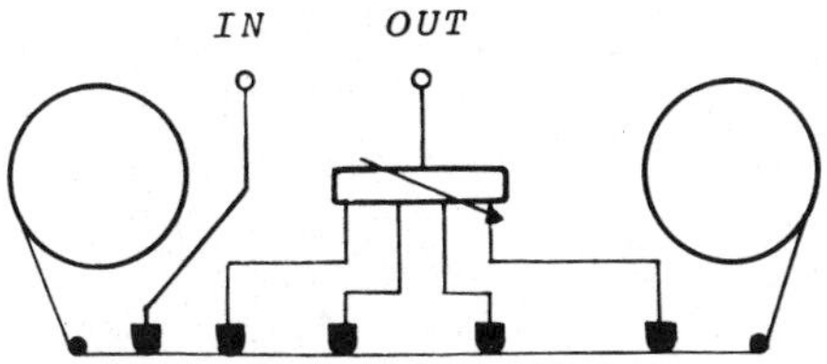

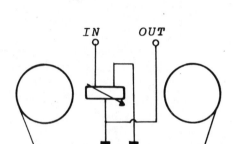

FIGURE 4.36

FIGURE 4.37

A four-channel, oscilloscope monitoring display circuit is shown in figure 4.38. This device finds many uses in everyday studio production, and the author highly recommends the circuit. It should be noted that $V+$ and $V-$ and $H+$ and $H-$ are differential outputs, and may be converted to two unbalanced outputs for a conventional x/y oscilloscope using differential amplifiers or transformers.

The electronic music studio should provide a proper monitoring envi-

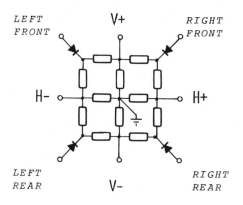

LEFT FRONT V+ RIGHT FRONT

H− H+

LEFT REAR V− RIGHT REAR

(all R's equal, 1%)

FIGURE 4.38

ronment, consistent with current acoustical engineering practice. Producing an electronic piece in a poor acoustical environment can obviously cause problems when the piece is performed in another monitoring environment with different acoustical characteristics, for example, in a concert hall, or in another electronic music studio for a competition, job interview, and so on. Electronic music studios are often assigned the least desirable spaces, which often have grave acoustical problems. Often the installation of draperies and carpeting will make workable an otherwise impossibly reverberant room. However, room equalization is an area fraught with pitfalls for the neophyte armed with his pink-noise generator and 1/3-octave filter set. The advice of a professional acoustical consultant is highly recommended if the studio's budget permits.

PROBLEMS

1. Mix approximately 8 sine-wave oscillators in a mixer. Adjust the frequencies of the oscillators to 100, 200, 300, 400, 500, 600, 700, 800 Hz, and adjust the amplitudes of the oscillators (using the mixer input attenuators) to A, 1/2A, 1/3A, 1/4A, 1/5A, 1/6A, 1/7A, 1/8A, respectively. Monitor the result both aurally and on an oscilloscope. Compare the result with a low-pass filtered (f_c = approximately 1 kHz) 100 Hz sawtooth wave and explain any differences between the two waveforms. If the eight oscillators described above have sync inputs, sync oscillators 2–8 to the fundamental and compare both the waveform and sound which result from this configuration.

2. Explain how the presence of offset voltage at the output of a direct-coupled device can produce undesired results when this instrument is used in conjunction with other devices.

3. Explain why it is desirable or not desirable to connect the output of a high impedance (approximately 100 K-ohm) device to the input of a device with an input impedance of 50 ohms.

4. Example 1 shows the summation of a pulse wave and a triangle wave. What two waveforms (of those we have discussed so far) were added to produce the waveform shown in example 2?

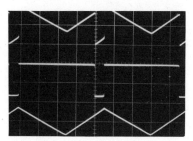 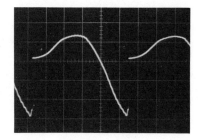

5. Explain how a balanced line may be converted to an unbalanced line.

6. What advantages and disadvantages do balanced lines provide as compared to other transmission line configurations?

7. Why should ordinary multiple jacks not be used for mixing? How can multiple jacks be adapted for mixing applications?

8. Describe a change of voltage from 3.97 volts to 0.073 volts in decibels.

9. Describe a change of power from 1.0 to 75.0 watts in decibels.

10. Describe some circuit features that characterize direct-coupled amplifiers. What advantages do such amplifiers provide for electronic music applications?

11. Describe three ways to achieve a rotating-sound effect using a four-channel playback system.

12. Using a VCA with a 1 db/volt gain versus control voltage characteristic, how much control voltage will be required to amplify a 0.5-volt signal to 1.2 volts?

13. What is the difference between the *linear* and *exponential* control modes in a VCA?

14. Describe some problems inherent in mixing an output from a low-impedance microphone with that of an oscillator (approximately 0.5-volt p-p output) in a mixer with high-impedance inputs.

15. Describe in general the proper operation of electronic music equipment in order to effect the maximum dynamic range and lowest signal-to-noise ratio.

16. What is the purpose of the pre/post switch in the auxiliary send circuit of a studio mixer?

17. When is impedance-matching necessary?

18. Describe the typical input/output structures used in electronic music synthesizers.

19. Describe a method for determining the output impedance of a device.

20. Patch a sine wave (1,000 Hz) through a mixer. Adjust the input fader so that clipping occurs (amplitude of sine-wave generator may have to be set high). Note the effect of clipping at several different sine-wave frequencies as well as with other waveforms of different frequencies. Decrease the sine-wave oscillator amplitude so that maximum input fader travel is required to achieve a 0 VU level on the mixer. How is the operation of the mixer affected? Explain the basic principles of obtaining the best dynamic range and signal-to-noise ratio from audio equipment.

21. Connect a program source (recorded music) to a VCA or mixer with complementary (push-pull) outputs. Mix the complementary outputs monaurally in various proportions and note the resulting effect. How could this effect occur accidentally in a studio?

NOTES

1. H. LeCaine, "The Sonde: A New Approach to Multiple Sinewave Generation," *Journal of the Audio Engineering Society* 18 (1970): 536–539.

2. J. Eargle, *Sound Recording* (New York: Van Nostrand Reinhold, 1976).

3. *Audio,* October 1972, p. 48.

4. Eargle, *Sound Recording.*

5. K. Blaukopf, "Space in Electronic Music," in *Music and Technology (La Revue Musicale)*, UNESCO Publications.

6. G. Bluthgen, "Unipot: A Panoramic Potentiometer for Quadrasonic Use," *Journal of the Audio Engineering Society* 20 (1972): 580–581.

7. F. Rzewski, "A Photoresistor Mixer for Live Performance," *Electronic Music Review,* no. 4 (October 1967), pp. 33–34.

8. J. M. Chowning, "The Simulation of Moving Sound Sources," *Journal of the Audio Engineering Society* 19 (1971): 2–6.

9. W. K. Connor, "Experimental Investigation of Sound–System-Room Feedback," *Journal of the Audio Engineering Society* 21 (1973): 27–32.

10. H. Bode and R. A. Moog, "A High-Accuracy Frequency Shifter for Professional Audio Applications," *Journal of the Audio Engineering Society* 20 (1972): 453–458.

11. R. Vermeulen cites an experiment demonstrating the power of the initial perceived sound to locate the perceived source location. Using a stereo playback system, the investigators fed a tone burst of up to approximately 4 seconds to the right speaker. The initial and final transients (approximately 40 milliseconds duration) are removed from the tone and fed to the *left* speaker. The listener is convinced that the entire tone burst then emanates from the left speaker (R. Vermeulen, "Stereo-Reverberation," *Journal of the Audio Engineering Society* 6 [1958]).

12. Chowning, "The Simulation of Moving Sound Sources."

13. Ibid.

14. See B. Hutchins, "Delay Module/Submodule, Option I," *Electronotes,* no. 72 (December 1976), pp. 17–20, for circuits involving the Matsushida MN3001 charge-coupled device.

15. D. Luce, "Dynamic Spectrum of Orchestral Instruments," *Journal of the Audio Engineering Society* 23 (1975): 565–568.

16. D. Norgaard, "The Phase-Shift Method of Single-Sideband Generation," *Proceedings of the IRE,* December 1956, pp. 1718–1735.

17. J. P. Davis, "Practical Stereo Reverberation for Stereo Recording," *Journal of the Audio Engineering Society* 10 (1962): 114–118.

18. H. F. Olson and J. C. Bleazey, "Synthetic Reverberation," *Journal of the Audio Engineering Society* 8 (1960): 37–41.

19. M. R. Schroeder, "An Artificial Stereophonic Effect Obtained from a Single Audio Signal," *Journal of the Audio Engineering Society* 6 (1958): 74–79.

20. B. Blesser and F. Lee, "An Audio Delay System Using Digital Technology," *Journal of the Audio Engineering Society* 19 (1971): 393–397.

SELECTED BIBLIOGRAPHY
Books

Audio Handbook (1976). Santa Clara, Calif.: National Semiconductor Corporation.

Eargle, J. *Sound Recording.* New York: Van Nostrand-Reinhold, 1976.

Everest, F. *Acoustic Techniques for Home and Studio.* Blue Ridge Summit, Pa.: Tab Books, 1973.

Hutchins, B. *Musical Engineer's Handbook.* Ithaca, N.Y.: Cornell University Press, 1975.

Lueg, R., and Erwin, A. *Basic Electronics for Engineers and Scientists.* San Francisco: Intext Publishers, 1972.

Nisbett, A. *The Technique of the Sound Studio.* New York: Hastings House, 1966.

Olson, H. *Modern Sound Reproduction*. New York: Van Nostrand Reinhold, 1972.

Slot, G. *Audio Quality*. New York: Drake, 1972.

Winckel, F. *Music, Sound, and Sensation*. New York: Dover, 1967.

Woram, J. *The Recording Studio Handbook*. New York: Sagamore, 1976.

Articles

Ajemian, R. "The New Breed of VU Meters." *dB*, October 1976, pp. 44–45.

Bauer, B., et al. "Recording Techniques for SQ Matrix Quadraphonic Discs." *Journal of the Audio Engineering Society* 21, no. 1 (January/February 1973): 19–26.

Balik, E. A. "Constructing a Peak-reading VU Meter." *Audio*, October 1972, p. 48.

Beauchamp, J. W. "Additive Synthesis of Harmonic Musical Tones." *Journal of the Audio Engineering Society* 14, no. 4 (October 1966): 332–342.

Blaukopf, K. "Space in Electronic Music." In *Music and Technology (La Révue Musicale)*, UNESCO Publications.

Bleazey, J. C. "Electronic Sound Absorber." *Journal of the Audio Engineering Society* 10, no. 2 (April 1962): 135–139.

Blesser, B., and Lee, F. "An Audio Delay System Using Digital Technology." *Journal of the Audio Engineering Society* 19, no. 5 (May 1971): 393–397.

Bluthgen, B. "Unipot: A Panoramic Potentiometer for Quadrasonic Use." *Journal of the Audio Engineering Society* 20, no. 7 (September 1972): 580–581.

Bode, H. "A Solid State Audio Spectrum Shifter." *Audio Engineering Society Preprint* 395.

Bode, H., and Moog, R. A. "A High-Accuracy Frequency Shifter for Professional Audio Applications." *Journal of the Audio Engineering Society* 20, no. 6 (July/August 1972): 453–458.

Chowning, J. M. "The Simulation of Moving Sound Sources." *Journal of the Audio Engineering Society* 19, no. 1 (January 1971): 2–6.

Connor, W. K. "Experimental Investigation of Sound–System-Room Feedback." *Journal of the Audio Engineering Society* 21, no. 1 (January/February 1973): 27–32.

David, E. "Applied Principles: Operational Amplifiers." *Electronic Engineering*, January 1971, pp. 48–51.

————. "Applied Principles: Operational Amplifiers." *Electronic Engineering*, March 1971, pp. 70–72.

Davis, D. "Impedance Matching for the Sound Engineer." *dB*, April 1974.

Davis, J. P. "Practical Stereo Reverberation for Stereo Recording." *Journal of the Audio Engineering Society* 10, no. 2 (April 1962): 114–118.

Eargle, J. "Equalizing the Monitoring Environment." *Journal of the Audio Engineering Society* 21, no. 2 (1973).

Fletcher, H., and Munson, W. A. "Loudness: Its Definition, Measurement, and Calculation." *Journal of the Acoustical Society of America* 5 (1933): 82–108.

Gardner, M. "Some Single- and Multiple-Source Localization Effects." *Journal of the Audio Engineering Society* 21, no. 6 (July/August 1973): 430–437.

Gerzon, M. A. "Periphony: With-Height Sound Reproduction." *Journal of the Audio Engineering Society* 21, no. 1 (January/February 1973): 2–10.

Jones, F. B. "Voltage Controlled Two-Phase Sawtooth Oscillator." *Wireless World* [Circuit Ideas], June 1973.

Jones, M. H. "A Frequency Shifter for 'Howl' Suppression." *Wireless World,* July 1971, pp. 317–322.

Kaegi, W. "A New Approach to the Theory of Sound Classification." *Interface* 1, no. 2 (November 1972): 93–109.

Kleis, D. "Modern Acoustical Engineering, Pt. I." *Phillips Technical Review* 20, no. 11 (1958–1959): 309–326.

————. "Modern Acoustical Engineering, Pt. II." *Phillips Technical Review* 21, no. 2 (1959–1960): 52–72.

Klipsch, P. W. "Stereophonic Sound with Two Tracks, Three Channels, by Means of a Phantom Circuit (2PH3)." *Journal of the Audio Engineering Society* 6, no. 2 (April 1958): 118–123.

Kuilenburg, W. "A New Studio Mixer: A New Mixing Desk for Studio II at the Institute of Sonology." *Interface* 1 (1972): 175–185.

Lancaster, D. E. "The Differential Amplifier." *Electronics World,* February 1968, pp. 53–57.

LeCaine, H. "The Sonde: A New Approach to Multiple Sine-wave Generation." *Journal of the Audio Engineering Society* 18, no. 5 (October 1970): 536–539.

Melis, J., and Nijholt, B. "Voltage-Controlled Gain in the Audio Channel." *Journal of the Audio Engineering Society* 20, no. 8 (October 1972): 629–633.

————. "Voltage-Controlled Gain in the Audio Channel: Appendix" [Letters to the Editor]. *Journal of the Audio Engineering Society* 20, no. 9 (November 1972): 759–761.

Naylor, J. "Digital and Analog Signal Applications of Operational Amplifiers." *IEEE Spectrum,* June 1971, pp. 38–46.

Norgaard, D. "The Phase-Shift Method of Single-Sideband Generation." *Proceedings of the IRE,* December 1956, pp. 1718–1735.

Olson, H. F. "Electronic Music Synthesis for Recordings." *IEEE Spectrum,* April 1971, pp. 18–30.

Olson, H. F., and Bleazey, J. C. "Synthetic Reverberation." *Journal of the Audio Engineering Society* 8, no. 1 (January 1960): 37–41.

Patten, D. L. "A Quadraphonic Oscilloscope Display Technique." *Journal of the Audio Engineering Society* 20, no. 6 (July/August 1972): 483–489.

Prestigiacomo, A. J., and McLean, D. J. "A Frequency Shifter for Improving Acoustic Feedback Stability." *Journal of the Audio Engineering Society* 10, no. 2 (April 1962): 110–113.

Schick, L. "Linear Circuit Applications of Operational Amplifiers." *IEEE Spectrum,* April 1971, pp. 36–50.

Schroeder, M. R. "An Artificial Stereophonic Effect Obtained from a Single Audio Signal." *Journal of the Audio Engineering Society* 6, no. 2 (April 1958): 74–79.

————. ''Improved Quasi-Stereophony and 'Colorless' Artificial Reverberation.'' *Journal of the Acoustical Society of America* 33, no. 8 (August 1961): 1061–1064.

————. ''Natural Sounding Artificial Reverberation.'' *Journal of the Audio Engineering Society* 10, no. 3 (July 1962): 219–223.

Seawright, J. ''Fundamental Concepts of Electronic Music Mixers.'' *Electronic Music Review,* October 1967, pp. 14–19.

Sedra, A., and Smith, K. C. ''Simple Digitally Controlled Variable Gain Linear DC Amplifier. *Electronic Engineering,* March 1969, pp. 362–365.

Shapiro, G. ''Functional Design of Electronic Music Mixers.'' *Electronic Music Review,* October 1967, pp. 20–24.

Vermeulen, R. ''Stereo-Reverberation.'' *Journal of the Audio Engineering Society* 6, no. 2 (April 1958).

5

MODULATION

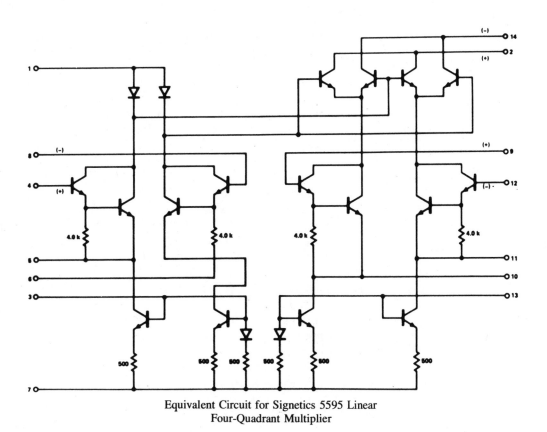

Equivalent Circuit for Signetics 5595 Linear
Four-Quadrant Multiplier

Modulation is used extensively as a means of generating complex sounds in electronic music. In general, modulation is the process by which some characteristic (amplitude, frequency, phase) of a signal is varied according to changes in some characteristic of another, or *modulating,* signal. It is possible and common to use combinations of various modulation methods in electronic music. The signal, which varies in accordance with the modulating signal, is called the modulated signal, or *carrier*.

Tremolo and vibrato are examples of traditional musical uses of amplitude and frequency modulation (at slow rates of change, approximately 5 to 8 times per second, and within limited ranges of effect. In the case of frequency modulation, the range of effect corresponds to the interval between the high and low limits of the vibrato). Although modulation is often used in electronic sound synthesis for similar effects (especially in popular music and electronic organ applications), its use as a means for producing complex sounds involves rates of change and ranges of effect far beyond human capabilities. For example, if a cellist could vibrate the A string (sliding his finger continuously back and forth) between the nut and bridge at 100 times per second (without serious damage to himself or his instrument), he would produce neither a tone with vibrato nor a glissando, but a continuous tone with a timbre quite different from that of the normal timbre of the A string on the cello. Similar analogies could be drawn for amplitude modulation, and the like. It is the production of complex tones by electronic means of changing frequency, amplitude, pulse width, and other variables which we will discuss in this chapter.

In communications, modulation is a means by which a message is converted into information-bearing signals for transmission over some medium. At the receiving end, the incoming information-bearing signal is demodulated to recover the information. In communications applications, the carrier, or modulated signal, is usually in the radio frequency range: approximately 10 kHz to 30 GHz. In electronic music work, both the modulated signal and modulating signals are commonly in the audio and sub-audio frequency range. Three types of modulation are usually employed in electronic music: *amplitude modulation, frequency modulation,* and *pulse-width modulation.*

AMPLITUDE MODULATION

Amplitude modulation is the process by which the amplitude of a signal is varied in accordance with changes in amplitude of another, or modulating, signal. This is a general definition that includes a large number of possible amplitude modulation systems using sinusoidal carriers, pulse carriers, or any type of carrier that has an amplitude factor capable of being varied. In addition, the variation of amplitude of the carrier may be related to the modulating signal in any unique manner.

Consider a case in which a carrier of maximum amplitude E_c and a radian frequency of ω_c is modulated by a sinusoidal signal of frequency ω_a. The maximum variation in amplitude of the carrier from its unmodulated value is ME_c, where M is the *modulation index:*

$$M = \frac{\text{rise (or fall) above the unmodulated carrier level}}{\text{carrier amplitude}}.$$

Thus, in figure 5.1, $M = E_a/E_c$. Often the term *percent modulation* is employed (% modulation = $100M$). When $M = 1$, the amplitude of the carrier varies between $2E_c$ and 0 (100% modulation). If $M = 1/2$, the amplitude of the carrier varies between $1.5E_c$ and $0.5E_c$ (50% modulation). If $M > 1$, the envelope† of the modulated signal is no longer sinusoidal in form, and the carrier is said to be *overmodulated*.

The amplitude of the modulated signal can be expressed by the following equation:

$$E = E_c (1 + M \cos \omega_a t) \cos \omega_c t.$$

Expanding the equation, we obtain

$$E = E_c \cos \omega_c t + ME_c \cos \omega_c t \cdot \cos \omega_a t.$$

Employing the trigonometric identity
$$\cos a \cos b = 1/2 \left[\cos (a + b) + \cos (a - b)\right],$$

we obtain

$$E = E_c \cos \omega_c t + ME_c/2 \cdot \cos (\omega_c + \omega_a)t + ME_c/2 \cdot \cos (\omega_c - \omega_a)t,$$

where E is the amplitude of the modulated wave, M is the modulation index, E_c is the amplitude of the unmodulated carrier, ω_c is the radian frequency of the carrier, and ω_a is the radian frequency of the modulating signal.

As can be seen from the above equations, three frequency components are present at the output of an amplitude modulator to which both a sinusoidal carrier and modulating signal are applied, the frequencies of these components being the *sum* of the carrier frequency and the modulating signal frequency; the *difference* of the carrier frequency and the modulating frequency; and the *carrier frequency itself*.

These sum and difference frequencies are called *sidebands*. (In the example above, the *upper sideband* is the sum of the carrier frequency and

†in figure 5.1, the two curves, one drawn through the positive, one drawn through the negative peaks of the modulated signal.

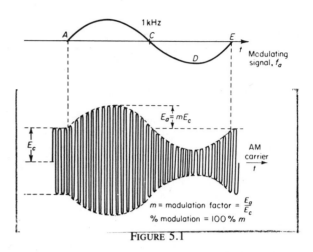

FIGURE 5.1

the modulating frequency; the *lower sideband* is the difference of the carrier frequency and the modulating frequency.) If the carrier is sinusoidal and the modulating signal is a complex wave, a pair of sidebands is produced for every component in the modulating signal. In this case, the upper side frequencies (sums of the carrier frequency and the frequencies of each of the components in the modulating signal) are known collectively as the upper sideband, while the lower sideband consists of the differences of the carrier frequency and every sinusoidal component in the modulating signal. (Certainly, complex-waveform carriers may be used—see patching 9 at the end of this chapter.)

Amplitude modulation is used for electronic modification of both electronically generated and natural sounds. In some cases, amplitude modulation effects are produced non-electronically, namely, the often-used contemporary instrumental technique of singing while playing a brass or wind instrument, or whistling while singing. We shall discuss two other types of amplitude modulation: *double-sideband suppressed carrier modulation* and *single-sideband suppressed carrier modulation*, which are useful, for example, in modifying natural sounds, where the presence of a continuous (carrier) signal from an ordinary AM system would be undesirable.

In mixing,† signals (time functions) are *added* together; in amplitude modulation, time functions are *multiplied* together. Figure 5.2a shows the result of the addition of two sine waves of different frequency; figure 5.2b shows the result of multiplication of the two signals in an amplitude modulator (the higher-frequency signal here is the modulated signal). With ordinary AM, the envelope of the modulated wave has the same shape as the waveform of the modulating signal (compare figure 5.3: sawtooth-wave amplitude modulation of a sinusoidal carrier; figure 5.4: triangle-

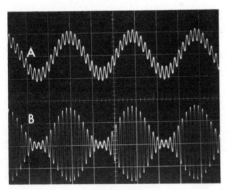

FIGURE 5.2

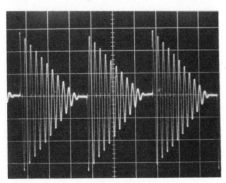

FIGURE 5.3

---

†*Mixing* is used throughout this book to mean addition of time functions. The reader should be aware that mixing may also be used to describe the case in which time functions are multiplied together.

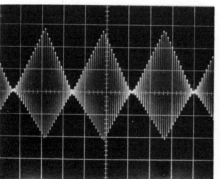

FIGURE 5.4

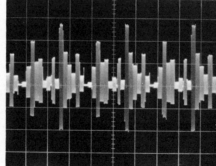

FIGURE 5.5

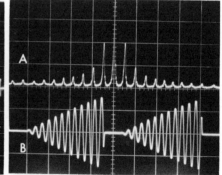

FIGURE 5.6

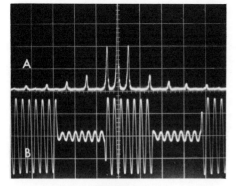

FIGURE 5.7

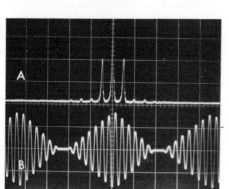

FIGURE 5.8

SUPPRESSED-CARRIER MODULATORS

wave amplitude modulation of a sinusoidal carrier; and figure 5.5: step function (sequencer) amplitude modulation of a sinusoidal carrier).

Figure 5.6b shows the time function of sawtooth-wave amplitude modulation of a sinusoidal carrier. The spectrum in figure 5.6a shows the distribution of the frequency components produced by such modulation. In figure 5.6a, the carrier is positioned in the center of the photograph, and the upper and lower sidebands are clearly visible. The first sideband pair is produced by the sum and difference of the carrier frequency and the fundamental frequency of the sawtooth wave; the second sideband pair is produced by the sum and difference of the carrier frequency and the second harmonic of the sawtooth wave, and so on. Notice that the upper-sideband group is the mirror image of the lower-sideband group.

Figures 5.7 and 5.8 show time functions and spectra for square-wave amplitude modulation and triangle wave modulation of a sinusoidal carrier. The modulation index of the waveforms in figures 5.6 and 5.8 is 1 (the percentage modulation = 100%). Compare these modulation spectra with the spectra of the sawtooth wave (figure 1.10, chapter 1), square wave (figure 1.14, chapter 1); and triangle wave (figure 1.17, chapter 1). Figures 5.9a through 5.9e show the time functions and spectra for a number of AM (sine-wave modulated sinusoidal carrier) signals with various modulation percentages.

Amplitude modulation is accomplished using various devices, for example, voltage-controlled amplifiers, integrated circuit modulators such as the Motorola MC1595 or Signetics 5595 and Motorola MC1596G or Signetics 5596, and passive diode modulators.

Suppressed-carrier modulators are of two general types: *double-balanced modulators,* which are balanced with respect to the carrier and the modulating signal; and *single-balanced modulators,* which are balanced only with respect to the carrier. One single-balanced modulator configuration, the

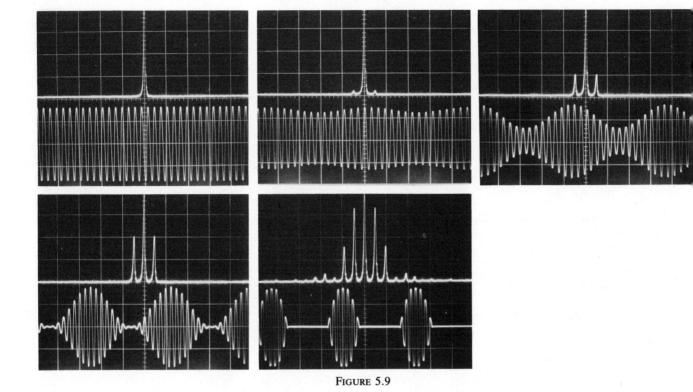

FIGURE 5.9

shunt quad modulator, is shown in figure 5.10. The output waveform of this modulator (sine-wave carrier and modulating signal) is shown in figure 5.11. (For optimum diode-switching characteristics, a square-wave carrier should be used.) The symbolic equivalent circuit for the shunt quad modulator is shown in figure 5.12. The frequency components present in the output of this modulator consist primarily of the sums and differences of the carrier frequency and modulating frequency, as well as the modulating signal itself. This type of modulator is most useful in applications in which the carrier is much higher in frequency than the modulating signal. Because the modulating signal appears in the output of the device, single-balanced modulators are not so useful in sound modifying applications.

The *ring-* or *lattice-type modulator* is shown in figure 5.13. An explanation of the operation of this circuit follows: When point A is positive, the carrier current into the center tap of T_1 divides. Half goes through the upper winding, through D_1, up through the lower half of T_3, through the center tap, and back to point B. The path of the other current is through the opposite half winding of T_1, through D_2, through the opposite half of T_3 to B. The current flow through both halves of the primary winding of T_3 is equal and opposite. Thus the output voltage at the carrier frequency is zero. During the next half-cycle when the carrier reverses polarity and point B is positive, diodes D_3 and D_4 conduct. Application of the modulating signal

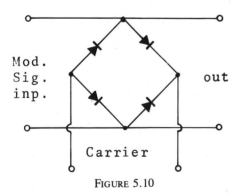

FIGURE 5.10

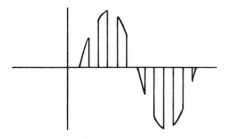

FIGURE 5.11

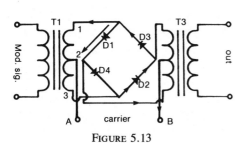

carrier-controlled switch

FIGURE 5.12

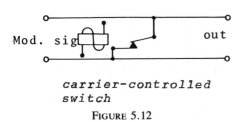

FIGURE 5.13

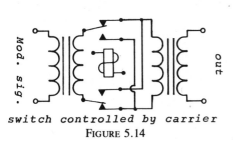

switch controlled by carrier

FIGURE 5.14

upsets the balance of the circuit. For example, if point 1 of T_1 is positive, and the carrier component at T_1 is also positive, more current flows through D_1 than D_2, thereby unbalancing the circuit. During the second half-cycle, when the carrier polarity reverses and the audio signal at point 1 is still positive, more current flows through D_2 than D_1. The symbolic equivalent circuit for the ring modulator is shown in figure 5.14. Figure 5.15c shows the waveform produced by this circuit's switching between sine waves of opposite polarity (figure 5.15 a and b), while figure 5.15d shows the switching signal.

The frequency components present in the output of the ring modulator consist primarily of the sums and differences of the carrier and modulating signal frequencies. However, because of the characteristics of the diodes, other frequency components are present (usually not to an objectionable degree) in the output.[1] The diode ring† modulator has been used in electronic music since the early 1950s. It is easily constructed and requires no power supply, although since it is a passive device it creates a loss (which can be easily overcome) when inserted in a circuit. Figure 5.16 shows a diode ring modulator with two carrier balance potentiometers added. Figure 5.17 shows the circuit configuration of figure 5.16 with the RCA CA3019 integrated-circuit diode array used for the diode ring. The use of the 3019 is recommended over discrete diodes, since no matching of forward resistances is required. Figure 5.18 shows the output waveform of this modulator, while figure 5.19 shows the output waveform of the modulator with the carrier balance potentiometers improperly adjusted.[2] Care should be taken in the construction of the modulator. Only high-quality transformers with a good frequency response should be used and the forward resistances of the diodes should be matched, since this affects the degree of carrier suppression. Hot carrier diodes are recommended for ring modulator design.

The MC1595 four-quadrant multiplier integrated circuit is recommended for electronic music applications. The MC1595 will accept both sinusoidal carrier and modulating signal inputs, while the MC1596G (5596) circuit is designed for sinusoidal modulating signal inputs but *square-wave* carrier inputs (although other waveforms may be used, provided sufficient drive is provided). Figure 5.20 shows a circuit of an active balanced modulator using the MC1595 integrated circuit. Voltage-controlled amplifiers with differential inputs and outputs may be connected to form a linear four-quadrant multiplier as shown in figure 5.21. The gain of each voltage-controlled amplifier should be equal (approximately 1/2). Carrier balance is adjusted by varying the input attenuators on the mixer. A squelch circuit may be used in conjunction with a balanced modulator to disable the carrier input when no modulating signal is present. The threshold of the squelch circuit can be varied to compensate for different modulating signal amplitudes.

†In this circuit, the four diodes form a ring in which they all "point" in the same direction.

a.

b.

c.

d.

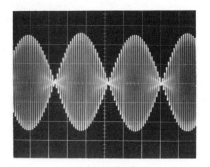

FIGURE 5.15

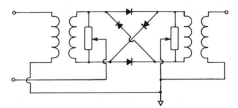

FIGURE 5.16

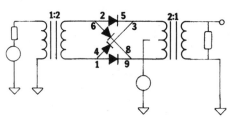

FIGURE 5.17

FIGURE 5.18

In a *single-sideband suppressed carrier (SSBSC) modulator,* or *frequency shifter,* or *Klangumwandler,* not only the carrier but one of the sidebands is suppressed, so that frequency components in the output of this device consist of either the sum or the difference of the carrier frequency and the frequency of the components in the modulating signal. Thus, with SSBSC modulation, the spectrum of the modulated wave is translated either inverted or non-inverted to a new location in the frequency spectrum. In figure 5.22, a complex wave consisting of harmonics at 0.3 kHz (300 Hz), 0.6 kHz, 0.9 kHz, 1.2 kHz, and 1.5 kHz (figure 5.22a) is fed to one input of a single-sideband suppressed carrier modulator, the other input of which is a 30.0-kHz sine wave. Figure 5.22b shows the spectrum of the modulator output with the attenuated lower sideband components at (30.0 − 0.3) = 29.7 kHz, (30.0 − 0.6) = 29.4 kHz, (30.0 − 0.9) = 29.1 kHz, (30.0 − 1.2) = 28.8 kHz, and (30.0 − 1.5) = 28.5 kHz; and the upper side-band components at (30.0 + 0.3) = 30.3 kHz, (30.0 + 0.6) = 30.6 kHz, (30.0 + 0.9) = 30.9 kHz, (30.0 + 1.2) = 31.2 kHz, and (30.0 + 1.5) = 31.5 kHz. Figure 5.22c shows the spectrum of the modulator after high-pass filtering to remove the residual lower sideband components. The upper sideband components (30.3, 30.6, 30.9, 31.2, and 31.5 kHz) are then heterodyned† using a multipler—the upper sideband components fed into one input of the multiplier, and (in this case) a 29.5 kHz sine wave is fed to the other input. The components resulting from the sum of the 29.5-kHz oscillator and the upper sideband components are easily removed with a lowpass filter (not shown in the diagram). The difference frequencies are shown in figure 5.22d. Notice that each component in the original signal (figure 5.22a) is translated up in frequency by 500 Hz (figure 5.22d) and that the translated components are no longer harmonically related.

The "detuning" effect of processing instrumental music with an SSB modulator has long been known to communication engineers and short-wave listeners. Gordon M. Russell writes:

> An incorrect reinserted carrier frequency is especially disturbing in the case of music transmission. Consider that the "overtones" which give color to the sound of musical instruments are [in most cases] exact harmonics of the pitch of the sound. . . . Any departure of the carrier frequency from the correct value will cause . . . the overtones to be displaced in frequency by the same amount, not proportionately. . . . The subjective effect is one of strangely *inharmonic* music. Perhaps some novel "musical" instrument will be invented making use of this effect.[3]

Single-sideband signals may be generated by several methods. Two of these methods, the *filtering* method and the *phasing* method are described below. The *filtering method* of SSB generation employs a sharp filter to pass the desired sideband and attenuate the other. The filter should be sufficiently sharp to suppress the unwanted sideband with the lowest frequency modulating signal employed (the distance between the two

---

†The time functions are multiplied together to produce the sum and difference frequencies.

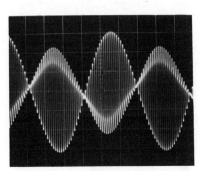

FIGURE 5.19

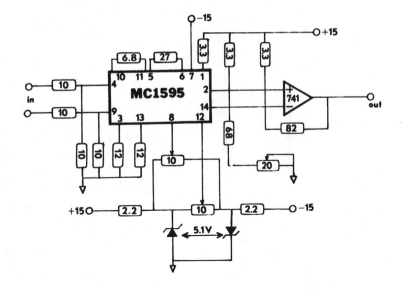

FIGURE 5.20
(all R's x 1000)

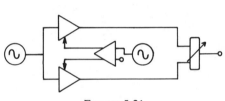

FIGURE 5.21

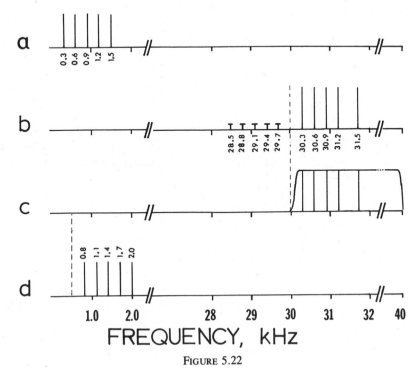

FIGURE 5.22

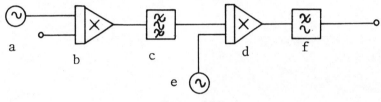

FIGURE 5.23

sidebands being twice the lowest frequency component in the modulating signal). The modulating signal is usually translated to a frequency that takes best advantage of the most discriminating range of the filter. Even with the most selective filters, a filter-type SSB generator designed for high-quality program inputs generally exhibits greatly reduced sideband suppression for low-frequency program inputs. A block diagram of a filtering-type SSB generator is shown in figure 5.23. In this diagram, the first oscillator (a) is set to position the double-sideband suppressed carrier output from the multiplier (b) at the correct point on the filter (c) response curve to achieve unwanted sideband suppression. The second, variable-frequency, oscillator (d) is used to heterodyne the SSB signal (using multiplier [e]) to the desired point in the audio-frequency range. The low-pass filter (f) eliminates unwanted high-frequency (sum of oscillator [d] and desired sideband) components.

A block diagram of the *phasing method* for SSB generation is shown in figure 5.24. In this system, both the modulating signal and carrier are fed to phase-shift networks ϕ^1 and ϕ^2, respectively. Signals appearing at the outputs of these networks are 90° out of phase with respect to each other. The phase-shift network ϕ^1 should provide a constant phase shift over the desired program bandwidth in order to maintain the desired degree of sideband suppression. Figure 5.25 shows a graph of phase-angle error versus sideband suppression. The phase-shift network associated with the carrier can be of more simple design, since the network operates at only one frequency. The resulting SSB signal may be retranslated to the audio frequency range as in the filtering system.

Given a sinusoidal carrier $A \cos \omega_c t$, and a sinusoidal modulating signal $B \cos \omega_m t$, where the coefficients of amplitude, A and B, are unity for the sake of simplification, at the outputs of ϕ^1 we have $\cos \omega_m t$ and $\sin \omega_m t$ ($\cos \omega_m t + 90° = \sin \omega_m t$). At the outputs of ϕ^2 we have $\cos \omega_c t$ and $\sin \omega_c t$. After multiplication in balanced modulator M_1, we obtain

$$E_{M_1} = \cos \omega_c t \cdot \cos \omega_m t.$$

Similarly, after multiplication in balanced modulator M_2, we obtain

$$E_{M_2} = \sin \omega_c t \cdot \sin \omega_m t.$$

Using the trigonometric identity cos a cos b = 1/2[cos $(a + b)$ − cos $(a - b)$],

$$E_{M_1} = 1/2[\cos(\omega_c - \omega_m)t + \cos(\omega_c + \omega_m)t].$$

Using the trigonometric identity sin a sin b = 1/2[cos $(a - b)$ − cos $(a + b)$],

$$E_{M_2} = 1/2[\cos(\omega_c - \omega_m)t - \cos(\omega_c + \omega_m)t].$$

Adding E_{M_1} and E_{M_2}, we obtain

$$1/2 \cos(\omega_c - \omega_m)t + 1/2 \cos(\omega_c + \omega_m)t + 1/2 \cos(\omega_c - \omega_m)t - 1/2 \cos(\omega_c + \omega_m)t = \cos(\omega_c - \omega_m)t,$$

the *lower* sideband. Exchanging points Δ and † (figure 5.24) results in *attenuation* of the *lower* sideband and *reinforcement* of the *upper* sideband. (The same effect may be achieved by exchanging the outputs ϕ^1.)

The filtering and phasing methods of SSB generation are often used in conjunction, as in figure 5.26. In this diagram, again, both the carrier and modulating signals are supplied to M_1 and M_2 in quadrature. The double-pole, double-throw switch controls sideband selection. Resistor R controls the suppression of the unwanted sideband. A sharp filter following R

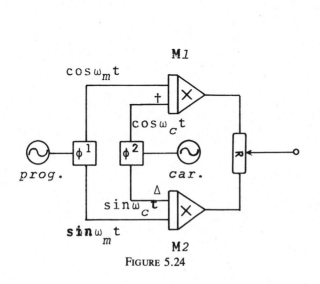

FIGURE 5.24

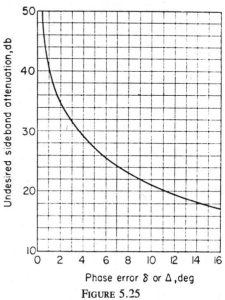

FIGURE 5.25

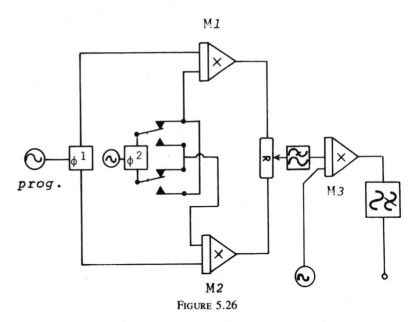

FIGURE 5.26

provides further sideband suppression. The resultant SSB signal is retranslated to the audio frequency range using modulator M_3. Oscillator 3, the local oscillator, may be voltage-controlled, in which case the amount of frequency shift may be a function of an external control signal.

Bode and Moog have described a frequency shifter capable of translating a program input continuously from -5000 Hz through 0 to $+5000$ Hz.[4] Whereas in figure 5.22 an ultrasonic frequency carrier is employed, necessitating subsequent heterodyning and low-pass filtering, the carrier in the Bode–Moog circuit translates the program *directly*. The quadrature carrier is produced by heterodyning a quadrature, fixed-frequency sine wave with a voltage-controlled oscillator. The desired sideband is obtained by summing or subtracting the two output signals from the multipliers.

FREQUENCY MODULATION

Frequency modulation synthesis is one of the most important techniques in electronic music production. Using FM synthesis, it is possible to create a large range of timbres, from sounds that consist of a few harmonic or nonharmonic components, to complex tones that sound like broadband noise. FM synthesis also provides a useful method for generating sounds with time-varying frequency components (number, amplitude, and frequency). We will discuss dynamic timbral differentiation using FM synthesis later in this chapter. FM synthesis is widely used in digital sound synthesis, in some cases as the sole sound generating process.

Unlike AM, DSB, and SSB, FM is not often employed for modification of natural sounds. Since FM is the modulation of a waveform along the time axis, natural sounds cannot be frequency modulated in *real time*, since such a modulation would require an accurate knowledge of both the past and future behavior of the signal. Analog or digital delay lines may be used, however, to preserve a record of the waveform, and the stored waveform may then be outputed either faster or more slowly than it entered the delay device. FM of natural (or electronically generated) sounds using delay devices is a relatively new and important tool for sound synthesis. The Lexicon Model 102–S is an example of a commercially produced digital delay device (see figure 5.27), and although the price of the unit is high at the time of this writing ($3,000 to $7,000, depending on the delay time and other features required), the Lexicon device provides a large dynamic and low distortion range. Several delay units employing analog (charge–transfer) delay lines are available at a more modest cost than digital units. Analog time delay devices are easily constructed[5] using readily available delay units such as the Matsushida MN3001 and Reticon SAD–1032 and TAD–32 integrated circuits. Analog delay lines are inherently noisy, and many commercial units such as the LOFT series 440 include a noise reduction system in their designs. In addition, maximum usable bandwidth of these devices is inversely proportional to the delay time. As we shall discuss later, FM of natural sounds may also be accomplished using a single-sideband frequency shifter.

Frequency modulation is usually accomplished in electronic music by using voltage-controlled oscillators (voltage-to-frequency converters). We will first consider the case in which the change of frequency (ΔF) of a VCO is related to control voltage (V) by the expression $\Delta F = F_0 V$, where F_0 is some starting frequency. The expression $\Delta F = F_0 k V$ includes the term k, a constant of proportionality that relates change in control voltage to change in frequency. A voltage-controlled oscillator with the above frequency-versus-control-voltage relationship is called a *linear* VCO.

FIGURE 5.27

Most VCOs used in electronic music provide an *exponential* control-voltage-versus-frequency response, $\Delta F = F_0 2^v$ (in this case, one octave per volt), unlike the linear response just described. A frequency-versus-control-voltage relationship of one octave per volt is standard for exponential VCOs used in electronic music.

Both linear and exponential VCOs are used in electronic music production. Applications of each type of oscillator are described below. For ease of description, we will first consider *linear* FM in explaining the spectra produced by FM processes.

As has been stressed throughout this book, it is important that the composer of electronic music understand and be able to control the processes involved in electronic music production in order to satisfy his compositional requirements. As we have mentioned before, an understanding of the technical processes involved in sound synthesis is certainly an important, though certainly not the only, approach to achieving such control. Some students might need only to be shown a few patchings and operations before proceeding on their own, working intuitively. Although a knowledge of technical information is helpful both for the student's understanding and later on in his own teaching, he does not have to understand the electronic engineering design refinements of a VCO, or to be fully conversant with the FM equations given below. The *result* of the equations, however, is important; they provide a general description of the capability of the FM process to produce certain distributions of frequency components (in this case, in the audio-frequency range). The spectrum analyzer photographs of FM spectra of an exponential VCO should be examined carefully as an aid to understanding this process.

The following expression shows how the magnitude of the voltage (E) of the frequency-modulated signal varies with time:

$$E = A \cos (\omega_c t + M_f \sin \omega_m t).$$

A is the carrier amplitude coefficient; $\omega_c t$ is the angular frequency of the carrier; $\omega_m t$ is the angular frequency of the modulating signal; and M_f is the *modulation index,* a quantity that relates the amplitude of the modulating signal to the amount of change it produces in the modulated signal.

The modulation index, M_f, is also known as the *deviation ratio,* that is, the peak difference between the instantaneous frequency of the modulated wave and its unmodulated frequency (carrier frequency). (For example, if a 2000-Hz sinusoidal carrier is frequency modulated by a 100-Hz sinusoid, causing the carrier to swing from 2000 to 2200 Hz, back to 2000 H, down to 1800 Hz, and back to 2000 Hz during one cycle of the modulating signal, the modulation index is:

$$\frac{\Delta f_c}{f_{mod}} = \frac{200 \text{ Hz}}{100 \text{ Hz}} = M_f = 2.$$

Expanding the expression $E = A \cos (\omega_c t + M_f \sin \omega_m t)$ using the trigonometric identity $\cos (a + b) = \cos a \cos b - \sin a \sin b$, we obtain

$$E = A[\cos \omega_c t \cdot \cos (M_f \sin \omega_m t) - \sin \omega_c t \cdot \sin (M_f \sin \omega_m t)].$$

However:

$$\cos (M_f \sin \omega_m t) = J_0(M_f) + 2J_2(M_f) \cos 2\omega_m t + 2J_4(M_f) \cos 4\omega_m t + \ldots,$$

and

$$\sin (M_f \sin \omega_m t) = 2J_1(M_f) \sin \omega_m t + 2J_3(M_f) \sin 3\omega_m t + \ldots.$$

$J_n(M_f)$ is the Bessel function of the first kind with order n and argument M_f. These Bessel functions may be obtained from a tabulation (see *Handbook of Mathematical Functions*[1]; figure 5.28 shows a graph of these functions). Substituting the Bessel function identities into the equation for the frequency-modulated wave above, we obtain:

$$E = A\{\cos \omega_c t[J_0(M_f) + 2J_2(M_f) \cos 2\omega_m t + 2J_4(M_f) \cos 4\omega_m t + \ldots]$$
$$- \sin \omega_c t[2J_1(M_f) \sin \omega_m t + 2J_3(M_f) \sin 3\omega_m t + \ldots]\},$$

which may be rewritten as:

$$E = A\{J_0(M_f) \cos \omega_c t - J_1(M_f)(2 \sin \omega_m t \cdot \sin \omega_c t) + J_2(M_f)(2 \cos 2\omega_m t \cdot \cos \omega_c t) - J_3(M_f)(2 \sin 3\omega_m t \cdot \sin \omega_c t) + J_4(M_f)(2 \cos 4\omega_m t \cdot \cos \omega_c t) - \ldots \}.$$

Using trigonometric product identities, we obtain:

$$E = A\{J_0(M_f) \cos \omega_c t +$$
$$J_1(M_f)[\cos (\omega_c + \omega_m)t - \cos (\omega_c - \omega_m)t] +$$
$$J_2(M_f)[\cos (\omega_c + 2\omega_m)t + \cos (\omega_c - 2\omega_m)t] +$$
$$J_3(M_f)[\cos (\omega_c + 3\omega_m)t - \cos (\omega_c - 3\omega_m)t] +$$
$$J_4(M_f)[\cos (\omega_c + 4\omega_m)t + \cos (\omega_c - 4\omega_m)t] +$$
$$+ \ldots\ldots\ldots\ldots\ldots \}.$$

The expression above shows that frequency modulation produces sideband pairs spaced on both sides of the carrier at integral multiples of the modulating frequency. The amplitudes of the sidebands are determined by the Bessel function coefficients. Figure 5.28 shows a plot of Bessel functions of integer order. In this graph, $J_0(M_f)$ shows the variation in amplitude of the carrier component with different modulation indices; $J_1(M_f)$ shows the variation in amplitude of the first sideband pair with different modulation indices, and so on. For example, a modulation index

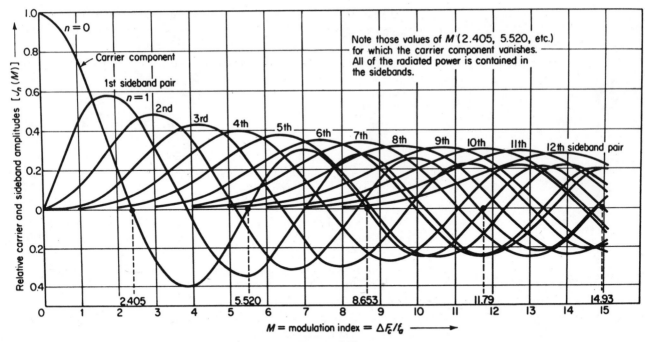

Note those values of M (2.405, 5.520, etc.) for which the carrier component vanishes. All of the radiated power is contained in the sidebands.

FIGURE 5.28

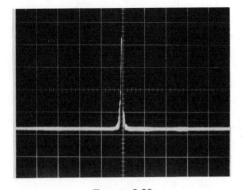

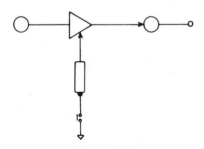

FIGURE 5.29

FIGURE 5.30

of 2 produces three significant pairs of sidebands. In this case, the carrier amplitude is 0.22389 times its unmodulated value; the amplitude of the first sideband pair is 0.5767 times the unmodulated carrier amplitude; the amplitude of the second sideband pair is 0.3528 times the unmodulated carrier amplitude; the amplitude of the third sideband pair is 0.1289 times the unmodulated carrier amplitude; the amplitude of the fourth sideband pair is 0.0339 times the unmodulated carrier amplitude; and so on.

By varying the amplitude of a modulating signal to the control port of a VCO, using the linear FM method described above, one can produce changes of timbre as a function of time. Figure 5.29 shows a simple patching using two sine-wave generators, a VCA, and an envelope generator to produce dynamic timbral effects with linear FM.

Figures 5.30 to 5.35 show frequency spectra produced by sine-wave FM (exponential VCO) of a sinusoidal carrier with different modulation indices.

Figures 5.36 to 5.38 show the time functions for sawtooth-wave FM of a sinusoidal carrier, square-wave FM of a sinusoidal carrier, and sine-wave FM of a sinusoidal carrier.

Figure 5.39 shows the time function of a sinusoidal carrier simultaneously sine-wave amplitude modulated and square-wave frequency modulated.

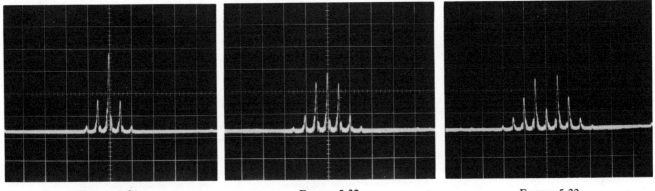

FIGURE 5.31   FIGURE 5.32   FIGURE 5.33

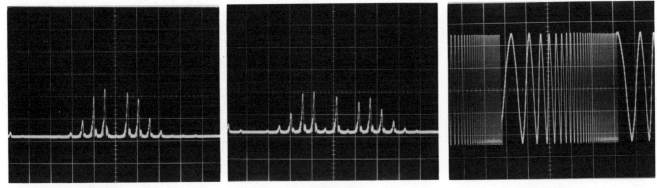

FIGURE 5.34   FIGURE 5.35   FIGURE 5.36

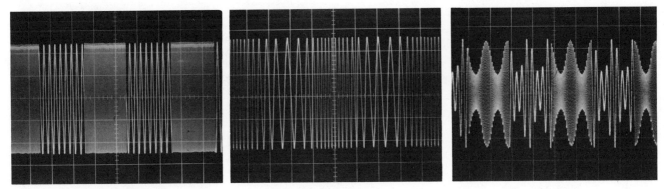

FIGURE 5.37   FIGURE 5.38   FIGURE 5.39

FM SYNTHESIS WITH EXPONENTIAL VCOS

Bernie Hutchins has made a thorough analysis of this topic in his article in the *Journal of the Audio Engineering Society*.[6] A summary of his results and their application to electronic music production techniques is given below:

1. As the modulating signal is increased in amplitude, there is an upward shift in frequency of the carrier and sidebands. (While such shifts might be a desirable effect in certain circumstances, the use of a *linear* VCO is recommended for the production of sounds with dynamic depth FM.)

2. Hutchins showed that the amount of carrier (and sideband) shift can be calculated using modified Bessel functions. For example, a frequency-modulated sine-wave oscillator (1000 Hz) with a one-octave-per-volt frequency versus control-voltage characteristic (exponential) modulated by a 3-volt peak-to-peak 100-Hz sine wave, would exhibit an upward spectral shift of 1.410 kHz. These shifts are not so noticeable for small values of modulating signal amplitude.

Hutchins illustrates several methods of providing a complementary "pitch pull down" to compensate for the spectrum shift described above. In addition, he shows the circuit (see figure 5.40) of a log amp that is used to drive the control input of an exponential VCO in order to convert its control-voltage/frequency response from exponential to linear.

Figure 5.41a (top) shows three spectra produced by sine-wave frequency modulation of an exponential VCO. From top to bottom, the control voltage (modulating signal) is gradually increased. Notice the upward shift of the carrier (F_c) and the sidebands. Figure 5.41b (bottom) shows a comparable set of spectra produced with a linear VCO. No carrier (F_c) shift is observed.

The one-octave-per-volt exponential VCO is a standard instrument in the electronic music studio today. Exponential VCOs have advantages where

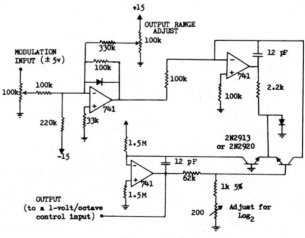

FIGURE 5.40

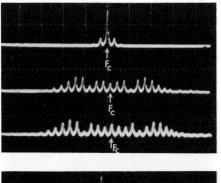

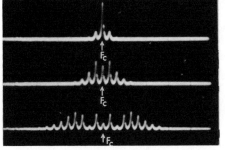

FIGURE 5.41

keyboard and other manual control devices are concerned, whereas linear VCOs are advantageous for FM synthesis applications involving dynamic timbral differentiation. Neither type of oscillator offers conspicuous advantages over the other as far as tracking capability is concerned, although the following case should be noted. Consider two pairs of VCOs, one exponential, one linear, both tuned in octaves (500 and 250 Hz). Each oscillator of a pair has its own control-voltage source, and both oscillators share a third control-voltage source. This configuration is the same for both the linear and exponential oscillator pairs. It is desired to increase the interval between the oscillators to *two* octaves by reducing the *control voltage* applied to the lower oscillator and then maintain tracking of the oscillators at the interval of a fifteenth (two octaves). Such control (transposition using changes of control voltage to one of the pair of oscillators) is possible with the exponential VCOs but impossible with the linear VCOs. However, the desired two-octave interval could be tuned using the frequency-adjust pot on the linear VCOs, and tracked using a common control signal. Both exponential and linear VCOs each are useful in various aspects of electronic music production: a VCO for electronic music should ideally offer the operator both modes of control. Studios with only exponential VCOs may add the linear VCO capability to their existing instruments at a moderate expense. Through-zero FM such as Chowning employed digitally[7] may be realized with analog equipment using several methods.

THROUGH-ZERO FM

Through-zero FM using a beat-frequency oscillator is easily demonstrated with equipment found in most studios. The beat-frequency oscillator (BFO) consists of two sine-wave oscillators tuned to the same frequency (for example, 25 kHz) with the outputs of the oscillators connected to the two inputs of a multiplier (2- or 4-quadrant). The multiplier output is low pass-filtered to block the upper sideband frequency and any 25 kHz component that might be present due to improper balance settings of the 4-quadrant multiplier, or if a 2-quadrant multiplier were used. Figure 5.42 shows the interconnection of the oscillators, multiplier, and filter described above. Note that one of the oscillators is voltage-controlled. Varying the voltage-controlled oscillator from 25,001 Hz (25.001 kHz) down to 25,000 Hz, and then to 24,999 Hz will produce a lower sideband frequency that starts at 1 Hz, decreases to 0 Hz, and increases to 1 Hz again. If we observe the BFO sine-wave output on an oscilloscope as it undergoes this 1-Hz-to-0-Hz-to-1 Hz change, we will see the sine wave slow down, stop momentarily, and resume its motion—in the opposite direction. Figure 5.43 shows an oscilloscope photograph of this zero-frequency transition and phase reversal. Through-zero FM is a very useful capability and does produce sounds which appear "richer" than those produced with conventional oscillators. As Hutchins puts it: "With the phase reversal the

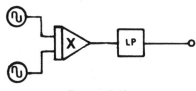

FIGURE 5.42

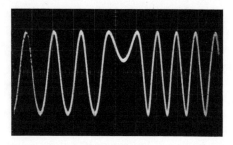

FIGURE 5.43

modulation depths seem much deeper, and there is much more . . . spectral content apparent."[8]

An alternative design for a through-zero oscillator is described in Electronotes.[9] Frequency modulation of natural sounds using a single-sideband frequency shifter is an important sound modification process. The Bode/Moog quadrature-BFO method described earlier (page 116) is well-suited to this purpose, since it permits through-zero modulation which results in upshifting and downshifting on alternate cycles of the (AC) modulating signal (assuming no offset present on the control input). Frequency shifters which do not employ through-zero oscillators are capable of only upshift or downshift, and although one may mix the upshifted and downshifted signals, the shifting does not occur alternately.

So far we have considered only FM with sinusoidal modulating signals. If the modulating signal contains more than one frequency component, the spectrum of the modulated wave will contain sidebands produced by the sum and difference frequencies of all the harmonics of the modulating frequencies, in addition to the sidebands produced by the modulating signals taken separately.

For example, a 2000-Hz carrier (f_c) is frequency modulated by a 320-Hz sinusoid (f_1) and a 520-Hz sinusoid (f_2). The modulation index for f_1 is 0.8, while the modulation index for f_2 is 0.2. Figure 5.44 shows the

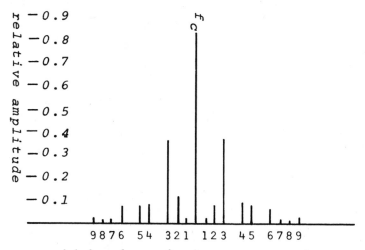

sideband-producing components	
1) $2f_1 - f_2$	6) $f_1 + f_2$
2) $f_1 - f_2$	7) $3f_1$
3) f_1	8) $2f_2$
4) f_2	9) $2f_1 + f_2$
5) $2f_1$	
	etc.

FIGURE 5.44

spectrum of the modulated wave, along with a tabulation of sideband-producing frequency components. The low modulation index was chosen to restrict the number of significant sidebands produced. Nevertheless, in figure 5.44 very low amplitude sideband pairs were omitted.

The reader might conclude from the FM spectra shown thus far that the sidebands of an FM wave are always distributed symmetrically about the carrier. Complex modulating signals may produce sideband components of the same frequency but different phase, resulting in partial or complete cancellation of certain sideband components. It is important to realize that the spectral contribution of an FM wave depend on the rate of change of frequency during the entire cycle: the longer the frequency of the FM signal remains in a certain frequency range, the greater the spectral density in that frequency range. Figure 5.45 shows an unsymmetrical sideband distribution in an FM wave produced by modulating a sinusoidal carrier with the complex wave shown in the drawing. It is important to note that in all the spectra of FM waves shown in this chapter, only the magnitude of frequency components is indicated, with no regard for the complex phase-relationships of the components.

With FM one can generate a great variety of sounds, from discrete-pitched sounds to wideband quasi-pitched and non-pitched sounds. The frequency components of FM-produced sounds are usually not harmonically related (except where $f_m = nf_c$, n being an integer). As a result, many FM-produced sounds resemble those of instruments of indefinite pitch, for example, gongs, bells, anvils, and so on, and have been referred to as "clangorous sounds." To be sure, "clangorous sounds" is a subjective term, and can by no means describe the great range of sounds producible by FM.

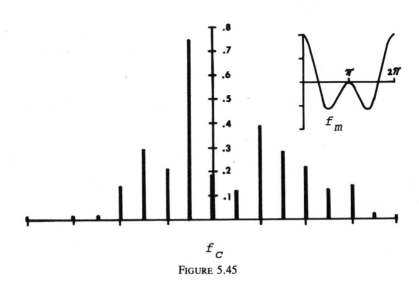

FIGURE 5.45

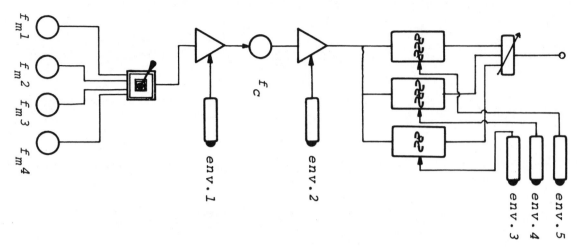

FIGURE 5.46

In preceding chapters we discussed some reasons why sounds produced by electronic means often seem artificial and lifeless in comparison with natural sounds. Although judgments concerning the value of sounds and their suitability for inclusion in a work are subjective and highly dependent on the context in which the sounds appear, there are procedures by which electronic sounds may be made to behave more like natural sounds, namely, by making not only the loudness of the total sound event change through time (as is the case in simple gating), but by making the amplitude, frequency, and phase of the individual components of a sound vary through time as well. To achieve such results with additive synthesis would require more transient generators and voltage-controlled amplifiers than are found in the usual electronic music studio. Although filters provide a practical means to accomplish timbral change through time, many studios are limited in their filter complement (see the filter array [figure 6.31] and related text in chapter 6). Due to the variation in number of sidebands and sideband amplitudes as the modulation index is varied in an FM patching, the composer may effect subtle timbral changes by varying M_f over a small range through time. For example, in figure 5.46 the following adjustments may be made as the sound is gated in VCA 2: $f_m{}^1, f_m{}^2, f_m{}^3$, and $f_m{}^4$ may be varied slightly; the quad panpot may be adjusted to alter the waveform of the modulating signal; env. 1 may be adjusted to vary the modulation index through time; envs. 3, 4, and 5 may be adjusted to vary the cutoff points of the filters; env. 2 may be adjusted to control the overall loudness of the sound.

OTHER TYPES OF MODULATION

Several types of pulse modulation are employed in electronic music; *pulse-width modulation* (PWM); *pulse-amplitude modulation* (PAM); and *pulse-position modulation* (PPM). Of these, pulse-width modulation is

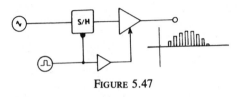

FIGURE 5.47

most commonly employed. In addition to being a built-in feature of many electronic music oscillators, pulse modulation is easily accomplished using standard electronic music instrumentation such as comparators, VCAs, sample-and-hold amplifiers, gates, and so on. Figure 5.47 shows a patching to produce pulse amplitude modulation. Figure 5.48 shows a patching to produce centered PWM using a comparator. Figure 3.9, chapter 3, illustrates the points at which the comparator switches, thus determining the pulse width. By employing an inverted sawtooth wave in the comparator diagram in figure 5.48, fixed-edge PWM may be produced. Figure 5.49 shows a patching to produce pulse-position modulation. Although the patchings to produce PPM and PAM do tie up several instruments to produce sounds that are not so different from the PWM usually available from electronic music oscillators, the patchings are good exercises and serve to increase the student's familiarity with the instruments involved.

No analytical discussion of the frequency components produced by the pulse modulation methods described above is presented here. Russell[10] and Black[11] have provided detailed analyses of pulse modulation systems. Figure 5.50 shows a pulse-width-modulated wave (a); the sine-wave modulating signal associated with the PWM wave (b); and the spectrum (c) of the PWM wave. In general, PWM produces phase modulation of each carrier harmonic. Figure 5.51 shows a detail of six harmonics of an unmodulated pulse wave (a) and the harmonics with the sidebands produced by PWM (b).

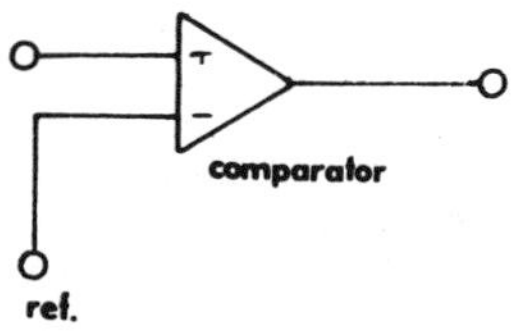

Formant modulation is a name often applied to a process in which the center frequency or half-power point of a voltage-controlled filter is changed in accordance with the amplitude of a modulating signal. We shall see in chapter 6 that the phase response (phase of output signal compared with that of the input signal) of filters varies with changes of operating point of the filter as well as with changes of frequency of the input signal.

In addition, sweeping a filter through a given program results in changes in amplitude at the output of the filter, due to the attenuation of program frequency components. Thus, formant modulation is a combination of

comparator

ref.

FIGURE 5.48

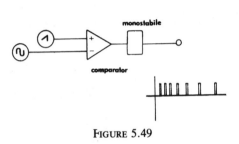

FIGURE 5.49

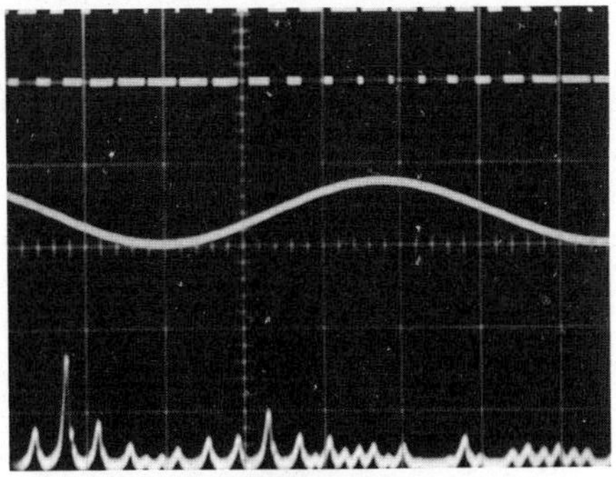

FIGURE 5.50

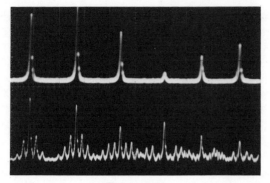

FIGURE 5.51

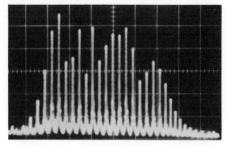

FIGURE 5.52

phase modulation and amplitude modulation. In addition, the usual exponential control-voltage-versus-operating-frequency response of the filter introduces further alteration of the sideband amplitudes produced by phase and amplitude modulation. Figure 5.52 shows a spectrum analyzer photograph of a sine wave, "formant-modulated" by a resonant low-pass filter (sinusoidal modulating signal).

PATCHINGS

1. Patching 1 shows a sine-wave oscillator amplitude modulated by another sine-wave oscillator. The percent modulation should be varied (from the 100% figure suggested) and the effect of changing this parameter noted.

636Hz   *100% AM*

360Hz

2. Patching 2 shows two amplitude modulators connected in parallel. The modulators share a common modulated signal (carrier).

252Hz

720Hz

177Hz

3. Patching 3 shows an amplitude modulation configuration that uses the sum of three sine-wave signals as a carrier, and the sum of four sine-wave signals as a modulating signal.

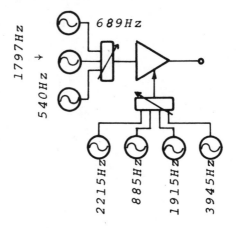

4. Patching 4 shows two amplitude modulators in series.

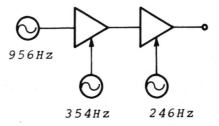

5. Patching 5 shows a sine-wave carrier that is amplitude modulated with an amplitude-modulated signal.

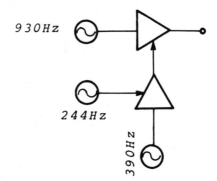

6. In patching 6, an amplitude-modulated signal is processed in a ring modulator (multiplier).

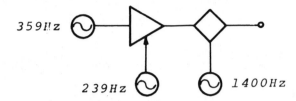

7. Patching 7 shows the output of a short-wave receiver processed with a multiplier. A *good* short-wave receiver (Hammarlund SP–600, Eddystone 1830, general-coverage receivers) is a useful sound source. Many of the signals in the 160 through 15 meter bands (approximately 1.8 MHz to approximately 21 MHz) are complex, for example, the HF (High-Frequency) carrier is modulated by, say, a frequency-modulated audio signal (AFSK facsimile, and so on).

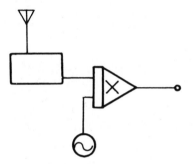

8. Patching 8 shows two VCAs connected as a four-quadrant multiplier. Carrier suppression in this configuration is adjusted with the fixed-control-voltage controls on the VCAs, as well as with the mixer input attenuators.

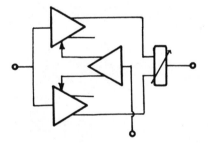

9. Patching 9 shows two multipliers used to process a transcribed signal. The first multiplier produces groups of sidebands centered around 30 kHz (the frequency of the suppressed carrier). The second multiplier serves to heterodyne the signal from the first multiplier down to the audio-frequency range. The low-pass filter at the output of the second multiplier attenuates the upper sideband components (approximately 30 kHz + 25–30–35 kHz) produced by that modulator. The low-pass filter at the output of the tape recorder limits the

bandwidth of the signal at the output of the first multiplier. (High-frequency components in the program often produce too harsh a timbre.)

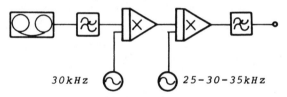

30kHz   25-30-35kHz

10. Patching 10 shows a multiplier arrangement in which any proportion of modulated/unmodulated program may be selected using a mixer (or panpot).

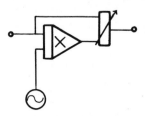

11. Patching 11 shows a multiplier, one input of which is connected to a quad panpot in which four sine waves are combined. The other multiplier input may be connected to the output from a microphone, tape reproducer, oscillator, short-wave receiver, and so on.

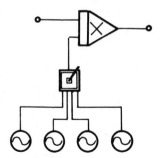

12. Patching 12 shows a low-pass-filtered random-signal source (for example, white noise generator) used to amplitude-modulate (DSBSC) a signal. The low-pass filtered signal may also be used to frequency-modulate a VCO. (Insert an amplifier in the line between the filter and the VCO FM-input in order to produce greater frequency deviation.)

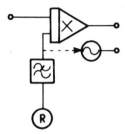

13. Patching 13 shows a sine-wave oscillator, the output of which is connected to: (a) an amplitude modulator and (b) two amplitude modulators in series. The outputs of the modulator branches are mixed, and the output of the mixer is connected to one of the inputs of a multiplier.

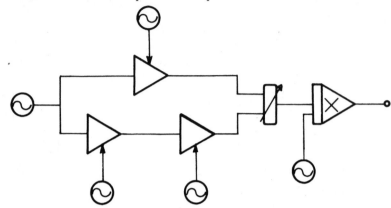

14. Patching 14 shows a sine-wave oscillator that is frequency modulated by a sine-wave modulating signal.

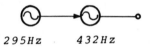

295Hz　　432Hz

15. Patching 15 shows a sine-wave oscillator that is frequency modulated by a frequency-modulated [$\sim f_m$] sine wave.

180Hz　　718Hz　　1125Hz

16. Patching 16 shows a sine-wave VCO, frequency modulated by the output of another sine-wave oscillator. A VCA is inserted in the modulating signal path. An envelope generator controls the amplitude of the modulating signal, resulting in a change of modulation "depth" through time. Use both exponential and linear VCOs for the modulated oscillator. Explain the results you encountered using the different types of VCOs in this patching (suggested operating points: 400 to 500 Hz for modulating signal, 1,000 Hz for modulated signal).

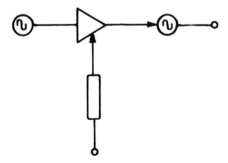

17. Patching 17 shows four sine-wave oscillators which share a common sine-wave modulating signal. The outputs of the four oscillators are combined in a quad panpot.

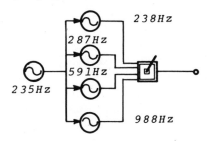

18. Patching 18 shows four sine-wave signals combined in a quad panpot. The output of the panpot is used to frequency modulate a sine-wave oscillator.

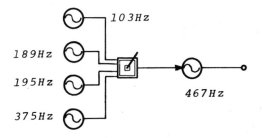

19. Patching 19 shows a variant of the preceding patching in which a voltage-controlled rotation mixer (see chapter 6) is substituted for the quad panpot. The speed of rotation (commutation) is controlled by a sine-wave modulating signal.

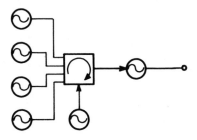

20. Patching 20 shows a sine-wave signal that is amplitude modulated by a frequency-modulated modulating signal.

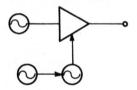

21. Patching 21 shows a sine-wave signal that is frequency modulated by an amplitude modulated signal.

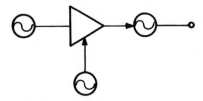

22. Patching 22 shows a frequency modulated signal that is amplitude modulated by a sine-wave signal.

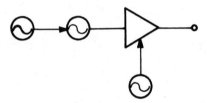

23. Patching 23 shows two mixtures of four frequency modulated sine-wave oscillators. The outputs of the mixers are then multiplied.

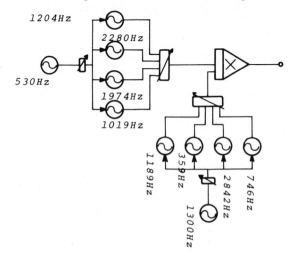

24. Patching 24 shows a mixture of four low-frequency square waves used to frequency modulate a triangle-wave oscillator. The resultant series of discrete pitches is gated by two low-frequency, frequency-modulated sawtooth waves that are summed and inverted (to produce a sharp attack characteristic).

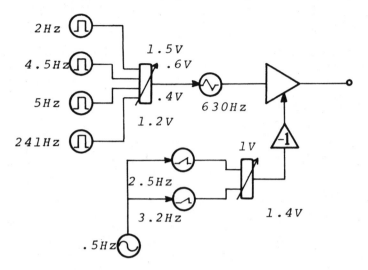

25. Patching 25 shows a patching demonstrating pulse-width modulation using a low frequency sine-wave modulating signal.

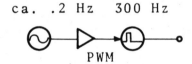

26. Patching 26 shows a pulse-width modulated oscillator, the output of which is passed through a band-reject filter. Two envelope generators are used to control both the duty cycle of the pulse wave and the filter.

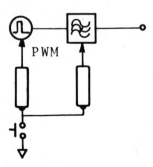

PROBLEMS

1. In amplitude modulation, what is the relationship between sideband power, carrier power, and percent modulation?

2. Explain in a general way how radio signals are transmitted and received through the use of (a) amplitude modulation and (b) frequency modulation.

3. What is the relationship between % modulation and the envelope of the modulated signal (AM, ~ carrier, ~ modulating signal)?

4. How may the percentage modulation of an amplitude-modulated signal (~ carrier, ~ modulating signal) be determined?

5. What factors affect carrier suppression in a diode-ring modulator?

6. Compare the characteristics of the two-quadrant multiplier with those of the four-quadrant multiplier.

7. Determine the frequency components in the output of the amplitude modulator shown in example 1.

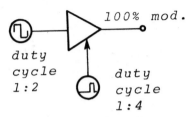

8. Two sine waves, f_c and f_m, are connected to the signal input and control input, respectively, of a VCA. Describe the output waveform: when $f_c \ll f_m$; when $f_c \gg f_m$; when $f_c \equiv f_m$.

9. Compare amplitude and frequency modulation as means for generating complex sounds for electronic music production.

10. What is the coefficient of amplitude of the third-order sideband pair in an FM signal with a modulation index of 4?

11. Compare the frequency components present in the output of the patchings in examples 2 and 3.

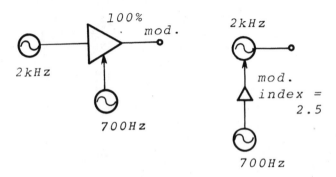

12. Describe the frequency components present in the output of the patching in example 4.

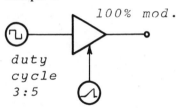

13. Under what conditions are the sidebands of a modulated (AM, FM) signal related one to the other by integers?[12]

14. Describe three types of amplitude modulation used in electronic music production and devise a patching using each of these types of AM.

15. A ring modulator is so called because of what characteristic?

16. What is the difference between a single-balanced modulator and a double-balanced modulator (AM)?

17. An oscilloscope display of a modulation envelope (ordinary AM, ~ carrier, ~ modulating signal) shows 4.9 cm peak-to-peak and 2.3 cm trough-to-trough. Determine the percentage modulation. What is the coefficient of amplitude of the sidebands with respect to that of the carrier?

18. How are the terms *modulation factor* and *percent modulation* related?

19. In general, describe the nature of the sound resulting from the patching shown in example 5. What effect does the mixture of the three sine-wave signals have on the three square waves? Criticize the settings of the three ~ oscillators.

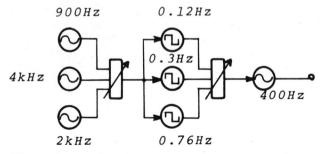

20. Discuss the operation of the patching shown in example 6.

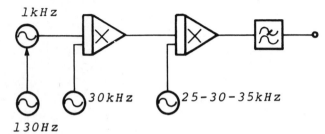

21. The bandwidth of an AM signal is determined by the _____ of the modulating signal, whereas the bandwidth of an FM signal is determined by the _____ of the modulating signal.

22. Describe two ways to control the percentage modulation using a VCA as an amplitude modulator.

23. What determines the frequency deviation of an FM wave produced by modulating a VCO? What effect does altering the frequency deviation have on the spectrum of the FM wave for linear and exponential VCOs?

24. What types of modulation are suitable for real-time electronic modification of natural sounds?

25. Determine the percentage modulation for the amplitude-modulated signal shown in example 7. How does percentage modulation relate to timbre in this case?

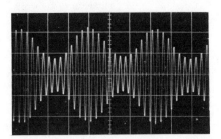

26. Using three sine-wave oscillators and two VCAs, devise a patching that will produce a spectrum similar to that shown in example 8.

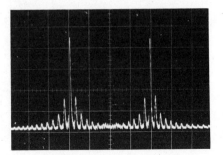

27. Using modulation techniques, devise a patching that will produce a spectrum similar to that shown in example 9. What resources would be required to produce this spectrum using additive synthesis?

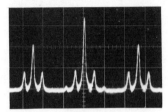

NOTES

1. P. F. Panter, *Modulation, Noise, and Spectral Analysis* (New York: McGraw-Hill, 1965); and R. E. Sentz, *Modern Communications Electronics* (San Francisco: Rinehart Press, 1971).

2. B. Hutchins, *Musical Engineer's Handbook*)Ithaca, N.Y.: Electronotes, 1975).

3. Gordon M. Russell, *Modulation and Coding in Information Systems* (Englewood Cliffs, N.J.: Prentice-Hall, 1962).

4. H. Bode and R. A. Moog, "A High-Accuracy Frequency Shifter for Professional Audio Applications," *Journal of the Audio Engineering Society* 20 (1972): 453–458.

5. B. Hutchins, "Delay Module/Submodule, Option I," *Electronotes* 8, no. 72 (December 1976), pp. 17–20.

6. B. Hutchins, "The Frequency Modulation Spectrum of an Exponential Voltage-Controlled Oscillator," *Journal of the Audio Engineering Society* 23 (1975): 200–206.

7. See J. M. Chowning, "The Synthesis of Complex Audio Spectra by Means of Frequency Modulation," *Journal of the Audio Engineering Society* 21 (1973): 526–534.

8. B. Hutchins, *Electronotes,* 9, no. 25: 17.

9. Ibid.

10. G. Russell, *Modulation and Coding in Information Systems* (Englewood Cliffs, N.J.: Prentice-Hall, 1962).

11. H. S. Black, *Modulation Theory* (Princeton, N.J.: Van Nostrand, 1953).

12. Chowning, "Synthesis of Complex Audio Spectra."

SELECTED BIBLIOGRAPHY

Books

Abramowitz, M., and Stegun, I. *Handbook of Mathematical Functions*. New York: Dover, 1965.

Black, H. S. *Modulation Theory*. Princeton, N.J.: Van Nostrand, 1953.

Cook, A., and Liff, A. *Frequency Modulation Receivers*. Englewood Cliffs, N.J.: Prentice-Hall, 1968.

CRC Standard Mathematical Tables. 12th ed. Cleveland, Ohio: Chemical Rubber Publication, 1962.

DeFrance, J. J. *Communications Electronics Circuits*. San Francisco: Rinehart Press, 1972.

Hund, A. *Frequency Modulation*. New York: McGraw-Hill, 1942.

Hutchins, B. *Musical Engineer's Handbook*. Ithaca, N.Y.: B. Hutchins, 1975.

Mandl, M. *Principles of Electronic Communications*. Englewood Cliffs, N.J.: Prentice-Hall, 1973.

Panter, P. F. *Modulation, Noise, and Spectral Analysis*. New York: McGraw-Hill, 1965.

Pappenfus, E. W.; Bruene, W. B., and Schoenike, E. O. *Single Sideband Principles and Circuits*. New York: McGraw-Hill, 1964.

RCA. *Linear Integrated Circuits*. RCA Technical Series, IC–42, 1970.

Rowe, H. E. *Signals and Noise in Communication Systems*. Princeton, N.J.: Van Nostrand, 1965.

Russell, G. *Modulation and Coding in Information Systems*. Englewood Cliffs, N.J.: Prentice-Hall, 1962.

Sentz, R. E. *Modern Communications Electronics*. San Francisco: Rinehart Press, 1971.

Tucker, D. G. *Circuits with Periodically Varying Parameters*. New York: Van Nostrand, 1964.

———. *Modulators and Frequency Changers*. London: McDonald, 1952.

Articles

Abramson, N. "Bandwidth and Spectra of Phase- and Frequency-Modulated Waves." *IEEE Transactions on Communications Systems* CS-11 (December 1963): 407–414.

Bedrosian, E. "The Analytic Signal Representation of Modulated Waveforms." *Proceedings of the IRE* 50 (October 1962): 2071–2076.

Bellamy, N. W., and West, M. J. "A High-Accuracy Four-Quadrant Time-Division Analogue Multiplier." *Electronic Engineering,* July 1970.

Bode, H., and Moog, R. A. "A High-Accuracy Frequency Shifter for Professional Audio Applications." *Journal of the Audio Engineering Society* 20, no. 6 (July/August 1972): 453–458.

Bode, H. "The Multiplier-Type Ring Modulator." *Electronic Music Review,* January 1967, pp. 9–15.

———. "A New Tool for the Exploration of Unknown Electronic Music Instrument Performances." *Journal of the Audio Engineering Society* 9, no. 4 (October 1961): 264–266.

———. "A Solid-State Audio Spectrum Shifter." *Audio Engineering Society Preprint,* no. 395.

Burhans, R. "A Pulse-Width Modulator." *Electronotes* 6, no. 44, p. 5.

Burkhard, M. D. "A Simplified Frequency Shifter for Improving Acoustic Feedback Stability." *14th Annual AES Convention,* October 1962.

Chowning, J. M. "The Synthesis of Complex Audio Spectra by Means of Frequency Modulation." *Journal of the Audio Engineering Society* 21, no. 7 (September 1973): 526–534.

Cohen, S. "Spectrum Conservation of Single–Side-Band Phase Modulation." *IEEE Conference on Signal Processing Methods for Radio Telephony,* May 1970.

Ehle, R. C. "A Preamp/Balanced Modulator for Audio Experimentation." *dB,* January 1970.

"Four-Quadrant Analogue Multiplier." *Electronic Engineering,* June 1972, p. 23.

Howson, D. P. "Rectifier Modulators and Switched Harmonic Generators Using a Single Idler Circuit." *IEE Conference on Electrical Networks,* September 1966, p. 266.

———. "The Generation of a Selected Harmonic or Subharmonic by Means of a Single Externally Driven Switch." *Radio and Electronic Engineering* 29 (1965): 247.

Hutchins, B. "Delay Module/Submodule, Option 1." *Electronotes* 8, no. 72 (December 1976): 17–20.

————. "The Frequency Modulation Spectrum of an Exponential Voltage-Controlled Oscillator." *Journal of the Audio Engineering Society* 23, no. 3 (April 1975): 200–206.

Jones, M. H. "Frequency Shifter for 'Howl' Suppression." *Wireless World,* July 1971, pp. 317–322.

Klein, G., and Kuijk, K. E. "Generating the Sum or Difference of Two Signal Frequencies." *Electronic Engineering,* March 1969, pp. 378–380.

Licklider, J. C. R., and Pollack, I. "Effects of Differentiation, Integration, and Infinite Peak Clipping upon Intelligibility of Speech." *Journal of the Acoustical Society of America* 20 (1948): 42–51.

Macario, R. C. V. "Unusual Forms of Analogue Modulation." *Wireless World,* June 1973.

Nelson, G. "A Program Library for Musical Data Processing." *Creative Computing,* March/April 1977, pp. 76–81.

Norgaard, D. "The Phase Shift Method of Single-Sideband Generation." *Proceedings of the IRE,* December 1956, pp. 1718–1735.

Prestigiacomo, A. J., and MacLean, D. J. "A Frequency Shifter for Improving Acoustic Feedback Stability." *Journal of the Audio Engineering Society* 10, no. 2 (April 1962): 110–113.

Saraga, W., and Houselander, L. S. "A Note on SSB Generation and Reception." *IEEE Conference on Signal Processing Methods for Radio Telephony,* 1970, pp. 119–123.

Weckler, G. "Making Music with Charge-Transfer Devices." *Audio Engineering Society Preprint,* no. 1166 (E5), 1976.

6

FILTERS

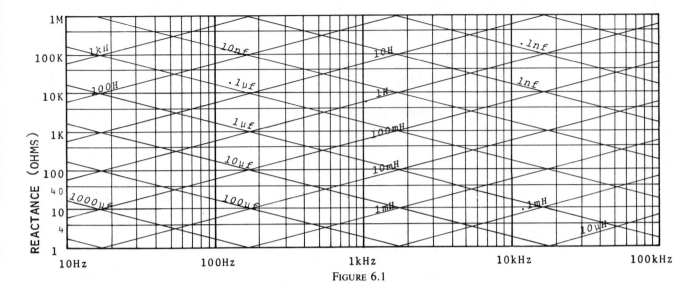

FIGURE 6.1

In general, an electrical *filter* is a frequency selective attenuator. As such, its function is to emphasize or de-emphasize certain parts of the frequency spectrum of a signal. Filters may be used to process practically all signals generated in the electronic music studio, namely, oscillator outputs, transcribed signals, microphone outputs, control signals, and so on. The process of filtering is sometimes referred to as *subtractive synthesis.*

In practice, a filtered complex signal will often exhibit less energy at some points in the frequency spectrum than the unfiltered signal. However, certain filters achieve their effect by emphasizing certain frequencies while simply passing all other frequencies unaltered. For this reason, the term subtractive synthesis can be confusing, since amplitude is not lost, but *gained*. We shall begin our discussion of filtering by considering how frequency selective circuits may be achieved.

The *capacitor* is by definition a frequency-sensitive component. It exhibits a capacitive reactance of $x_c = 1/2\pi fC$, where x_c is the capacitive reactance in ohms, $\pi = 3.1416$, f is the frequency, measured in Hz, and C is the capacitance, measured in farads. Notice that the value of this expression is infinite at $f = 0$ Hz, or DC. A capacitor does not pass direct current and consequently is often used to pass signals between circuits whose DC levels do not match. Under these circumstances, a capacitor is often referred to as a *blocking* capacitor, or *coupling* capacitor.

The *inductor,* sometimes called a coil, also exhibits reactance. However, the inductor has an inverse characteristic from the capacitor, the inductor having an inductive reactance ot $X_L = 2\pi fL$, where X_L is the inductive reactance in ohms, $\pi = 3.1416$, f is the frequency, measured in Hz, and L is the inductance, measured in henries. Figure 6.1 diagrams the reactance of the capacitor and inductor versus frequency.

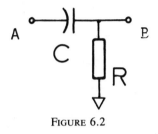

FIGURE 6.2

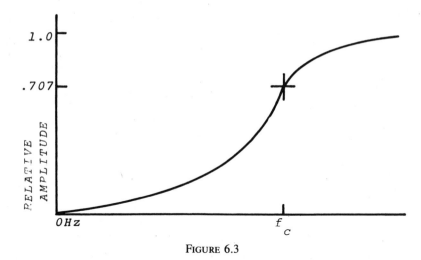

FIGURE 6.3

In general, inductors have been supplanted in modern frequency-selective circuits by less expensive active components. However, many passive inductor/capacitor filter sets such as the Allison Model 2ABR are still in service in many studios.

In general, inductors have been supplanted in modern frequency-selective circuits by less expensive active components. However, many passive *inductor/capacitor filter* sets such as the Allison Model 2ABR are still in service in many studios.

A frequency-sensitive attenuator is shown in figure 6.2. At low frequencies, the reactance of the capacitor is high with respect to the value of the resistor, causing a great amplitude reduction from *A* to *B*. As the frequency of the signal applied to *A* increases, the reactance of the capacitor decreases, and the voltage division ratio between *A* and *B* diminishes.

Figure 6.3 diagrams the amplitude-versus-frequency characteristics of the circuit in figure 6.2. However, the response of a filter is usually graphed logarithmically, as in figure 6.4. Because this filter passes more of a signal as the frequency of the signal increases, this filter is called a *high-pass* filter. By convention, the frequency at which the filter characteristic reduces the signal amplitude to 0.707 of maximum value is called the *cutoff frequency,* or *break frequency*. The break frequency may be calculated from the expression $f_c = 1/2\pi RC$, where f_c is the break frequency in Hz, *R* is the value of the resistor in ohms, and *C* is the value of the capacitor in farads. Assuming a resistive load on the filter, the power of the signal at the break frequency is proportional to the amplitude of the signal squared, that is, $(0.707)^2 \simeq 1/2$. Consequently, the break frequency is also called the *half-power point*. All frequencies above the cutoff frequency of this filter (figure 6.2) are said to lie within the *passband* of the filter, while those frequencies below the break frequency are said to lie in the *stopband* of the filter.

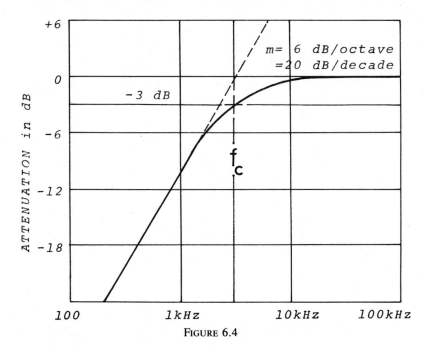

FIGURE 6.4

Below the break frequency, the high-pass filter response (figure 6.4) closely approximates a straight line. In the case of the simple resistor-capacitor (RC) filter, this line has a characteristic slope of 6 dB/octave, or 20 dB/decade. By placing two of these filters in series (with buffering amplifiers between each RC element to prevent loading effects), one obtains a filter with a slope of 12 dB/octave or 40 dB/decade. Connecting three filters in series produces a filter with a slope of 18 dB/octave, or 60 dB/decade, and so on.

By simply reversing the resistor and capacitor (figure 6.5), one obtains the filter characteristic shown in figure 6.6. Notice that the break frequency and slope of this filter are identical with those of the previous example, but in this case, frequencies higher than the break frequency are attenuated. Consequently, this filter is known as a *low-pass* filter. The stopband of the high-pass filter corresponds to the passband of the low-pass filter and vice versa.

By placing the high-pass and low-pass filters in series (with buffering stages between RC elements to prevent loading effects [figure 6.7]) one obtains a filter with a response that is a composite of the two filter characteristics (figure 6.8). Such a filter is called a *band-pass* filter. If the two filters are of differing break frequencies, the passband will exhibit various characteristics, two examples of which are shown in figures 6.9 and 6.10. Usually, these simple filters are provided with input and output amplifiers to effect a high input impedance and a low output impedance. Such a circuit is still referred to as a filter, although it is often called an *active*

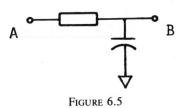

FIGURE 6.5

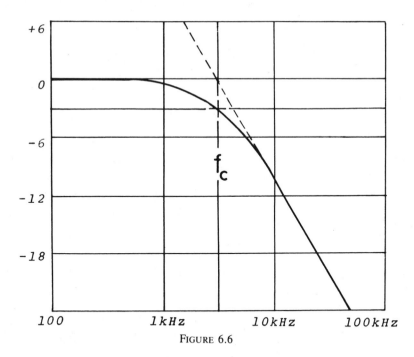

FIGURE 6.6

filter because of the buffer amplifiers. A more complex active filter will be discussed later in this chapter.

The filter symbols shown in figure 6.11 are used throughout this book. Figures 6.11c and 6.11d show two notations for the band-pass filter. In general, the first symbol implies two separate filters, in which case the high and low frequency cutoff points may be varied independently. The second notation implies a band-pass filter with a fixed passband characteristic, although the center frequency of the passband may be variable.

If a high-pass filter and a low-pass filter are connected in parallel, one may obtain a wide variety of response characteristics by varying the two break frequencies. If two separate filters are used, a mixer must be employed to avoid mutual loading effects (figure 6.11e). Figure 6.12 shows some filter characteristics produced by the arrangement of figure 6.11e. Curves 6.12c and 6.12d are characteristic of a *band-stop*, or *band-reject*, filter, so called because frequencies between its two break points are attenuated. Figures 6.11e and 6.11f show symbols for the band-reject filter.

Connecting an inductor and a capacitor in series (figure 6.13a) or parallel (figure 6.13b) produces a resonant circuit. Referring to the reactance chart (figure 6.1), one notices that with the capacitor and inductor in series, circuit impedance decreases with increasing frequency, until at the resonant frequency the impedance of the capacitor equals that of the inductor. As the frequency continues to rise, the impedance of the coil becomes dominant, and the impedance increases. With the capacitor and inductor in

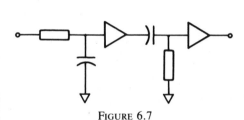

FIGURE 6.7

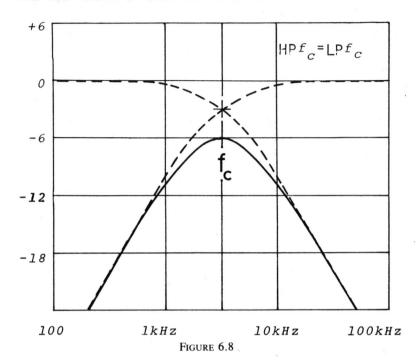

FIGURE 6.8

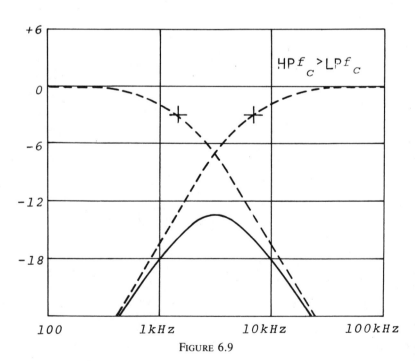

FIGURE 6.9

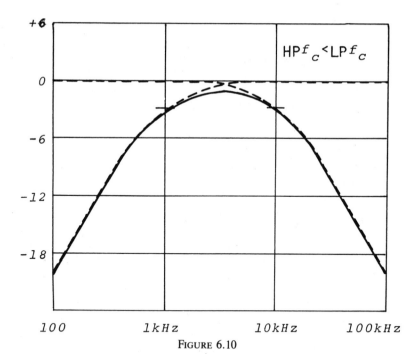

FIGURE 6.10

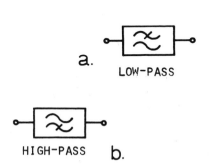

a. LOW-PASS

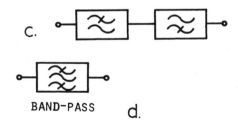

HIGH-PASS b.

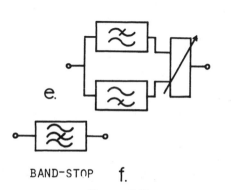

c.

BAND-PASS d.

e.

BAND-STOP f.

FIGURE 6.11

parallel, the resonant frequency is not the frequency at which the impedance is lowest, but rather that at which circuit impedance is maximum. In either case, the resonant frequency is $f = 2\pi\sqrt{LC}$. Resonant circuits may be used to construct versions of the band-pass and band-reject filters called *peak* filters and *notch* filters, respectively.

Figure 6.14a shows an amplifier with a resonant circuit connected in the positive feedback loop, with a control to limit the amount of feedback. The response of this circuit for various amounts of feedback is shown in figure 6.14b. Notice that the greater the amount of feedback, the greater the gain at the resonant frequency. If the gain of the amplifier is great enough to overcome the power loss of the inductor-capacitor (*LC*) network, the circuit will oscillate at the resonant frequency of the filter. If the feedback is decreased just below the point at which the circuit oscillates and a narrow-width pulse is fed to the amplifier, the circuit will *ring*; that is, energy from the pulse will cause the circuit to oscillate at the resonant frequency. However, because the amplifier's gain is not sufficient to supply the energy required to maintain oscillation, the oscillations will decay as energy is dissipated into the *LC* network. The greater the amount of feedback, the longer the time required for the oscillations to be damped out (figure 6.15).

The greater the energy of the input pulse, the greater will be the

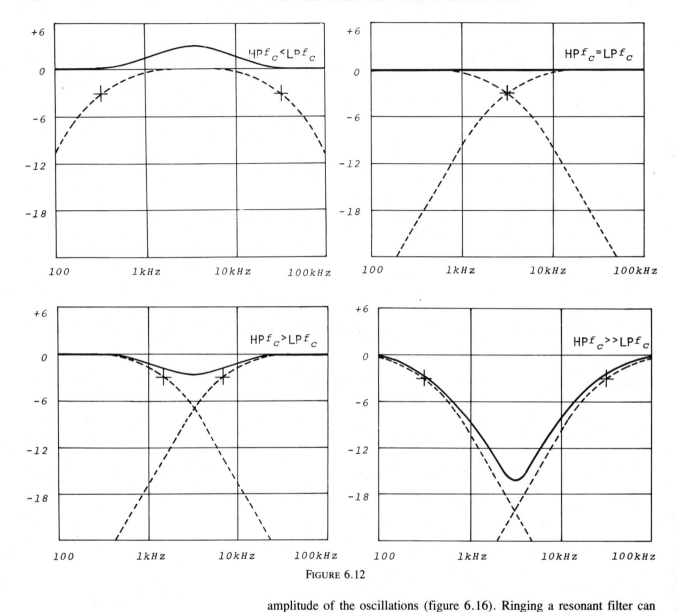

FIGURE 6.12

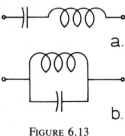

FIGURE 6.13

amplitude of the oscillations (figure 6.16). Ringing a resonant filter can produce a variety of percussive sounds, since the response of many filters is that of a natural acoustic resonator. For example, ringing a filter (cutoff frequency ≃ 150 Hz) produces a sound similar to that of a marimba in the low register.

This principle is used in electronic rhythmic percussion devices to produce the sounds of wood blocks, bongos, floor and ride toms, claves, and so on.† However, since inductors used in audio-frequency resonant circuits

†Several types of percussion synthesizers employing resonant filters are currently available.[1]

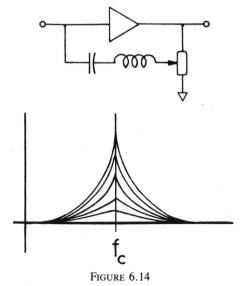

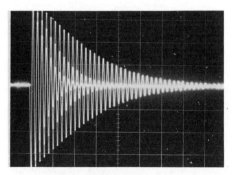

$$f_c$$

FIGURE 6.14

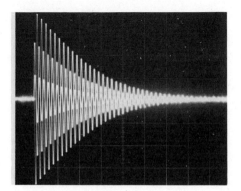

FIGURE 6.15

FIGURE 6.16

are relatively expensive, an RC network known as the *Twin-T* can be used to produce a resonant circuit. Figure 6.17 shows a typical circuit for a percussive tone generator using a Twin-T filter (the filter is enclosed within the dashed line).

The Twin-T configuration is a type of band-stop filter. However, by placing this filter in a negative, rather than a positive, feedback loop (figure 6.17), those frequencies in the stopband do not reduce the gain of the amplifier to so great a degree as the frequencies passed by the filter, resulting in a bandpass filter response.

Certain filters may be modified to produce a resonant filter. Figure 6.18a shows a method for resonating a filter by means of a variable resistor that couples the output of the filter to the input of the filter. Figure 6.18b shows another method for resonating a filter using a mixer. In some cases, the fed-back signal must be inverted to bring the combined signals into the proper phase relationship.

Figure 6.19 is an amplitude-versus-frequency display produced by sweeping a VCO with a sawtooth wave through the passband of a low-pass filter. The output of the filter is connected to the *y*-axis input of the oscilloscope, and the control signal that sweeps the VCO is connected to the *x*-axis input of the oscilloscope. Because the VCO in this case has an exponential control-voltage-versus-frequency characteristic, the frequency display in figure 6.19 is logarithmic. In figure 6.20, the filter has been resonated, producing a peaked response. The filter adjustments used for figure 6.20 were changed from those of figure 6.19; thus, the resonant peak in figure 6.20 does not occur at the point which corresponds to the -3 dB point in figure 6.19.)

Some filters provide a control called *regeneration, Q,* or *resonance,* for resonating the filter. Q is defined for a band-pass filter as the ratio of the center frequency of the filter to its -3 dB bandwidth. For example, a peak filter with a center frequency of 1000 Hz, and 1/2-power points of 500 Hz and 1500 Hz has a Q of $1000 \div (1500 - 500) = 1$. A peak filter with a center frequency of 1000 Hz and 1/2-power points of 100 5Hz and 995 Hz has a Q of $1000 \div (1005 - 995) = 100$.

Figure 6.21 shows the amplitude-versus-frequency response of a high-Q band-pass filter. (This display was produced by the same technique used to generate figure 6.19.) Passing white noise through this filter results in a signal of random amplitude (figure 6.22b), but well-defined pitch (see spectrum, figure 6.22a). Figure 6.23 shows the responses of two band-pass filters. The selectivity (Q) of filter A is less than that of filter B.

An important filter specification is *insertion loss,* which is defined as the ratio of signal level input to signal level output for signal frequencies within the filter's passband. Commercially available filters typically exhibit 0 dB insertion loss, that is, signal input and output levels are identical within the passband of the filter. If such a filter is resonated, the filter will exhibit gain at the resonant frequency. For example, if a band-pass filter with a Q of 1 and 0 dB insertion loss at the center frequency is supplied

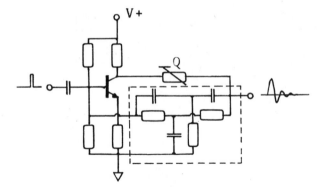

FIGURE 6.17

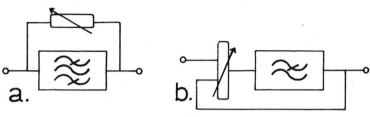

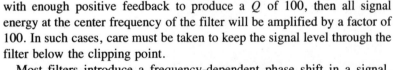

FIGURE 6.18

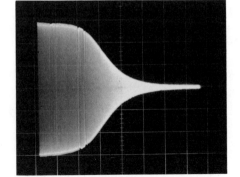

FIGURE 6.19

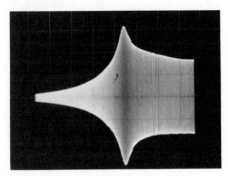

FIGURE 6.20

with enough positive feedback to produce a Q of 100, then all signal energy at the center frequency of the filter will be amplified by a factor of 100. In such cases, care must be taken to keep the signal level through the filter below the clipping point.

Most filters introduce a frequency-dependent phase shift in a signal. Figure 6.24, for example, graphs normalized signal frequency versus the phase of the filter output signal (with reference to the phase of the signal entering the filter) for a simple RC filter. Notice that at the break frequency, the filter introduces a 45° phase shift in the passed signal. In the high-pass configuration (figure 6.24), the output signal leads the input signal by 45°, while in the lowpass configuration (figure 6.24), the output signal lags the input signal by 45°.

Since these phase shifts are additive, placing four RC low-pass filters in series with suitable buffering to minimize loading effects produces a filter with an attenuation slope of 24 dB/octave. Attenuation at the break frequency, f_c, is 12 dB, and the phase shift at this point is $-180°$ (4 · [$-45°$]). Figure 6.25 shows the characteristics of a high-pass filter and low-pass filter connected in parallel to form a band-stop filter. In this case, each filter consists of four series RC elements like those described above. The low-pass break frequency is set to approximately twice the filter center frequency, while the high-pass filter break frequency is adjusted to approximately one-half the center frequency. With the filter adjusted in this man-

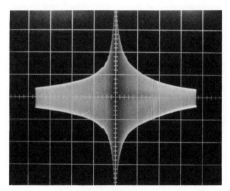

FIGURE 6.21

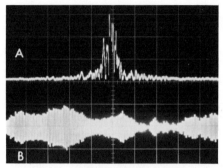

FIGURE 6.22

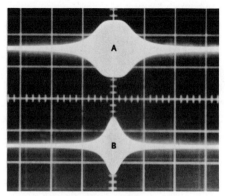

FIGURE 6.23

ner, signals from the two filter elements are 180° (−90°, +90°) out of phase at the center frequency. Thus, signals of this frequency exactly cancel, resulting in a deep notch characteristic at the center frequency. Such filters are useful not only for rejecting undesired signals (for example, power-line hum), but also for producing effects to be discussed later in this chapter.

By altering the spectral characteristics of a signal, filters provide the composer a powerful means for timbral control. The *filter bank* consists of a number of fixed-frequency (usually band-pass) filters, all fed from a common input. The outputs from each of the filters are combined in an internal mixer, and in some cases, the output of each filter is individually accessible (figure 6.26). Filter banks are often referred to as formant filters.†

By mixing the filter outputs of a filter bank in various proportions, one may selectively alter the spectrum of a signal. Figure 6.27 shows a possible response for a formant filter that consists of peak filters spaced at octave intervals. In this diagram, the overall frequency response of the filter is indicated by the dashed line, while the contribution of each peak filter is shown by the solid line. Passing a 100-Hz square wave (spectrum, figure 6.28a) through this filter distorts the spectrum of the square wave (figure

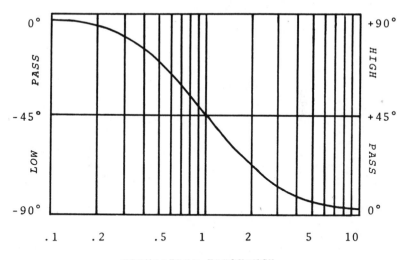

NORMALIZED FREQUENCY

FIGURE 6.24

Normalized frequency

†The term *formant* refers to the resonant frequency bands produced by a mechanical sound generator. At one time, these frequency regions were thought to define the timbre of a sound. However, it is now believed that these resonances contribute to, but do not completely define, the distinctiveness of a sound.

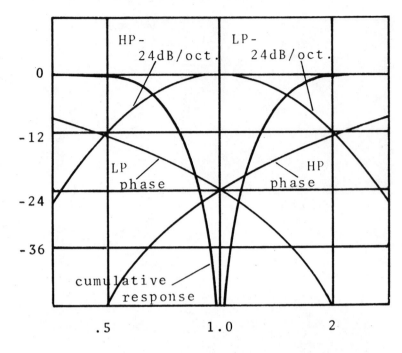

NORMALIZED FREQUENCY
FIGURE 6.25
Normalized frequency

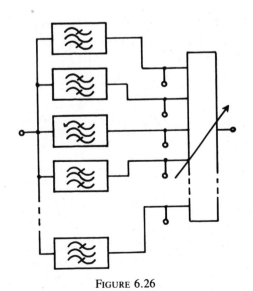

FIGURE 6.26

6.28b), producing a concomitant timbral change. Figure 6.29 shows an amplitude-versus-frequency display produced by sweeping a VCO through a Moog 907 fixed filter bank on which all filter output controls were set to maximum. In figure 6.30, all controls except those affecting the high and low extremes of the filter range have been set to minimum, producing a wide stopband characteristic. (Note that the horizontal and vertical scales of figures 6.29 and 6.30 are not the same.) Mixing of filter outputs should not always be associated with the filter bank configuration shown in figure 6.26. A large degree of timbral interest can be achieved by the mixing of several different types of filters.

A filter bank with a large number of elements, for example, one every 1/2 or 1/3 octave throughout the audio range, permits subtle timbral control of sound events. Many commercial sound systems utilize such filter banks to compensate for uneven response, both in the sound system itself and in the environment in which the system must operate. Such filter banks are known as *graphic equalizers*.

Typical graphic equalizers incorporate 24 of more 1/3-octave band-pass filters covering the audio range. Each filter is carefully designed so that with all filter controls at their median position, the overall response of the

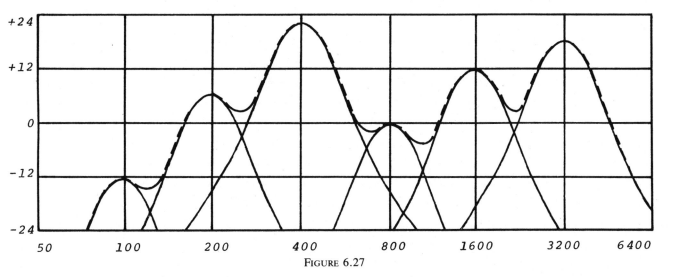

FIGURE 6.27

unit is flat, exhibiting 0 dB insertion loss over the entire audio range. The settings of the controls provide a visual display of the overall filter response, enabling the composer to "draw" a desired frequency response characteristic—hence the term *graphic equalizer*. (See the chapter-opening photograph of the Albis filter).

Graphic equalizers are often used (1) in the treatment of the studio monitoring environment (with the equalizers permanently connected before the power amplifiers); (2) in making adjustments for concert performances of electronic pieces; and (3) in general production work as a means of timbral control.

Some graphic equalizers permit a boost or attenuation (peak or dip) with each of the filter sections, while others provide only peak or only dip response. For general production work, a peak-and-dip-type equalizer such as the UREI Model 527–A 1/3-octave equalizer is recommended, while the UREI Model 529 (band-reject type) is recommended for equalization applications. John Eargle made the following observations about equalizers:

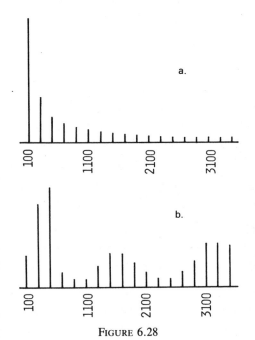

FIGURE 6.28

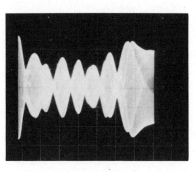

FIGURE 6.29

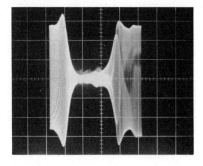

FIGURE 6.30

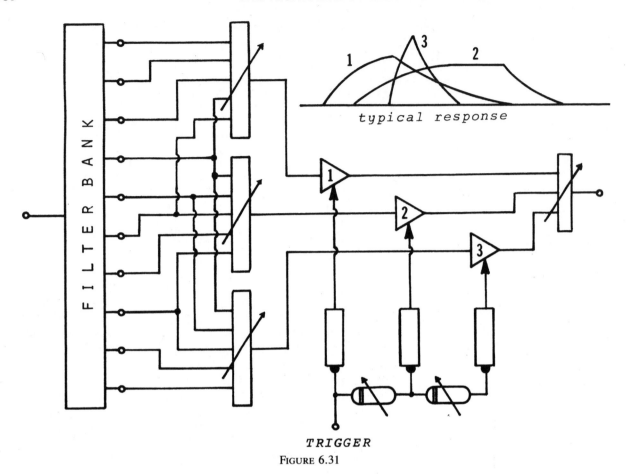

TRIGGER

FIGURE 6.31

An equalizer is a device which alters the frequency response of a recording or monitoring channel. It is easy to lose sight of the original meaning and application of the term: the first equalizers were used in telephony and were for the purpose of making the output of a transmission line equal to the input. . . . The term equalizer has been applied over the years to devices both fixed and variable which provide variations in frequency response.[2]

A filter bank that provides access to each filter output is highly desirable. Figure 6.31 shows a patching in which an input signal is broken down into spectral segments by means of the elements in the filter banks. Several frequency bands are then combined in each mixer, and each combination is given a separate envelope. The individual events are then combined to produce a sound the power spectrum of which has been modified to vary through time.

The *vocoder* is a device which was designed to improve the efficiency of voice transmission by reducing the bandwidth necessary to retain intelligibility.[3] The design of the instrument was suggested by research that demonstrated that the envelope of the power spectrum of speech, rather than the absolute frequencies themselves, conveyed information to the listener. Basically, a vocoder consists of a number of fixed-frequency bandpass filters, for example, 27 third-octave filters distributed throughout the audio frequency range. The filters share a common input, and the output of each filter is connected to its own envelope detector (see chapter 7, page 190) which provides a control voltage proportional to the amount of energy passing through the filter to which the detector is connected.

The remaining section of the vocoder consists of a set of bandpass filters identical to those just described. These filters share a common input, and the output of each filter is connected to its own voltage-controlled amplifier, the program (audio signal) outputs of which are summed together. The second part of the vocoder is thus a format filter with the capability of scaling the amplitude of the program output of the individual filter sections by voltage control. The filter/detectors in section one of the vocoder provide control signals that can control the amplitude of the program coming from the filters in section two of the instrument.

For example, assume that white noise is used as program material for section two of the instrument (filter/VCA section), and the output of a microphone is connected to the input of section one (filter/detector section). The control voltage output from each filter/detector is connected to the control voltage input of the filter/VCA of corresponding passband frequency. Speaking into the microphone causes each filter/detector to produce a control signal proportional to the amount of energy in the speech program that occurs within the passband of the filters. Each control voltage causes an increase in gain of the VCA to which it is connected, permitting filtered white noise to pass to the output. The output of the summer to which all the filter/VCAs are connected will thus consist of filtered white noise having the characteristics of the speech inputed to the first section of the instrument. The outputs of the filter/detectors may, of course, be connected to the filter/VCA control inputs in other arrangements to provide a wide range of timbral control possibilities. Alvin Lucier used a Sylvania Electronic Systems vocoder in his *North American Time Capsule 1967* (Odyssey 32160156). At this writing, commercially manufactured vocoders are available from the E.M.S. Company and Sennheiser.

If a composer has access to only one small filter bank in a studio, he may tire of the sameness of the (fixed) ''pitch areas'' emphasized by the filter in processed program material. *Parametric* equalizers provide the usual boost and cut (peak and dip) in addition to control of center frequency and bandwidth. The sameness of fixed pitch areas of a filter bank/equalizer is less of a problem with filter banks that contain a large number of sections. On the other hand, it is difficult using two hands to control, for instance, a 36-element filter bank over a fairly short time interval to produce a complex sound by filtering using such a device.

Figure 6.32 shows the Krohn-Hite Model 3550 tunable multi-function

FIGURE 6.32

filter. This instrument consists of independent high-pass and low-pass tunable filters that may be switched into one of four configurations: *low-pass, high-pass, band-pass* (filter elements in series), and *band-reject* (filter elements in parallel). The break frequency of each filter is tunable over a one-decade frequency range. Each filter section has a five-position switch to control the factor by which the dial indication is multiplied. Thus, the break frequency may be tuned from 2 Hz to 200 kHz in five ranges: 2 Hz to 20 Hz; 20 Hz to 200 Hz; 200 Hz to 2 kHz; 2 kHz to 20 kHz; and 20 kHz to 200 kHz. Each filter element exhibits an insertion loss of 0 dB within its passband, while providing a roll-off rate of 24 dB/octave. Although voltage-controlled filters (VCFs) designed specifically for electronic music production are available, a laboratory-grade filter such as the Krohn-Hite Model 3550 is a useful addition to the filter complement of the studio.

In previous chapters we discussed some differences between natural sounds and (most) electronically generated sounds. In chapter 5 we described some techniques by which a composer may generate complex sounds, the components of which can be made to vary dynamically. In the 1950s and early 1960s several articles were published that suggested modulating electronic sounds with random functions in order to simulate what were thought to be analogous random conditions in the behavior of natural sounds.

The ear is accustomed to dealing with sounds of a complex nature. Naturally occurring sounds are accompanied by a reverberation envelope that is unique to each acoustical environment, as well as to the position of the listener in that environment. As we have mentioned, the listener can often determine information from a sound regarding the sound source's distance and angular location. Reproducing a sound in a room will give a sound a reverberation envelope, which will, to a certain extent, add to a sound's complexity. However, room acoustics are steady-state, in the sense that at any given point within a room a specific set of phase cancellations and summations exists, so that the room behaves as a fixed, although highly complex, filter. Consequently, as a sound reverberates in a room, its quality is altered, but altered in a consistent manner that the ear will quickly learn to recognize. In one respect this effect attests to the ability of the ear to process and recognize patterns so complex as to be statistical in nature. The composer, on the other hand, is faced with the task of producing sounds that will interest the demanding ear. The problem is not to imitate nature, but rather, in the words of John Cage, "to imitate nature in her manner of operation."

Electronic modification of natural sounds can result in sound events that possess the qualities of electronically generated sounds, while retaining the complex, non-steady-state characteristics of the original natural sound. In this regard, many composers choose to employ *both* electronically generated and electronically modified natural sounds in their works. In addition, the use of electronically modified natural sounds in real-time-produced electronic music provides the composer access to a wide range of sounds, and mitigates many of the technical difficulties inherent in real-time performance of purely electronically generated works.

According to Winckel, the hearing process seems to involve successive integrations over the frequency spectrum of the sound present to the ear.[4] This integration is analogous to determining the envelope of a line spectrum of the sound in question. For example, an unmodified sawtooth wave would present a fixed spectrum at each sampling, and since no new information is presented to the ear upon successive samplings, the steady-state condition is quickly recognized. Thus, if it is desired to maintain a flow of information to the ear, the frequency components of a sound must be varied from sampling to sampling (although, in a contextual sense, no new information can constitute meaning).

Figure 6.33a shows the amplitude-versus-time characteristics of the first five harmonic components of a violin tone during the first 100 milliseconds following the initiation of the tone. Figure 6.33b shows a similar diagram for a trumpet tone. Note that each harmonic reaches a relatively steady value only after the first 50 milliseconds or so. This onset behavior is unique to each type of instrument. It is thought that the transient behavior

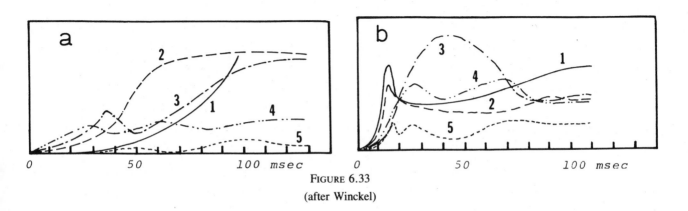

FIGURE 6.33
(after Winckel)

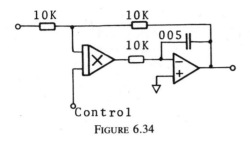

FIGURE 6.34

of frequency components at the initiation of the tone is a factor that largely determines the distinctive qualities of sounds.

It is difficult to produce sound events comparable in complexity with those shown in figure 6.33 by using the filter complement found in most electronic music studios; it is possible, however, to disrupt the steady-state qualities of certain electronically generated sounds by, for example, tuning several notch filters through the spectrum of the sound. Comb filters and other devices are useful for such applications and will be discussed later in this chapter.

Filters provide the composer with an important means for "finishing" sounds. In this regard, mixing consoles usually have filtering (equalization) capabilities for each input channel. These filters, usually peak and dip filters, one each for the high-band, mid-band, and low-band frequencies (see chapter 4), are used both during recording and mixdown.

Application notes published by various manufacturers contain much data concerning the design of fixed frequency active filters. (National Semiconductor application notes for the LM3900 integrated circuit and the Krohn-Hite Corporation catalog are particularly recommended.)

Figure 6.34 shows a circuit of a simple voltage-controlled low-pass filter.[5] The multiplier in the feedback loop varies the time constant of the filter, allowing voltage control of f_c over a decade or more. Several other VCF circuits have been described in the literature (see the selected bibliography at the end of this chapter). For a discussion of design principles of VCFs for electronic music applications, see R. A. Moog, "Voltage-Controlled Electronic Music Modules,"[6] and Dennis P. Colin, "Electrical Design and Musical Applications of an Unconditionally Stable Combination Voltage Controlled Filter/Resonator."[7]

The circuit shown in figure 6.35 is known as a *state variable filter*. This filter may be tuned over a decade or more by varying R_f, and the Q of the filter may be adjusted to $>>1$ by varying R_q. This filter provides simul-

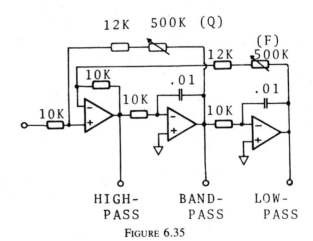

FIGURE 6.35

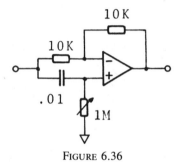

FIGURE 6.36

taneous high-pass, low-pass, and band-pass outputs. By connecting a linear taper pot between the high-pass and low-pass outputs, a notch output may be obtained. The notch frequency may be tuned above or below the center frequency of the filter by changing the setting of this control. This circuit provides an attenuation slope of 12 dB/octave for the low-pass and high-pass outputs, and a 6 dB/octave characteristic for the band-pass output.

Several companies sell state variable filters that feature voltage control of the filter center frequency over a wide range, as well as voltage control of the filter Q over a range from approximately 1/2 to over 500.

In patchings that employ voltage-controlled filtering, envelope shaping is usually accomplished by a VCA/envelope generator following the filter. If a filter is used as the only program gate in a patching, unwanted residual program material may appear after gating, due to the presence of frequency components in the program which lie outside the passband of the filter. For example, consider a voltage-controlled filter through which pink noise is passed. The break frequency of the filter is controlled by an envelope generator. The fixed control voltage of the VCF is adjusted to minimum, yet low frequencies present in the pink noise continue to be heard. In addition, lowering the fixed control voltage to its minimum value decreases the point to which the break frequency will rise when the VCF control input is driven by the envelope generator. By using the VCA/envelope generator following the filter, the remanent low frequency components may be blocked when the VCA receives no control voltage.

In addition, many sounds whose timbral qualities are to be altered may already possess a desired envelope. In this case, an envelope follower may be used to provide a reasonably accurate replica of the desired envelope, and this control signal may be used to drive a VCA following the filter.

The inherent noise level of some VCFs is high, and low-level inputs cannot be processed if a satisfactory signal-to-noise ratio is to be maintained. This problem can be diminished by envelope shaping after filtering as described above, taking advantage of the masking of the noise when a program is present. In certain cases, noise reduction instruments such as the dBX 150 series or the less-effective Phase Linear 1000 may be used to reduce noise contributed by a VCF.

Figure 6.36 shows a circuit that introduces a frequency-dependent phase shift in a signal while introducing no insertion loss. Replacing the variable resistor with a photoresistor or field effect transistor (FET) permits voltage control of the phase shift introduced by the circuit. Most voltage-controlled phase shifting devices are intended only to produce flanging effects (see below), and are not suitable for producing accurate phase shifts over a wide frequency range.† Commercially available phase-shifting devices employ

†Networks designed to produce a constant phase shift over a wide frequency range employ two or more phase-shifting networks, designed so that the phase shift between the networks is constant.

several elements like that shown in figure 6.37, with the frequencies of effect of these elements staggered.

Figure 6.37 shows a typical application of the circuit of figure 6.36 in a phase shifter. In this circuit, the phase-shift networks are tuned in octaves. The output of the networks is summed with the original signal in amplifier 2. As in this circuit, many commercially produced phase shifters intended for musical instrument modification include a low-frequency control oscillator as part of the design.

If a periodic signal is delayed by an interval t, the phase angle between the delayed and undelayed signals is $\phi = 2\pi ft$, where ϕ is the phase angle, f is the frequency of the signals, and t is the delay interval in seconds. If $\phi/180°$ is an odd integer, and both signals are of equal amplitude, the addition of the original and delayed signals produces a cancellation.

If the two signals are of equal amplitude A, and in phase ($\phi/180°$ is an even integer), the addition of the original and delayed signals results in a signal of amplitude $2A$. In general, the amplitude of the summed signals is equal to $(2 \cdot \cos \pi ft)A$.

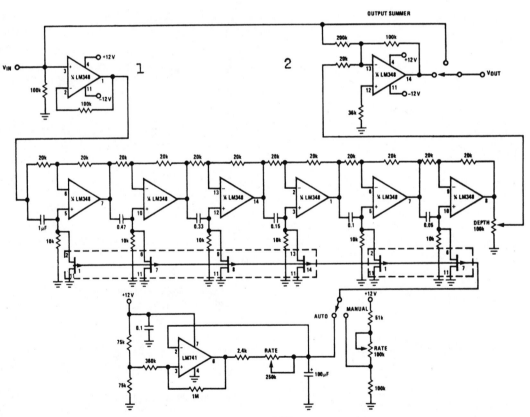

FIGURE 6.37

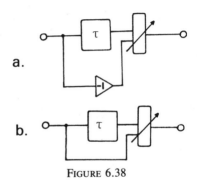

FIGURE 6.38

The result of this phase shifting (and subsequent mixing of the delayed and original signal) of a complex signal is a series of cancellations similar to that produced by a comb filter or a number of notch filters connected in series. The frequencies at which cancellation occurs may be varied by altering the time delay. The effect that results when the frequencies at which cancellation occurs are varied through time is called *phasing,* or *flanging.*

A delay may be introduced in a signal by playing two tapes with identical program material on two tape reproducers and varying the speed of one recorder so that it leads or lags the other machine. (The change of capstan motor speed should be accomplished using a power oscillator, although some composers prefer to use their hands to brake the reel flange or pinch roller, a technique the author does not recommend.) The outputs of the tape reproducers should be mixed down to one channel, and the output levels should be adjusted to be nearly equal. Flanging effects may also be produced by using disc reproducers in a similar manner (an effect often used by disc jockeys). Two microphones (mixed down to one channel) may be used to produce phasing effects by moving the microphones relative to the sound source until the desired effect (caused by sound waves reaching the microphones at different times) is achieved.

Analog and digital delay lines find many applications in electronic music production. Their use has recently become affordable for most electronic music studios. Typical applications of delay lines include simulation and enhancement of reverberation,[8] flanging, spatial positioning,[9] and filtering.

Several filter configurations can be implemented using delay lines.

Figure 6.38a shows a delay line, the output of which is summed with the inverted undelayed signal to produce the comb filter response to a swept sine wave shown in figure 6.39a (patching 10, page 167 shows the swept

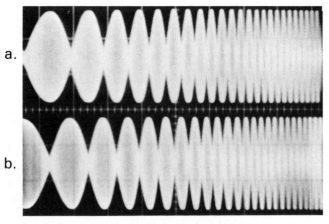

FIGURE 6.39

sine wave and oscilloscope configuration—minus the diode—used to produce this figure). The frequencies (F) of nulls in the response of this filter are integer multiples of $F = 1/$delay time. In figure 6.39a, the first null is not at the origin, but between the first two crests of the filter response.

Figure 6.38b shows a delay line, the output of which is summed with the undelayed signal (noninverted) to produce the comb filter response to a swept sine wave (figure 6.39b). The frequencies of nulls in the response of this filter are odd integer multiples of $F = 1/2 \cdot$ delay time. Thus, if a composer wanted two comb filter responses, one with nulls at, say, 1,000, 2,000, 3,000, 4,000, 5,000 Hz and so on, he would choose the configuration of figure 6.38a and set the delay time to 0.001 second, or 1 millisecond. If nulls at 1,000, 3,000, 5,000, 7,000, 9,000 Hz, and so on, are desired, he would choose the configuration of figure 6.38b and set the delay time to half the value of the delay used in the first case, that is, 0.001 second/2, or 0.5 millisecond.

In the case of the configuration of figure 6.38a with a sine-wave input, the delayed sine wave may be represented as $\sin(\omega t + \omega T)$, where T is the delay time and the inverted nondelayed sine wave is $-\sin t$. Using the trigonometric identity for the difference of two sines,

$$\sin x - \sin y = 2 \sin\left(\frac{x-y}{2}\right) \cos\left(\frac{x+y}{2}\right)$$

we substitute $(\omega t + \omega T)$ for x, and ωt for y to obtain:

$$\sin(\omega t - \omega T) - \sin(\omega t) = 2 \sin\left(\frac{\omega T}{2}\right) \cos\left(\omega t + \frac{\omega T}{2}\right).$$

The term $\sin \omega T/2$ is responsible for the amplitude of the expression, and when $\omega = 2n\pi/T$ (where n is any integer), the value of $\sin \omega T/2$ is zero. (Recall that the value of the sine function is zero at π radians (180 degrees), 2π radians (360 degrees), 3π radians (540 degrees), and so on.) Thus, null frequencies for configuration 6.38a occur at integer multiples of $1/$delay time. In the case of the configuration of figure 6.38b with a sine-wave input, using the trigonometric identity for the addition of two sines,

$$\sin x + \sin y = 2 \cos\left(\frac{x-y}{2}\right) \sin\left(\frac{x-y}{2}\right),$$

we substitute $(\omega t + \omega T)$ for x, and ωt for y to obtain:

$$\sin(\omega t + \omega T) + \sin \omega t = 2 \cos\frac{\omega T}{2} \cos \omega t + \frac{\omega T}{2}.$$

The term $\cos T/2$ is responsible for the amplitude of the expression, and when $\omega = (2n - 1)\pi/T$ (where n is any integer and $(2n - 1)$ is, therefore, any odd integer), the value of cos $\omega T/2$ is zero. (Remember that the value of the cosine function is zero at $\pi/4$ radians [90 degrees] $3\pi/4$ radians [270 degrees], $5\pi/4$ radians [450 degrees], and so on.) The null frequencies for configuration 6.38b occur at odd integer multiples of $1/2$·delay time.

The integer-related frequencies at which the nulls occur in the comb filter may be voltage controlled. As noted above, the effect resulting from the changing of the null frequencies through time is called phasing, or flanging. Voltage control of comb filters used in flanging instruments is usually accomplished using slow periodic control signals, foot-operated potentiomenters, or, more rarely, envelope generators. The effect associated with the term *flanging* is limited to certain rates of change, whereas the use of comb filters in electronic music extends beyond flanging applications—from making subtle timbral changes to producing complex phase and amplitude modulation of program material.

Time delay devices may be used to produce comb filters (recursive filters), that have sharp resonant peaks, rather than nulls, as in the examples described above. For this response, the output of the delay device is fed back to its input using an input summer (mixer). The signal to be filtered is applied to another input of the mixer.

In general, filters provide the composer with an effective method for altering the spectral characteristics of sound events through time, as well as the direct generation of sound events (resonant filter synthesis). The use of VCFs in simple gating operations involving oscillator waveforms is a device that has well fertilized the repertory of electronic music transcriptions, popular music, electronic organ technology, radio and television logos, and other commercial advertising, creating a type of sound that the layman associates with ''synthesizers'' and ''electronic music.''

PATCHINGS

1. Patching 1 shows a band-pass filter used to process a random signal source (white noise). Figure 6.22, chapter 6 shows a typical spectrum and time function produced by this arrangement. Used as an input signal to a filter, white noise is useful in demonstrating filter operation.

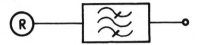

2. Patching 2 shows a sawtooth wave whose frequency components may be selected by using a tunable high-Q band-pass filter.

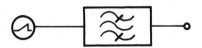

3. Patching 3 shows an amplitude-modulated sine wave processed by a band-pass filter.

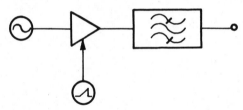

4. In patching 4, a band-pass filter is rung with a pulse from a monostable multivibrator.

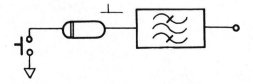

5. In patching 5, the output of a rung band-pass filter is routed to the input of an envelope detector. The detected signal is then used to control the gain of a VCA.

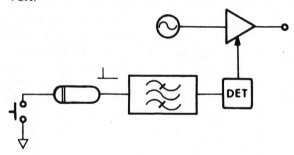

6. In patching 6, two random function generators are low-pass filtered ($f_c = 5$ HZ) to produce two separate low-frequency random signals, one of which is passed through a Schmitt trigger to produce a train of random-width pulses, which are then used to ring a high-Q band-pass filter. The other random signal is used to control the center frequency of the band-pass filter, thereby determining the pitch of the resulting sounds. The Q of the filter (which determines the duration of the sounds) is controlled by the difference of the two random signals. The cutoff frequency of the low-pass filters may be varied to alter the rate of change of pitch as well as the rate of events.

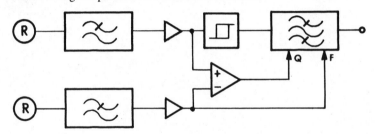

7. Patching 7 shows a panning arrangement using two low-pass filters (see figure 4.30, chapter 4).

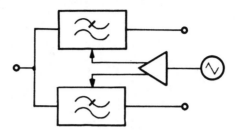

8. Patching 8 shows a high-pass filter, the cutoff frequency of which is controlled by the output of a sine-wave oscillator. If the frequency of the sine-wave oscillator is sufficiently great, sidebands will be produced.

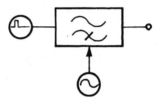

9. Patching 9 shows a spectrum analyzer that uses a high-Q band-pass filter, the center frequency of which is swept over a given frequency range by a low-frequency sawtooth wave. The internal horizontal sweep of the oscilloscope is disabled, and the sawtooth signal from the oscillator is used for the horizontal sweep. The output of the band-pass filter is half-wave rectified (to produce a display more like those shown throughout this book, that is, ___ rather than __◇__) and connected to the vertical input of the oscilloscope. If the control-voltage-versus-frequency response of the band-pass filter is exponential (for example, one volt per octave), the resulting display will be a plot of amplitude (y=axis) versus the logarithm of frequency (x=axis).

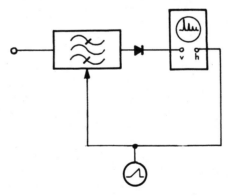

10. Patching 10 shows a configuration that may be used to display the amplitude-versus-frequency characteristics of a band-pass filter. The input signal to the filter is a sine wave, the frequency of which is swept through the passband of

the filter by a low-frequency sawtooth wave. (It may be necessary to amplify the signal from the sawtooth oscillator to the control input of the VCO in order to obtain sufficient frequency deviation.) As in patching 9, the sawtooth oscillator is also used to provide a horizontal sweep for the oscilloscope.

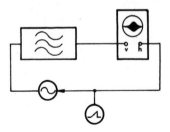

11. Patching 11 shows a configuration of three band-reject filters connected in parallel to process a signal. (No specific signal source is indicated.)

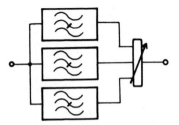

12. Patching 12 shows a configuration similar to that of patching 11. In this configuration, however, the processed signal may be selectively distributed to four signal lines by means of a quad panpot.

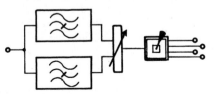

13. Patching 13 shows a rotation mixer used to distribute a signal among four separate band-pass filters.

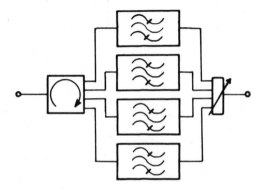

14. Patching 14 shows four notch filters connected in series to produce a *flanging* or *phasing* effect. If voltage-controlled filters are employed, their control inputs may be connected in parallel to simplify simultaneous control of the filters.

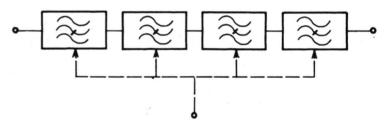

15. Patching 15 shows a group of patchings which may be used for live electronic modification of natural sounds.

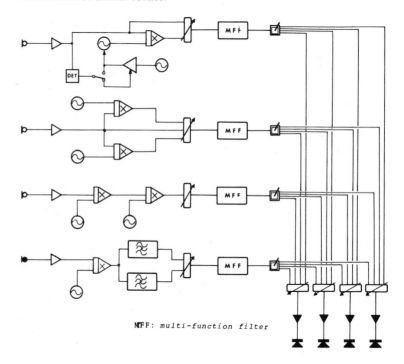

MFF: *multi-function filter*

PROBLEMS

1. With an adjustable filter such as the Krohn-Hite Model 3550 multifunction filter, to what point on the filter's response curve does the scale setting on the filter refer?

2. A band-pass filter can be produced by connecting a high-pass filter and a low-pass filter in what configuration? How may a band-reject filter be derived from a high-pass filter and a low-pass filter?

3. Describe the stop band of the following filters: high-pass, low-pass, band-pass, band-reject.

4. What is the Q of a filter? What effect does increasing the Q of the filter in example 1 have on the resulting sound?

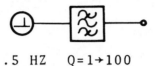

.5 HZ   Q=1→100

5. Generate approximately the following loudness-versus-time function using a sequencer, filter, and voltage-controlled amplifier (see example 2).

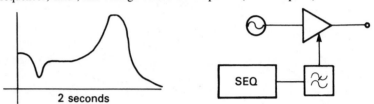

2 seconds

6. Connect the patching shown in example 3 and vary the cutoff point of the filter over the range indicated. Explain the changes in the modulated signal that result from changing the filter setting.

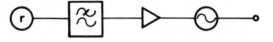

5Hz→50Hz   ca. 1kHz

7. What is *ringing?* How does one ring a filter?

8. How was the sound (purely electronically generated—not the electronically modified ethnic music sounds that also occur in this section) in Stockhausen's *Telemusik*, at about 117 seconds from the beginning of the work, produced? Speculate, or look up, the patching in the realization score (UE 14807).

8. Duplicate the section in Stockhausen's *Kontakte* from 17 feet, 0.5 inch to 17 feet, 38.5 inches using the realization score (UE 13678; see chapter 11).

9. How may filters be employed to produce a flanging effect?

10. Describe how the patching in example 4 enables variable filter cutoff frequency operation using a fixed-frequency filter.

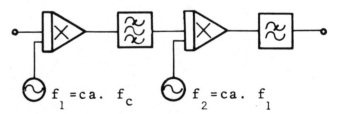

f_1 =ca. f_c f_2 =ca. f_1

11. Using a tunable multifunction filter (with separate low-pass and high-pass sections), which filter section determines the low cutoff frequency for a band-reject configuration and for a band-pass configuration?

12. Regenerate a low-pass filter, a band-pass filter, a high-pass filter, and a band-reject filter. What effect does introducing regeneration have on the frequency response of these filters? (If the filter oscillates, decrease the regeneration or put an inverter in the feedback line.)

13. Using the patching shown in example 5, demonstrate the frequency-response characteristics of a band-reject filter, a fixed filter bank, a high-pass filter, and so on.

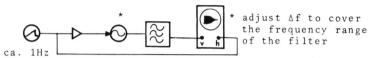

14. Discuss the differences between the spectral modification capabilities of a single VCF (low-pass, high-pass, band-pass, notch) and those of the patching shown in figure 6.30, chapter 6.

NOTES

1. R. W. Burhans, "Simple Bandpass Filters," *Journal of the Audio Engineering Society* 21 (1973): 275–277; H. Haussman and M. C. Y. Kuo, "Variable Filter Characteristics with an Operational Amplifier," *Electronic Engineering,* February 1972.

2. J. Eargle, *Sound Recording* (New York: Van Nostrand-Reinhold, 1976).

3. G. M. Russell, *Modulation and Coding in Information Systems* (Englewood Cliffs, N.J.: Prentice-Hall, 1962).

4. F. Winckel, *Music, Sound, and Sensation,* trans. T. Binkley (New York: Dover, 1967).

5. "Multiplier as a Variable Resistor Voltage-Controlled Active Filter." *Electronic Engineering,* October 1972, p. 27.

6. T. Orr and D. W. Thomas, "Electronic Sound Synthesizer," *Wireless World* 79 (1973): 485–490.

7. D. Colin, "Electrical Design and Musical Applications of an Unconditionally Stable Combination Voltage-Controlled Filter/Resonator," *Journal of the Audio Engineering Society* 19 (1971): 923–927.

8. M. Schroeder, "Natural Sounding Artificial Reverberation," *Journal of the Audio Engineering Society* 10 (1962): 219–223.

9. Lexicon, Inc., "Studio Applications of Time Delay," *Lexicon Applications Note* AN-3 (1976).

SELECTED BIBLIOGRAPHY
Books

Botos, B. *Low Frequency Applications of Field-Effect Transistors.* Motorola Application Note AN–511.

Craig, J. W. *Design of Lossy Filters.* Cambridge, Mass.: MIT Press, 1970.

Eargle, J. *Sound Recording.* New York: Van Nostrand-Reinhold, 1976.

Eimbinder, J. *FET Application Handbook,* 2nd ed. Blue Ridge Summit, Pa.: TAB Books, 1970.

Geffe, P. R. *Simplified Modern Filter Design*. New York: Hayden, 1967.

Burr-Brown Research Corp. *Handbook of Operational Amplifier Active RC Networks*. Tucson, Ariz., 1966.

Haykins, S. *Synthesis of RC Active Filters*. New York: McGraw-Hill, 1966.

Jung, W. *IC Op-Amp Cookbook*. Indianapolis, Ind.: Howard W. Sams, 1976.

Krohn-Hite Corporation. *Catalog, 1970–71*. Cambridge, Mass.

Mitra, S. K., ed. *Active Inductorless Filters*. New York: IEEE Press, 1971.

Russell, G. M. *Modulation and Coding in Information Systems*. Englewood Cliffs, N.J.: Prentice-Hall, 1962.

Winckel, F. *Music, Sound, and Sensation*. Translated by T. Binkley. N.Y.: Dover, 1967.

Articles

"Active Filters with Gain." *Electronic Engineering*, February 1972, p. 56.

Adams, Karl-Heinz. "Filter Circuits for Electronic Sound Production." *Technische Hausmitteilungen des Nortwestdeutschen Rundfunks*, 6 (1954): 18–23. Translated by D. Sinclair, National Research Council of Canada, Technical Translation TT–605 (of historical interest).

Albersheim, W. J., and Shirley, F. R. "Computation Methods for Broad-Band 90° Phase-Difference Networks." *IEEE Transactions on Circuit Theory* CT16, no. 2 (May 1969): 189–196.

Al-Nasser, F. "Tables Shorten Design Time for Active Filters." *Electronics*, 23 October 1973, pp. 113–118.

Ashley, J., and Kaminsky, A. "Active and Passive Filters as Loudspeaker Crossover Networks." *journal of the Audio Engineering Society* 19, no. 6 (June 1971): 494–501.

Ashley, J. R., and Henne, L. M. "Operational Amplifier Implementation of Ideal Electronic Crossover Networks." *Journal of the Audio Engineering Society* 19, no. 7 (1971).

Artusy, M. "Tunable Active Filter Has Controllable High Q." *Electronics*, 31 January 1972, p. 57.

Barbarello, J. "Electronic Percussion Synthesizer." *Popular Electronics*, August 1977.

Brandt, R. "Active Resonators Save Steps in Designing Active Filters." *Electronics*, 24 April 1972, pp. 106–110.

Burhans, R. W. "Simple Band-pass Filters." *Journal of the Audio Engineering Society* 21, no. 4 (May 1973): 275–277.

―――. "Low-Cost Comb Filter Methods." *Journal of the Audio Engineering Society* 22, no. 5 (1974).

Burton, L. T., and Treleaven, D. "Active Filter Design Using Generalized Impedance Converters." *Electronic Design News*, 5 February 1971.

Cate, T. "Voltage Tune Your Band-pass Filters with Multipliers." *Electronic Design News*, 1 March 1971, pp. 45–47.

Colin, D. "Electrical Design and Musical Applications of an Unconditionally Stable Combination Voltage Controlled Filter/Resonator." *Journal of the Audio Engineering Society* 19, no. 11 (November 1971): 923–927.

———. "On the Stability of a Voltage Controlled Filter/Resonator" (Letters to the Editor [J. R. Ashley/Dennis P. Colin]). *Journal of the Audio Engineering Society* 20, no. 4 (May 1972): 304.

Cook, R. E. "Cascaded Active Circuits Yield 90-Degree Phase-Difference Networks." *Electronic Design News,* 9 April 1973.

Crawford, D. "Constructing a Room Equalizer." *Audio,* September 1972, pp. 18–22.

Crowhurst, N. H. "Theory and Practice of Twin Tee Networks." *db,* December 1970.

DeBoo, G. J., and Hedlund, R. C. "Automatically Tuned Filter Uses IC Operational Amplifiers." *Electronic Design News,* 1 February 1972, pp. 38–41.

Dome, R. B. "Wideband Phase Shift Networks." *Electronics,* December 1946, pp. 112–115.

Doyle, N. "360° Video Phase Shifter Uses No Transformers." *Electronic Design,* 15 March 1969.

Ellern, F., and Hazony, D. "Active Notch Filters for Eliminating Noise." *Electronic Engineering,* September 1972.

Erickson, R., ed. "Timbre Seminar Readings." *Synthesis* 1 (1971).

Foster, E. J. "Active Low-Pass Filter Design." *IEEE Transactions on Audio,* AU–13 (1965): 104.

Franco, S. "Hardware Design of a Real-Time Musical System." Urbana, Ill.: University of Illinois, Department of Computer Science, 1974.

Gabrielson, B. "A Patchable Electronic Music Synthesizer." *Journal of the Audio Engineering Society* 25, no. 6 (June 1977): 395–399.

Georgiou, V. J. "Voltage-Tuned Filter Varies Center Frequency Linearly." *Electronics,* 6 November 1972, p. 104.

Haussman, H., and Kuo, M. C. Y. "Variable Filter Characteristics with an Operational Amplifier." *Electronic Engineering,* February 1972.

Ioannides, P. G. "RC Elements Improve Active Filter Performance." *Electronic Engineering,* May 1972, pp. 43–46.

Jones, D. L. "Use of Operational Amplifiers in Narrow-Band Filter Systems for Spectrum Analysis at Audio and Sub-Audio Frequencies." *Electronic Engineering,* January 1969, pp. 97–101.

Lexicon, Inc. "Studio Applications of Time Delay." *Lexicon Applications Note AN–3,* 1976.

Loe, J. M. "FET's Call the Tune in Active Filter Design." *Electronics,* 3 October 1966, pp. 98–101.

Luce, D. "Dynamic Spectrum Changes of Orchestral Instruments." *Journal of the Audio Engineering Society* 23, no. 7 (September 1975): 565–568.

Macario, R. C. V., and Yusuf, T. "High-Q N-Path Filter Using Diode Bridges." *Electronic Engineering,* January 1969, pp. 76–81.

Macken, W. J. "FET's as Variable Resistances in Op Amps and Gyrators." *Electronic Engineering,* December 1972, pp. 60–61.

Maynard, F. B. "Twin-T Oscillators." *Electronics World,* May 1963.

———. "Twin-T Oscillators for Electronic Musical Instruments." *Electronics World,* June 1964.

_____. "Twin-T's." *Electronics World,* August 1968.

Moog, R. A. "Electronic Music: Its Composition and Performance." *Electronics World,* February 1967, pp. 42–46.

_____. "Voltage-Controlled Electronic Music Modules." *Journal of the Audio Engineering Society* 13, no. 3 (July 1965): 200–206.

"Multiplier as a Variable Resistor Voltage-Controlled Active Filter." *Electronic Engineering,* October 1972, p. 27.

Orr, T., and Thomas, D. W. "Electronic Sound Synthesizer." *Wireless World* 79, no. 1455 (September 1973): 429–434.

_____. "Electronic Sound Synthesizer." *Wireless World* 79, no. 1456 (October 1973): 485–490.

Pease, R. "An Easily Tunable Notch-Pass Filter." *Electronic Engineering,* December 1971, p. 50.

Ribbens, W. "An Electronically Tunable Band-pass Filter." *Journal of the Audio Engineering Society* 16, no. 10 (1968): 440–442.

Rowe, N. B. "Designing a Low-Frequency Active Notch Filter." *Electronic Engineering,* April 1972, p. 43.

Schroeder, M. "Natural Sounding Artificial Reverberation." *Journal of the Audio Engineering Society* 10, no. 3 (July 1962): 219–223.

Shirley, Fredrick R. "Shift Phase Independent of Frequency." *Electronic Design,* 1 September 1970, pp. 62–66.

Stephenson, F. W. "IC's Encourage RC Active Filter Design." *Electronic Engineering,* September 1970, pp. 63–67.

Thoren, U. "Banish Inductors from Resonant Circuits." *Electronic Design,* 16 August 1973, pp. 72–74.

"A Voltage Tuned Active Filter." *Electronic Engineering,* February 1972, p. 45.

Williams, F. "Active Filter Design and Use, Part II." *73 Magazine,* July 1972, pp. 97–106 (73 Inc., Peterborough, N.H. 03458).

_____. "Active Filter Design and Use, Part III." *73 Magazine,* September 1972, pp. 76–87.

_____. "Active Filter Design and Use, Part IV." *73 Magazine,* October 1972 pp. 43–47.

7

CONTROL
SIGNALS

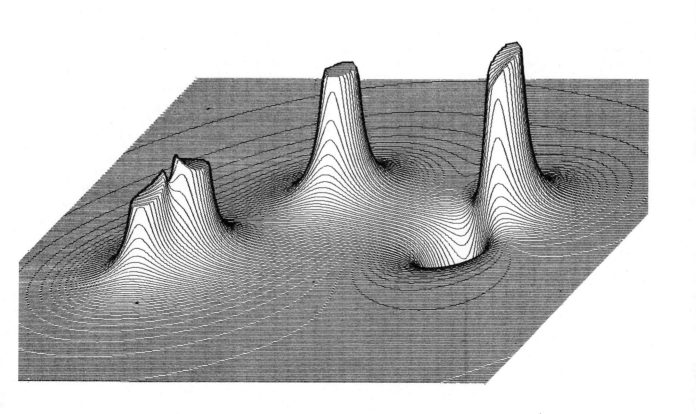

In previous chapters certain voltage-controlled devices were discussed in connection with amplitude and frequency modulation and mixing. In modulation applications the signals applied to the control input of a device are periodic waveforms or combinations of periodic waveforms obtained from oscillators or from microphones, tape or disc reproducers, radios, and other sources. Other types of control signals are employed to vary the operating points of voltage-controlled instruments. These control signals include transient functions, step functions, and sub-audio-frequency periodic functions.

The production and subsequent widespread availability from the mid-1960s onward of voltage-controlled signal generating and modifying instruments designed specifically for electronic music production was a major development in the history of electronic music. However, to reckon the beginnings of electronic music from the issue of the first voltage-controlled packaged studio is erroneous, since, as the author has pointed out, many excellent electronic music works were produced in the 15 years or so preceding the production of such equipment. Karlheinz Stockhausen, in his article "The Origins of Electronic Music," writes:

> Electronic Music began in Cologne in 1952–53.... Scarcely anybody in America is now aware of this; they act as though it had dropped out of the American sky at some time or another.[1]

On the other hand, Allen Strange, in his manual *Electronic Music: Systems, Techniques, and Controls,* states:

> In the early days of electronic music, composers were limited to very basis [?] classical techniques that were quite time-consuming, and often the end results did not justify the means [*production time*] involved.[2]

Although much important work in electronic music occurred in Europe, as Stockhausen relates, the reader should have an appreciation of the important early contributions to electronic music by American composers such as Vladimir Ussachevsky, Otto Luening, Milton Babbitt, and others.

While much new equipment designed specifically for electronic music production includes certain features of automation designed to facilitate generation of sounds, some composers who use this equipment are slow to progress beyond the superficial capabilities of such time-saving refinements. A musically vapid synthesizer-produced work that may have taken three weeks to produce can be equally numbing as its inane counterpart that may have taken three months to produce in a classical studio.

Figure 7.1† shows a simple step voltage generator that consists of a voltage divider with switches to select various points on the divider string. For example, given the battery voltage $E = 3$ volts, $R_1 = 200$ ohms, $R_2 = 400$ ohms, $R_3 = 800$ ohms, and $R_4 = 1$ kilohm, let us investigate the

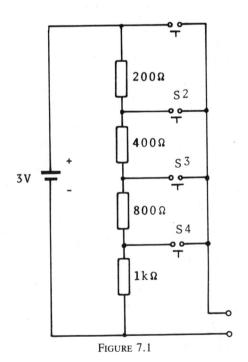

FIGURE 7.1

†In this and several other circuits in this chapter, no output buffering is shown.

voltage drop across each resistor. From Ohm's Law, the total current flowing in the circuit is

$$I = E \div R = 3 \div (200 + 400 + 800 + 1000) = 0.00125 \ A.$$

Then

$$E_1 = I \cdot R_1 = 0.00125 \cdot 200 = 0.25 \ \text{volt}$$
$$I \cdot R_2 = 0.00125 \cdot 400 = 0.5 \ \ \text{volt}$$
$$I \cdot R_3 = 0.00125 \cdot 800 = 1.0 \ \ \text{volt}$$
$$I \cdot R_4 = 0.00125 \cdot 1000 = 1.15 \ \text{volts}$$

and

$$E_{\text{tot.}} = 3 \ \text{volts} = (E_1 + E_2 + E_3 + E_4).$$

Referring to figure 7.1, if switch S_1 were closed, the full battery potential (3 volts) would appear at the output. Closing switch S_2 causes a 2.75-volt potential $(E_2 + E_3 + E_4)$ to appear at the output. Closing switch $S3$ causes a 2.25-volt potential $(E_3 + E_4)$, and closing S_4 causes a 1.25-volt potential to appear at the output.

Applying these control voltages one at a time to the control input of a voltage-controlled oscillator† with a one-volt-per-octave control voltage versus frequency response, the following pitches would be produced, the oscillator being set initially to 440 Hz:

Control Voltage	Frequency
0.0 volts	440 Hz
1.25 volts	$2^{1.25} \cdot 440 \simeq 1047$ Hz
2.25 volts	$2^{2.25} \cdot 440 \simeq 2090$ Hz
2.75 volts	$2^{2.75} \cdot 440 \simeq 2961$ Hz
3.00 volts	$2^{3.00} \cdot 440 \simeq 3520$ Hz

The same control voltages applied to the control input of a voltage-controlled amplifier with a 1-dB-per-volt control voltage versus gain characteristic would produce changes in amplifier gain (from some initial value) of 1.25 dB, 2.25 dB, 2.75 dB, and 3.0 dB, respectively. Similarly, these control voltages applied to the control input of a voltage-controlled

---

†taking care to set any internal, or "fixed control voltage," associated with the oscillator to a value which when added to the external control voltage will not exceed the maximum permitted control voltage. Exceeding the control voltage range might result in inaccurate control voltage versus frequency response, or might cause the oscillator to produce spurious signals.

filter with a half-power-point-versus-control-voltage characteristic of one octave per volt will raise the half-power point $2^{1.25}$, $2^{2.25}$, $2^{2.75}$, and $2^{3.00}$ times the initial frequency setting, respectively.

A voltage divider producing 1/12 volt increments could be used with the above-mentioned VCO to produce a scale of equal temperament. Such a divider in its simplest form would resemble the circuit of figure 7.2. The output of the divider can be scaled, that is, each voltage step is multiplied by the same constant, by using an attenuator or a direct-coupled amplifier with variable gain. For example, if the output of the 1/12-volt increment divider were amplified by a stage having a voltage gain of 2, and the amplifier output connected to the control input of the above-mentioned VCO, the set of pitches produced by the divider/VCO would be a series of twelve whole steps. Conversely, if the amplifier in series with the divider is set to a voltage gain of one-half, a set of twelve quarter-steps results. Division of the octave into any number of discrete and equal steps down to and beyond just-noticeable differences is possible with this configuration. Conversely, the limit of expansion with this configuration is the point at which the entire controllable range of the oscillator is controlled by two adjacent switch positions. Notice that it is not possible to produce more than one control voltage simultaneously using the simple circuits illustrated above that have all divider tap switches connected to a common output bus.

A step-voltage generator that allows individual adjustment of the magnitude of control-voltage steps is shown in figure 7.3. In addition to electronic music applications, such a control-voltage generator with a suitable number of steps might be useful, for example, in ethnomusicological studies to construct various tuning systems (in conjunction with a VCO). The generator in figure 7.3 employs 10-turn potentiometers to achieve a high degree of resolution.

Figure 7.4 shows a step-voltage generator in which the battery is replaced by a transistor constant-current source. As in previous examples, switches select control voltages from the divider string. The voltage at the switch bus charges capacitor C through the relay (which is activated whenever any switch is closed). The switch contacts that control the relay are not shown in the drawing. When a switch is opened, the capacitor retains its charge until another switch is closed, and capacitor C is charged to a new value. The high-impedance FET amplifier/buffer stage isolates the capacitor from the load.

The voltage divider examples above are simple models of keyboard control voltage generators, or keyboard controllers. Many commercially available keyboard control-voltage generators feature such refinements as touch-sensitive key switches (capacitance switches, semiconductor pressure-sensitive switches, and so on) to select elements in the voltage-divider chain. Many keyboard control-voltage generators produce a trigger pulse or provide a switch closure when any key is depressed, the trigger being used, for example, to fire an envelope generator (see Patchings

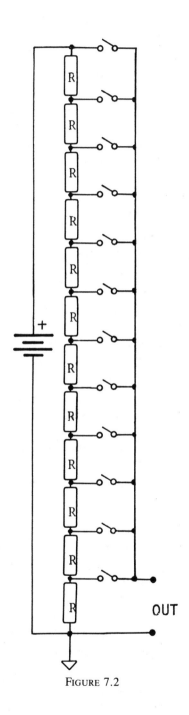

FIGURE 7.2

OUT

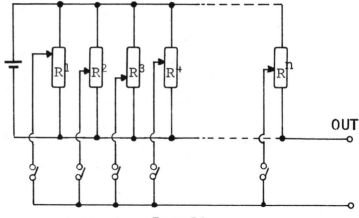

FIGURE 7.3

section at the end of this chapter). Some keyboard control-voltage generators include a provision to hold the voltage associated with the last key depressed (see figure 7.4). Some keyboards produce several independent control-voltage signals simultaneously, permitting, for example, the control of two VCOs. Several manufacturers produce polyphonic keyboards, which allow the operator to play simultaneous and independently variable (usually *pitch*) events. The E.M.S. Company markets a keyboard control-voltage generator that allows the storage and playback of a large number of control-voltage steps. The events are played back in the rhythmic sequence in which they were ''read in'' by the operator playing on the keyboard. In addition, the rate of playback of control-voltage steps may be varied.

Several digital-control signal-storage devices are commercially available at somewhat high cost: for example, the Technical Hardware Company's Model MMC–1 256-event digital storage device sells for $1,200 at this writing. The Oberheim Polyphonic Synthesizer Programmer permits the storage of a number of simultaneous control-voltage settings for instruments such as VCOs, VCFs, and envelope generators. A maximum of sixteen different programs may be stored using the Oberheim device.

A *sequencer* is a step-voltage generator that produces a series of independently adjustable control-voltage steps, one after another in sequence. A mechanical model of a sequencer is shown in figure 7.5. In this drawing, the rotating switch S_r, or *commutator*, contacts the wipers of the potentiometers in turn to produce a series of adjustable DC voltage steps. The control-voltage sequences may be: *repetitive,* in that the same set of voltage steps is repeated ad infinitum (although, as we shall see, within a given period, durations of events may be unequal); *continuous,* in that the elements within the sequence change from period to period (see problem 7 at the end of this chapter); or *nonrepetitive,* that is, one-shot. By using

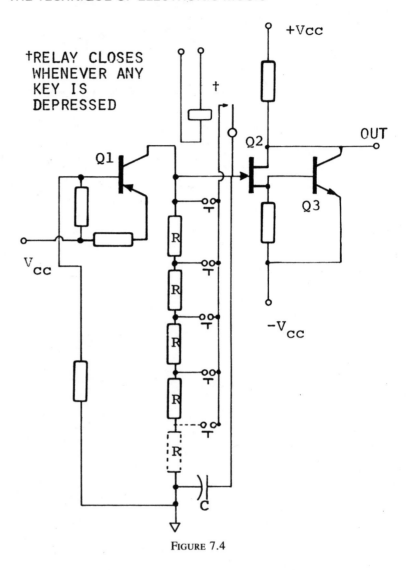

FIGURE 7.4

complex patching configurations, one may produce complex sequences, the periods of which may be quite long, obscuring the cyclic quality of the sequence.

The use of sequencers to produce repetitive pitch sequences, or *ostinati,* has become rather a cliché. The capabilities of sequencers range far beyond that of producing simple ostinati; the capability to produce several independent control signals simultaneously, permitting the composer accurate and presettable control of the operating points of voltage-controlled instruments, makes the sequencer a most useful control-signal generator.

The time interval between sequencer events may be altered in several

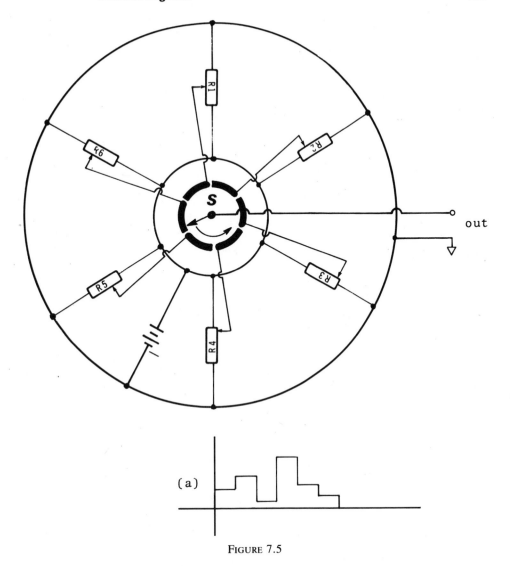

(a)

FIGURE 7.5

ways. The 555 timer-sequencer shown in figure 7.11 provides this capability as an integral part of the design.

Many sequencers employ a frequency-modulatable clock, the control input of which may be connected to the sequencer's control-voltage output to vary the duration of events. Figure 7.6a shows one of three separate and independently variable waveforms produced by a Moog Music Model 960 sequencer. In figure 7.6b, the voltage steps are equal in amplitude but different in frequency from those of waveform 7.6a. To obtain the waveform in figure 7.6b, the output from the *second* series of dividers was connected to the frequency-modulation input of the clock oscillator. Thus,

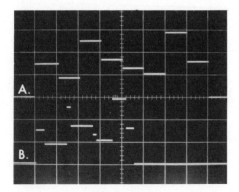

FIGURE 7.6

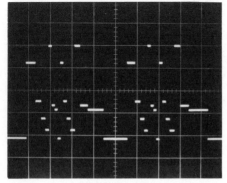

FIGURE 7.7

the higher the control voltage present, the shorter will be the event. (The control voltage may be inverted so that higher control voltages produce longer-duration events.)

The waveform in figure 7.7 was produced by frequency modulating the sequencer clock with a sine wave (clock frequency $\gg$ modulating frequency).

For example, it is desired to generate the following set of pitches with the indicated durations (figure 7.8) using Moog 900 series instrumentation. After setting the control voltages for the pitches, the control voltages for the durations are determined. After these control voltages have been determined, the operator should adjust the clock rate of the sequencer for the desired tempo. The control voltage for the longest duration events (figure 7.8a, events 2 and 4) are set to a low value, say 0.2 v (the greater the control signal, the higher the sequencer clock frequency; the higher the clock frequency, the shorter the period [time duration per cycle]). The remaining voltages are then determined from this value as follows:

Event	Control Voltage (Duration)
2, 4	0.2
8	$0.2 \cdot 14/11 = 0.254$
1	$0.2 \cdot 3/2 = 0.3$
6	$0.3 \cdot 14/11 = 0.38$
3	$0.3 \cdot 4 = 1.2$
5	$0.4 \cdot 14/11 = 0.5$
7	$1.2 \cdot 14/11 = 1.52$

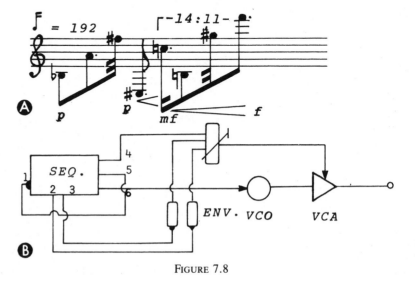

FIGURE 7.8

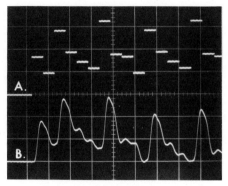

FIGURE 7.9

The control voltages for the dynamic levels should be adjusted by ear. We emphasize that the computations above are included mainly for pedagogical reasons, and that highly developed aural skills are essential tools for the composer, regardless of the medium for which he writes.

A block diagram for the patching to generate the above sequence of pitches is shown in figure 7.8b. One control voltage "channel" of the sequencer (6) controls the frequency of the VCO, while the other two channels control the sequencer clock frequency (5) and dynamic level (4), respectively. The voltage levels associated with events 4 and 5 (figure 7.8a; channel 2 [5], figure 7.8b) should be set to zero, thus allowing the envelope generators that are triggered on events 4 and 5 to assume full control over the gain of the VCA. (Trigger outputs are shown at numbers 2 and 3 in figure 7.8b.) A positive voltage is present at these outputs when the sequencer reaches the count corresponding to the event number with which the trigger is associated. The envelope generators used in this patching (Moog 900 Series) are triggered by grounding a trigger contact, and cannot be triggered directly by the voltage outputs from 2 and 3 without the intervening voltage-to-switch device (transistor switch).

The sequencer may be used to generate audio frequency signals if the period of the sequence is made suitably short. Although the switching speed of most commercially available sequencers is adequate for this application, the high frequency range of many sequencers' internal clocks is limited. An external pulse generator with an adequate frequency range and with an output waveform that meets the amplitude, switching time, and pulse-width requirements of the sequencer should be employed. For example, to generate a 440-Hz signal with a 36-event sequencer requires a clock frequency of $440 \cdot 36 = 19,840$ Hz. Figure 7.9a shows the output waveform of an 8-event sequencer, while figure 7.9b shows this sequencer waveform low-pass-filtered to produce a continuous function. The output waveform of this configuration may be altered by adjusting the individual voltage levels associated with different sequencer events, as well as by changing the filter setting. This process of generating signals with the sequencer is called *waveform synthesis*. With the sequencer set in the nonrepetitive mode, and the clock frequency set to a slow scanning rate, the low-pass-filtered sequencer output may be used as a transient generator. The large number of published sequencer plans attest that sequencer design is a matter of personal preference and intended application.

Schematic diagrams for two sequencers are shown in figures 7.10 and 7.11. The sequencer in figure 7.10 employs TTL logic circuits, while the sequencer in figure 7.11 uses Signetics 555 timing circuits. The sequencer in figure 7.10 is advanced from event to event by a clock pulse applied to the 7493 counter. Rotary switch *A* selects the number of events in the sequence in the nonrepetitive mode, and rotary switch *B* selects the number of events in the sequence in the repetitive mode.

In the 555 timer-sequencer, a pulse associated with the termination of an

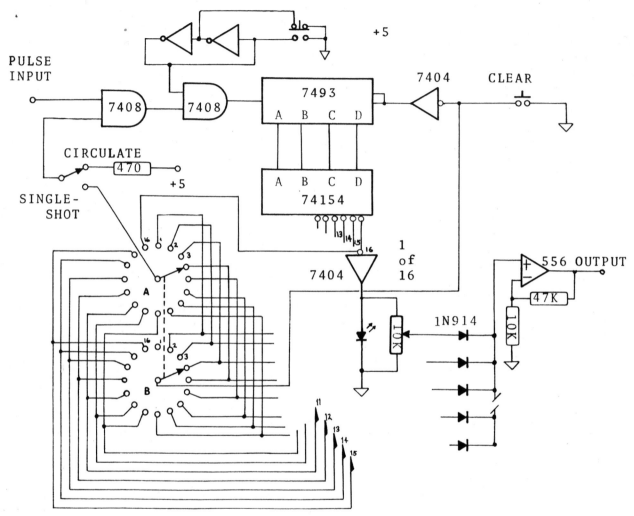

FIGURE 7.10

event triggers the next event in sequence, and so forth. The TTL counter sequencer may be in only one state at a time, while the 555 timer-sequencer may be retriggered in the middle of a cycle, allowing several events to occur simultaneously (although in the configuration shown in figure 7.11, this aspect is of little advantage). The 555 timer-sequencer is well suited to producing events of different durations and may be employed as a timer to control the firing of, for example, a group of envelope generators, provided that each timing circuit output is accessible (and the triggering requirements of the envelope generator are respected).

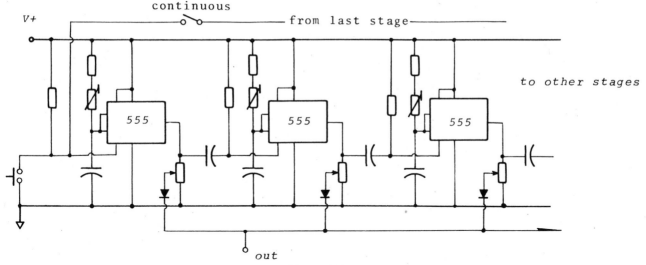

FIGURE 7.11

The sequencer is often employed as a timer. Figure 7.12 shows a sequencer used to control the firing of four envelope generators. This configuration may be used for quad panning. It should be noted that the attack and decay times of the envelope generators in this patching must be carefully set to the desired values. Changing the panning (sequencer clock) rate necessitates changing the time constants of the generators. Of course, if the envelope generators are voltage-controllable, the envelope generator and sequencer clock control inputs may be supplied with a common control signal to regulate the envelope shaping and panning rate together.

Transient signals are an important class of control signals used in electronic music production. Transient generators, or envelope generators, produce a voltage-versus-time function that varies over a certain interval but does not repeat. Transient generators are usually activated by grounding a trigger input or by supplying a triggering pulse to the device. The output of a Moog Music envelope generator is shown in figure 7.16a. With this type of transient generator, one may specify the rise (attack) time Tr; the initial fall (decay time T_{f1}; the level (E_{sus} [sustain] to which T_{f1} decays and holds before the final fall (decay) time T_{f2} occurs. With many envelope generator designs, the first three functions occur while the trigger is applied (removing the trigger causes the output of the generator to reset to zero). The fourth function occurs after the trigger is removed. Such generators are often called attack/decay/sustain release (ADSR) envelope generators, or simply ADSR. Voltage control of the time constants and sustain levels of envelope generators is a useful refinement offered by several manufacturers of electronic music instrumentation.[3]

Figure 7.13 shows a family of curves produced by varying the rise time

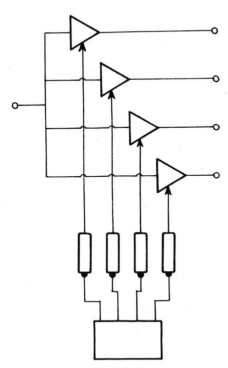

FIGURE 7.12

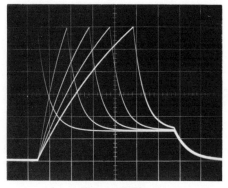

FIGURE 7.13

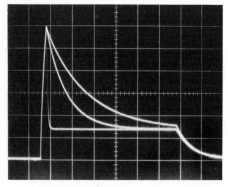

FIGURE 7.14

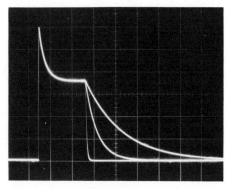

FIGURE 7.15

and holding the two fall times constant as the generator is triggered several times.

Figure 7.14 shows a family of curves produced by varying the first fall time and holding the rise time and the second fall time constant.

Figure 7.15 shows a family of curves produced by varying the second fall time and holding the rise time and the first fall time constant. The values for E_{sus} are equal in figures 7.13 and 7.14, while the E_{sus} value was altered in figure 7.15 for clarity.

The transient generator is commonly used in conjunction with a voltage-controlled amplifier for gating operations. Patching 2 at the end of this chapter shows a transient generator connected to the control input of a VCA, through which a program could be gated. Figure 7.16a shows the output waveform of a certain transient generator. Figure 7.16b shows the amplitude-versus-time function of a sine-wave signal, its amplitude controlled by the transient signal by means of a voltage-controlled amplifier. The process by which the amplitude of signals is controlled (usually) by a transient function is called *gating*. Most gating operations involve a transient-controlled amplitude change between two limits—a maximum, and a minimum, usually zero, amplitude.

Figure 7.17b shows the output of a transient generator adjusted to produce a fast rise and medium decay. Figure 7.17a shows the effect on a sine wave passed through a VCA when this same transient function is applied to the VCA control input (the VCA fixed control voltage is set to zero). As we have seen, the VCA is a two-quadrant multiplier, which in this case provides multiplication of the instantaneous values of the sine-wave program and the (positive-going) transient generator output. Figure 7.17a (#2, outer trace) was produced by a gated VCA with a linear control-voltage-versus-frequency characteristic; figure 7.17a (#1, inner trace) was produced by a gated VCA with an exponential control-voltage-versus-frequency characteristic (envelope generator settings were unchanged). For example, if every centimeter along the x axis denotes 1/4 second (250 milliseconds), we could say that figures 7.17a, 1 and 2, represent two musical events: two 32 Hz (approximately C_1, or subcontra C) tones, one approximately a half-note with a decrescendo at quarter = approximately MM 89; the other approximately a quarter-note, *sfp*, at the same tempo. We determined the frequency, 32 Hz, by counting approximately eight complete cycles of the sine wave per centimeter (each centimeter represents 250 milliseconds); dividing eight into 250 to determine the period of one cycle (31.25 milliseconds); and dividing 0.03125 into 1.000000 to obtain the quotient, 32. The use of the half-note analogy is completely arbitrary; but once this value was decided upon, the duration of the sound event described by the outer trace of figure 7.17a was measured (approximately 1.35 seconds, although at this point the sine wave has not decayed to extinction), divided into two parts, each part corresponding to one quarter-note, and the appropriate metronome setting in beats-per-minute was determined (60 ÷ 0.675 = 88.88). The preceding analogy, although somewhat gratuitous, illustrates the use of electronic sound synthesis for musical purposes, and reminds us that electronic music was developed through the efforts of forward-looking composers who were interested in this new sound resource as a vehicle for serious musical expression.

It should be noted that some timbral change accompanies the amplitude shaping, or gating, process. The spectrum of a gated waveform, say a sine-wave tone burst, contains more than the single frequency component of the sine wave itself. In some cases, the additional frequency components (clicks) add desirable transient interest to the gated waveform. In general, the strength of these switching-produced components depends on how abruptly the waveform is switched on (to full amplitude) and off: the shorter the attack and decay, the stronger the clicks. Such transients can be eliminated by simply rounding off the corners of the gated waveform (increasing the attack and decay times of the envelope generator). This process may, however, result in "too soft" an attack where a more percussive onset is desired. Of course, spurious transients (clicks) can be caused by improper DC offset of the gating device (see the Glossary under *offset voltage*).

Often, slow periodic signals may be used for gating. In figure 7.18, the transient generator is used to gate a complex sub-audio-frequency control signal that, in turn, gates a prerecorded signal.

Figure 7.19 shows a schematic diagram of a simple envelope generator that produces a waveform that rises, holds at a certain level, and falls. Commercially available envelope generators differ in the number of events (rise time, hold time, and fall time) they produce, as well as in the type of

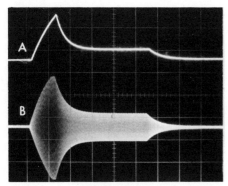

FIGURE 7.16

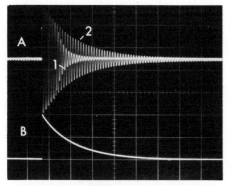

FIGURE 7.17

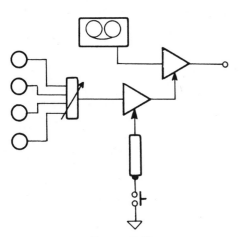

FIGURE 7.18

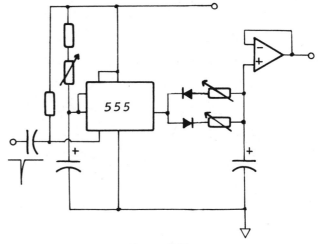

FIGURE 7.19

triggering they require. The transient generator is used as a control signal source for other voltage-controlled instruments besides voltage-controlled amplifiers. Since many envelope generators do not have provisions for scaling their output level, it is often necessary to route the output of the transient generator through an attenuator or direct-coupled amplifier.

Different types of envelope generators require different means of triggering (causing the generator to output the desired function): some generators require the grounding of a triggering contact; others require application of a triggering voltage. It is often desirable to trigger envelope generators with level-sensitive devices (Schmitt triggers, comparators) as well as outputs of sequencers and timers, the outputs of which usually consist of a voltage. A voltage-controlled switch must be inserted in the line between the voltage output of the triggering device and the trigger input of the envelope generator that requires contact grounding. Switches that trigger the envelope generators should be mounted within easy reach of the operator (in some cases, multiple switches or a plug-in remote-control switchbox may be necessary).

As we shall see in the patchings section at the end of this chapter, transient signals themselves may be modified by such processes as addition, multiplication, and so on.

Often VCAs used in gating applications may be replaced by or used in conjunction with voltage-controlled filters. For example, it is difficult using some voltage-controlled low-pass filters to achieve gating from zero amplitude to some desired level, especially when processing wideband signals that contain low-frequency components. In this case, a VCA with its own envelope generator should be placed in series after the VCLPF. The two transient generators are then triggered in parallel (or with a desired time delay), and the envelope generator controlling the VCA is adjusted to turn off the amplifier after the filter event is over.

The use of voltage-controlled filters in conjunction with transient generators adds timbral interest to electronically generated sounds, causing them to behave more like natural sounds, the decays of which are usually associated with a gradual loss of higher number partials. Furthermore, each partial in the natural sound will possess an individual amplitude-versus-time function, or attack-and-decay curve. To provide analagous conditions for the electronically generated sound would require more filters and transient generators than are usually found in the electronic music studio. As mentioned before, herein lies a basic problem of working with electronic sound: not simply to imitate instrumental timbres by synthesis, but to make electronically generated sounds behave in ways that make them appear more natural and alive, to use subjective descriptions, and to avoid the steady-state conditions that characterize many electronically generated sounds.

A sample-and-hold circuit is diagrammed in figure 7.20. This circuit is

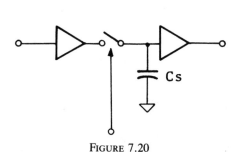

FIGURE 7.20

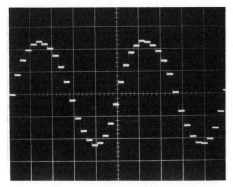

FIGURE 7.21

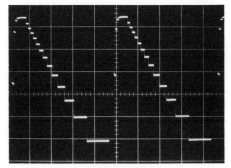

FIGURE 7.22

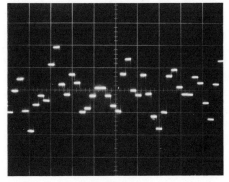

FIGURE 7.23

comprised of an input buffer, a switch, a storage capacitor, C_s, and an ouput buffer. In the *sample* mode, the switch is closed, permitting the input buffer to make the storage capacitor voltage equal to the analog input voltage. In the *hold* mode, the switch is opened, isolating the storage capacitor from the input and leaving it charged to a voltage equal to the last analog input voltage present at the input before entering the hold mode. The output buffer amplifier isolates the charge on the capacitor from the load. The National Semiconductor LH0023C sample-and-hold integrated circuit (about $25) is highly recommended. A workable sample-and-hold circuit may be constructed using the RCA CA3080 operational transconductance amplifier (see *RCA Application Note ICAN-6688*).

Figure 7.21 shows a sine wave of frequency f sampled at a rate $\simeq 20f$. Figure 7.22 shows a sampled sawtooth wave. In this case, the sampling rate is controlled by the waveform being sampled. Figure 7.23 shows low-pass-filtered white noise sampled at a constant rate. Figure 7.24 shows low-pass-filtered white noise sampled at a random rate. The patching used to generate the waveform of figure 7.24 is shown at the end of this chapter (patching 10). The sample-and-hold circuit allows the composer to transform continuous-function control voltages into step functions. These sampled waveforms are often used to produce sequences of discrete pitches. Notice that as long as the switch (see model, figure 7.20) is closed, the output of the sample-and-hold device follows the analog input signal. Consequently, if the sampling period is an appreciable portion of the hold time, a step function will not result. The composer may wish to utilize this effect to produce, for example, a sequence of pitches with glissandi between events. While sample-and-hold control-voltage sequences may be quite complex, they are not so easy to control and specify as sequencer-produced control voltages.

A *quantizer* is a device that compares an input signal to a limited set of discrete values and outputs the magnitude of the value closest to the magnitude of the input signal. For example, a set might consist of 12 values (twelve 1/12-volt increments). A random-function generator connected to the quantizer input would produce random sequences of the 1/12-volt increments, resulting in random series of 12 equal-tempered pitches when the quantizer is connected to the control input of a one-octave-per volt VCO (or a high-Q VCF filtering a noise source or used for resonant-filter synthesis). The operation of a quantizer is similar to that of an analog-to-digital converter. However, whereas the output of the A/D converter consists of digital words, the quantizer output consists of discrete voltages (which could be obtained by using a digital-to-analog converter at the A/D converter output).

A series of frequency dividers, the outputs of which are summed together, can be used to generate complex step functions such as the one shown in figure 7.23. Although it is difficult to predict the step waveshape

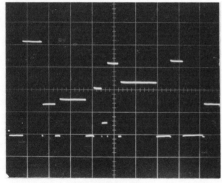

FIGURE 7.24

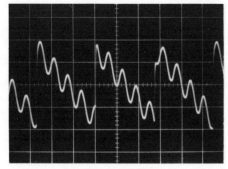

FIGURE 7.25

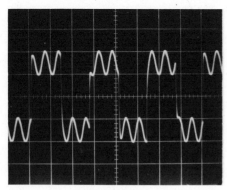

FIGURE 7.26

resulting from such an arrangement, frequency dividers are inexpensive to construct, and this type of control-voltage generation may find favor with some composers.

Some composers employ mixtures of sub-audio signals as control voltages, both in real-time performance and in the generation of sound events for tape pieces. Although the addition of slow periodic signals will produce a more complex yet periodic signal, the inherent periodicity may not be perceivable. Figure 7.25 shows the addition of a sine and a square wave. Figure 7.26 shows the addition of a sawtooth and a sine wave. Figure 7.27 shows the addition of four square waves of different amplitudes and frequencies.

Figures 7.28 and 7.29 show the addition of a sine wave, sawtooth wave, triangle wave, and square wave (each with a different frequency and amplitude). The summed signal may be made more complex by modulating the signals to be summed, as well as by modulating the summed waveform itself.

While control signals of the type discussed above can be useful, one should keep in mind that it is extremely difficult to generate or alter such complex waveforms predictably. (Of course, the composer may work interactively with such a configuration until he achieves the desired result.) Nevertheless, since small deviations in the amplitude and frequency of the summed components will alter the resultant waveform, problems of equipment stability and repeatability may make this approach unsuitable for some applications. Figure 7.30 shows the addition of two sawtooth waves, one of greater amplitude and lower frequency than the other. The addition of these two waveforms results in the *staircase wave* shown in figure 7.30b. Unless the component waveforms are mixed in the proper proportions, the ''steps'' of the staircase wave will be slanted up or down.

The *envelope detector,* or *envelope follower* is a device that produces a voltage proportional to the instantaneous amplitude of some (usually audio- or higher-frequency) input signal. Figure 7.31 shows a simple detector circuit. The step response of envelope detectors depends on the time-constant of the smoothing filter, RC. Figure 7.32 shows an oscilloscope photograph of an envelope detector with a fast time-constant processing a sine-wave signal with a certain envelope that was produced by controlling the gain of a VCA with two envelope generators triggered sequentially. Figure 7.33 shows the same gated sine-wave signal processed by an envelope detector with a longer time-constant.

Although with a fast time-constant the detector accurately follows the signal envelope, some ripple is present. On the other hand, the longer time-constant smoothes out the ripple at the expense of transient response.

The problem of pitch-to-voltage conversion is extremely complex compared to that of envelope detection, and most pitch-to-voltage converters, or *pitch followers,* operate accurately only within certain ranges. Pitch followers find many applications in live electronic music, especially that

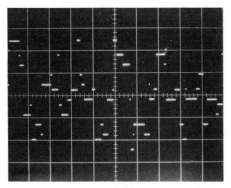

FIGURE 7.27

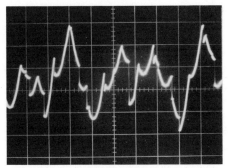

FIGURE 7.28

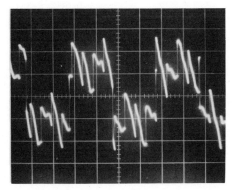

FIGURE 7.29

which uses discrete pitch material: for example, a guitar player can produce pitches on his instrument that are converted to the appropriate control voltages to produce the same (or different) pitches or intervallic relationships on a voltage-controlled oscillator. The oscillator may be gated using a VCA or a VCF controlled by an envelope detector driven by the guitar.

Control signals may be stored on magnetic tape using several methods. The frequency response of tape recorders and reproducers designed for audio-frequency recording is not adequate for control-signal recording, which demands a frequency response down to 0 Hz, or DC. One method of recording control signals involves amplitude modulating an audio frequency or ultrasonic signal with the control voltage to be recorded, recording the resultant amplitude-modulated signal, and demodulating the signal upon playback with an envelope detector. As discussed above, the trade-off between transient response and ripple suppression makes amplitude modulation and detection less useful for control-voltage recording than other processes.

Scientific instrumentation recorders have long employed FM recording to achieve wide bandwidth (for example, 0 Hz to 1 MHz). Figure 7.34 shows a block diagram of a three-channel FM recording system. In this system, a VCO is frequency modulated by the signal to be recorded, and the resultant FM signal is recorded on tape. In this three-channel system, the FM signals of different carrier frequencies are routed from the tape reproducer through band-pass filters to provide additional isolation from channel to channel. After amplification following the band-pass filters, the signals are passed through limiters, which eliminate amplitude variations in the signal fed to the detector. Of course, up to a certain point, increases in the input signal to the limiter will produce changes in the limiter's output. Above this point, however, further increases in the amplitude of the input signal will produce no change in the limiter's output. The *discriminator,* or frequency detector, converts changes in frequency to changes in amplitude. The discriminator is tuned to the unmodulated frequency of the carrier (VCO). When the frequency of the VCO rises above the unmodulated value, the discriminator produces a positive voltage that is proportional to the frequency deviation. Conversely, when the frequency of the VCO falls below the unmodulated value, the discriminator produces a negative voltage that is proportional to the frequency deviation. Thus, unlike the amplitude modulation and detection system described above, the FM recording system can record and reproduce both negative- and positive-going signals, and is capable of much better transient response. In addition, several FM channels may be stored on one audio channel of a recorder. Several manufacturers of electronic music instrumentation produce frequency-to-voltage converters that may be used to an FM recording system.

Another method for the storage of control-voltage signals involves representing the magnitude of the signals as numbers, storing the numbers, and reconverting the digitized signals to analog signals. Control signals

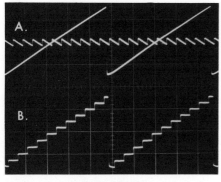

FIGURE 7.30

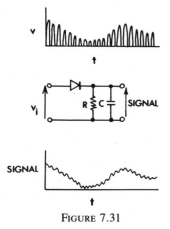

FIGURE 7.31

may be stored in this way using punched paper tape. Figures 7.35 and 7.36 illustrate this conversion/recovery process. Figure 7.37 shows a punched paper tape reader.

Many composers, in attempting to ameliorate what they feel are unsuitable social and psychological aspects of concert presentations of electronic music, have become interested in real-time performance with electronic sound generating and modifying equipment. Such composers feel that the playing of a tape piece in concert is stifling due to the lack of visual interest usually present in the concert situation. Other composers have become interested in integrating extramusical elements such as dance, sculpture, architecture, graphic arts, film, and video tape into their works. Many such integrated works are not designed specifically to be performed in concert, but rather to be exhibited, and many of these works are designed to react to the presence of an audience (for example, audience-produced sounds, the position of the audience with respect to the work, and so on, may trigger devices or initiate sequences of events).

In order to achieve the high degree of differentiation (assuming this to be a compositional goal) evidenced in many instrumental and tape pieces, a large amount of programmable signal-generating and modifying equipment, as well as large number of control-voltage channels to specify the operating points of voltage-controlled instruments is necessary. Much real-time electronic music lacks integrity and continuity, manifested in problems of getting from one sound event to another, of producing simultaneous and independently variable sound events, and of distributing the resultant sounds among the playback channels (to name only a few considerations). Two hands are not capable of much speed in transition from one complex patching to another using currently available electronic music production equipment. Several authors have described hybrid electronic music systems in which patching and setting of operating points of instruments is accomplished or aided by a digital computer.

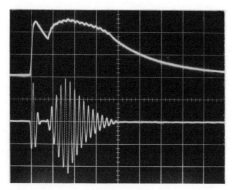

FIGURE 7.32

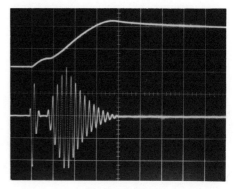

FIGURE 7.33

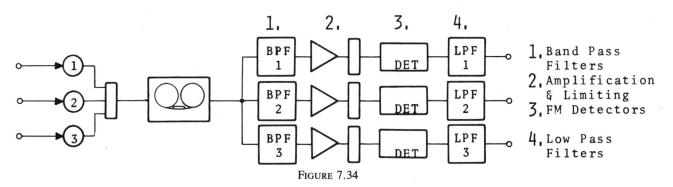

FIGURE 7.34

1. Band Pass Filters
2. Amplification & Limiting
3. FM Detectors
4. Low Pass Filters

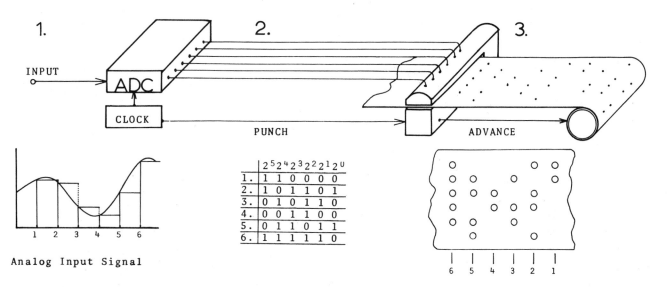

Analog Input Signal

	2^5	2^4	2^3	2^2	2^1	2^0
1.	1	1	0	0	0	0
2.	1	0	1	1	0	1
3.	0	1	0	1	1	0
4.	0	0	1	1	0	0
5.	0	1	1	0	1	1
6.	1	1	1	1	1	0

1. The analog input signal is sampled at points determined by the clock pulses.

2. The Analog to Digital Converter (ADC) translates the sampled voltage into a binary figure represented by a group of six signal levels.

3. Then the punch is triggered, causing the binary number to be punched into the paper tape. (Here a hole represents a binary one, and no hole represents a binary zero.) The tape is then advanced one space to prepare for the next number.

FIGURE 7.35

Recording an Analog Signal on Punched Paper Tape

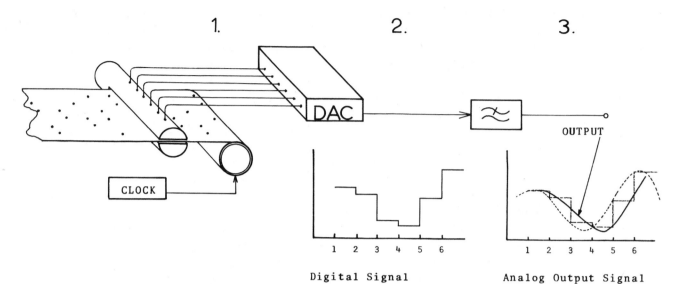

1.   **2.**   **3.**

Digital Signal   Analog Output Signal

1. On cue from the clock the
paper tape is advanced one
space. The punched holes
are detected and these
signals are passed to the
Digital to Analog Converter
(DAC). By varying the clock
rate, the original data
may be temporally compressed or expanded.

2. The DAC sums these
individual signals
in a weighted manner
such that the original
output from the ADC is
exactly reproduced.

3. The resulting step
voltage is low pass
filtered, smoothing the
curve into a close
approximation of the
original analog signal.

FIGURE 7.36

Recovering the Analog Signal from the
Punched Paper Tape

Certainly, technical complexity in itself should not be a criterion by
which the success of a real-time-generated electronic piece is judged. Accuracy of repeatability, on the other hand, *is* in most cases an important
design consideration for real-time performance equipment.

In general, real-time electronic pieces employ the following techniques:
real-time modification of instruments and sound sources (for example,
electronic organs, pianos, shortwave receivers, and the like); simple
amplification; and real-time generation of electronic music by performers
using a variety of control devices. Real-time pieces may also utilize prerecorded audio and control signals, which may be modified in the course of
performance.

The simple light-controlled control-voltage device shown in figure 7.38
may be used in a variety of electronic music applications. The device
provides an output voltage proportional to the amount of light falling on the
phototransistor. The unit is considerably more sensitive than a photoresistor or photovoltaic cell, and its narrow light-sensitive bandwidth and in-

FIGURE 7.37

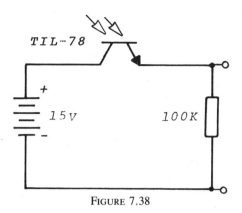

FIGURE 7.38

frared sensitivity (9400 angstroms) make it attractive for this application. For example, using a suitable transmitter and modulator, control signals may be transmitted over a light beam. Several light-controlled control voltage devices have been discussed in the literature. Beyer and Sennheiser currently market stereo cordless headphones that use an infrared light transmission medium. While many of these configurations are useful for live electronic music situations, where "hands-on" capability is useful for a theatrical effect, these devices are not commonly employed in electronic music studio production work.

The so-called *Photoformer,* described by David Sunstein in 1949,[4] is an interesting system that uses a photomultiplier tube in conjunction with an oscilloscope to produce complex waveforms. The photomultiplier tube and its associated circuitry cause the oscilloscope trace to follow an opaque mask, the edge of which is cut to the shape of the desired waveform. The resulting waveform might be used as an audio signal or a transient signal to produce complex envelopes. Sunstein lists several interesting applications of his device among them a volume compressor/expander, a frequency modulator, and bandwidth compressor.

However, a more versatile and easily controllable waveform generator may be built by electronically commutating a large number (approximately

FIGURE 7.39

Joel Chadabe in the electronic music studio at the State University of New York at Albany. Several Moog 960 sequencers with sequential switches and interfaces may be seen behind and to the right of Professor Chadabe.

60) straight-line potentiometer voltage dividers. Using this device, the operator may set up a model of a desired waveform by positioning the potentiometer sliders. The resulting step function would require low-pass filtering to produce a smooth waveform (see figure 7.9).

A group of direct-coupled voltage amplifiers (gain variable from 0 to approximately 10) is very useful for amplifying and attenuating control signals, since many control-voltage generators such as envelope generators, envelope detectors, sample-and-hold amplifiers, and so on, do not provide a built-in output level control. Control signal amplifiers are also useful for FM synthesis applications in which large frequency deviations are required, since many types of electronic music instrumentation include oscillators capable of a large control range without providing control signals of sufficient amplitude to take advantage of such control capabilities. The direct-coupled amplifiers should be of both the inverting and non-inverting types to provide maximum flexibility. Ordinary 741 op-amps are ideal for this application. Several groups of multiple jacks should be included on the panel with the amplifiers for convenience.

PATCHINGS

1. Patching 1 shows an envelope generator (transient generator) used to control the center frequency of a voltage-controlled band-pass filter.

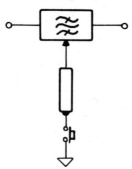

2. Patching 2 shows an envelope generator used to control the gain of a voltage-controlled amplifier. The amplitude of a signal processed through this VCA will be altered according to changes in gain of the amplifier.

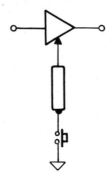

3. In patching 3, the outputs of three envelope generators are summed (in a direct-coupled mixer) to produce a more complex control signal.

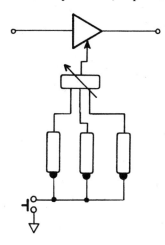

4. In patching 4, the outputs of two envelope generators are summed in a mixer. A (variable) delay may be introduced between the firing of the two envelope generators. This configuration was used to produce the control signal employed to generate the amplitude-versus-time characteristic shown in figures 7.32 and 7.33 (the lower waveform in both photographs).

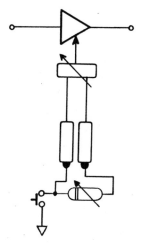

5. Patching 5 shows a patching for panning a signal from one channel to another. The amplitude-versus-time characteristics for each channel, as well as the time

delay between the firing of the envelope generators, may be varied to produce different panning characteristics.

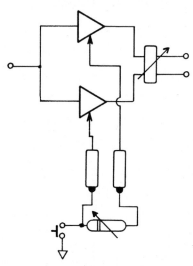

6. Patching 6 shows a four-channel version of the panning arrangement shown in patching 5.

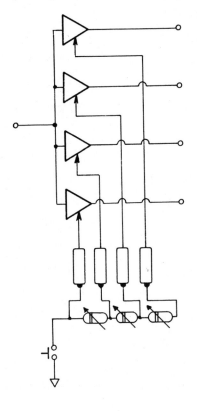

7. In patching 7, the outputs of two transient generators are processed in a multiplier.

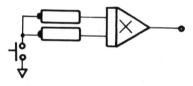

8. Patching 8 shows a configuration in which a control signal is produced by detecting the output of a rung band-pass filter.

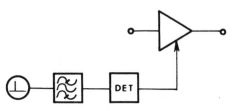

9. Patching 9 shows a patching for use with the Moog 960 sequencer and 962 sequential switch to generate an n-event sequence ($n \leqslant 24$). At the beginning of the sequence, the 960 counts eight clock pulses. On the ninth pulse, the sequential switch advances (turning row 1 of the sequencer *off* and turning row 2 of the sequencer *on*). At this point, the VCA (the fixed control-voltage setting of which is set to minimum) is turned on by a DC voltage associated with event 2 of the sequential switch. Consequently, when the sequencer reaches count 5 on the second pass, the marker (DC) voltage associated with the fifth event is passed by the VCA to a voltage-to-switch trigger that is set to produce a short switch closure (B column, Model 961), approximately 70 milliseconds. The output of the voltage-to-switch device is connected to the input of a switch-to-voltage interface, and the pulse from this device is routed to the *set* input of event 1 (if a *repetitive* sequence is desired), or to the *clock disable* input (if a *nonrepetitive* sequence is desired).

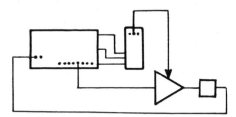

10. Patching 10 produces a train of pulses of random width and amplitude. The frequency with which events occur is determined by the settings of the low-pass filters.

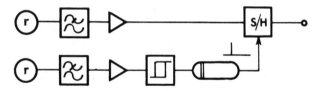

11. In patching 11, signals from a microphone are detected and then conditioned by a Schmitt trigger. The output of the Schmitt trigger is used to advance a sequencer. The microphone signal is multiplied with the output of a sine-wave oscillator, the frequency of which is controlled by the sequencer. The resulting modulated signal is low-pass filtered by a filter, the break frequency of which is also controlled by the sequencer. Each time the sequencer advances, an envelope generator is triggered, gating the sound.

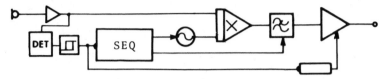

12. In patching 12, the clock output from a sequencer is employed to ring a filter, the Q and f_c of which are controlled by the sequencer.

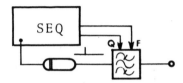

13. In patching 13, a sequencer controls both the Q and center frequency of a band-pass filter to which a noise generator is connected. An envelope generator driven by the sequence clock controls the gain of a VCA which gates the sound event. The small square indicates a voltage-to-switch interface required in some equipment designs in which envelope generator triggering is accomplished by grounding a terminal, while the sequence clock output is a positive-going pulse.

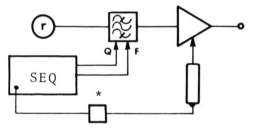

14. In patching 14, the trigger output from a keyboard control-voltage generator is used to ring a high-Q band-pass filter, the center frequency of which is set by the control signal output from the KBCVG.

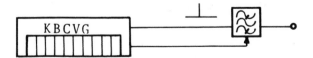

15. In patching 15, a KBCVG is employed to control the center frequency of a high-Q band-pass filter. With white noise as the input signal, the filter pro-

duces an output of defined pitch but random amplitude. The trigger output of the KBCVG is used to trigger an envelope generator, which is used in conjunction with a VCA to gate the signal.

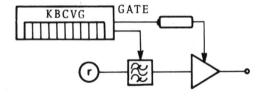

16. Patching 16 shows a typical configuration for a small keyboard synthesizer (Electrocomp, MiniMoog, and so on). In this patching, a keyboard control-voltage generator controls the frequency of a sawtooth wave. The timbre of the resulting sound is controlled by a low-pass filter, and the output of the filter is gated by a VCA.

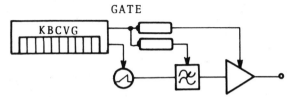

17. Patching 17 shows a patching in which a group of sine waves are combined in a panpot and are employed to frequency modulate a VCO ($\sim$). Three manually advanced sequencers are employed to control (a) the modulation index of the FM signal and (b) the time-constants for the voltage-controlled envelope generators.

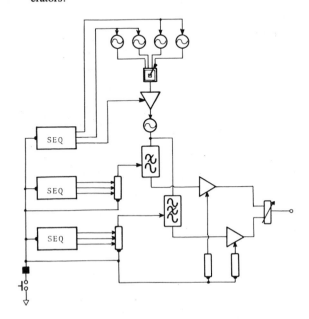

PROBLEMS

1. Using a VCO with a 1-octave/volt frequency-versus-control-voltage characteristic, what control-voltage changes are required to produce the following changes in frequency:

   a. 172 Hz→3720 Hz

   b. 16 Hz→256 Hz

   c. 1560 Hz→100 Hz

2. Using a keyboard control-voltage generator, VCO, and other equipment as required, generate: a 1/4-tone scale; a 23-note-to-the-octave scale; a 3-note-to-the-octave scale.

3. Using the AM recording and detection method described in chapter 7, record a series of control voltages, and apply the control voltages to the control input of a VCO to produce a series of discrete pitches. Describe the limitations of this type of modulated-carrier recording.

4. Using a sequencer (Moog 960) generate: a 7-event repetitive sequence; a 7-event nonrepetitive sequence; a 13-event repetitive sequence; a 13-event nonrepetitive sequence.

5. Generate a chromatic scale over the range $C_2 \to C_7$: (a) using a sample-and-hold circuit; (b) using a staircase wave; and (c) using another method you devise.

6. Generate a sequence of 8 pitches, events 1, 3, and 5 having an envelope approximately ⌒⌍, and events 2, 4, 6, 7, and 8 having an envelope approximately ⌐⌍

7. Describe the operation of the patching in example 1.

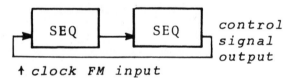

8. Example 2 shows a waveform produced by processing a sawtooth wave with the configuration shown in example 3. Explain the operation of the patching.

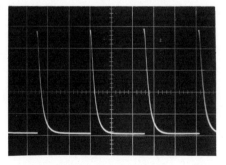

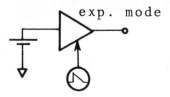

9. Example 4 shows a waveform produced by processing a triangle wave with the configuration shown in example 5. Explain the operation of the patching.

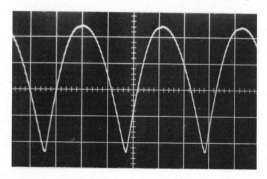

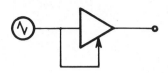

10. Using a sequencer that produces 3 independently adjustable control voltages per event, harmonize an ascending major scale (3 voices, scale in the soprano).

11. Using a sample-and-hold circuit in conjunction with other instruments, produce a series of random- (discrete-) pitch, random-duration sound events.

12. Realize the musical example shown in figure 7.8.

13. Explain the operation of the patchings in examples 6, 7, 8, and 9.

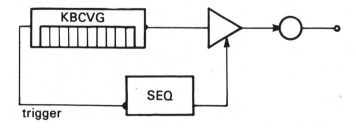

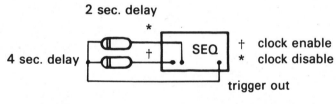

clock rate: CA. 3 Hz.

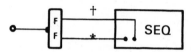

+   clock enable
*   clock disable

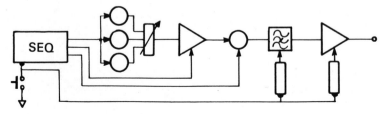

Manual Advance

14. Using the patching in example 10, compare oscilloscope displays of the linear and exponential response modes of a VCA.

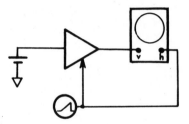

15. Name three ways by which a staircase wave may be produced. Why is additive synthesis of a staircase wave not practical using most oscillators designed for electronic music production?

16. Process a preamplified signal from a microphone through a squaring circuit (for example, a Schmitt trigger) and use the processed signal to clock a sequencer. Monitor the output of the sequencer through a loudspeaker. Adjust (if possible) the number of events per cycle of the sequencer, and note the resulting changes in the monitored signal.

17. Describe the differences between the output signals of the patchings in examples 11 and 12.

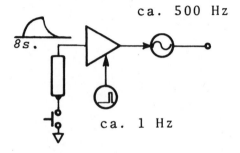

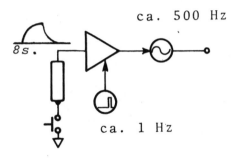

18. Record a series of sounds, each sound having its own attack-and-decay characteristic on channel 2 of a recorder. Play back channel 2 (sel sync), and use this signal to trigger the patching shown in example 13. Explain the operation of this patching.

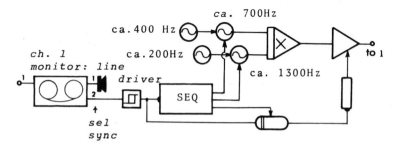

19. Explain the operation of the patching in example 14.

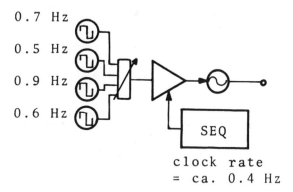

20. Using summed frequency dividers, generate a staircase wave (use divide-by-multiples-of 2). Name two other ways by which a staircase wave may be produced.

21. Regarding the gated 32-Hz sine wave in figure 7.17a, page 187, comment on possible perceptual difficulties regarding the duration of this gated event at the 32 Hz frequency. Experimentally determine the limit of how short this duration can be before the perception of the 32-Hz tone is affected.

NOTES

1. K. Stockhausen, "The Origin of Electronic Music." *Musical Times* 112 (1971): 649–650.

2. Allen Strange, *Electronic Music: Systems, Techniques, and Controls* (DuBuque, Iowa: Brown, 1972).

3. B. Hutchins, "Voltage Control of Envelope Generator Parameters," *Electronotes* 10 (1976).

4. D. E. Sunstein, "Photoelectric Waveform Generator," *Electronics,* February 1949, pp. 100–103.

SELECTED BIBLIOGRAPHY

Books

Belove, C., et al. *Digital and Analog Systems, Circuits, and Devices: An Introduction.* New York: McGraw-Hill, 1973.

Burr-Brown Research Corporation. *Operational Amplifiers.* New York: McGraw-Hill, 1971.

Cleary, J. F. *General Electric Transistor Manual,* 7th ed. New York: General Electric, 1969.

Hutchins, B. *Musical Engineer's Handbook.* Ithaca, N.Y.: B. Hutchins, 1975.

Motorola Linear Integrated Circuits Data Book, 1st ed. Phoenix, Ariz.: Motorola, 1971.

National Semiconductor Corporation, *Linear Applications,* February 1973.

The Optoelectronics Data Book for Design Engineers, 1st ed. Texas Instruments, CC405 71065–52–IS, 1972.

Philbrick Researches, Inc. *Applications Manual for Computing Amplifiers for Modelling, Measuring, Manipulating, and Much Else.* Dedham, Mass.: Philbrick Researches, 1966.

RCA. *RCA Solid State Databook, Series SSD–201 and SSD–202A.* Somerville, N.J.: RCA, Solid State Division, 1974.

Signetics Corporation. *Signetics Digital, Linear, MOS Applications* (and *Supplement*). Sunnyvale, Calif.: Signetics Corporation, 1973.

Strange, Allen. *Electronic Music: Systems, Techniques, and Controls.* DuBuque, Iowa: Brown, 1972.

Vassos, B. H., and Ewing, G. W. *Analog and Digital Electronics for Scientists.* New York: Wiley Interscience, 1972.

Articles

Ball, J. "The Digital Divider in Music Synthesis." *Electronotes* 5, n. 34, p. 8.

Barnes, J. "Improve Single-Slope A/D Accuracy. *Electronic Design 2,* 18 January 1973, pp. 58–62.

Bilateral Switch as Sample-Hold Element." *Electronic Engineering,* October 1972, p. 31.

Blesser, B., and Lee, F. "An Audio Delay System Using Digital Technology." *Journal of the Audio Engineering Society* 19, no. 5 (May 1971): 393–397.

Ehle, R. C. "An Electronic Music Sequencer." *dB,* March 1969, pp. 26–28.

"The 'Electronic Poem' [Varèse] Performed in the Phillips Pavillion at the 1958 Brussels World Fair." *Phillips Technical Review* 20, no. 2–3 (1958/1959): 34–49.

Grth, W. "*Das Halophon.*" *Melos,* January 1973.

Goldberg, J. "Build the N-Flop, a Multiple Pulse-Input, Level-Output Device That Uses Simple Gates." *Electronic Design* 17, (16 August 1973): 84.

Grover, D. J. "Ring Counters Using One Transistor Per Stage." *Electronic Engineering,* June 1969, pp. 23–27.

Hall, K. S. "New Non-Linear Feedback Shift-Register Circuits." *Electronic Engineering,* February 1969, pp. 194–197.

Hillen, P. "A Microprocessor-Based Sequencer for Voltage-controlled Electronic Music Synthesizer." *Audio Engineering Society, Preprint no. 1229,* 1977.

Hutchins, B. "Voltage Control of Envelope Generator Parameters." *Electronotes* 66, no. 10 (June 1976).

———. "Some Notes on Sequencers." *Electronotes* 31, no. 3 (November 1973).

Ibrahim, O. E. "Low-Frequency Signals Can Be Recorded on Standard Commercial Tape Recorder." *Electronic Engineering,* January 1973, pp. 37–39.

Johnson, D. "A Voltage-Controlled Sequencer." *Electronic Music Reports,* no. 4 (September 1971).

Johnson, W. "First Festival of Live-Electronic Music, 1967." *Source* 2, no. 1 (January 1968).

Kubo, A. M. "Inexpensive FM Telemetry with Active Circuits." *Electronic Engineering,* July 1970, pp. 26–29.

Landrieu, W. G., and Goethals, L. "Electronic Programming of Electroacoustical Music." *Interface 2,* 1973, pp. 71–99.

Le Caine, H. "Apparatus for Generating Serial Sound Structures." *Journal of the Audio Engineering Society* 17, no. 3 (June 1969): 258–264.

———. "Some Applications of Electrical Level Controls." *Electronic Music Review,* October 1967, pp. 25–32.

———. "Touch-Sensitive Organ Based on an Electrostatic Coupling Device." *Journal of the Acoustical Society of America* 27, no. 4 (July 1955): 781.

"Mixed Media Composition." Panel discussion. *American Society of University Composers Proceedings,* 1968.

Moog, R. A. "Electronic Music: Its Composition and Performance." *Electronics World,* February 1967, pp. 42–46, 84–85.

"Programmed Control. Symposium in *Electronic Music Review,* January 1967.

Rakovich, B. D. "A Wide-Range Linear Time Delay Circuit." *Electronic Engineering,* April 1970, pp. 57–60.

Schaeffer, M. S. "The Hamograph." *IRE Transactions on Audio,* AU–1092 (January/February 1962): 22.

Stockhausen, K. "The Origin of Electronic Music." *Musical Times* 112, no. 1541 (July 1971): 649–650.

Sunstein, D. E. "Photoelectric Waveform Generator." *Electronics,* February 1949, pp. 100–103.

Turino, J. L. "Design Versatile D/A Converters." *Electronic Design 2,* 18 January 1973, pp. 66–68.

"Unijunctions Simplify Sequential Control." *Electronic Engineering,* October 1972, pp. 18–19.

Wells, T. "Review of *Electronic Music: Systems, Techniques, and Controls* by Allen Strange." *Journal of Music Theory* 15, nos. 1 and 2 (1971): 274–281.

Wittlinger, H. A. "Applications of the CA3080 and CA3080A High Performance Operational Transconductance Amplifiers." *RCA Application Note ICAN-6668,* Somerville, N.J.: RCA Solid State Div., 1974.

8

TAPE RECORDING

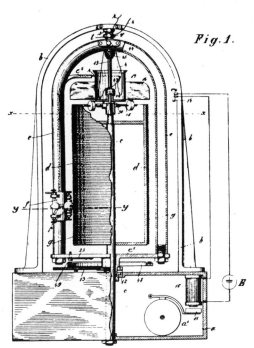

No. 661,619.   Patented Nov. 13, 1900.
V. POULSEN.
METHOD OF RECORDING AND REPRODUCING SOUNDS OR SIGNALS.
(Application filed July 8, 1899.)
(No Model.)   3 Sheets—Sheet I

Fig.1.

Witnesses:

Inventor:
Valdemar Poulsen

Detail of Valdemar Poulsen's *Telegraphone*,
from the U.S. Patent Office application.

The availability of practical tape recording and reproducing equipment after World War II was an important development in the history of electronic music. It should be noted, however, that early *musique concrète* work by Pierre Schaeffer and others employed disc recording and reproduction.[1]

The first magnetic recorder/reproducer was built in 1898 by a Danish engineer, Valdemar Poulsen. Poulsen's device, called the *Telegraphone,* used steel piano wire as the recording medium, and had a limited frequency response and dynamic range. Poulsen's recorder (see frontispiece, this chapter) employed a record head, that slid along a rod, parallel to a drum on which the piano wire was wound. The head could slide up the cylinder, guided by the wire with which it was in contact. In 1909, Poulsen found that the addition of a small direct current fed to the recording head along with the audio signal improved the linearity of the system. With the development of the triode vacuum tube by DeForest, amplifiers were used in conjunction with the Telegraphone to overcome its low output. However, the inherently poor signal-to-noise ratio of the Telegraphone was not improved by amplification, and proved to be a serious defect of the device. In 1927, Carson and Carpenter made an important contribution to magnetic recording technique with the development of AC biasing, which made possible the subsequent development of high-quality recording instruments.

In general, tape recording offers the following advantages over other signal recording methods: (1) wide frequency and dynamic range; (2) low inherent distortion; (3) immediate and repeatable playback; (4) high density storage; (5) economy of operation; and (6) the ability to change the time rate of playback. The magnetic recording process is not discussed in this chapter; rather, the reader is referred to the selected bibliography (3, 5, 6, 7) for detailed discussions of this topic.[2]

Magnetic recording is, at this writing, the most practical means for structuring sounds through time an an electronic piece. However, high-quality digital recording is currently technically feasible, although expensive. The high signal-to-noise ration, capacity for microediting, and infinite shelf life of a digital recording make this method extremely attractive. It is not hyperbolic to say that digital recording is likely to supersede the analog method for professional applications in the future.

As was discussed in chapter 7, currently available electronic music instrumentation is limited in the number of simultaneous and independent sound events, that may be produced. In addition, using complex patchings that involve several variables, it is difficult to predict precisely the nature of a sound event produced by particular settings of sound generating and modifying equipment. For these reasons, the most practical approach is an interactive one, in which the composer varies the settings of the instruments involved in a patching until he achieves a desired result and then records the results on magnetic tape. This is not to say that a piece of electronic music should be produced one sound at a time: through the use of voltage-controlled devices in conjunction with appropriate control signal generators, it is possible to produce large numbers of individually controllable sounds from one patching. The composer may employ naturally or electronically generated material, which he may modify electronically and by tape manipulation. With a suitable complement of voltage- or current-controlled instruments and inter-connection devices, along with a sufficient number of control channels and control signal storage devices, it is possible to specify through time the patchings and instrument settings for an entire electronic piece. Such a system, while certainly technically feasible at this writing, would be rather expensive. Systems of this type generally use a digital computer for switching and for generation of control signals. One such hybrid system has been described in the literature.[3] The E.M.S. Company currently markets a hybrid system using a PDP–11 computer (see frontispiece, this chapter). The availability of microcomputers and used minicomputers has made this hybrid approach economically feasible for many electronic music studios. The RCA Mark II synthesizer is an example of such a system capable of storing the specifications for sound events in a piece (using punched paper tape) and playing the result back.[4]

Hybrid, partially or fully automated systems are not so useful for a composer who relies to some extent on electronically modified natural sounds for his sound material. This is an important consideration if one of the goals of a hybrid system is to provide real-time performance capability to produce results equal to that of the best tape music. This is not to imply any conflict between hybrid systems and the tape studio. Certainly, composers of tape music will appreciate any additional facility in generating sounds. The difficulty of integrating electronically modified natural sounds in an automated system might be solved using digital sound synthesis techniques, in which the natural sounds may be processed through a digital-to-analog-converter, stored, and modified as desired within the limits of the program.

Electronic modification of natural sounds is still a most valuable technique for electronic music production. The electronically modified natural sounds exhibit many of the characteristics of the original natural sound event; in particular, these sounds usually do not exhibit the steady-state quality inherent in many purely electronically produced sounds. Karlheinz Stockhausen's *Telemusik* (UE 14807) is an example of a work that integrates electronically modified natural sounds with purely electronically generated sounds in such a way as not to emphasize obvious differences between the two types of sounds. In another regard, the disparity between electronic and instrumental timbre presents problems that few composers have solved in integrated (electronic + instrumental) works (see Davidovsky's *Synchronisms No. 6* and Stockhausen's *Kontakte* for examples of what the author feels are successful works in this genre).

Multitrack tape recorders have been used in electronic music studios since the early 1950s. In the last 15 years or so, the demand by the recording industry for multitrack professional-quality machines has made such recorders readily available. Current interest in four-channel reproduction for home entertainment has made available many semiprofessional tape machines suitable for electronic music use. Of these machines, the Sony 854–4S, the Crown CX-844, and the Teac 2340 are recommended. In addition, 8-track machines such as the Otari MX–7308 (1'' tape; see figure 8.1) and semiprofessional machines such as the Otari MX–5050 and Teac/Tascam 80–8 (both 1/2'' tape) are widely used in electronic music. Sixteen- and twenty-four track machines are the industry standard for commercial recording but due to their expense are used in only a few electronic music studios.

Multitrack recording makes possible the storage of independently variable sound events that can be ordered in time as the composer desires. Channel-to-channel synchronization is achieved in most cases by playing back the transcribed material on one channel on the record head while recording the new material on an adjacent channel on the same record head. This technique is called *selective synchronization,* abbreviated *sel sync* (Sony: *synchro-track*; Teac: *simul-sync*). Although some signal degradation may be noticed in playing back a signal from the record head, due to the wider gap of the record head, † the signal is certainly usable for synchronization purposes. After synchronization, all channels may be played back from the reproduce head.

Many machines provide remote (relay) control of the switching involved in selective synchronization. However, a more common feature on professional and semiprofessional machines is remote control of the tape transport. Remote-control units, which generally consist of four normally open and one normally closed pushbutton switch, may be obtained from recorder manufacturers or may be easily constructed. Remote control of the tape transport enables the composer to remain close to the sound generating equipment in order to make adjustments on the sound material he is recording. In addition, remote control facilitates starting several tape machines at approximately the same time.

While tape editing remains an important and necessary skill for the composer of electronic music, the importance of tape manipulation as a primary means to produce sequences of sound events has been diminished, due to the capabilities of voltage-controlled instruments and the widespread use of multichannel recording. Editing is employed now mainly to make certain types of adjustments in sound events, to remove spurious transient

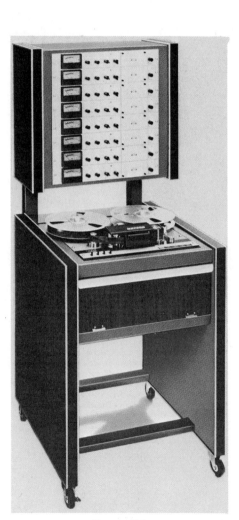

FIGURE 8.1

† As Lowman puts it: "The width of the gap is dependent upon the intended use of the head. In a record head it must be wide enough to permit the magnetic flux to fringe (leak) far enough away from the gap to provide deep penetration into the oxide coating of the magnetic tape. On the other hand, the gap must be small enough so that sharp changes or gradients of the flux may be generated, to permit small changes in . . . level to be recognized. Thus it is that the record gap width is a compromise between a wide gap, for strong recorded signals, and a narrow one, for definition of small increments of change."[5]

noises, and to order groups of events and individual events in time. The employment of tape editing as a self-sufficient means to order sound events in time often produces a homophonic result, depending on the degree to which the individual sound events to be spliced together consist of independent events. Since the composer must rely on juxtaposition of sound events, transitions are usually more difficult to achieve using only tape manipulation (again, the degree to which the juxtaposition is perceivable depends on the nature of the sound events).

The following items are required for tape editing: single-edged razor blades; editing block, or editing jig; splicing tape (AMPEX type recommended) or Editabs (pre-cut splicing material with peel-off backing to expose the adhesive); marker (yellow or white china-marker); empty reels; and leader tape. With professional machines (preferably mounted horizontally for editing use), the location of cutting points is accomplished by moving the tape manually, slowly back and forth past the playback head (figure 8.2), or, more infrequently, the *record* head (if the machine is in the sel sync mode) until the beginning of the sound is heard. Due to the inertia of the take-up and supply reel systems, moving the tape manually with the transport stopped requires the use of both hands, one to move the supply and one to move the take-up reel. By placing the tape on the other side of the capstan (figure 8.3) so that the tape will not be caught between the capstan and pinch roller, the tape may be easily moved by hand when the transport is put in the playback mode. However, searching in the *stop* mode is preferred. For searches involving long segments of tape, the fast forward and rewind motors may be used with the tape lifter defeated (figure 8.4).

While the beginner should practice editing electronic sounds, editing speech is a good exercise. The student might record several sentences with mistakes and corrections, spurious noises, and so on, which he will edit out

FIGURE 8.2

FIGURE 8.3

FIGURE 8.4

FIGURE 8.5

FIGURE 8.6

FIGURE 8.7

to restore the sentence to its intended form. However, editing speech, while easy to do in a superficial way, is fraught with subtle problems. Joel Tall discusses speech editing in detail.[6] W. Meyer-Eppler has discussed the identification of speech sounds played backwards as an aid to editing.[7]

Having located the cutting point (just before the sound to be isolated) at the playback head, the cutting point should be marked (figure 8.5). To avoid fouling the head, it is not advisable to mark the tape directly at the head gap. Rather, the edge of the head housing near the playback head is a convenient spot. The distance from the playback head gap to the marking spot should be carefully measured off from the center of the 45° cutting slot to some other point on the editing block. It is not necessary to make another mark for the 90° cutting slot: one needs simply to mark the tape at the 45° slot and then slide the tape over to make the 90° cut. Having been marked, the tape is placed in the editing block (figure 8.6) and cut cleanly with a sharp razor blade (figure 8.7). The tape yields more easily to cutting if the blade is held down at a 45° angle and the point of the blade edge is used to pierce the tape. Cutting tools employed for editing should not be magnetized, to avoid spurious noises at the joint as the spliced section is played back. In most cases, however, the blade will wear out long before it becomes magnetized from cutting tape. Care should be exercised, nevertheless, to avoid exposing the cutting tool to the fields of bulk erasers and transformers.

The tape segments to be joined together are butted up against one another and covered with a piece of splicing tape (figure 8.8). AMPEX splicing tape is recommended because of its strength, good adhesive properties, and durability. Splicing tape is available in full and narrow widths, for example, for 1/4 inch-tape, 1/4-inch and 7/32-inch widths. When using full-width or larger splicing tape, care should be taken to avoid overlapping the edge of the magnetic tape. Overlapping may permit adhesive material to contact the heads, tape guides, and rollers, causing tape drag and deposits of adhesive, oxide, and foreign matter. Figure 8.9 shows the cutting of the splicing tape after sealing the joint. Most editors prefer to use a splicing tape dispenser. If oversize splicing tape is used, the splicing tape may be trimmed to the edges of the magnetic tape with the tape in the editing block. The practice of cutting small arcs into the top and bottom of the splice using scissors or a splicing jig is not recommended. None of these methods affords any protection against splicing-tape oozing.

The 45° cut is most commonly used in editing, since this cutting angle provides a smooth transition from tape segment to segment, avoiding transients that might appear to be the result of an abrupt discontinuity. However, the 90° cut is often employed purposely to produce an abrupt attack. When 45° and 90° cuts are juxtaposed, a piece of leader tape should be inserted between the cuts to provide a buffer between the splicing tape adhesive and the points of contact along the tape path (figure 8.10).

Cuts other than 45° and 90° are possible, and certain editing blocks (see

FIGURE 8.8

FIGURE 8.9

FIGURE 8.10

FIGURE 8.10

figure 8.11) make provision for these cutting angles. A 45-degree cut on a
1-inch, 8-track tape might produce an audible sequencing of tracks as the
tracks are exposed to the playback head one after the other in order, 1
through 8. Tape editing has been employed for envelope control using
various tape-cutting angles. Although this method is hardly practical today
as a self-sufficient means for amplitude control, it still finds occasional
uses. For example, with a full-track recording, it is possible to effect
decreases in recorded signal amplitude by paring down the width of the
tape (and cutting and splicing a complementary piece of leader tape to fill
out the normal tape width to avoid tape breakage). In addition to being
time-consuming, envelope control using tape editing often results in
mechanical problems: an acute-angle splice, approximately $10°$, say is
less durable because the long, sharp corners of the tape so cut are susceptible to peelback. Peelback is often troublesome even with normal splices; in
general, the shorter the length of splicing tape used, the more vulnerable to
peelback the joint becomes. The tendency toward peelback is, of course,
aggravated as the tape passes around rollers and tape guides.

Figure 8.12 shows a patching consisting of one sine-wave oscillator that
is frequency-modulated by the addition of four sinusoidal modulating signals. This patching is capable of generating a wide range of sounds, and,
with the appropriate changes of settings, it might be used to generate a
section of a piece. The frequency-modulated signal is routed through a
voltage-controlled multifunction filter and then through the gate, VCA 2.
The sequencer controls: the frequency deviation of VCO 1 by regulating
the gain of VCA 1; the -3-dB point(s) of the filter; and the frequency of
VCO 1. Other instruments may be independently controlled by the sequencer, depending on the number of individual control voltages available
per event. (Of course, the outputs of the sequencer may be fanned out to
control instruments in parallel.) Thus, in this patching, the operator may
specify a sequence of sound events by setting the operating points of

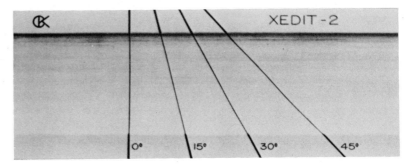

FIGURE 8.11

instruments both manually and with the sequencer (which in this case is manually triggered). The envelope of the resultant sound may be varied manually by adjusting the time-constants of the envelope generator, or automatically, if a voltage-controlled envelope generator is used.

Figure 8.13 shows an amplitude-versus-time graph of a four-channel segment produced one channel at a time by tape overlaying. The tape was started and stopped several times during the production of the individual tracks to permit resetting of the instruments in the patching. The graph was produced by connecting the inputs of the chart recorder to the outputs of four envelope detectors that were driven by the outputs of the four channels of the tape recorder. The process involved in producing the segment in figure 8.13 is described below:

1. Record channel one segments. Playback monitor in line driver position. Play back channel one on channel one of the *record* head (sel sync).

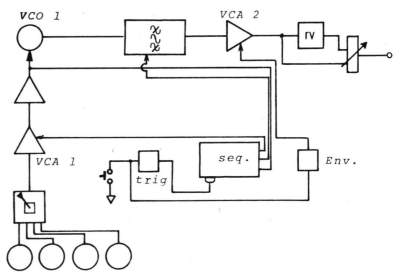

FIGURE 8.12

2. Record channel two segments in desired time relationship to channel one. Playback monitor in line driver position. Play back channel two on channel two of the record head (sel sync) along with channel one (sel sync, channel 1).

3. Record channel three segments in the desired time relationship to channels one and two. Play back channel three on channel three of the record head (sel sync) along with channel one (sel sync, channel 1) and channel two (sel sync, channel 2).

4. Record channel four segments in the desired time relationship to channels one, two, and three. Set all four monitor selectors on the recorder to play back from the reproduce head, and monitor the four-channel overlay.

This section may be used just as it was generated, edited† to adjust the timing of sound events, mixed down and combined with other sound events, or subjected to further modification (tape speed change, modulation, filtering, and so on).

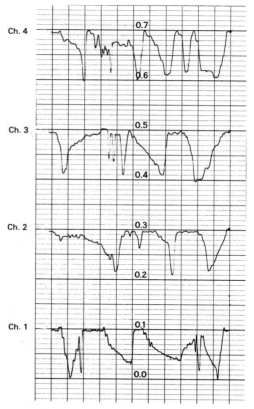

FIGURE 8.13

† In this case, editing must be done with the realization that any editing of one channel will affect the other channels. Individual channels may be dubbed on another machine and the second generation tape edited. The edited version may be rerecorded on the original four-channel tape in the proper time relationship to channels 2, 3, and 4 (although the exact resynchronization of events may prove difficult). This dubbing and editing procedure is time-consuming, and the third generation edited result will probably be of poor audio quality, although better results may be obtained by using a noise reduction system (Dolby, dBx).

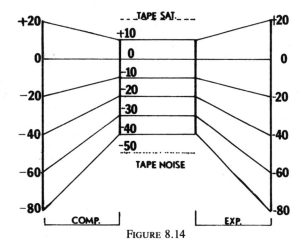

FIGURE 8.14

Practical audio systems are subject to certain types of distortion at extremes of operating range. A magnetic recording system is subject to distortion due to high signal amplitudes and tape noise at small signal amplitudes. In working with magnetic recording, one should choose a level such that high input levels will not overload the system and tape noise will not be obtrusive with small signal levels. Recording at high levels increases the possibility of spurious printing, or print-through, which will be discussed later in this chapter.

One method of extending the dynamic range of a recording system entails decreasing the dynamic range of the original program material to conform to the usable dynamic range of the tape recorder, thereby keeping the weakest parts of the program above the noise level and the strongest parts of the program from saturating the tape. This process is called *compression*. During the playback process, a complementary process called *expansion* is used to restore the original dynamic range of the program. The combined process of compression and expansion is called *companding*.

Figure 8.14 illustrates the process by which 2:1 compression and 1:2 expansion can theoretically result in enhancement of a recorder's dynamic range, compressing a 100-dB-dynamic-range program to fit the limited 50-dB range of a recorder, and the subsequent expansion to the original 100-dB dynamic range. Although this system seems attractive, the instantaneous noise level in the system varies according to changes in loudness in the program, causing annoying noise level modulation. The companding process was employed by recording engineers for many years before automatic level controls were commonly employed. The engineer would be responsible for remembering level changes during recording and would make complementary changes during playback. This manually expanded version would then be rerecorded.

The amount of compression is measured numerically in terms of in-

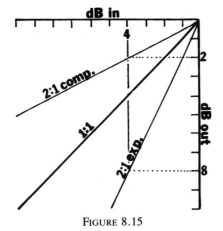

FIGURE 8.15

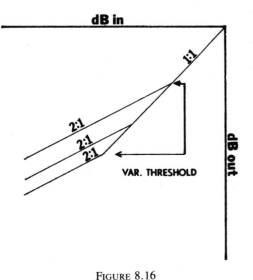

FIGURE 8.16

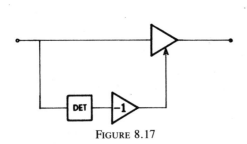

FIGURE 8.17

put:output level. Figure 8.15 shows the input-versus-output curves for a 2:1 compressor, unity-gain amplifier, and 1:2 expander. In figure 8.15, a 4-dB input plotted against the compression curve results in a 2-dB output level, hence 4:2, or a 2:1 compression. The same 4-dB input level plotted against the expansion curve results in an 8-dB output level, hence 4:8, or 1:2 expansion. Some compressors provide a threshold adjustment which allows the operator to select the program level at which compression or expansion action begins. Variable-threshold expansion is available in most professional compressors as well as several semiprofessional units such as the dBx Model 119. The Phase Linear Autocorrelator Noise Reduction device includes a "peak unlimiter," or expander with variable threshold to allow the user to compensate for compression used during the recording process. Figure 8.16 shows a plot of dB-in versus dB-out for a compressor with variable threshold.

For purposes of illustration, figure 8.17 shows how a simple compressor may be patched in the classroom using equipment normally found in the electronic music studio: a voltage-controlled amplifier; envelope follower (detector); and inverting amplifier. The program to be compressed is routed both to the signal input of the VCA and to the input of an envelope detector. The output of the detector is inverted and connected to the control port of the VCA with the result that the gain and subsequent output of the VCA will decrease with increased signal input.

To be effective, a compressor must perform its gain-limiting function very quickly to prevent distortion from high-input signals with fast attacks, for example, piano, guitar, and electronic sounds. Compressors are usually designed so that, after entering the gain-limiting portion of their response, they return slowly to the initial state. This slow decay prevents undesirable rapid gain fluctuations that would be obvious to the ear. The raising and lowering of the gain of a system results in a characteristic modulation of the noise floor called *breathing*. Many compressors provide panel controls of attack and decay times. RMS (root-mean-square) detection is often employed in compressors today. Because the detection process requires a certain amount of time, the operation of the compressor can never be instantaneous.

Compressors are useful in electronic music production in many ways. For example, the use of a compressor for recording natural sounds for processing (filtering, modulating, and so on) can smooth out variations in amplitude that the composer might find undesirable. In the making of a tape loop to produce a continuous sound from some part of a natural sound that has amplitude variations, a limiter (a compressor with a compression ratio of around 10:1 or greater) can be used to good advantage to hold the amplitude of the natural sound to a constant level both during recording and during playback of the loop. Compressors are also useful for works involving real-time electroacoustical modification of instrument sounds when it is important to have a constant level for processing. The dynamic characteristics of the compressor itself are often used purposefully to impart different attack-and-decay characteristics to sounds, for example, in commercial recording, to impart a ''punchier'' sound to a bass. Compression should be used with discretion, however, to avoid the condition of undifferentiated musical dynamics—the deadly mezzo-forte.

R. M. Dolby described in 1967 his audio noise reduction system.[8] This system employs a refined companding process. The system uses fast attacks and decays in the compressor and expander circuits. The Dolby system reduces the noise modulation problem by dividing the recorded spectrum into four bands: 30 Hz–90 Hz; 90 Hz–3 kHz; 3 kHz–9 kHz; and 9 kHz–15 kHz, with each segment having its own compressor/expander circuitry. The Dolby system avoids distortion problems of compressors in handling high-level signals by bypassing high-level signals around the companding circuits. Figure 8.18 shows a block diagram of the Dolby A system (c), along with a diagram of the input and output characteristics of the device (b), and a block diagram (a) of the compressor/expander circuit feature used to bypass high-level signals.

The Dolby system can reduce high-frequency hiss, hum, crosstalk, print-through, and other types of noises by at least 10 dB. The Dolby A

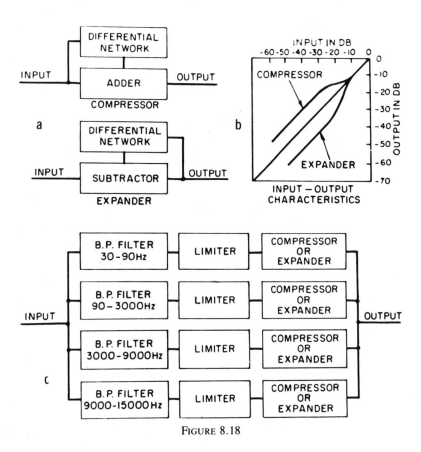

FIGURE 8.18

system described above is widely used in recording studios and in some electronic music studios. The device costs $1,200 for a two-channel processor.

A less expensive version, the Dolby B system, employs compression and expansion from 600 Hz upward. Either Dolby system is most useful in electronic music production. Using the Dolby system, it is possible to make dubs for overlays and mixdowns with no appreciable degradation in quality due to tape noise intrusion. The system is highly appropriate for the production of master tapes of electronic pieces. Of course, the *Dolbyized,* or compressed, recording should be played back through a Dolby expander circuit to restore the original dynamic (and timbral) relationships in the program, and to take advantage of the noise reduction capability of the device.

In using the Dolby B unit, the following sequence of steps is typical: A Dolby alignment tape is provided to calibrate the output level of the tape recorder and the playback amplifier in the Dolby unit. The recorder is adjusted so that the signal from the calibration tape produces a 0 - dB reading on the recorder's VU meter. The Dolby playback calibration control is then set for a 0 - dB reading on the Dolby unit's VU meter. The calibration tape is then replaced with a tape of the type the operator will use in recording. The recorder is placed in the record mode with the recorder's VU meter still monitoring the playback head amplifier. A test tone generated by the Dolby unit is then applied to the recorder line input, and the recorder's VU meter is adjusted to read 0 VU. The above calibration is typical and need not be repeated, provided the operator records the settings of all input and output attenuators involved in the calibration.

The dBx noise reduction system employs 2:1 compression and 1:2 expansion over the entire audio range. The dBx system offers several advantages over the Dolby system: no calibration tape or calibration tone is required: level matching for the dBx system is not critical.

Much of the noise inherent in tape recording consists of high-frequency noise, or hiss. It has been shown that tape noise varies with program level and spectral content. Although most broadband audio signals tend to mask tape noise (recall listening to a loud program over a weak FM station), hiss does become apparent with program material that consists of strong low-frequency signals alone, a condition that occurs not infrequently in electronic music (see chapter 2, pages 34–36). With the dBx system in the record mode (compress), high-frequency components in the program material are *attenuated* (through the use of pre-emphasis in the control circuit), not *boosted* as in the Dolby B system.

As mentioned above, with a dynamic compression system, changes in amplitude of a low-frequency program will cause the compressor to alter the gain of the entire system, resulting in a perceptible change in the level of background hiss. This modulation of background noise, or breathing (described above) is noticeable especially with certain types of programs, such as a low guitar tone, isolated timpani stroke, or gated, low-frequency oscillator.

The dBx noise reduction system (see figure 8.19) employs high-frequency pre-emphasis before recording and complementary de-emphasis upon playback. Using high-frequency de-emphasis on playback helps filter out high-frequency noise in the recording system while restoring the original frequency response of the program. To alleviate the problem of high-frequency self-erasure caused by boosting high-frequency program components (pre-emphasis), the dBx designers included high-frequency pre-emphasis before the level sensing circuit in the compressor. Thus, the higher the amplitude of the high-frequency program components, the more the compressor action. The expander performs the complement of the functions described above, restoring the original amplitude and frequency characteristics of the program through the de-emphasis networks in the control and program lines. The dBx noise reduction system is preferred for electronic music studio applications, both for its simplicity of operation and the large increase in dynamic range it provides: 30 to 40 dB as compared to 10 dB for the Dolby system.

Applications of the dBx noise reduction system are not restricted to tape recording: for example, the unit may be used for noise reduction with a filter or a reverb system (although reverb time will be halved due to the action of the expander, most reverbation units provide sufficient reverb time to allow the settings of the unit to be doubled).

The Burwen noise reduction system is another companding type unit

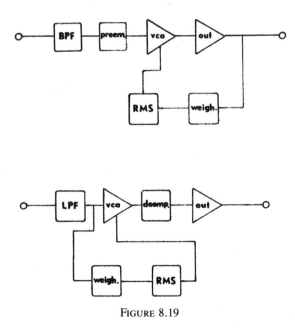

FIGURE 8.19

using pre-emphasis and de-emphasis. The Burwen system employs 3:1 compression and 1:3 expansion.

The Dolby, dBx, and Burwen systems are all *two-way* devices involving compression and expansion. They cannot be used *directly* to remove noise from program material, for example, connected between the output of a tape or disc reproducer and a monitoring system. The transcribed program must first be compressed. The Phase Linear Autocorrelator Noise Reduction System and the SAE Impulse Noise Reduction System are examples of *one-way* systems that do not rely on companding and that may be used in the application described immediately above.

A *noise gate* is a device that behaves like a unity-gain amplifier in the *presence* of program and causes gain reduction in the *absence* of program. Most noise gates permit adjustment of the threshold at which the noise gate "opens" in the presence of program, as well as the amount of gain reduction in the absence of program. Some noise gates provide for control of the attack-and-decay characteristics associated with the two states of the device, as well as adjustable slope over the gain-varying range. The Allison Research Kepex noise gate is widely used in commercial recording. The Kepex unit provides for external control of the gating function: a program may be gated on and off according to amplitude variations of another program.

Concerning noise reduction, Eargle has observed that

> practical noise reduction was not possible until the recording art had progressed to a fairly refined point where shifting of the noise floor would be relatively inaudible. In other words, a noise reduction system might easily extend the effective dynamic range of a 65-dB recording system to 75 dB; it would have a difficult job, however, increasing the dynamic range of a 45-dB system to 55 dB because of the relative audibility of the noise-floor shift.[9]

Many professional tape recorders have a provision for operating the capstan motor from an auxiliary alternating-current power supply. Such operation might be necessary if the frequency of the power line were not constant within tolerable limits. The speed of the capstan motor may be varied intentionally by altering the frequency of the sinusoidal signal that powers the motor, using a high-voltage, high current-capacity, variable-frequency AC supply called a *power oscillator*. Power oscillators may be purchased from recorder manufacturers or assembled from a test oscillator (of the appropriate frequency range), power amplifier, and an impedance-matching device. McProud describes a power oscillator, or variable frequency power source, using a modified high-fidelity power amplifier.[10] The power inverter (figures 8.20) using Signetics integrated circuits may be adapted for use as a power oscillator. The 566 oscillator may be voltage-controlled (although some modification is necessary to permit the use of control signals down to DC). A control range of approximately 25 to 140 Hz is common for capstan motor speed control. Such a control range would vary the relative motor speed by $\log_2 140/25 \simeq 2.4$

octaves. Figure 11.4 chapter 11 shows an excerpt from Stockhausen's *Telemusik* in which variations in the frequency of a power oscillator† are indicated. Variable-speed tape drive is particularly useful in flanging and other tape-delay applications.

, The *Melotron* is a keyboard instrument in which prepared tapes are used to generate tones. Depressing a key on this instrument causes the appropriate tape to be drawn across a reproduce head at a constant rate. Because the tape is not a loop, the tape may be sounded for a finite amount of time (approximately 8 seconds), after which the tape stops moving. Releasing the key resets the tape by causing a weight attched to one end of the tape to draw the tape back to its original position. Each key controls its own tape, clutch, and playback head assembly. Usually, a chromatic scale from an instrument (violin, trumpet, and the like) is recorded on each set of tapes, with one note in the chromatic scale per tape per key. Different timbres are selected by bringing the entire head assembly in line with the appropriate track on each tape. Since no provision is made for reproducing the characteristic attacks and decays of the prerecorded instrument sounds, Melotron-produced sounds differ from those of the original instruments. Several variable-speed tape recorders utilizing keyboard control of the capstan motor speed have been described in the literature.

The *information-rate changer* is another device employed for tape modification of signals. Such a device consists of a tape player that employs a rotating reproduce head to change the motion of the tape relative to the reproduce head gap. Figure 8.21 shows the device in the condition in

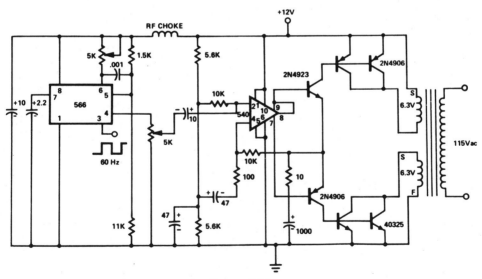

FIGURE 8.20

† *Steuerfrequenz*

COMPRESSION

EXPANSION

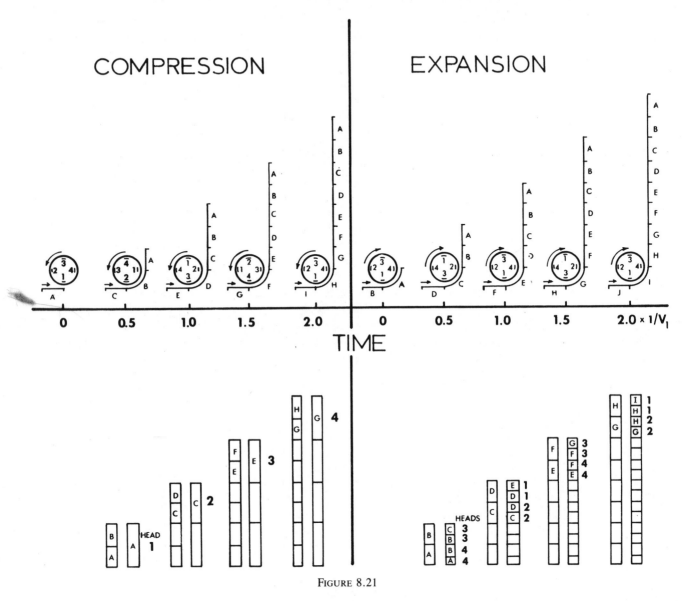

TIME

FIGURE 8.21

which the playback heads move in the same direction as the tape. The velocity, V_5, of the rotating head in this case is one-half that of the tape velocity, V_t, resulting in an effective tape velocity of $1/2V_t$. The transcribed information will be lowered in frequency by a factor of two. For purposes of illustration, assume that the information on the tape is divided into segments called A, B, C, D, E, F, G, and H. At the beginning of the example, head 1 is in contact with segment A of the tape. Since both tape and head are moving in the same direction, segment A is reproduced

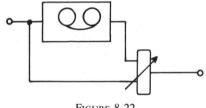

FIGURE 8.22

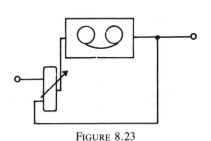

FIGURE 8.23

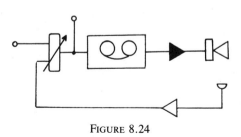

FIGURE 8.24

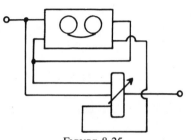

FIGURE 8.25

by head 1 in the time normally required for segments A and B to pass a stationary head. At the next point of observation, head 1 has rotated 90°. Segment B occurs between the gaps of heads 1 and 2, and is not reproduced. Then head 2 begins reproducing segment C. The process continues in a similar fashion, with even-numbered sections omitted and odd-numbered sections reproduced. The pitch of the original transcribed signal is lowered one octave, while the total duration is unaltered. This *compressed* version may be recorded and played back at double speed, restoring the pitch to its original value while halving the duration.

In the next example, the playback heads move in a direction opposite to that of the tape. In this case, V_r is equal to that of v_t, resulting in a tape velocity relative to that of the rotating head of $2V_t$. At the beginning of the example (figure 8.21, Expansion), head 4 is beginning to reproduce segment A. Head 4 will reproduce segments A and B before leaving the tape. Head 3 will reproduce segments B and C, and so forth. In this case the frequency of the original transcribed signal will be raised one octave. This *expanded* version may be recorded and played back at one-half the original tape speed, restoring the original pitch while doubling the duration. German engineers developed the rotating head reproducer in the late 1930s and 1940s. A similar German device made by Springer is part of the tape-machine complement at the W. D. R. Cologne Electronic Music Studio. A similar machine, called the *Tempophon,* is used in the Studio di Fonologica Musicale in Milan. The Eltro Company markets an information-rate changer for $4,000. This device consists only of the rotating-head assembly and must be used with a tape transport. A digital information-rate changer has been described in the literature.[11] Although more expensive than the rotating head device, the digital system is not subject to mechanical problems and slip-ring electrical noise inherent in the mechanical unit.

Tape echo is an interesting, although somewhat overworked, technique. Several basic configurations for producing tape echo are shown below. Figure 8.22 shows an interconnection to produce a single echo. With the recorder in record mode and the monitor selector set to playback (monitoring the signal from the reproduce head), the signal applied to the input is recorded on the record head and played back on the reproduce head after a delay in seconds equal to the distance in inches between the record and reproduce head gaps divided by the tape speed in inches per second. Figure 8.23 shows an interconnection to produce multiple echoes using a three-head recorder. In this configuration, the delayed signal is mixed with the program input, and the resultant addition is recorded, delayed, played back, mixed, recorded, and so on. The configuration of figure 8.24 is similar to that of figure 8.23, except that the feedback is accomplished electroacoustically.

Figure 8.25 shows a configuration for producing two echoes using a two-channel machine. Figures 8.26 and 8.27 show configurations to pro-

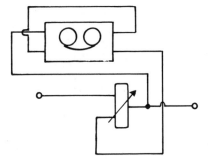

FIGURE 8.26

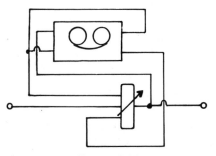

FIGURE 8.27

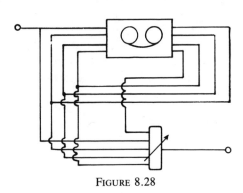

FIGURE 8.28

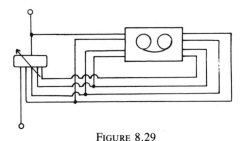

FIGURE 8.29

duce multiple echoes using a two-channel tape machine. In Figure 8.26, the signal is delayed twice before being fed back. Figure 8.27 resembles figure 8.26 except that the signal is monitored and fed back after both the first and second delays. Figure 8.28 shows the double-echo configuration of figure 8.25 expanded to four channels. Figure 8.29 is a four-channel version of figure 8.27.

Tape-delay systems may also be employed to distribute signals to achieve limited spatial effects. Figure 8.30 shows the interconnections for sound distribution in which the delayed signal is recirculated through the system, as in figure 8.29. Figure 8.31 shows a sound distribution configuration without regeneration, similar to the arrangement of figure 8.28. A feedback path (dashed line, figure 8.31) may be inserted between the output of channel 4 and the input of channel 1 to recirculate the echo.

Signal modification devices such as multipliers, frequency dividers, frequency shifters, clippers, filters, and so forth, may be connected in series in the feedback lines of regenerative tape-echo systems to produce certain iterative effects. Figure 8.32 shows a multiplier inserted between the playback amplifier and the recorder line input in a multiple echo arrangement similar to that of figure 8.23. The delayed signal in figure 8.32 is routed to the multiplier, the other input of which is connected to a sine-wave generator. The signal is modified every time it circulates through the system, and in general the resultant signal becomes more complex with each iteration.

Dedicated tape-echo systems are commercially available. These units generally employ a tape loop and consist of erase, record, and multiple playback heads, although other designs make use of magnetic disc recording to avoid tape wear, head wear, and splice noise. Many complex tape delay systems have been devised by composers for specific works (see Stockhausen's *Solo, für Melodie-instrument mit Ruckkoppelung,* Universal Edition 14789). *Solo* uses a special reel-to-reel tape-delay device with a number of playback heads and variable-position tape guides to control the tape path length from head to head. Delayed signals are mixed, re-recorded, and recirculated through the system. Figure 8.33 shows the tape-delay system employed in early versions of *Solo* (facsimile of composer's manuscript). A recent performance of this work in London in which the performers substituted several tape recorders for the special delay apparatus was plagued by tape breakage due to differences in recorder tape speeds. The commercially available recording of *Solo* includes excerpts from the composer's *Hymnen,* interpolated by the composer, who felt that the realization in this case was not self-sufficient.

The purpose of Stockhausen's delay system is to produce a polyphonic result. Through the use of long delays, approximately 1-1/2 minutes, and by selective mixing, the result is *not* characteristic of most tape-delay systems which employ comparatively short delays and periodic repetition.

While tape delay can be a useful device for simulating reverberation,

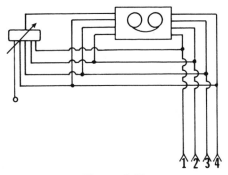

FIGURE 8.30

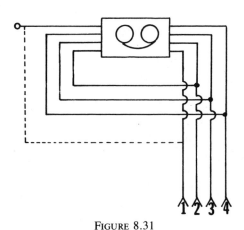

FIGURE 8.31

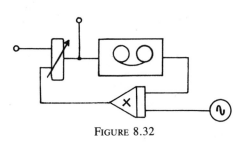

FIGURE 8.32

other devices that produce effects more like that of natural reverbation are preferred. Tape reverberation, unlike natural reverberation, is usually characterized by periodic repetitions, and even though the inherent periodicity may be obscured by employing multiple playback heads, or by simultaneous use of several tape-echo devices running at different speeds, the resultant reverberation simulation is still different from natural reverberation (although the complex tape-delay system may be used for other purposes). In addition, tape reverberation systems produce comparatively low echo densities (see chapter 4).

Commonly used reverberation devices include reverberant rooms, plate reverberation units, spring reverberation units, digital and analog delay lines, acoustical delay lines, so-called water-tank reverberators (an ultrasonic carrier is amplitude-modulated with the program material, propagated through water using a sonar transducer, picked up by another transducer, and demodulated), and tape delay systems.

Reverberation should be used with discretion in electronic music. A useful technique for employing reverberation is shown in figure 8.34. With this configuration, the operator may select any proportion of reverberated sound to non-reverberated sound, or *wet* signal to *dry* signal. In figure 8.34, the proportion of wet:dry signal is voltage-controllable. (See chapter 4 for a general configuration of a voltage-controlled panpot.) Of course, the wet:dry proportion may be manually controlled in a mixer or manual panpot.

For audio signal recording, a plastic-base tape such as polyester (polyethylene terephthalate), acetate (cellulose diacetate, cellulose triacetate), or polyvinyl chloride† of thickness 0.0005 to 0.0015 inch (0.5 to 1.5 mil [1 *mil* = 1/1000 inch]) is employed. This base is coated with a magnetic oxide (Fe_2O_3 gamma) of thickness approximately 0.0007 to 0.002 inch. Table 1 lists some differences between acetate and polyester backings.

For electronic music applications, 1/4-inch, 1/2-inch, and 1-inch tape widths are common. In practice, tape is always cut undersize, that is, for 1/4-inch tape approximately 0.246 inch ± 0.002-inch; for 1/2-inch tape, approximately 0.498 inch ± 0.002 inch; for 1-inch tape, approximately 0.998 inch ± 0.002 inch to ensure that the tape width will not exceed tape guide size.

Audio tape is generally divided into classes according to application demands. *Mastering tape* is used in commercial recording applications to produce master tapes from which records and prerecorded tapes are made. Scotch 250 or Ampex Grand Master tape is recommended for all electronic music work. *Professional tape* is used in broadcast work and in less stringent mastering applications. *Consumer tape* is used in home entertainment applications, cassettes, and so on. The frequency response, dynamic range,

† used in many European-produced tapes

Table 1

	Acetate	*Polyester*
Tensile strength	≈5 lb	11 lb
Tear strength	4 g	25 g
Effect of exposure to high temperatures	Becomes brittle; tends to contract	Remains flexible; relatively unaffected
Thermal dimensional stability	Coefficient of thermal expansion for 1° temp. change = $3.0 \times 10^5 \dfrac{\text{in}}{(\text{in}) (°F)}$	Coefficient of thermal expansion for 1° temp. change = $1.5 \times 10^5 \dfrac{\text{in}}{(\text{in}) (°F)}$
Uniformity of thickness	Excellent	Good
Length tolerance	$\dfrac{-0+30 \text{ ft}}{\text{reel}}$	$\dfrac{-0+30 \text{ ft}}{\text{reel}}$

SOURCE: C. F. Lowman, *Magnetic Recording* (New York: McGraw-Hill, 1972).

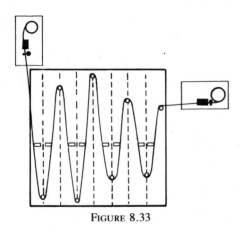

FIGURE 8.33

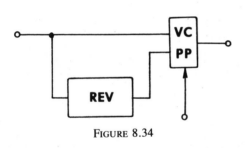

FIGURE 8.34

susceptibility to print-through, and so forth, of these tapes differ, with mastering tape having the best specifications. A tape with thinner backing is more susceptible to print-through, the magnetization by one layer of tape of adjacent tape layers. (Oxide-impregnated tape is no longer used because of its extreme vulnerability to spurious printing.) The signal represented by the changes in flux on the tape will be transferred to adjacent layers and will either precede or follow the original signal as the tape is played. Storage and handling of tape at high temperatures considerably accelerates the printing process, with a correspondence of approximately 1-dB increase in spurious printing for every 10° F temperature increase. Shock caused by dropping reels of tape will also contribute to spurious printing. To provide maximum protection from print-through for valuable master tapes, leader tape may be interwound with the magnetic tape on the reel.

It is good practice to store magnetic tapes *tail out,* that is, the tape should be stored without rewinding after playing in order to take advantage of the more even-winding tension of the transport in the play mode. In addition, should print-through occur with the tape wound tail out, the stronger of the two printed-through signals will occur *after* the original sound.

Tapes should be stored at a constant cool ambient temperature, in a dust-free and smoke-free environment, and should be kept away from stray magnetic and electrostatic fields. A tape affected by print-through may in part be salvaged by running the tape through the transport past a lightly-energized erase head. The amount of erase head current should be adjusted so the printed-through signal will be just erased. Of course, the level of the original signal will also be affected, resulting in a degradation of signal-to-noise ratio. This method represents a last-ditch solution, and should be employed with caution.

A comprehensive program of recorder maintenance will ensure optimum performance from and will prolong the life of the instrument. Careful maintenance is most important in the case of electronic music studio tape recorders that are used regularly. Although the user should refer to his particular machine's manual for detailed maintenance information, the following list of procedures is suggested:

1. Daily clean heads, tape guides, capstan, and rollers that come in contact with the tape. Xylene (dimethylbenzene) is recommended for cleaning heads, tape guides, and the capstan. Use ethanol (ethyl alcohol) to clean rubber parts. Carbon tetrachloride is *not* recommended, since it has been shown to cause liver damage. Besides clogging the tape head, oxide from the tape can form highly abrasive buildups at points of contact along the tape path.

2. Demagnetize tape heads (and all magnetizable surfaces that contact the tape) after about every 10 hours of use. One may determine if a head or heads is/are magnetized by playing the same segment of virgin tape repeatedly on the machine. If the tape noise increases perceptibly after about 10 playings, one of the heads (or some part of the transport that contacts the tape) is magnetized. This operation does not, however, identify *which* head is magnetized. In practice, the demagnitization process is less time-consuming than the above test. Head demagnetization should be carried out as follows: turn on the demagnetizer *away* from the head assembly; slowly bring the demagnetizer into proximity with the tape head and slowly move the pole pieces of the demagnetizer up and down the heads for about 30 seconds (it is good practice to cover the pole pieces with tape or plastic to avoid scratching the heads); slowly remove the demagnetizer from the vicinity of the heads and remove power to the device; *do not* switch the demagnetizer on or off while the device is in proximity with the heads. The state of magnetization of the heads and points of contact along the tape path can be checked with a small magnetometer such as the Annis Company (Indianapolis, Indiana) Model 20/5–0–5.

3. Align the recorder periodically. As the heads wear, the head gaps widen, resulting in high-frequency loss (see Appendix 5). Up to a certain point, the high-frequency loss may be compensated for by equalization of the recorder electronics. Head misalignment can cause uneven wear, resulting in permanent damage to the head if the misaligned head is used for long periods of time. The tape azimuth adjustment also affects the high-frequency response and should be checked periodically.

4. Ensure that the capstan is properly aligned (90° to the direction of tape travel and parallel to the tape surface). Misalignment of the capstan angle can cause tape to ride up and down on the heads and guides, possibly causing damage to the tape (wrinkling of the edges), as well as improper tracking. The force of the pressure roller on the capstan should be set to the manufacturer's specifications and periodically checked. Excessive force can cause wear on the capstan motor bearings as well as cause wear and deformation of the pressure roller. Insufficient force can cause slow starting and speed variations (especially when splices pass the capstan/pressure roller). The Tentelometer Model T2–H20–ML (around $180 at this writing) tape tension gauge is highly recommended for tape machine maintenance.

The bulk demagnetizer, or degausser, is a necessary device for reclaiming used tape. The user should not assume that the erase head of his tape recorder will completely erase previous signals. High recording levels, improper erase current, and other factors influence the effectiveness of erasure. As standard practice, the recordist should degauss all recycled tapes before recording new program material on them. Tape to be bulk-erased should be brought slowly into proximity with the degausser, rotated on the spindle of the device, turned over, rotated again, and removed slowly from the immediate area of the degausser. The degausser should not be switched on or off while the tape is in its new field. Since magnetizing force is proportional to the rate of change of flux, the rapidly increasing or collapsing field of the degausser will cause intense magnetization of the tape, resulting in hard-to-erase thumping or clicking during playback.

PROBLEMS

1. Record a sound that has a sharp attack characteristic. Play the sound back in reverse, and process this signal through a reverberation unit. Then record the reverberated signal on another tape recorder (or channel of the same machine). Play the second generation recording back *backwards* and note the character of the resultant sound.

2. Why is the track configuration on many in-line 4-channel 1/4-inch-tape machines 1 3 2 4 rather than 1 2 3 4 (tracks numbered from the top of the head to the bottom)?

3. How may the speed of a tape recorder's capstan motor be varied? Why should an autotransformer (*Variac, Powerstat*) not be used for this purpose?

4. Record a piano sound. Remove the initial transient from the sound by editing and note the resulting effect.

5. Record each of the pitches in figure 7.8, chapter 7, one at a time, and edit these tones together in the relationships shown in the score.

6. Why is tape manipulation not a preferred technique for control of the amplitude-versus-time characteristics of sounds?

7. Describe a daily program of maintenance for a professional tape recorder.

8. What is FM recording? What advantages does this type of recording offer for electronic music applications?

9. Record a sentence read with several mistakes (false starts, mispronounciations, and corrections [normally, corrections will be emphasized]). Edit the tape to make the delivery as normal and natural as possible.

10. Describe the operation of the Dolby A and B noise reduction systems.

11. How may one increase the duration of a sound event without altering its pitch?

12. How does the high-frequency response of a tape recorder change with head wear? How may this effect be compensated for?

13. Describe "tape reverberation." How does this type of reverberation differ from natural reverberation?

14. Describe the reaction of polyester- and acetate-base recording tapes to a sudden increase in tape tension.

15. What is the effect of playing a "Dolbyized" (compressed) tape on a normal machine (without expanding). Assume the Dolby system in this case to be the A system.

16. In general, what recording levels should be used in order to achieve the maximum signal-to-noise ratio with least distortion in a magnetic recording system?

17. When playing a tape piece in a large hall, it is advisable for the composer to regulate the levels of the channels from a position in the middle of the listening area. Describe several ways in which such a playback system may be constructed (use different types of attenuators [electronic attenuators, photoresistors]) and describe the types of cables required.

18. Contrast the operation of the dBx and Dolby B noise reduction systems.

19. Describe the process of compression. How is the compression ratio defined?

20. Why will simple 2:1 compression during recording and subsequent 1:2 expansion upon playback not double the dynamic range of a recording system?

21. Describe the effect of the threshold control on a compressor.

22. What is a limiter? What applications do limiters have in electronic music?

23. What is the effect of playing a tape on a machine with magnetized heads?

24. From outside readings,[12] what is the effect of (1) too little bias and (2) too much bias on the frequency response of a magnetic recorder?

25. Amplitude modulate a 1000-Hz sine wave with an approximately 3-Hz triangle wave (100 percent modulation). Connect the output of the modulator to a multiple, one tap from which is routed to the x-axis input of an oscilloscope, and the other from which is routed to the input of a compressor/expander. Connect the output of the compressor/expander to the y-axis input of the oscilloscope. With the compander set to 1:1, separately adjust the x- and y-axis deflections on the scope to be equal. Replace the x and y connections as described above, and observe the resultant traces on the oscilloscope for various compression and expansion ratios, as well as for various threshold settings. Explain what you observe on the oscilloscope.

NOTES

1. L. Cross, "Electronic Music: 1948–1953," *Perspectives of New Music,* Fall/Winter 1968.

2. See, especially, J. Eargle, *Sound Recording* (New York: Van Nostrand-Reinhold, 1976); N. Hayes, *Elements of Magnetic Tape Recording* (Englewood Cliffs, N.J.: Prentice-Hall, 1957); C. F. Lowman, *Magnetic Recording* (New York: McGraw-Hill, 1972); and C. D. Mee, *The Physics of Magnetic Recording* (New York: Interscience Publishers, 1964).

3. D. Friend, "A Time-Shared Hybrid Sound Synthesizer," *Journal of the Audio Engineering Society* 19, no. 11 (1967).

4. M. Babbitt, "An Introduction to the R.C.A. Synthesizer," *Journal of Music Theory* 8, no. 2 (Winter 1964).

5. Lowman, *Magnetic Recording.*

6. J. Tall, *Techniques of Magnetic Recording* (New York: Macmillan, 1958).

7. W. Meyer-Eppler, "Reversed Speech and Repetition Systems as a Means of Phonetic Research," *Journal of the Acoustical Society of America* 22 (1950): 804–806.

8. R. M. Dolby, "An Audio Noise Reduction System," *Journal of the Audio Engineering Society* 15 (1967): 383.

9. Eargle, *Sound Recording.*

10. C. G. McProud, "Build a Variable Frequency Power Source," *Audio* 54 (1970): 30, 34, 36.

11. F. F. Lee, "Time Compression and Expansion of Speech by the Sampling Method," *Journal of the Audio Engineering Society* 20 (1972): 738–742.

12. Eargle, *Sound Recording*; F. Everest, *Handbook of Multichannel Recording* (Blue Ridge Summit, Pa.: Tab Books, 1975); and Hays, *Elements of Magnetic Tape Recording*.

SELECTED BIBLIOGRAPHY

Books

Borwick, J. *Sound Recording Practice*. London: Oxford University Press, 1976.

Dwyer, T. *Composing with Tape Recorders: Musizue Concrète for Beginners*. London: Oxford University Press, 1972.

Eargle, J. *Sound Recording*. New York: Van Nostrand-Reinhold, 1976.

Everest, F. *Handbook of Multichannel Recording*. Blue Ridge Summit, Pa.: Tab Books, 1975.

Hayes, N. *Elements of Magnetic Tape Recording*. Englewood Cliffs, N.J.: Prentice-Hall, 1957.

Lowman, C. F. *Magnetic Recording*. New York: McGraw-Hill, 1972.

Mee, C. D. *The Physics of Magnetic Recording*. New York: Interscience Publishers, 1964.

Nisbitt, A. *The Technique of the Sound Studio*. New York: Communication Art Books–Hastings House Publishers, 1966.

Olson, H. F. *Modern Sound Reproduction*. New York: Van Nostrand-Reinhold, 1972.

Pear, C. B. *Magnetic Recording in Science and Industry*. New York: Van Nostrand-Reinhold, 1967.

Stewart, W. E. *Magnetic Recording Techniques*. New York: McGraw-Hill, 1958.

Tall, J. *Techniques of Magnetic Recording*. New York: Macmillan, 1958.

Articles

Babbitt, M. "An Introduction to the R.C.A. Synthesizer." *Journal of Music Theory* 8 no. 2 (Winter 1964).

Blesser, B. "Audio Dynamic Range Compression for Minimum Perceived Distortion." *IEEE Transactions on Audio Electroacoustics* AU–17 (1969): 22–32.

———. "An Ultraminiature Console Compression System with Maximum User Flexibility." *Journal of the Audio Engineering Society* 20 no. 4 (May 1972): 297–302.

Buff, P. C. "A Combination Limiter." *dB*, February 1972, pp. 22–24.

Cross, L. "Electronic Music: 1948–1953." *Perspectives of New Music*, Fall/Winter 1968.

Dolby, R. M. "An Audio Noise Reduction System." *Journal of the Audio Engineering Society* 15 (1967): 383.

Friend, D. "A Time-Shared Hybrid Sound Synthesizer." *Journal of the Audio Engineering Society* 11 (December 1971).

Lee, F. F. "Time Compression and Expansion of Speech by the Sampling Method." *Journal of the Audio Engineering Society* 20, no. 9 (November 1972): 738–742.

Malanowski, G. W. "Sound Level Compression with Low-Cost AGC." *Electronic Engineering,* January 1973, pp. 40–42.

Meyer-Eppler, W. "Reversed Speech and Repetition Systems as a Means of Phonetic Research." *Journal of the Acoustical Society of America* 22, no. 6 (November 1950): 804–806.

McProud, C. G. "Build a Variable Frequency Power Source." *Audio* 54, no. 1 (January 1970): 30, 34, 36.

Oliveros, P. "Tape Delay Techniques for Electronic Music Composition." *The Composer* 1, no. 3 (December 1969).

Olson, H. F. "Electronic Music Synthesis for Recordings." *IEEE Spectrum,* April 1971, pp. 18–30.

Poullin, J. "The Application of Recording Techniques to the Production of New Musical Materials and Forms. Applications to Musique Concrète." Translated by D. Sinclair. *National Research Council of Canada, Technical Translation TT-605* (of historical interest).

Poulsen, V. "The Telegraphone: A Magnetic Speech Recorder." *Electrician* 46 (November 1900): 208–210.

Ristad, C. H. "Volume Compressor with 50 dB Range Built Around a Single Op Amp." *Electronic Design 10* (Ideas for Design), 10 May, 1973, p. 110.

"Tape Recording." *Electronic Music Review* 6 (April 1968).

Yamazaki, M., and Masuda, E. "A New Automatic Noise Reduction System (ANRS)." *Journal of the Audio Engineering Society* 21 no. 6 (July/August 1973): 445–449.

9

STUDIO LAYOUT AND DESIGN

The E.M.S. Studio in London. The PDP 11 computer, DecTape drives, and other computer and test equipment appear in the upper left of the photograph. To the right are an E.M.S. 100 synthesizer and various recording equipment. A portable E.M.S. synthesizer is in the foreground.

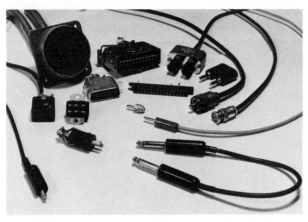

FIGURE 9.1a

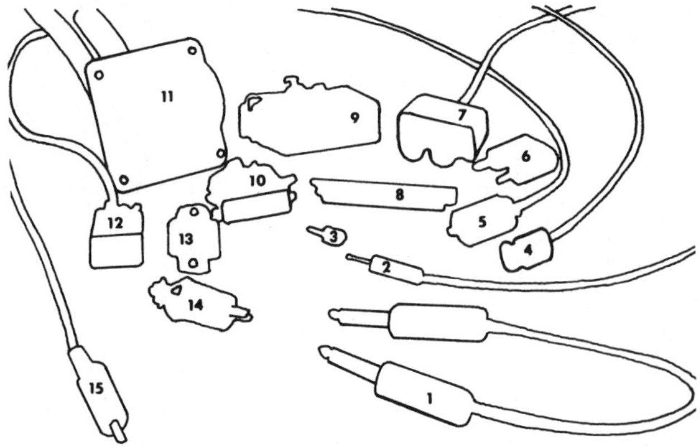

1. Telephone plug patch cord
2. Miniature phone plug
3. Phono pin (RCA) plug
4. BNC plug
5. PL-259 (UHF) plug
6. Double banana plug
7. Double banana jack
8. Printed circuit board edge connector
9. Blue Ribbon connector plug
10. Blue Ribbon connector plug
11. Amphenol cylindrical multi-contact connector
12. Cinch-Jones plug
13. Cinch-Jones jack
14. Cinch-Jones plug
15. Alligator clip head

FIGURE 9.1b

Although the availability of small, modular electronic music instrumentation has simplified the problem, the installation of an electronic music studio requires careful consideration of both the physical layout of the studio and the electrical interconnections of studio instruments.

A basic component in the design of most electronic music studios is the patch panel, a collection of connectors of the same type, to which the inputs and outputs of most studio equipment are connected. The patch panel thus facilitates the interconnection of studio instruments both by bringing the inputs and outputs in close proximity, and by providing the same type of connectors for all inputs and outputs.

Figure 9.1 (a and b) shows several types of connectors used in the electronic music studio. (The Cannon XLR–3 connectors were omitted from the photograph.) The following adaptor cables find many uses in the studio: phone plug to phono pin plug; phone plug to miniature phone plug; phone plug to BNC plug; phone plug to banana plug; phone plug to Cannon XLR male; phone plug to Cannon XLR female; phone plug to alligator clips; Cannon XLR male to phono pin plug; Cannon XLR female to phono pin plug; BNC plug to alligator clips; banana plug to alligator clips; and PL–259 plug to alligator clips. In addition, an adaptor panel with panel-mounting XLR plugs and recepticles, 1/4″ telephone jacks, miniature telephone jacks, banana jacks, BNC jacks, RCA phono jacks, and so forth, along with a small 1/4-inch telephone jack patch panel to allow the interconnection of any combination of connectors on the panel, is a useful addition to the patch panel. Groups of multiple jacks may be added to this panel if needed.

The standard telephone jack is commonly used in patch panel construction. Telephone jacks are available in several configurations, the simplest of which is shown in figure 9.2. A ring-tip-sleeve jack with plug inserted is

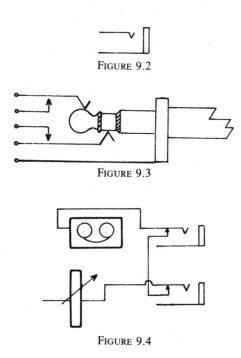

FIGURE 9.2

FIGURE 9.3

FIGURE 9.4

shown in figure 9.3. This particular jack includes a set of *normal* contacts that contact the ring and tip swingers (contacts) when no plug is inserted. Inserting the telephone plug will push the swingers away from the normal contact springs, breaking the normal connections. Normal jacks are used to interconnect instruments routinely used in conjunction with each other. Of course, these instruments may be used separately simply by the insertion of a plug that breaks the normal connection. Other types of jacks include switches (for controlling lamps, relays, and so on) that are operated by the insertion of a plug. Figure 9.4 shows a tape recorder and mixer connected together using normal jacks. The use of normalled connections for routine interconnection of electronic music equipment is highly recommended.

A diagram of a simple signal monitoring system is shown in figure 9.5. It may be desirable to use such a switching system on a limited basis for routine patchings involved in signal generation. The use of multiple-bus solid state crosspoint switches under microprocessor control provides an efficient means of routing signals in the electronic studio. Arrays of pre-mounted telephone jacks called jack bays are commercially available. These jack bays are usually designed for standard 19-inch rack mounting. Figure 9.6 shows a patch panel used in a small recording studio which employs balanced lines. Most electronic music studios use unbalanced lines. (See Hiller, "The Experimental Music Studio at the University of Illinois" for a layout of a studio employing balanced lines.)

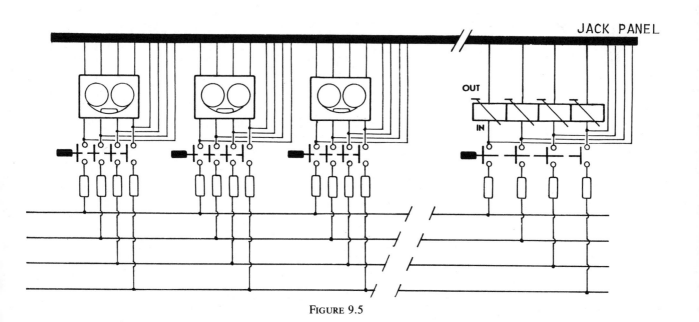

FIGURE 9.5

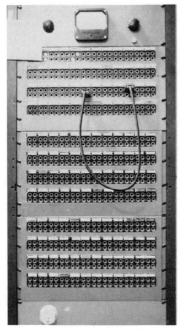

FIGURE 9.6

The layout of various instrument inputs and outputs on the patch panel is determined both by the studio's complement of equipment, and by the need for a logical and convenient arrangement. In the case of commercially available "packaged" studios, even though patching may be accomplished at the "synthesizer" itself, it is highly desirable that the synthesizer inputs and outputs appear on the patch panel. It is desirable to join the lines from the synthesizer to the patch panel with electrical connectors (such as the Amphenol cylindrical multicontact unit shown in Figure 9.1b [no. 11], especially if it is desirable to retain the portability of the synthesizer.

Patch-panel labeling may be accomplished using cards that fit into designation strips on some jack panels. Embossed plastic adhesive labeling may also be used. A greater variety of typefaces and symbols is available using pressure lettering. The lettering is, of course, difficult to apply to the jack panel directly. The lettering should be applied to a smooth surface, and then lifted off with a strip of transparent tape. The tape is then applied to the desired surface. Jacks may be color-coded to identify, for example, control-signal inputs, control-signal outputs, audio-signal inputs, and so forth. (Some of these distinctions will overlap: for example, an oscillator output may be used both as an audio signal and a control-signal source.) Colored tape used for graphic design work may be used to separate groups of instruments. The completed panel should be protected with a transparent finish (taking care not to get paint on the jack contacts). Figure 9.7 shows the layout of the patch panel of a large electronic-music studio.

A useful addition to the patch panel is a simple continuity tester made by connecting a transformer, buzzer, and two jacks in series, so that plugging a patch cord into the two jacks completes the circuit. This tester checks center-conductor continuity only, and will give no indication of a center-conductor-to-shield short.

Other means besides patching may be used to interconnect instruments. The *matrix switch* is used in some *Tonus* (ARP) equipment to effect patching. A photograph of a 10 × 10 matrix switch is shown in Figure 9.8. A matrix switch is composed of two groups of contacts that are bussed in parallel rows. The contact rows of one group are oriented perpendicular to those of the other group so as to obtain switching crosspoints. Electrical connections of the bussed-contact rows are effected by moving a sliding contact to the desired crosspoint. Figure 9.9 shows the matrix board of the E.M.S. Synthi AKS. A matrix board is similar to a matrix switch except that crosspoint connections are effected with the matrix board by inserting shorting pins in holes. The interconnection of instruments may also be accomplished using crossbar switches or electronic switches which may be driven by digital circuitry to permit rapid patching changes.

Interconnecting signal-carrying cables in a studio are susceptable to electrical noise. Most spurious signals, such as power-line hum, fluorescent-light interference, crosstalk, and so forth, can be excluded

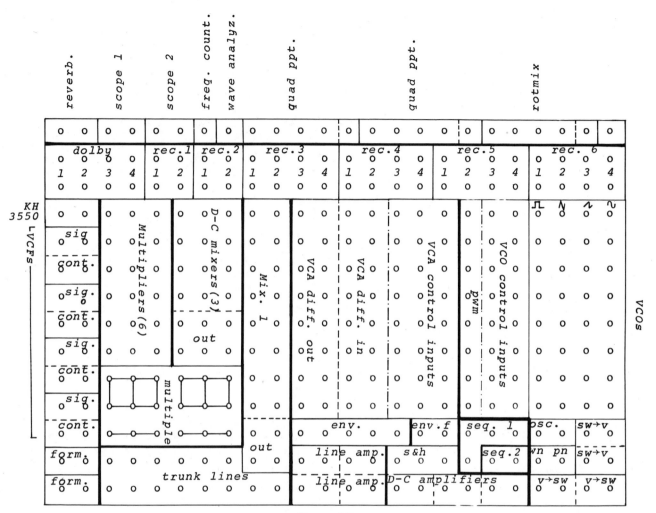

FIGURE 9.7

from studio lines by using shielded cable. As was mentioned in chapter 4, interference from spurious signals presents fewer problems if signal input and output impedances are kept low. While the elimination of noise in an electronic system may seem to involve a certain amount of hocus-pocus, there are systematic approaches to the problem (see Morrison, *Grounding and Shielding Techniques in Instrumentation*[2]).

The *ground loop* is a major source of electrical interference. In general, ground loops are caused by grounding a signal-carrying shielded cable at more than one point. Figure 9.10 shows a system in which the shield of the cable connecting the signal source and signal destination is grounded at both ends. In this example, differences in potential between the two

FIGURE 9.8

grounding points cause noise currents to flow. These noise currents are then coupled to the inner conductor, resulting in noise on the signal. In Figure 9.10, the flow of noise currents in the shield is eliminated by lifting the ground connection at the signal destination.

The capacitance per foot of interconnecting audio cables should be considered when long cable runs are used. The capacitance of the cable acts as a low-pass filter, limiting the high-frequency response of the line.[3] Most electronic music studio installations, however, do not require long runs of cable, a typical length being about 10 to 20 feet. Typical capacitance-per-foot values for selected cables are shown below.

Belden 8451	67 pf/ft
Belden 8776	55 pf/ft
Belden 8219–RG58A/U	26 pf/ft
Belden 8641	42 pf/ft

The following cables are recommended for electronic music studio use: two conductor-shielded cables—Belden 8451 and 8641; microphone cable—Belden 8402; multiple-pair individually shielded cable—Belden 8778 (6 pairs), Belden 8776 (15 pairs), Belden 8773 (27 pairs); coaxial cable (suitable for patch cords with telephone plug terminations)—Belden 8219 RG58A/U.

It is desirable to rack-mount most studio equipment. Figures 9.11 and 9.12 show a typical rack-mounted installation of tape machines and other equipment. Since most "synthesizers" are usually supplied with their own

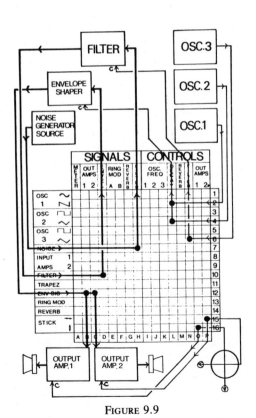

FIGURE 9.9

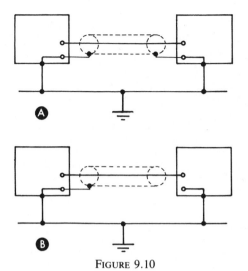

FIGURE 9.10

FIGURE 9.11

FIGURE 9.12

enclosures, these units probably need not be rack-mounted, especially if it is desired to retain their portability. However, rack mounting enclosures are available from several synthesizer manufacturers. Rack mounting is not desirable for tape machines that are used extensively for editing, horizontal or slanted mounting being preferred for this application.

Although professional mixing consoles are readily available, many studios employ mixers built by their own personnel. Professional-quality mixing equipment is expensive. One can spend several thousand dollars even for a small unit. Sony and Tascam have recently marketed inexpensive mixing equipment in the $500 to $3,000 range suitable for electronic-music use. Figure 9.13 shows a bare-bones version of the Tascam Model 10B mixer which is used in many electronic-music studios in this country. Accessories for this unit include: quad panner module; slate/talkback module; 8-channel mixdown module; auxiliary console to permit up to 24 inputs; and headphone amplifier. Figure 9.14 shows a Fairchild mixer used in a small commercial recording studio. The studio mixer is the central audio-signal distribution device in the studio. The mixer is connected at all times to the monitor amplifiers, and monitor levels are regulated by controls on the mixer itself, the adjustment of which does not affect the level of the signal passing through the mixer. Signals to be recorded are routed through the mixer, and then to the tape machines. By using a test tone (often built into the mixer), readings on mixer and re-

FIGURE 9.13

FIGURE 9.14

corder VU meters are set to correspond, permitting the operator to monitor levels from the mixer only. (See chapter 4 for a lengthier discussion of mixers.)

All wiring and other technical work in the studio should be done to the highest professional standards. If professional help is not available, touring several recording studios and radio stations to observe proper installation techniques will be instructive.[4] Exposed wiring should be avoided, and separate cable trays should enclose low-level signal-carrying cables, high-level signal-carrying cables, and power and remote control cables. A false (computer) floor is ideal for running and concealing wiring.

A main power switch to disconnect power from all studio equipment is desirable. This switching may be relay-controlled and operated from the central console in the studio.

Physical layout of the studio depends, of course, on the equipment on hand, as well as personal preference. Again, rack mounting, either in

FIGURE 9.15
The Buchla Electronic Music System, CBS
Musical Instruments.

FIGURE 9.16
The EMS 100 synthesizer.

standard rack cabinets or in sloping-front desk type racks is very desirable. Track lighting with 150- or 300-watt floodlights and spotlights is ideal for the studio situation.

The value of documentation in the studio cannot be overstated. Every instrument in the studio should be assigned a file that contains specifications, schematics, and a chronology of failures and the circumstances under which the failures occurred, as well as the diagnosis and remedy, including any substituted parts or changes in the schematic. A log sheet, to be signed by all studio users, should be placed in a conspicuous place. Entries in the log should include the name of the user, time in and out (registered on an elapsed-time meter connected to the main power switch), equipment used, and comments (faulty equipment, and so on) that may aid the technician in servicing the equipment. Depending on the amount of use and personnel available, studio instruments should be checked at least every two weeks, and the results recorded in the maintenance file.

NOTES

1. R. C. Ehle, "Live Electronic Music Equipment," *dB*, December 1971, pp. 21–25.

2. R. Morrison, *Grounding and Shielding Techniques in Instrumentation* (New York: Wiley, 1967).

3. W. Kuilenburg, "A New Studio Mixer: A Description of the Design for a New Mixing Desk for Studio II at the Institute of Sonology," *Interface 1* (1972): 175–185.

4. See H. Tremaine, *Audio Cyclopedia* (Indianapolis, Ind.: Howard W. Sams, 1969); J. Woram, *The Recording Studio Handbook* (New York: Sagamore, 1976).

SELECTED BIBLIOGRAPHY

Books

Eargle, J. *Sound Recording*. New York: Van Nostrand-Reinhold, 1976.

Harper, C., ed. *Handbook of Wiring, Cabling, and Interconnecting for Electronics*. New York: McGraw-Hill, 1972.

Morrison, R. *Grounding and Shielding Techniques in Instrumentation*. New York: Wiley, 1967.

Slot, G. *Audio Quality*. New York: Drake, 1972.

Tremaine, H. *Audio Cyclopedia*. Indianapolis, Ind.: Howard W. Sams, 1969.

Woram, J. *The Recording Studio Handbook*. New York: Sagamore Publishing, 1976.

Articles

Alexandrovich, G. "How to Specify a Custom Audio Console." *dB*, December, 1970.

Anderton, C. "Low-Cost Compander Enhances Hi-Fi Recordings." *Popular Electronics,* April 1975.

Bottje, W. G. "Equipment in the Electronic Music Studio at Southern Illinois University." *Electronic Music Reports,* no. 2, Utrecht State University, Institute of Sonology, Utrecht, Netherlands.

Burhans, R. W. "Simplified Educational Music Synthesizer." *Journal of the Audio Engineering Society* 19, no. 2 (March 1971), 127–132.

Chadabe, J. "New Approaches to Analog Studio Design." *Perspectives of New Music* 7, no. 1.

———. "Das Elektronische Musik Studio von Albany." *Melos,* May 1971.

Cherry Switch Catalog C70. Cherry Electrical Products Corp., 3600 Sunset Ave., P. O. Box 718, Waukegan, Ill. 60035.

Ciamaga, G. "Kennwort UTEMS." *Melos,* December 1971.

Ehle, R. C. "An Electronic Music Synthesizer." *dB,* November 1968, pp. 22–25.

———. "Live Electronic Music Equipment." *dB,* December 1971, pp. 21–25.

Eimert, H. "Electronic Music," (1956). *National Research Council of Canada, Technical Translation TT–601.*

Electronic Music Reports. Utrecht State University, Institute of Sonology, Utrecht, Netherlands.

Enkel, F. "The Technical Facilities of the Electronics Music Studio of the Cologne Broadcasting Station." *Technische Hausmitteilungen des Nortwestdeutschen Rundfunks,* no. 6 (1954): 8–15. Translated by D. Sinclair. *National Research Council of Canada, Technical Translation TT–603* (of historical interest).

Friend, D. "A Time-Shared Sound Synthesizer." *Journal of the Audio Engineering Society.* 19, no. 11 (December 1971): 928–935.

Gabura, J., and Ciamaga, G. "Digital Computer Control of Sound Generating Apparatus for the Production of Electronic Music." *Electronic Music Reports,* no. 1, p. 54.

Hiller, L. A., Jr. "An Integrated Electronic Music Console." *Journal of the Audio Engineering Society* 13, no. 2 (April 1965): 142–150.

Ketoff, P. "The Synket." *Electronic Music Review* 4 (October 1967).

Kindlmann, P. J., and Fuge, P. H. "Sound Synthesis: A Flexible Modular Approach." *IEEE Transactions on Audio and Electroacoustics* AU–16, no. 4 (December 1968): 507–514.

Kuilenburg, W. "A New Studio Mixer: A Description of the Design for a New Mixing Desk for Studio II at the Institute of Sonology." *Interface* 1 (1972): 175–185.

Landrieu, W. G., and Goethals, L. "Electronic Programming of Electro/ Accoustical Music." *Inteface* (1973): 71–79.

Lietti, A. "The Technical Equipment of the Electronic Music Studio of Radio Milan." Translated by D. Sinclair. *National Research Council of Canada, Technical Translation TT–603.*

Moog, R. A. "Electronic Music: Its Composition and Performance." *Electronics World,* February 1967, pp. 42–46, 84–85.

Mumma, G. "An Electronic Music Studio for the Independent Composer." *Journal of the Audio Engineering Society* 12: 240.

Rampazzi, T. "Elektronische Musik in Padua." *Melos,* February 1971.

Schaeffer, M. "The Electronic Music Studio at the University of Toronto." *Journal of Music Theory* 8, no. 1 (Spring 1963).

Schwartz, A. "The Feedback Loop" [cable losses]. *dB,* May 1971, pp. 14–15.

Seawright, J. "What Goes Into an Electronic Music Studio?" *Music Educator's Journal* 55, no. 3 (November 1968).

Stockhausen, K. "Elektronische Musk aus Studios in aller Welt." *Texte zur Musik, Band 3*. Cologne: DuMont Schauberg, 1971.

"Synthesizers." *Synthesis* 1, no. 2 (July 1971).

Tempelaars, S. "Voltage Control in the Utrecht University Studio." *Electronic Music Reports,* no. 1 (September 1969).

Vercoe, B. "Electronic Sounds and the Sensitive Performer." *Music Educator's Journal* 55, no. 3 (November 1968).

Voss, R. M. "The Brandeis University Electronic Music Studio." *Journal of the Audio Engineering Society* 13, no. 1 (January/February 1965), 65–68.

Wiggan, K. "The Electronic Music Studio at Stockholm: Its Development and Construction." *Interface* 1, no. 2 (November 1972): 127–165.

Zinovieff, P. "A Computerized Electronic Studio." *Electronic Music Reports*, no. 1 (September 1969), p. 5.

10

TEST EQUIPMENT
AND
MEASUREMENTS

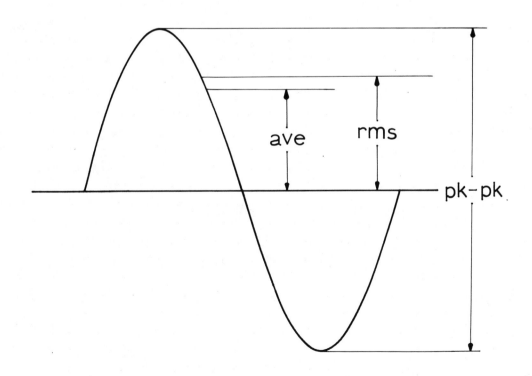

FIGURE 10.1

A good complement of test equipment is useful both for studio maintenance and for instruction. Many composers have the technical ability and experience to build and maintain their studio equipment, while many studios employ a full-time technician who may do design, construction, and maintenance work. Still other studios rely on factory maintenance; this can deprive the studio of needed equipment, since few manufacturers provide "loaners" to replace malfunctioning equipment being repaired. Ideally, the electronic music studio should contain shop facilities for the maintenance and construction of studio equipment. Several types of test equipment, as well as test equipment applications in the electronic music studio, are discussed below.

The *cathode-ray oscilloscope* (figure 10.1) is a device that permits the graphic display of various types of signals. The oscilloscope finds many uses in the electronic music studio—for testing and repair, as well as for teaching and checking the operation of certain patchings. The visual display is the result of a narrow beam of electrons striking a luminescent coating on the face of the cathode ray tube. There are several types of fluorescent coatings that vary in color and persistence (the length of time the trace remains after excitation is removed), common colors being green, blue, blue-white, blue-green, orange, and yellow. For measurements associated with electronic music, a medium-persistence phosphor is suitable.

A schematic drawing of a cathode-ray tube (CRT) is shown in figure 10.2. The electron beam (dashed line) passes between two sets of deflection plates, one pair of which is aligned at a right angle to the other, thereby permitting a two-dimensional display. Since electrons are negatively charged particles, they will be attracted by a positive charge and repelled by a negative charge. This process is called *electrostatic deflection,* and is employed in cathode-ray tubes used in most oscilloscopes. (Television-receiver CRTs, on the other hand, use *electromagnetic deflection*.) A usual

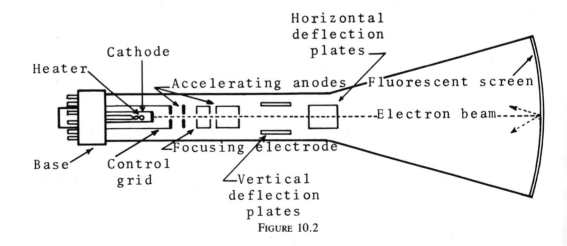

FIGURE 10.2

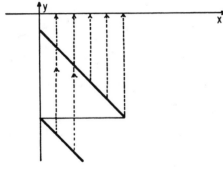

FIGURE 10.3

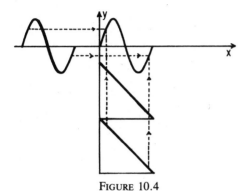

FIGURE 10.4

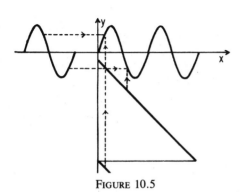

FIGURE 10.5

deflection-versus-voltage (applied to the deflection plate) characteristic for electrostatic-deflection CRTs is approximately 50 volts/inch. Amplifiers are required both for the examination of small amplitude signals and to assure a linear correspondence between deflection and amplitude of the signal applied to the deflection plates.

In order to display signals that vary with time, provision must be made to move the electron beam at a uniform rate, usually horizontally, across the face of the CRT. The sweeping of the electron beam is accomplished by applying a sawtooth-wave signal to the horizontal (x-axis) deflection plates. Figure 10.3 shows sawtooth-wave motion projected against the x-axis. Figure 10.4 shows a sine-wave signal applied to the vertical axis projected against a sawtooth-wave sweep signal applied to the horizontal axis. In most applications, the retrace, or flyback, is eliminated by interrupting the electron beam during flyback. In figure 10.4 the sine-wave signal and sawtooth sweep signal are of the same frequency. In figure 10.5 the sine-wave signal is twice the frequency of the sawtooth sweep signal.

The sweep signal may be run continuously, often called *recurrent sweep*; one cycle at a time, called *single sweep*; or triggered by some portion of the signal to be observed, called *triggered sweep*. The use of a triggered sweep precludes the possibility of the sweep cycle starting after the signal cycle, eliminating a part of the signal to be observed. The frequency of the sawtooth sweep is accurately determinable with high-quality instruments, permitting the operator to make accurate measurement of the frequency of a signal being analyzed. The sweep frequency is usually specified in terms of the amount of time required for the beam to travel one division on a ruled screen, called a *graticule,* positioned in front of the CRT face. Figure 10.6 shows two sine waves viewed on an oscilloscope, the sweep frequency (time base) of which is set to 1 millisecond per centimeter (1ms/cm). The y-axis scale is set to read one volt per centimeter. One cycle of the top (lower frequency) sine wave requires about 6.6 centimeters, that is, 6.6 milliseconds. One cycle of the other (higher frequency) sine wave requires 4 centimeters, that is, 4 milliseconds. Thus, the frequency of the top sine wave is

$$f = 1 \text{ (cycle)} \div \text{second} = 1/6.6 \text{ ms} = 1/0.0066 \text{ s} = 150 \text{ cycles per second}$$
$$(150 \text{ Hz}),$$

and the frequency of the lower (higher frequency) sine wave is

$$f = 1/4.0 \text{ ms} = 1/0.004 \text{ s} = 250 \text{ cycles per second (250 Hz)}.$$

The peak-to-peak amplitude of the top sine wave is $\simeq 1.8$ Volts, while the peak-to-peak amplitude of the lower sine wave is $\simeq 3.3$ volts.

The oscilloscope may be employed for frequency comparison measurements through the use of *Lissajous figures*. Lissajous was a

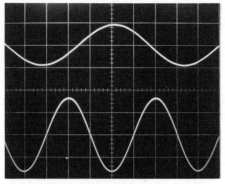

FIGURE 10.6

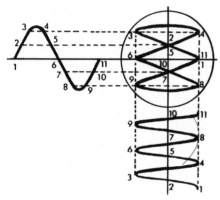

FIGURE 10.7

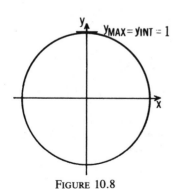

FIGURE 10.8

nineteenth-century French physicist who first generated these figures by optical means using mirrors attached to tuning forks. To obtain Lissajous figures on an oscilloscope, apply a sine wave of known frequency to the *x*-axis input (sweep generator *off*), and adjust the horizontal gain to obtain a convenient deflection. Disconnect the signal from the *x*-axis input and apply a sine wave of unknown frequency to the *y*-axis input. Adjust the vertical deflection to the same length as that produced by the signal applied to the *x*-axis. Connect both inputs and observe the pattern on the screen. The pattern will probably be moving. Adjust the frequency of the unknown oscillator until the pattern becomes stationary. The pattern is stationary when the known and unknown frequencies are related by integers, for example, 3:5, 10:11, 2:7, and so on. Figure 10.7 illustrates the generation of a Lissajous figure showing a 3:1 frequency ratio.

To determine a frequency ratio using Lissajous figures, count the number of horizontal loops in the pattern and make this number the *numerator* of a fraction. Count the number of vertical loops in the figure and make this number the *denominator* of that fraction. Thus for the example in figure 10.7,

known frequency/unknown frequency = number of horizontal loops/number of vertical loops = 3/1.

Of course, the use of Lissajous figures is limited to the comparison of frequencies that are integer related. As the integer values in both the numerator and denominator of the fraction increase, the number of loops becomes increasingly difficult to determine, and the pattern may be difficult to stabilize. Certain types of displays, such as the modulated ring pattern, the broken ring pattern, and the broken line pattern, may be employed when Lissajous figure loop counting becomes difficult.

The configuration for producing Lissajous figures may be employed for measurement of the phase difference between two signals. To measure phase difference with the oscilloscope, first remove all signal inputs and center the trace (a point) on the graticule. Connect one signal to the *y*-axis input and adjust the vertical deflection to a convenient length. Disconnect the *y*-axis input, connect the second signal to the *x*-axis input, and adjust the horizontal deflection to equal the vertical deflection caused by the *y*-axis input. Reconnect the *y*-axis input. If the two signals are equal in frequency and maintain a constant phase difference, a steady circular or elliptical pattern will result. If either or both of the signals drift slightly in frequency, the pattern will move, producing a three-dimensional effect. The phase difference between the two signals is determined by the relation: sine $\theta = y_{\text{intercept}}/y_{\text{maximum}}$, where $y_{\text{intercept}}$ means the distance from the origin to the point where the figure intersects the *y*-axis; y_{maximum} means the height of the figure in *y*-axis units, measured from the *x*-axis; and θ is the *phase angle* between the two signals. Figure 10.8 shows a Lissajous

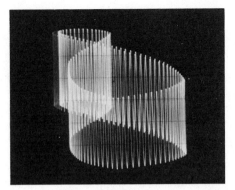

FIGURE 10.9

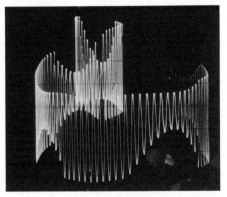

FIGURE 10.10

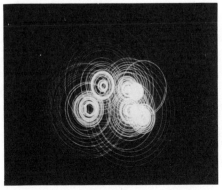

FIGURE 10.11

figure obtained from measuring two sine waves of phase difference θ. In this example the $y_{\text{intercept}} = $ the $y_{\text{maximum}} = 1$. We know that $\sin^{-1}$ (read arcsin 1, or angle whose sine is 1) equals 90°. Thus, the two sine waves differ in phase by $\theta = 90°$.

Lissajous figures have been used by some composers to generate graphic art for inclusion in their works. Figures 10.9 and 10.10 are illustrations of simple "oscillographic art" produced by modification of Lissajous figures. Figures 10.11 and 10.12 were generated using a multifunction filter.

The *volt-ohm-milliammeter* (acronym: VOM) and the *vacuum-tube voltmeter* (VTVM) are most useful test instruments for electronic music applications. In many applications, the internal resistance of a voltmeter must be sufficiently high in order to minimize errors caused by current drawn by the meter itself. The vacuum-tube voltmeter is characterized by a high (about 100-megohm) input resistance, so that, for most measurement applications, the current drawn by the VTVM is negligible. Some VTVMs, like the Hewlett-Packard Model 412A, also measure current and resistance directly. Many transistorized multi-function meters, such as the Hewlett-Packard Model 427A and the Heath Models IM 16 and IM 25, have high (about 10-megohm) input impedance and have the advantage of portability over the VTVM, which usually requires an AC supply. VOMs, such as the Simpson 260 and Triplett 630–A, (figure 10.13) are suitable for applications that do not require a high input measuring device.

Digital multimeters are available at reasonable ($150 and up) prices and provide portability, high input impedance, and much greater accuracy than a meter-indicating device. The Fluke 8020A (about $170), the Weston 4440 (about $300), and Simpson 360–2 (about $300) digital multimeters are recommended.

A *frequency counter* finds many uses in the electronic music studio. Many oscillators designed for electronic music production are either not calibrated in hertz, or the calibration and control devices do not permit precise and repeatable settings. Often the replacement of the 270°–turn oscillator vernier control with a 5– or 10–turn control of the same resistance and taper will improve the oscillator frequency resolution. Most frequency counters operate by totalizing the number of cycles of the input signal for a precisely determined length of time. The operation of a typical frequency counter is shown in figure 10.14. The signal to be measured is applied to the input and is shaped by the Schmitt trigger. This signal is then applied to the gate, which is opened for a precisely known time interval, or power-of-ten times this interval. In this example, a 400.3-Hz signal is applied to the input of the counter, the gate of which is open for 10-second intervals (0.1 Hz time base). The decade counters thus count 4,003 cycles of the measured signal and display the number 400.3 (positioning of the decimal point is accomplished automatically by the instrument). The Hewlett-Packard Model 5300–A counter system with Model 5310-A battery pack is shown in figure 10.15.

FIGURE 10.12

Most composers who employ specified discrete pitches in their work, as well as composers who write works for combined electronic and instrumental forces, have a need for a frequency counter. The counter is also useful in preparing documentation for a realization score for an electronic piece. In this case, frequency measurements are generally made *after* the operating points of the oscillators involved in a certain patching have been set by the composer, who works interactively with the equipment—using his senses of aural discrimination.

The wave analyzer and the spectrum analyzer have many applications in the electronic music studio. The *wave analyzer,* or frequency-selective voltmeter (or tuned voltmeter), may be considered to be a very narrow bandwidth filter that can be tuned throughout a particular frequency range. (Many practical wave analyzer designs employ a *fixed-frequency* filter to whose passband frequency signals under analysis are heterodyned.[1] The wave analyzer filter is followed by a meter that is often calibrated in volts, or decibels. If the filter is tuned through the components of a signal being analyzed, and the frequency and amplitude of each component is recorded, the resulting tabulation will be a frequency spectrum. The operation of a *spectrum analyzer* is similar to that of a wave analyzer with automatic sweeping. The spectrum analyzer employs a CRT display which presents a visual tabulation of how the energy of a signal is distributed as a function of frequency. Spectrum analyzers are available both as self-contained units and as oscilloscope plug-ins. The frequency spectra in this book were made using a Tektronix Model 1L5 spectrum analyzer plug-in unit. Other types of spectrum analyzers divide the spectrum under consideration into discrete frequency bands using sharp fixed-frequency band-pass filters. The signal under analysis is applied to all filter inputs simultaneously, and the outputs of the filters are displayed on a CRT which indicates the signal energy distribution in all bands simultaneously. Spectrum analysis may also be performed using digital computers to perform a fast Fourier transform of the input signal under consideration. Self-contained instruments called Fourier analyzers contain the necessary analog-to-digital converters and digital processors, as well as a display device. At this writing, however,

FIGURE 10.13

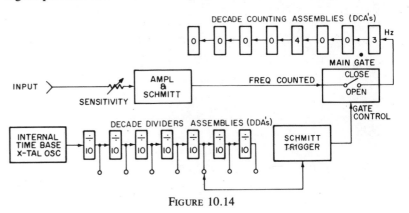

FIGURE 10.14

FIGURE 10.15

such analog/digital analyzers are prohibitively expensive for studio budgets.

The following hand tools and materials are useful for the repair and construction of electronic music equipment. This list is by no means exhaustive: the complement of tools required depends, of course, on the amount and type of construction and maintenance work undertaken.

- soldering station (Weller Model WTCPL)
- soldering iron, temperature controllable, about 25 to 50 watts
- soldering iron or gun, high wattage, about 200 to 300 watts
- solder vacuum (de-soldering device)
- solder, resin-core, no. 22
- sponge, for cleaning soldering iron tips
- pliers, needle-nose
- pliers, small diagonal cutting
- pliers, diagonal needle-point cutting
- pliers, electrician's side cutting
- pliers, combination
- seizer (hemostat)
- tweezers
- metal nibbling tool
- tool set (Xcelite 99MP Multi-Purpose Set [nut drivers, allen screwdrivers, bristol screwdrivers, spline screwdrivers, phillips screwdrivers, reamers, awl scriber])
- center punch
- cold chisel
- chassis punches
- wrenches, open end
- set of files
- electrician's knife
- metal shears
- dividers
- hacksaw and blades
- X-acto knife
- bench vise
- 3/8" electric drill
- assorted round shank drills
- cutting oil
- heat gun
- heat-shrinkable tubing
- hammer, ball peen
- DREMEL Moto-Tool with drill-press holder

FIGURE 10.16

Figure 10.16 is illustrative of a good workbench layout, and figure 10.17 shows a selection of useful integrated circuits.

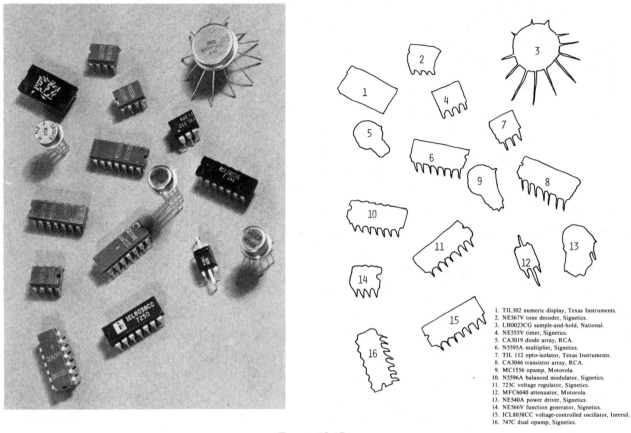

1. TIL302 numeric display, Texas Instruments.
2. NE567V tone decoder, Signetics.
3. LH0023CG sample-and-hold, National.
4. NE555V timer, Signetics.
5. CA3019 diode array, RCA.
6. N5595A multiplier, Signetics.
7. TIL 112 opto-isolator, Texas Instruments.
8. CA3046 transistor array, RCA.
9. MC1556 opamp, Motorola.
10. N5596A balanced modulator, Signetics.
11. 723C voltage regulator, Signetics.
12. MFC6040 attenuator, Motorola.
13. NE540A power driver, Signetics.
14. NE566V function generator, Signetics.
15. ICL8038CC voltage-controlled oscillator, Intersil.
16. 747C dual opamp, Signetics.

FIGURE 10.17
A selection of useful integrated circuits.

NOTES

1. W. Ribbens, "An Electronically Tunable Bandpass Filter," *Journal of the Audio Engineering Society* 16 (1968): 440–442.

SELECTED BIBLIOGRAPHY
Books

Blake, M. P., and Mitchell, W. S. *Vibration and Acoustic Measurement Handbook.* Chapter 29, "The Oscilloscope, Camera, . . . and Signal Generator." Chapter 30, "Wave Analyzers." Chapter 31, "Homemade Instrumentation." Chapter 32, "The Tape Recorder, Pen Oscillograph, and Level Recorder." New York: Spartan Books, 1972.

Buchsbaum, W. H. *Buchsbaum's Complete Handbook of Practical Electronic Reference Data.* Englewood Cliffs, N.J.: Prentice-Hall, 1973.

Davis, D. *Acoustical Tests and Measurements*. Indianapolis, Ind.: Howard W. Sams, 1965.

Magrab, B., and Blomquist, D. S. *The Measurement of Time Varying Phenomena: Fundamentals and Applications*. New York: Wiley-Interscience, 1971.

Prentiss, S. R. *How To Use Vectorscopes, Oscilloscopes, and Sweep-Signal Generators*. Blue Ridge Summit, Pa.: TAB Books, 1971.

Tremaine, H. M. *Audio Cyclopedia*, 2nd ed. Indianapolis, Ind.: Howard W. Sams, 1969.

11

ELECTRONIC MUSIC SCORES

Traditionally, the purpose of a musical score is to provide the performer(s) the information required (depending on performance practice) to carry out the composer's musical intentions. In the case of tape music, however, the composer's intentions are presumably manifested on magnetic tape, thus making a written score gratuitous in many respects.

Scores for electronic music pieces range from a simple graphic "representations" of sound events to complete *realization scores* that contain all the information necessary to reconstruct the work (the degree of success in this regard depending on the limitations of the studio equipment involved). Reconstructing short sections of an electronic piece from a score can be an instructive process, one the author recommends for teaching electronic music. In the case of electronic music works that include live instrumental music (with or without electroacoustical modification) the composer is obliged to indicate the relationships between the electronic sounds and the instrumental parts. Still another type of score is required for live electronic music works (see *Source Magazine - Music of the Avant Garde*. Sacramento, California, 95818.).

The excerpt in figure 11.1 (Ligeti, *Arkikulation*) shows the use of graphic symbols to represent the relationship of sound events though time. (This score was prepared by a professional artist.) The distribution of sounds among the four channels is shown by shaded quadrants of a circle.

Figure 11.2 shows excerpts from the realization score and performance score of Karlheinz Stockhausen's *Kontakte* (Universal Edition UE 13678). The complete score (*Realisationspartitur* and *Afführungspartitur*) required about 7 years to prepare; much credit for the production of the realization score goes to Mr. Jaap Spek. In this score, numbers and letters (see X, 44a, 44b, and so on) in the *Afführungspartitur* refer to sections in the *Realisationspartitur,* which shows interconnections and settings of equipment. Most of this section of *Kontakte* was generated by passing low-frequency pulse waveforms through a band-pass filter (with adjustable

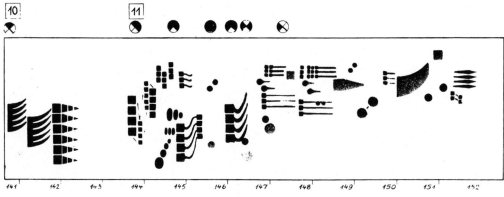

FIGURE 11.1

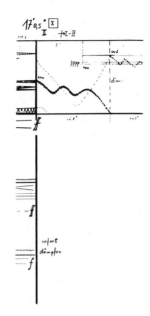

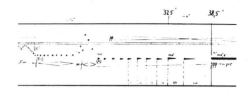

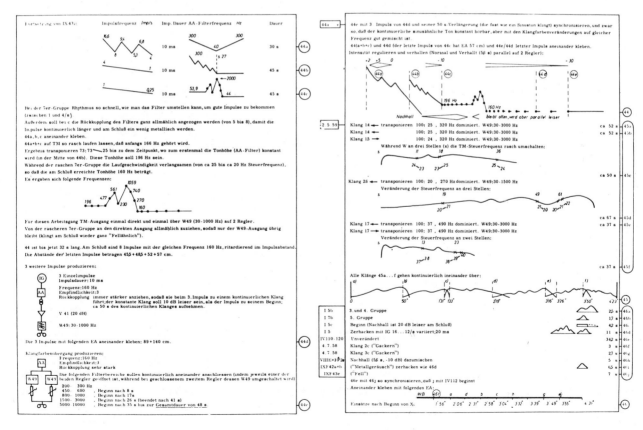

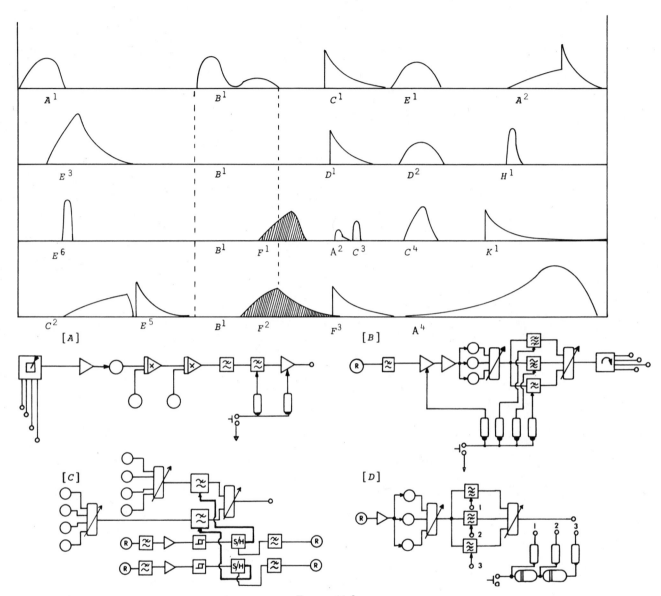

FIGURE 11.3

regeneration), the cutoff frequency of which is varied (see realization score). The realization score, 44a to e, shows the complete sequence of events from 17 min., 0.5 seconds to 17 min., 38.5 seconds. Notice the level indications +2, +5, 0 and so on, and the indication for amount of reverberation (*Nachhall*).

Figure 11.3 shows an excerpt from Thomas Wells's *12.2.72, Electronic Music*. This score plots the amplitude-versus-time characteristics for sound

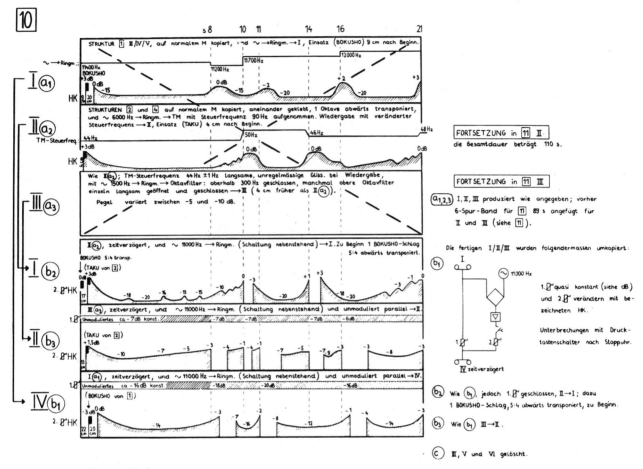

FIGURE 11.4

From TELEMUSIK by Karlheinz Stockhausen. Copyright © 1969 by Universal Edition A.G., Wien. All rights reserved for the USA and Canada controlled exclusively by European American Music Distributors Corp. Used by permission.

events on each of the four channels used in the work. Letters in the score refer to patchings, some of which are shown on the page with the score. Letters with superscripts refer to tabulations of the instrument settings for a particular patching as well as instructions showing how a patching is controlled through time. As is the case with many electronic music scores, while all the information required for the reconstruction of the piece is given, such a reconstruction would probably require more time than was spent in the original composition of the work. As we have mentioned, the preparation of a complete realization score for an electronic piece is a lengthy process, and many composers, unless they are specifically commissioned to prepare a score of an electronic piece, are content with the magnetic tape version of their work.

Figure 11.4 shows an excerpt from Karlheinz Stockhausen's *Telemusik,*

FIGURE 11.5

UE 14807. Although this score can be "followed" through time, one gains little information from such an endeavor. In this score, complex sound events are represented only by their loudness-versus-time curves, with no graphic representation of the microstructure of sound events being given. Numbers in boxes (for example, $\boxed{10}$) indicate the sequence of structures that follow one another without pause. Roman numerals I to VI indicate the six channels of the tape recorder used in the production of *Telemusik* (at the Studio for Electronic Music: Nippon Hoso Kyokai, Denshi Ongaku Studio, Tokyo). I, II means perform on channel I and II, one after the other. I/II/III means perform on channels I, II, and III simultaneously. Although a six-channel tape recorder was employed in the production of this work, the original version of *Telemusik* is a five-channel work. Channel six was used only in the production of the work. Each page of the score details a sequence of processes (encircled lower-case letters) that were followed in the composition of the work. I→II means copy channel I onto channel II; V & ~ → Ringm. means patch channel V and a sine-wave signal to both ring modulator inputs.

Figure 11.5 shows an excerpt from Karl Korte's *REMEMBRANCES*, for

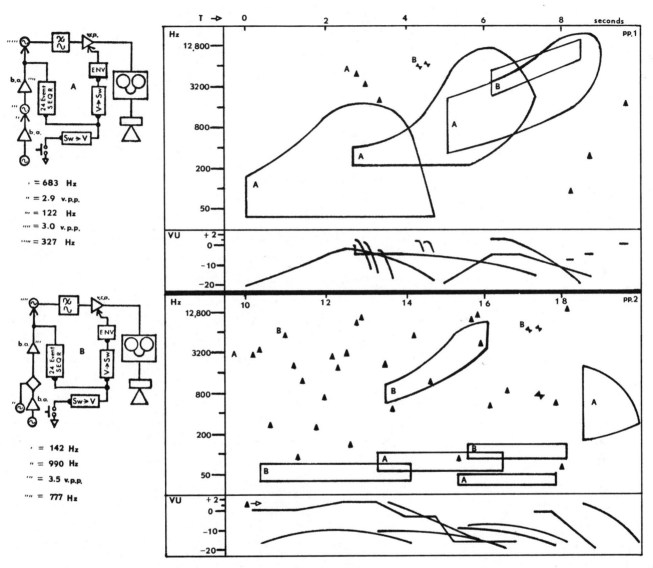

FIGURE 11.6

flute (alto, soprano, and piccolo) and synthesized and processed sound (Elkan-Vogel, Inc., Bryn Mawr, Pa.). This score is an example of a performance score in which careful attention is given to solving performance problems. There are abundant cues, as well as verbal instructions, for example, "*Do not rush. The tendency may be to reach the B-flat too soon,*" and "*Connection with next tape entrance should be as close as possible. If necessary repeat last few notes even if overlap occurs.*"

Figure 11.6 shows an excerpt from *Electronic Music: 1973* by Bruce L. Faulconer. This score includes separate amplitude and frequency scales.

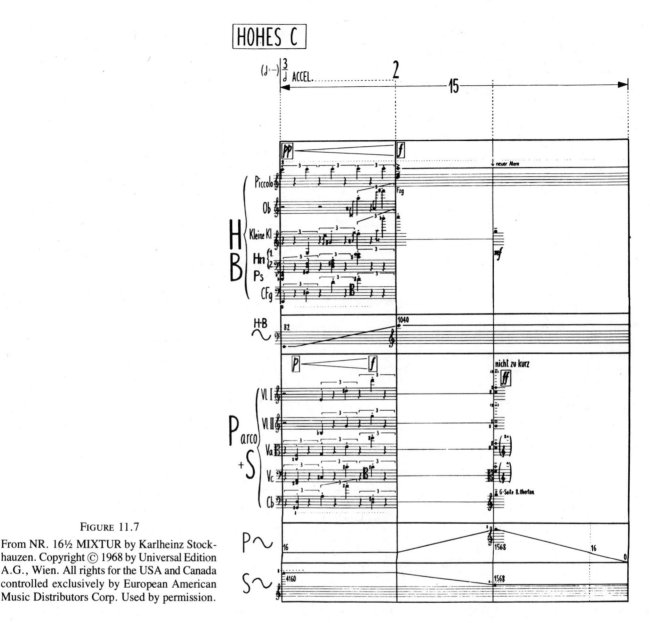

FIGURE 11.7

From NR. 16½ MIXTUR by Karlheinz Stock-hauzen. Copyright © 1968 by Universal Edition A.G., Wien. All rights for the USA and Canada controlled exclusively by European American Music Distributors Corp. Used by permission.

The patchings used to generate the sound events of pages one and two are shown at the right-hand side of the page.

Figure 11.7 shows an excerpt from Karlheinz Stockhausen's *Mixtur* (*kleine Besetzung* [version for chamber orchestra]), for orchestra, sine-wave generators, and ring modulators (UE 13847). In the score, H = Woodwinds; B = Brass; P = Strings (sempre pizzicati); S= Strings (arco). The score contains the following instructions:

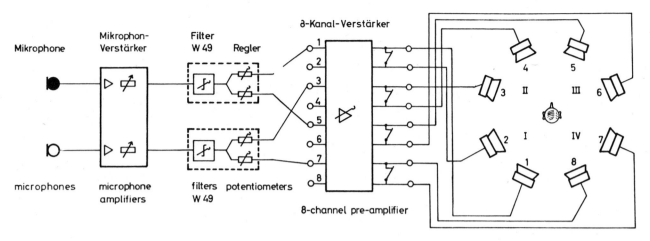

Jeder Lautsprecher hat seinen eigenen Verstärker.

Each loudspeaker has its own amplifier.

FIGURE 11.8

From KURZWELLEN by Karlheinz Stock-
hauzen. Copyright © 1969 by Universal Edition
A.G., Wien. All rights for the USA and Canada
controlled exclusively by European American
Music Distributors Corp. Used by permission.

Each of the groups, H, B, P, S, should sit concentrated and be separated from
the others as much as possible. Every woodwind and brass player and every desk
of violins and violas has a microphone; all Vc and Cb have individual microphones. The 4 microphone groups H, B, P, S, are each balanced in a mixer by
a sound technician sitting with his group. The sum of each group is connected to
a separate ring-modulator (if possible, special modulators which give only the
primary sum and difference frequencies [multiplier?]). 4 further players, who sit
with their groups, each operate a beat-frequency oscillator. Each of these BFOs
is connected to one of the modulators. The oscillators are indicated in the score
by

In this example the tuning of the BFO is particularly apparent (see measure
2, figure 11.7).

Figure 11.8 shows a block diagram of the electroacoustic apparatus used
in the performances of Stockhausen's *Kurzwellen,* for electric viola and
shortwave radio, piano and shortwave radio, tam-tam and shortwave radio,
electronium and shortwave radio, and filters and potentiometers (UE 14806);
and *Prozession*, for electric viola, piano, tam-tam, elektronium, and filters
and potentiometers (UE 14812).

Figure 11.9 shows an excerpt from Thomas Wells' *Systems of Electronic and Instrumental Music* (1968). The instruments (piano, 'cello,
tam-tam) are each processed through separate sound-modifying configurations consisting of a balanced modulator (the other input of which is a sine
wave) and multifunction (LP, HP, BP, BR) filter. Settings of instruments
are suggested by lines that vary between certain limits, namely, frequency
of the sine-wave oscillator, distribution of the sound between the two
speakers (L & R), volume, and ratio of modulated signal to unmodulated
signal. The duration of this excerpt is about 18''.

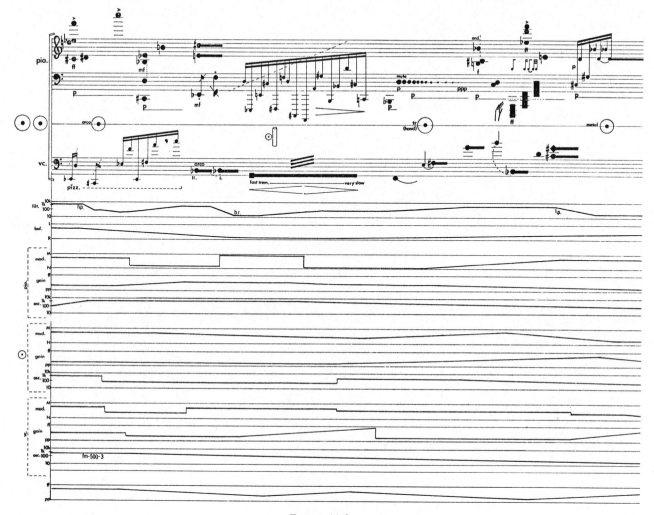

FIGURE 11.9

SELECTED BIBLIOGRAPHY

Books

Baer, C. *Electrical and Electronic Drawing,* 3rd ed. New York: McGraw-Hill, 1973.

Davies, H. *International Electronic Music Catalog.* Cambridge, Mass.: MIT Press, 1967.

Karkoschka, E. *Das Schriftbild der neuen Musik.* Moeck Verlag.

Articles

Behrman, D. "What Indeterminate Notation Determines." *Perspectives of New Music,* Spring/Summer, 1965.

Darmstädter Beiträge zur neuen Musik IX. Notation. Schott.

Fennelly, B. "A Descriptive Language for the Analysis of Electronic Music." *Perspectives of New Music* 6, no. 1.

Karkoschka, E. "*Ein Hörpartitur Elektronischer Musik.*" *Melos*, November 1971, pp. 470–471.

Leitner, B. "Sound Architecture—Space Created Through Traveling Sound." *Artforum* 9, no. 7 (March 1971): 44–49.

Smalley, R. "Pulses for 5X4 players; Transformation I for Piano." *Temp* 90.

Stockhausen, K. "The Concept of Unity in Electronic Music." *Perspectives of New Music,* Fall/Winter 1962.

————. "*Komposition 1953 Nr. 2, Studie I: Analyse.*" *Texte.* Band 2. Cologne: DuMont Schauberg, pp. 23–42.

————. "*Musik und Sprache III*" [Analysis of *Gesang der Jünglinge*]. *Texte, Band 2,* Cologne: DuMont Schauberg, pp. 58–68.

Stone, K. "Problems and Methods of Notation." *Perspectives of New Music,* Spring/Summer, 1963.

Ussachevsky, V. "Notes on A Piece for Tape Recorder." Reprint from *The Musical Quarterly* 46, no. 2 (April 1960).

APPENDIXES

APPENDIX 1   TRIGONOMETRIC TABLES

Angle	Radians	Sine	Cosine	Angle	Radians	Sine	Cosine
0°	.0000	.0000	1.0000	35°	.6109	.5736	.8192
1°	.0175	.0175	.9998	36°	.6283	.5878	.8090
2°	.0349	.0349	.9994	37°	.6458	.6018	.7986
3°	.0524	.0523	.9986	38°	.6632	.6157	.7880
4°	.0698	.0698	.9976	39°	.6807	.6293	.7771
5°	.0873	.0872	.9962	40°	.6981	.6428	.7660
6°	.1047	.1045	.9945	41°	.7156	.6561	.7547
7°	.1222	.1219	.9925	43°	.7505	.6820	.7314
8°	.1396	.1392	.9903	45°	.7854	.7071	.7071
9°	.1571	.1564	.9877	47°	.8203	.7314	.6820
10°	.1745	.1736	.9848	49°	.8552	.7547	.6561
11°	.1920	.1908	.9816	51°	.8901	.7771	.6293
12°	.2094	.2079	.9781	53°	.9250	.7986	.6018
13°	.2269	.2250	.9744	55°	.9599	.8192	.5736
14°	.2443	.2419	.9703	57°	.9948	.8387	.5446
15°	.2618	.2588	.9659	59°	1.0297	.8572	.5150
16°	.2793	.2756	.9613	61°	1.0647	.8746	.4848
17°	.2967	.2924	.9563	63°	1.0996	.8910	.4540
18°	.3142	.3090	.9511	65°	1.1345	.9063	.4226
19°	.3316	.3256	.9455	67°	1.1694	.9205	.3907
20°	.3491	.3420	.9397	69°	1.2043	.9336	.3584
21°	.3665	.3584	.9336	71°	1.2392	.9455	.3256
22°	.3840	.3746	.9272	73°	1.2741	.9563	.2924
23°	.4014	.3907	.9205	75°	1.3090	.9659	.2588
24°	.4189	.4067	.9135	77°	1.3439	.9744	.2250
25°	.4363	.4226	.9063	81°	1.4137	.9877	.1564
26°	.4538	.4384	.8988	83°	1.4486	.9925	.1219
27°	.4712	.4540	.8910	85°	1.4835	.9962	.0872
28°	.4887	.4695	.8829	87°	1.5184	.9986	.0523
29°	.5061	.4848	.8746	89°	1.5533	.9998	.0175
30°	.5236	.5000	.8660				
31°	.5411	.5150	.8572				
32°	.5585	.5299	.8480				
33°	.5760	.5446	.8387				
34°	.5934	.5592	.8290				

APPENDIX 2   VOLTAGE AND POWER RATIOS TO DECIBELS

Voltage Ratio	− Power Ratio	dB	Voltage Ratio	+ Power Ratio
1.0000	1.0000	0.00	1.0000	1.0000
0.9886	0.9772	0.1	1.012	1.023
0.9772	0.9550	0.2	1.023	1.047
0.9661	0.9333	0.3	1.305	1.072
0.9550	0.9120	0.4	1.047	1.096
0.9441	0.8913	0.5	1.059	1.122
0.9333	0.8710	0.6	1.072	1.148
0.9226	0.8511	0.7	1.084	1.175
0.9120	0.8318	0.8	1.096	1.202
0.9016	0.8128	0.9	1.109	1.230
0.8913	0.7943	1.0	1.122	1.259
0.8810	0.7762	1.1	1.135	1.288
0.8710	0.7586	1.2	1.148	1.318
0.8610	0.7413	1.3	1.161	1.349
0.8511	0.7244	1.4	1.175	1.380
0.8414	0.7079	1.5	1.189	1.413
0.8318	0.6918	1.6	1.202	1.445
0.8222	0.6761	1.7	1.216	1.479
0.8128	0.6607	1.8	1.230	1.514
0.8035	0.6457	1.9	1.245	1.549
0.7943	0.6310	2.0	1.259	1.585
0.7499	0.5623	2.5	1.334	1.778
0.7079	0.5012	3.0	1.413	1.995
0.6310	0.3981	4.0	1.585	2.512
0.5623	0.3162	5.0	1.778	3.162
0.5012	0.2512	6.0	1.995	3.931
0.4467	0.1995	7.0	2.239	5.012
0.3981	0.1585	8.0	2.512	6.310
0.3548	0.1259	9.0	2.818	7.943
0.3162	0.1000	10.0	3.162	10.000
0.1000	10^{-2}	20.0	10.000	10^2
0.03162	10^{-3}	30.0	31.620	10^3
0.01	10^{-4}	40.0	100.00	10^4
0.003162	10^{-5}	50.0	316.20	10^5
0.001	10^{-6}	60.0	1000.00	10^6

APPENDIX 3 FREQUENCIES OF NOTES IN THE TEMPERED SCALE

Note	Freq	(sharp)		Note	Freq	(sharp)		Note	Freq		Note	Freq	(sharp)
C_0	16.352	17.324		D_0	18.354	19.445		E_0	20.602		F_0	21.827	23.125
C_1	32.703	34.648		D_1	36.708	38.891		E_1	41.203		F_1	43.654	46.249
C_2	65.406	69.296		D_2	73.416	77.782		E_2	82.407		F_2	87.307	92.499
C_3	130.81	138.59		D_3	146.83	155.56		E_3	164.81		F_3	174.61	185.00
C_4	261.63	277.18		D_4	293.66	311.13		E_4	329.63		F_4	349.23	369.99
C_5	523.25	554.37		D_5	587.33	622.25		E_5	659.26		F_5	698.46	739.99
C_6	1046.5	1108.7		D_6	1174.7	1244.5		E_6	1318.5		F_6	1396.9	1480.0
C_7	2093.0	2217.5		D_7	2349.3	2489.0		E_7	2637.0		F_7	2793.8	2960.0
C_8	4186.0	4434.9		D_8	4698.6	4978.0		E_8	5274.0		F_8	5587.7	5919.9

Note	Freq	(sharp)		Note	Freq	(sharp)		Note	Freq
G_0	24.5	25.957		A_0	27.5	29.135		B_0	30.868
G_1	48.999	51.913		A_1	55.000	58.270		B_1	61.375
G_2	97.999	103.83		A_2	110.00	116.54		B_2	123.47
G_3	196.00	207.65		A_3	220.00	233.08		B_3	246.94
G_4	392.00	415.30		A_4	440.00	466.16		B_4	493.88
G_5	783.99	830.61		A_5	880.00	932.33		B_5	987.77
G_6	1568.0	1661.2		A_6	1760.0	1864.7		B_6	1975.5
G_7	3136.0	3322.4		A_7	3520.0	3729.3		B_7	3951.1
G_8	6271.9	6644.9		A_8	7040.0	7458.6		B_8	7902.1

APPENDIX 4 SOUND POWER OUTPUT FROM A SIMPLE SOURCE IN TERMS OF THE MAXIMUM VOLUME DISPLACEMENT

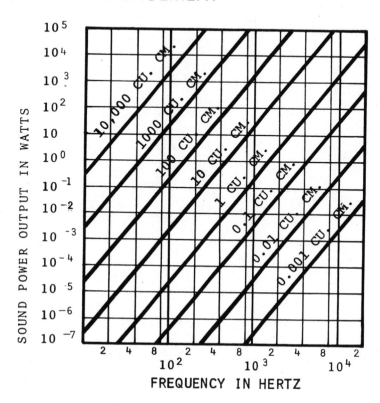

APPENDIX 5   TAPE HEAD GAP LENGTH VERSUS RESPONSE

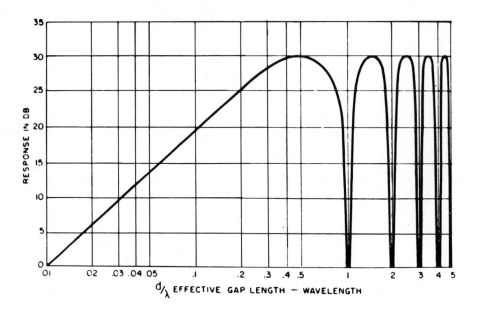

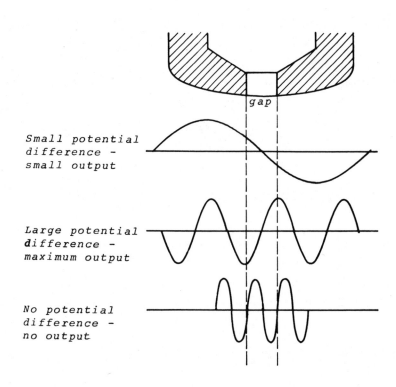

Small potential
difference -
small output

Large potential
difference -
maximum output

No potential
difference -
no output

APPENDIX 6 LOGARITHMS

A logarithm is an exponent.

If $a^x = y$, x is said to be the logarithm of y to the base a, or $\log_a y = x$.

The term *log* implies that $a = 10$, the base of *common* logarithms.

The term *ln* implies that $a = e = 2.718281828459\ldots$, the base of *natural* logarithms.

Properties of logarithms:

$$\log x^y = y \log x$$
$$\log^y \sqrt{x} = [1/y]\log x$$
$$\log x \cdot y = \log x + \log y$$
$$\log x \div y = \log x - \log y$$
$$\log_x x = 1$$
$$y^{\log_y x} = x$$
$$\log_x 1 = 0$$

EXPONENTS AND ROOTS IN ALGEBRA

$$a^0 = 1$$
$$(a \cdot b)^x = a^x \cdot b^x$$
$$(a^x \cdot a^y) = a^{(x+y)}$$
$$a^{-x} = 1/a^x$$
$$[a \div b]^x = a^x \div b^x$$
$$a^{1/x} = {}^x\sqrt{a}$$
$$a^{x/y} = {}^y\sqrt{a^x}$$

SCALING FACTORS, PREFIXES, AND ABBREVIATIONS

10^{12}	tera	T
10^{9}	giga	G
10^{6}	mega	M
10^{3}	kilo	k
10^{2}	hecto	h
10^{1}	deka	da
10^{-1}	deci	d
10^{-2}	centi	c
10^{-3}	milli	m
10^{-6}	micro	μ
10^{-9}	nano	n
10^{-12}	pico	p
10^{-15}	femto	f
10^{-18}	atto	a

INEQUALITIES

$a > b$	a is greater than b
$a < b$	a is less than b
$a \gg b$	a is much greater than b
$a \ll b$	a is much less than b
$a \geqslant b$	a is equal to or greater than b
$a \leqslant b$	a is equal to or less than b
$a \neq b$	a is not equal to b
$a \simeq b$	a is approximately equal to b

OHM'S LAW

$$E = IR = P/I = \sqrt{PR}$$
$$I = E/R = P/E = \sqrt{P/R}$$
$$R = E/I = E^2/P = P/I^2$$
$$P = IE = I^2R = E^2/R$$

TRIGONOMETRIC IDENTITIES

$$\sin x + \sin y = 2 \sin \tfrac{1}{2}(x + y)\cos \tfrac{1}{2}(x - y)$$
$$\sin x - \sin y = 2 \cos \tfrac{1}{2}(x + y)\sin \tfrac{1}{2}(x - y)$$
$$\cos x + \cos y = 2 \cos \tfrac{1}{2}(x + y)\cos \tfrac{1}{2}(x - y)$$
$$\cos x - \cos y = -2 \sin \tfrac{1}{2}(x + y)\sin \tfrac{1}{2}(x - y)$$

$$(\sin x)(\sin y) = \tfrac{1}{2} \cos (x - y) - \tfrac{1}{2} \cos (x + y)$$
$$(\cos x)(\cos y) = \tfrac{1}{2} \cos (x - y) + \tfrac{1}{2} \cos (x + y)$$
$$(\sin x)(\cos y) = \tfrac{1}{2} \sin (x - y) + \tfrac{1}{2} \sin (x + y)$$

APPENDIX 7 JOURNALS

Analog Sound. 12 West 17th Street, N.Y., N.Y. 10022.

Audio, 134 North 13th Street, Philadelphia, Pa. 19107.

The Composer, 3705 Strandhill Road, Cleveland, Oh. 44122.

Computer Music Journal, P.O. Box E, Menlo Park, Ca., 94025.

dB, the Sound Engineering Magazine, 980 Old Country Road, Plainview, L.I., N.Y. 11803.

Die Reihe, English Translation, Theodore Presser Co., Bryn Mawr, Pa., 19010. (Discontinued)

Electronic Music Review, Trumansburg, N.Y. Discontinued.

Electronotes, 1 Pheasant Lane, Ithaca, N.Y. 14850.

Gaudeamus Information, Contemporary Music Center, P.O. 30, Bilthoven, Netherlands.

Interface (formerly *Electronic Music Reports*), Utrecht State University, Institute of Sonology, Utrecht, Netherlands.

Journal of the Acoustical Society of America, American Institute of Physics, 335 East 45th St., N.Y. 10017.

Journal of the Audio Engineering Society, 60 East 42nd Street, Room 428, N.Y., N.Y. 10017.

Journal of Music Theory, Yale School of Music, Yale University, New Haven, Ct. 06520.

The Music Educators Journal, 1201 16th Street, Washington, D.C. 20036.

Numus West, PO Box 146, Mercer Island, Wa. 98040.

Perspectives of New Music, PO Box 231, Princeton, N.J. 08540.

Source Magazine, Music of the Avant Garde, 1201 22nd Street, Sacramento, Ca. 95818.

Synapse, 2829 Hyans Street, Los Angeles, Ca. 90026.

Synthesis Magazine, Sculley-Cutter Publications, 1315 4th Street, Minneapolis, Mn. Discontinued.

APPENDIX 8   MANUFACTURERS

ARP Instruments, 320 Needham Street, Newton Highlands, Ma. 02161.

Buchla Associates, Box 5051, Berkeley, Ca. 94705.

CBS Laboratories, 1300 East Valencia Street, Fullerton, Ca. 92631.

Electronic Music Labs, Inc., Box H, Vernon, Ct. 06080.

Electronic Music London, Ltd., 49 Deodar Road, London, SW15 2NU, England

Electronic Music Studios of Amherst, Inc., 460 West Street, Amherst, Ma. 01002.

Eμ Systems, 3455 Homestead Road, no. 59, Santa Clara, Ca. 95051.

Ionic Industries, 128 James Street, Morristown, N.J. 07960.

Moog Music, Inc., PO Box 131, Williamsville, N.Y. 14221.

Noumenon Electronics, PO Box 7068, Austin, Tx. 78705.

PAIA Electronics, PO Box 14359, Oklahoma City, Ok. 73114.

Southwest Technical Products Corp., 219 West Rhapsody Street, San Antonio, Tx. 78216.

Serge Modular Music Systems, 1107½ N. Western Avenue, Hollywood, California 90029.

GLOSSARY

The information in this glossary includes material assimilated from various sources. This glossary is offered only as a convenience and not as a standard. In general, terms defined in the text are not included here.

AC: Electricity, the value of which varies periodically about some reference level. More precisely, AC means a periodic or random signal or signal component having no net integral. A particular signal may contain AC, DC, and transient components.

Amplifier, voltage-controlled: An amplifier, the gain of which is a function of the voltage applied to its control input.

Amplitude: A measure of the deviation of a signal from its zero value.

Analog-to-digital converter (ADC): A device that converts an analog input signal to a digital representation of the value of the analog signal, either for storage or further processing.

Attenuation: A loss in signal energy.

Audio frequency range: The range of frequencies of soundwaves that are perceived as sound (this range is usually considered to be about 20 Hz to 20 kHz).

Azimuth loss: A high-frequency loss produced by misalignment of the recording and reproducing head gaps (of a magnetic recorder) such that the gaps are not parallel to each other in the plane of the tape.

Balanced line: A transmission line consisting of two identical conductors operated such that signal voltages at any given point along the conductors are equal in magnitude but of opposite sign with respect to ground. With this type of transmission line (balanced grounded line) the output terminals can be reversed without disturbing the circuit, whereas reversal of the output terminals of a single-ended grounded line is not possible.

Balanced modulator: An amplitude modulator constructed such that the carrier signal does not appear in the output of the device. With a *single-balance* modulator, the modulating signal appears in the output, whereas with a *double-balanced* modulator, the output of the device consists entirely of modulation products.

Band-pass filter: A filter that passes frequencies above and below its lower and upper cutoff points, respectively, while attenuating all other frequencies.

Band-reject filter (band-stop filter): A filter that attenuates frequencies above and below its lower and upper cutoff points, respectively, while passing all other frequencies.

Bandwidth: The difference between the upper and lower cutoff frequencies of a device, such as an amplifier, tape recorder, and so on.

Bias: A signal (AC or DC) applied to a device to establish an operating point.

Bias, AC: A high-frequency signal (approximately 3 to 5 times the frequency of the highest frequency component to be recorded) that is added to the signal to be recorded and fed to the record head of a magnetic recorder to compensate for the hysteresis effect of the tape.

Bouncing tracks: In multitrack recording, the transferring of several previously recorded tracks to a vacant track on the same tape, permitting the previously recorded tracks to be erased and used again. Bouncing between adjacent tracks is not recommended, since (even with state-of-the-art equipment) feedback due to lack of separation between tracks may occur.

Buffer: A circuit or component that is used to isolate one circuit from another.

Bus: A conductor used for the distribution of signals to several destinations.

Cannibalization: A method of maintenance or modification in which required components are removed from one system for installation in another system.

Capstan: An electromechanical system that pulls magnetic tape (at a constant rate) past the heads of a recorder.

Clipping: A type of distortion (often intentionally introduced as a sound modification procedure) produced as a result of a device being operated in a nonlinear amplitude region. In general, clipping-generated products consist mainly of odd harmonics.

Common-mode rejection: A measure of the signal output of an amplifier with differential outputs when the same signal is applied to both inputs of the device.

Comparator (voltage comparator): A circuit used to compare the amplitude of an input signal with a reference voltage. The output of the comparator changes from logical 0 (output of the comparator full *off*) to logical 1 (output of the comparator full *on*), and vice versa.

Contact microphone: A transducer designed to be attached to a vibrating body to convert the mechanical vibration of the body into electrical signals.

Crossfader: A panpot.

Counter, frequency: A device that measures the frequency of a periodic signal by counting the number of cycles of the signal over a precisely measured time interval and displaying this count on a readout (LED, Nixie Tube, neon bulb).

Crosstalk: A measure of the interference between two signal paths, for example, two conductors in a cable, two amplifier channels, and so forth, caused by stray electromagnetic or electrostatic coupling.

CRT: Cathode-ray tube.

Degaussing: The reduction of all residual magnetization of an object to zero.

Demodulation: Recovery of the modulating (program) signal from the modulated signal. Also called detection.

Detection: See demodulation.

DC: An unchanging signal. A steady, unchanging voltage or current.

Discriminator: A type of detector used to recover the program signal from a frequency-modulated signal.

Distortion: Any alteration in a given waveform. *Harmonic distortion* produces new frequency components which are integrally related to the frequency components of the original signal. *Intermodulation distortion* produces new frequency components that correspond to the sums and differences of the fundamentals and harmonics of two or more frequencies passed through a system (also called *Heterodyne distortion*).

Dropout: A (temporary) loss of signal in a magnetic recorder caused by imperfections in or foreign bodies on the tape surface.

Dynamic range: Ratio of maximum signal level (for a given level of distortion) to minimum signal level which can be processed by a system. The dynamic range of a device is usually measured in decibels.

Echo: A delayed repetition (or repetitions) of a sound or signal.

Electroacoustic: Having to do with the process of conversion from sound (mechanical) energy to electrical energy, and vice versa.

Envelope: A curve drawn through the points of maximum positive and/or negative excursion of a signal.

Envelope follower: A device consisting basically of a rectifier and low-pass filter which produces an output voltage proportional to the amplitude of an input signal.

Equalizer: A device (usually an electrical filter) used to alter the frequency-response chracteristics of a system.

Exponential: A relationship between two variables such that one variable, say y, changes according to a constant raised to the power of the other variable, x, that is, $y = a^x$. For example, the relationship between pitch and frequency is exponential. See *logarithmic*.

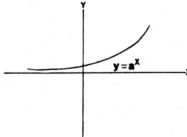

Feedback: The application of some proportion of the output signal of a device back to the input of the device.

Fletcher-Munson curves: A family of curves showing the characteristics of the human ear for different intensity levels between the threshold of hearing and the threshold of feeling.

Floating: Having no established reference potential (including ground).

Floating input: An input circuit not connected to ground at any point. With such an input, both conductors are free from any reference potential.

Flutter: Periodic variations in tape speed at rates of greater than or equal to 10 Hz, caused by friction between the tape and heads or guides.

Flux, magnetic: The magnetic induction (measured in gauss) in a material. A change in flux will induce an electromotive force in a conductor placed in the magnetic field.

Frequency response: The variation of sensitivity of a system with changes in signal frequency.

Full-track recording: Recording in which the track width is essentially equal to the tape width. (Applies specifically to ¼-inch tape.)

Gain: The ratio of the voltage, power, or current at the output of a device to the voltage, power, or current at the input of a device. Gain is often expressed in dB.

Gate: Any device or number of devices (for example, VCA and transient generator) used to control the amplitude-versus-time characteristics of a signal. The telegraph key used by Stockhausen in *Telemusik* is a simple gating device.

Graticule: The scale placed in front of the face of a cathode-ray tube to permit measurements of signals.

Ground: That point in a circuit used as a reference point in voltage measurements; the (conductive) chassis on which a circuit is mounted and to which one point in the circuit is connected; the earth, or a low-resistance conductor connected to the earth (for example, through a cold-water pipe, and so on).

Ground loop: The generation of spurious signals in a ground conductor, usually resulting from the connection of two separate grounds to a signal circuit.

Half-track recording: Recording in which the track width is approximately 40 percent of the tape width. Such a configuration permits the recording of two simultaneous channels in one direction, or the recording of a single channel in both directions. (Applies specifically to ¼-inch tape.)

.25 | .03 | .1 | .01

Track Configuration, Half-track recording, ¼" tape.

Harmonic: A sinusoidal frequency component which is an integral multiple of the lowest frequency component, or fundamental.

Harmonic distortion: See *distortion*.

Heterodyning: The mixing (non-linear) of two signals so as to produce new frequency components equal to the sum and difference of the frequencies of the two signals.

High-pass filter: A filter that passes signals of frequency greater than its cutoff frequency and attenuates signals of frequency less than its cutoff frequency.

Hysteresis synchronous motor: See *synchronous motor*.

Impedance: The total AC resistance (measured in ohms) of a circuit.

Inverting amplifier: An amplifier which multiplies the input signal by $-A$, where A is the voltage gain of the amplifier.

Klangumwandler: A single-sideband suppressed carrier generator (frequency shifter) used as a sound modification device.

Linearity: The property that the output resulting from the sum of two inputs is the sum of the outputs which would result from each input alone.

Logarithmic: A relationship between two variables such that one variable, say y, changes as the logarithm to a certain base of the other variable, x, that is, $y = \log_a x$. See *exponential*.

Loudness: A measure of the sensitivity of the ear to the intensity of a sound.

Low-pass filter: A filter that passes signals of frequency less than its cutoff frequency and attenuates signals of frequency greater than its cutoff frequency.

Mixer: A device used to produce the algebraic summation of two or more signals.

Modulated carrier recording: A process in which information is recorded in the form of a modulated carrier which is subsequently demodulated upon playback.

Modulation: A process by which a characteristic or characteristics (amplitude, frequency, phase) of a signal (called the *carrier*, or modulated signal), is (are) varied according to changes in a characteristic or characteristics of another, or modulating, signal. Modulation is used extensively as a sound modification process in the production of electronic music.

Multiplier, two-quadrant: A multiplier, one input of which is restricted to a single sign. The Moog 902 voltage-controlled amplifier is an example of a two-quadrant multiplier. Two quadrant multipliers may be connected to form a four-quadrant multiplier.

Multiplier, four-quadrant: A multiplier in which operation is not restricted with regard to the signs of the input signals.

Multitrack recording: A process by which several independent tracks are recorded on a single magnetic tape.

Musique concrète: A type of electroacoustical music that employs natural sounds that are recorded, processed, and assembled into a piece, as opposed to electronic music, which employs electronically generated sounds exclusively. Nowadays, these terms are not mutually exclusive, and much electroacoustical music employs both types of sound sources, the term *electronic music* being preferred for all types of electroacoustical musics.

Non-linear: Having an output which does not vary in direct proportion to the input.

Notch filter: A band-reject filter which is designed to attenuate a single, narrow band of frequencies.

Null: To oppose an output with its complement such that the result of the addition of these quantities is zero; to bring a circuit into a balanced condition, such that its output is zero.

Octave: A relationship between two frequencies such that $\log_2 [F_2/F_1] = 1$, where $F_2 > F_1$. For example, the distance in octaves from 100 Hz to 3,200 Hz is equal to $\log_2 32$, or 5.

Offset voltage: The DC potential remaining across the inputs of a differential amplifier when the input signals are adjusted so that the output level is zero. Some instruments, such as VCAs and multipliers, provide an offset adjustment control to adjust the offset voltage to zero.

Output impedance: The impedance presented by a device to a load (see *impedance*).

Patch cord: A short length of cable with connectors on both ends, used for the temporary interconnection of instruments.

Patching: A temporary connection made between two lines or circuits with a patch cord.

Period: The time (usually measured in seconds) required for a complete single oscillation or cycle of events. Period is the reciprocal of frequency. For example, a 1,000-Hz square wave has a period of 1 millisecond.

Periodic signal: A signal which exactly repeats itself every T seconds, where T is the period. In other words, $f(t) = f(t + T)$, where T is the period of the function, and t is time.

Phase: In a periodic wave, the fraction of the period that has elapsed, measured from some fixed origin. If the time required for one period is represented as $360°$ along a time-axis, the phase position is called the phase angle.

Phase angle: The phase difference in degrees between corresponding stages of progress of two periodic waveforms.

Phasing (flanging): A process in which a signal is delayed and then summed with the undelayed signal to produce phase cancellations. For example, a 1-millisecond delay results in a $180°$ phase shift at 500 Hz, producing a cancellation at this frequency when the delayed and undelayed signals are mixed. This effect may be accomplished by tuning a number of notch filters through a signal; by using a frequency shifter (mixing a shifted [approximately 0.2 Hz] signal with its unshifted version); by playing back identical signals on two tape recorders, one of which leads or lags the other by a small time interval (this time interval may be adjusted by varying the speed of one recorder by using a variable-frequency AC power supply).

Potentiometer (POT): A resistive element along which a contact (called a *wiper*) moves, providing an adjustable division of any potential present across the resistive element. Potentiometers are commonly employed as volume controls, panning devices, and so forth.

Power oscillator: A variable-frequency (usually sine-wave) oscillator, used in conjunction with a power amplifier to provide a variable-frequency power supply for speed control of a tape-recorder capstan motor.

Pulse: An abrupt change in signal level.

Quantization: A process in which a (continuous) function is transformed into a series of discrete values.

Quarter-track recording: Recording in which the track width is approximately 15% of the tape width. Such a configuration permits the recording of four simultaneous channels in one direction, or the recording of two simultaneous channels in both directions (as well as other track allocation schemes). (Applies specifically to ¼-inch tape.)

Track Configuration, Quarter-track recording, ¼" tape.

Repeatability: The ability of a device to be reset to some previously determined operating point.

Resolution: A measure of the smallest possible increment of change in the variable output of a device.

Resonant frequency: The frequency at which a peak filter exhibits maximum gain.

Ringing: A damped oscillation induced in a resonant circuit by an abrupt change in the input signal.

Ring modulator: A type of balanced modulator, so named because it employs four diodes connected anode to cathode, anode to cathode, and so on, to form a ring.

Roll off: An increase in attenuation over a given frequency range.

Saturation (tape): The point in the response of a magnetic tape at which an increase in the magnetizing force causes no increase in the magnetic intensity exhibited by the tape.

Schmitt trigger: A comparator with hysteresis (see text).

Scrape flutter: The "rubber band" effect produced by the movement of the tape under tension past heads and guides.

Slew rate: The maximum rate at which the output level of a device can change from minimum to maximum.

Spectrum: The frequency components that make up a description of a complex waveform; also a graphical representation of those components.

Stereo: A prefix meaning three-dimensional.

Synchronous motor: An induction motor that runs at constant speed. A *hysteresis synchronous motor* is a type of synchronous motor without salient poles or direct current excitation.

Synchronous speed: A speed value which is a function of the frequency of the AC mains and the number of poles in the motor.

Transducer: A device that converts data from its natural form into electrical signal analogs.

Tremolo: Amplitude modulation at rates of change of approximately 1 to 12 Hz.

Variac: An autotransformer that permits adjustment of the AC line voltage from 0 to 117% of the normal value. (Trade name of the General Radio Company.) An autotransformer should not be employed for tape recorder capstan motor speed control.

Vernier: An auxiliary scale or control that represents subdivisions of another tuning scale. Use of the vernier permits greater resolution in tuning than can be realized with the main, or coarse, tuning scale.

Voltage-controlled device: A device, the operating point of which can be adjusted by the application of a voltage applied to a control input.

Waveform: The amplitude-versus-time function of a signal.

Wire recorder: A magnetic recorder that utilized a stainless-steel wire (outer diameter 0.004 or 0.0036 inch) as a recording medium. (see Poulsen's Telegraphone). Wire recorders were used into the mid-1950s. The performance of wire recorders approached that of a modern cassette recorder. Splicing was accomplished by tying a knot in the recording wire.

Wow: Instantaneous variations of tape speed at relatively slow rates, approximately 0.1 Hz to 10 Hz.

Zero beat: A condition in which two frequencies being mixed are exactly the same, and therefore produce no beat frequency.

Zero level: A reference level used for comparing sound or signal intensities. For example, in sound measurement the zero level is the threshold of hearing.

SELECTED
DISCOGRAPHY

AMM–London. Cardew *et al*. MAINSTREAM MS–5002.

Arel, Bülent. *Electronic Music Number 1; Music for a Sacred Service (Prelude and Postlude); Fragment.* SON NOVA 3.

———. *Stereo Electronic Music Number 1.* COLUMBIA MS–6566.

Babbitt, Milton. *Composition for Synthesizer.* COLUMBIA MS–6566.

———. *Ensembles for Synthesizer.* COLUMBIA MS–7051.

———. *Philomel.* DEUTSCHE GRAMMOPHON 0654–083.

Beaver, P., and Krause, B. *The Nonesuch Guide to Electronic Music.* NONESUCH HC–73018.

Berio, Luciano. *Visage.* TURNABOUT TV–34046S.

———. *Ommagio à Joyce.* TURNABOUT TV–34177.

Brün, Herbert. *Futility 1964.* HELIODOR HS–25047.

Cage, John. *Fontana Mix.* TURNABOUT TV–34046S.

———. *Variations II,* Columbia MS–7051.

Davidovsky, Mario. *Electronic Study I,* COLUMBIA MS–6566.

———. *Synchronisms No. 1; Synchronisms No. 2; Synchronisms No. 3.* CRI S–204.

———. *Electronic Study No. 3; Synchronisms No. 5; Synchronisms No. 6.* TURNABOUT TV–S 34487.

Dodge, Charles. *Changes* (computer-generated sounds). NONESUCH H–71245.

———. *Earth's Magnetic Field.* NONESUCH H–71250.

Druckman, Jacob. *Animus III.* NONESUCH H–71253.

Eimert, Herbert. *Sechs Studien.* WERGO WER–60014.

El Dabh, Halim. *Leiyla and the Poet.* COLUMBIA MS–6566.

Erb, Donald. *In No Strange Land.* NONESUCH H–71223.

Ferrari, L. *Tête et Queque du Dragon.* CANDIDE 31025.

Gaburo, Kenneth. *Antiphony III, etc.* NONESUCH H–71199.

Gerhard, Roberto. *Collages* (Symphony No. 3 for Orchestra and Electronic Music). ANGEL S–36558.

Henry, Pierre. *Mass.* PHILLIPS 4FE8004.

Ichyanagi, Toshi. *Extended Voices.* ODYSSEY 32–16–0156.

Kagel, Mauricio. *Transición I.* MERCURY SR2–9123.

———. *Transición II.* MAINSTREAM MS–5003.

———. *Acustica.* DEUTSCHE GRAMMOPHON 2DG 2707059.

Koenig, Gottfried Michael, *Terminus II; Funktion Grün.* DEUTSCHE GRAMMOPHON DG 137011.

Korte, Karl. *Remembrances, for Flute (Alto, Soprano, and Piccolo) and Synthesized and Processed Sound.* NONESUCH H–71289.

League of Composers, *ISCM National Competition Electronic Music Winner*. *ODYSSEY Y34139*.

Lucier, Alvin. *Vespers*. MAINSTREAM MS-5010.

Luening, Otto. *Tape Music*. DESTO 6466.

Martirano, Salvatore. *L's GA*. POLYDOR 24-5001.

Mimaroglu, Ilhan. *Le Tombeau d'Edgar Poe*. TURNABOUT TV-34004S

Oliveros, Pauline. *I of IV*. ODYSSEY 32-16-0160.

Pousseur, Henri. *Rimes pour différentes sources sonores*. RCA VICTROLA VICS-1239.

Powell, Mel. *Events; Second Electronic Setting*. CRI 227.

Randall, J. K. *Lyric Variations for Violin and Computer*. CARDINAL C-1-57.

Rudin, Andy. *Tragoedia*. NONESUCH H-71198.

Stockhausen, Karlheinz. *Gesang der Jünglinge; Kontakte* (electronic sounds only). DEUTSCHE GRAMMOPHON DG 138811.

———. *Hymnen*. DEUTSCHE GRAMMOPHON 2DG 2707037.

———. *Kurzwellen*. DEUTSCHE GRAMMOPHON 2DG 2707045.

———. *Mantra*. DEUTSCHE GRAMMOPHON DG 2530208.

———. *Solo, für Melodieinstrument mit Ruckkoppelung*. DEUTSCHE GRAMMOPHON DG 137005.

———. *Telemusik; Mixtur*. DEUTSCHE GRAMMOPHON DG 137012.

———. *Mikrophonie I; Mikrophonie II*. COLUMBIA MS 7355.

Subotnick, Morton. *Sidewinder*. COLUMBIA MS-30683.

———. *Touch*. COLUMBIA MS-7316.

Ussachevsky, Vladimir. *A Piece for Tape Recorder*. CRI 112.

Varèse, Edgard. *Poème électronique; Deserts*. COLUMBIA MG-31078.

Vercoe, Barry. *Synthesism*. NONESUCH H-71245.

Wuorinen, Charles. *Time's Encomium*. NONESUCH H-71225.

Xenakis, Iannis. *Electro-Acoustic Music*. NONESUCH H-71246.

INDEX